G000123507

To Govern China

How, practically speaking, is the Chinese polity – as immense and fissured as it has now become – being governed today? Some analysts highlight signs of "progress" in the direction of a more liberal, open, and responsive government, whereas others dwell instead on the many remaining "obstacles" to a transition to democracy. Drawing together cutting-edge research from an international panel of experts, the essays in this volume argue that both approaches rely upon starkly drawn distinctions between democratic and non-democratic regime types, concentrating too narrowly on institutions as opposed to practices. The current focus on adaptive and resilient authoritarianism – a neo-institutionalist concept – fails to capture and accommodate processes of political change in contemporary China. In its place, the authors offer a more open-ended, fluid approach that privileges nimbleness, mutability, and an openness to institutional invention and procedural change, both proactive and reactive, illuminating the repertoires and practices of governing in China today.

Vivienne Shue is Professor Emeritus of Contemporary China Studies at the University of Oxford, and is an Associate of the University's China Centre.

Patricia M. Thornton is Associate Professor in the Department of Politics and International Relations at the University of Oxford.

To Govern China

Evolving Practices of Power

Edited by

Vivienne Shue
University of Oxford

Patricia M. Thornton
University of Oxford

CAMBRIDGE
UNIVERSITY PRESS

University Printing House, Cambridge CB2 8BS, United Kingdom

One Liberty Plaza, 20th Floor, New York, NY 10006, USA

477 Williamstown Road, Port Melbourne, VIC 3207, Australia

4843/24, 2nd Floor, Ansari Road, Daryaganj, Delhi – 110002, India

79 Anson Road, #06–04/06, Singapore 079906

Cambridge University Press is part of the University of Cambridge.

It furthers the University's mission by disseminating knowledge in the pursuit of education, learning, and research at the highest international levels of excellence.

www.cambridge.org
Information on this title: www.cambridge.org/9781107193529
DOI: 10.1017/9781108131858

© Cambridge University Press 2017

First published 2017

Printed in the United Kingdom by Clays, St Ives plc

A catalogue record for this publication is available from the British Library.

Library of Congress Cataloging-in-Publication Data
Names: Shue, Vivienne, editor. | Thornton, Patricia M., editor.
Title: To govern China : evolving practices of power / edited by Vivienne Shue, University of Oxford; Patricia M. Thornton, University of Oxford.
Description: Cambridge, United Kingdom ; New York, NY : Cambridge University Press, 2017. | Includes bibliographical references and index.
Identifiers: LCCN 2017012402 | ISBN 9781107193529 (hardback)
Subjects: LCSH: Zhongguo gong chan dang. | China – Politics and government – 1976– | BISAC: POLITICAL SCIENCE / Government / International.
Classification: LCC JQ1519.A5 T6 2017 | DDC 320.951–dc23
LC record available at https://lccn.loc.gov/2017012402

ISBN 978-1-107-19352-9 Hardback

We dedicate this volume to *all* of our students.

May the Force be with you.

Contents

Contributors

JOEL ANDREAS is an Associate Professor in the Department of Sociology at Johns Hopkins University. He is the author of the award-winning *Rise of the Red Engineers: The Cultural Revolution and the Origins of China's New Class,* as well as other notable contributions on culture, education, labor and class in China. He is currently completing a study of changing modes of industrial governance since 1949.

YIGE DONG holds an MA from the University of Chicago and is currently completing the PhD in Sociology at Johns Hopkins University. Her research interests are centered on social relations in urban China under Mao, examining in particular changing structures and norms of community and family, of social welfare, and gender relations.

CHRISTIAN GÖBEL is a Professor of Modern China Studies at the University of Vienna. The author of *The Politics of Rural Reform in China* and *The Politics of Community Building in Urban China* (with Thomas Heberer), his more recent publications have included studies of collective action in urban China, of anti-corruption in Taiwan, and of the uses of digital technology in Chinese local governance.

THOMAS HEBERER is a Professor of East Asian Politics at the University of Duisburg-Essen. A former translator and seasoned field researcher of politics and economy in rural, urban, and ethnic minority areas, his many publications in German, Chinese and in English include *Doing Business in Rural China: Liangshan's New Entrepreneurs, The Politics of Community Building in Urban China* (with Christian Göbel), and *Rural China: Economic and Social Change in the Late Twentieth Century* (with Fan Jie and Wolfgang Taubmann).

SEBASTIAN HEILMANN is a Professor of Chinese Political Economy at the University of Trier, and founding President of the Mercator Institute for Chinese Studies in Berlin. Known for his influential earlier journal articles on policy experimentation and on development planning in China, he is the author (with Dirk Schmidt) of *China's Foreign*

Political and Economic Relations and the principal author most recently of the very highly regarded comprehensive text *China's Political System*.

CHING KWAN LEE is a Professor of Sociology at UCLA, and the author of two award-winning books on labor conditions in China, protests and party-state strategies for containing unrest: *Gender and the South China Miracle*, and *Against the Law: Labor Protest in China's Rustbelt and Sunbelt*. Her current research examines issues of labor, politics, and Chinese state capital investment in Africa.

ELIZABETH J. PERRY is a Professor of Government at Harvard University and Director of the Harvard-Yenching Institute. A prolific scholarly author and editor of works on 20th and 21st century Chinese history and politics, pursuing research themes traversing the study of popular rebellion, protest, labor and class politics, as well as changing relations of state and society through revolution and reform, her major publications have included the award-winning *Shanghai on Strike*, *Patrolling the Revolution: Worker Militias, Citizenship and the Modern Chinese State*, and more recently *Anyuan: Mining China's Revolutionary Tradition*.

JEAN-LOUIS ROCCA is a Professor of Sociology at the Centre de Recherches Internationales at Sciences Po. The author of numerous works in French devoted to investigating and rethinking questions of labor, class, and the standards and conditions of life in urban China, his recent publications in English also include the very wide-ranging *A Sociology of Modern China*, and the intricately-argued *The Making of the Chinese Middle Class: Small Comfort and Great Expectations*.

VIVIENNE SHUE is Professor Emeritus of Contemporary China Studies at the University of Oxford. Best known for *The Reach of the State*, on state and society under Mao, she has published also on agrarian reform, county-level government, and small town development in China; on theorizing the evolving nature of China's "local state" under reform; on the political economy of charity in China, the plural techniques of rule deployed in Chinese governance practice, and the philosophical underpinnings of contemporary state legitimation.

PATRICIA M. THORNTON is an Associate Professor of Chinese Politics at the University of Oxford. The author of *Disciplining the State: Virtue, Violence and State-making in Modern China*, she has published studies also on patterns of protest and dissent across China; on contemporary urban geographies of power and consumption in Beijing; on shifting practices of contemporary grassroots party-building; on modern survey methods and the construction of "public opinion"; and on "crisis" as a mode of governance in contemporary China.

LUIGI TOMBA is a Professor of Chinese politics and society and Director of the China Studies Centre at the University of Sydney. His prize-winning book, *The Government Next Door: Neighborhood Politics in Urban China*, is among the most recent of many studies he has authored focused on China's urbanization processes, tracing the consequences of accompanying evolutions in labor, housing, land, class, and grass-roots governance.

ROBERT P. WELLER is a Professor in the Department of Anthropology at Boston University. Frequently probing, in his research, our under-standings of the nature and limits to authority in contrasting historical and social settings, he is the author of numerous studies theorizing Chinese and Taiwanese cultures in comparative perspective, including *Discovering Nature: Globalization and Environmental Culture in China and Taiwan*, and more recently, *Rethinking Pluralism: Ritual, Experience, and Ambiguity* (with Adam Seligman).

YONG HONG ZHANG (张永宏) is an Associate Professor of Sociology at Sun Yatsen University in Guangzhou. The central concerns of his research and writing have been with organizational behavior, the chang-ing local state, and state-citizen relations in urban and urbanizing China. His research projects and publications have examined, in parti-cular, the dynamics of contemporary contentious politics and social protest, including labor disputes, local-state corruption, and land grabs.

Introduction: Beyond Implicit Political Dichotomies and Linear Models of Change in China

Vivienne Shue and Patricia M. Thornton

How, practically speaking, amid all the economic and political turbulence of the twenty-first century, is the Chinese polity – as immense and as formidably fissured as it has now become – being governed? And what are the soundest approaches students and scholars can now choose to employ in the quest for fuller answers to all the many dimensions of this puzzling question? These are the unsolved problems of understanding that pre-occupy us in this volume.

The essays to come have their origins in a conference convened at Oxford University in the spring of 2012,[1] but each one has been revised in light of more recent political developments. As late as 2011, as we were sending out the invitations, we still thought of the research task we and our conference participants would face as essentially exploratory – one of mapping an expanding universe of changing political practices widely recognized to be emerging in China. Our initial charge to our conference contributors was simply that they consider the complex of *processes* entailed in "governing and being governed" in the contemporary Chinese context, and utilize their own most recent research investigations and data to illuminate *some* dimension of how governance is currently being approached and realized. This investigative and empirical orienta-tion was not chosen with a view to building a comprehensive character-ization of the deep nature or final trajectory of the governing system as a whole, but instead intended to sample what we suspected would be a broad and unevenly choreographed *repertoire* of governing practices. The open-endedness of that initial approach has, we still believe, encour-aged our authors to feature in their essays here some of those governing

---

[1] The conference on "Power in the Making: Governing and Being Governed in Contemporary China" was organized by the University of Oxford's Contemporary China Studies Programme, a ten-year research development initiative generously funded by the Leverhulme Trust. We are grateful to all those who attended and took part in that meeting for their many insights, and wish to record our thanks also to Christopher Kutarna who served as rapporteur.

practices that have previously been relegated to the margins of view. And it has allowed us all to highlight some of the fascinating, occasionally ironic, internal inconsistencies and jarring anomalies of a decidedly mixed system that is still in the making.

As of this writing in 2016, however, we have concluded that it has become possible, indeed necessary, to press our modest initial conceptual agenda still further forward. On the basis of what we have learned from the diverse studies collected here, as well as from other recent work in the fields of Chinese and comparative political and social studies, we wish to suggest a refreshed framework for approaching the study of governance in China, and what we hope may serve as a progressive new orientation for future research. But before presuming to point to any new way forward, it is necessary for us to provide an overview and reconsideration of just where our field of study has lately been.

In the Anglophone scholarship on Chinese society and politics over recent decades, with its emphasis on the Chinese Communist Party (CCP)-led effort at "system reform," some analysts have chosen to highlight signs of "progress" in the direction of a more liberal, open, and popularly responsive future for the Chinese polity. Others have dwelt instead on system reform failures and the many remaining "obstacles" to achieving a genuine transition to democracy. As we hope this volume may help serve to illustrate, these undeniably complex and seemingly contradictory trends that scholars based in the West have observed and recorded have often been conceptualized and debated against the backdrop of overly drawn distinctions between democratic and non-democratic *regime types*. And they have tended to concentrate too narrowly on governing *institutions* as opposed to governing *practices*. They have failed, thereby, to capture adequately the wide assortment of idioms and the interlaced array of channels through which political evolution may proceed.

From Transition Studies to Authoritarian Resilience

A quarter of a century ago the entire world, much taken by surprise, witnessed the spectacle of serial socialist state breakdowns that the esteemed American political scientist Ken Jowitt was prompt to label the "Leninist extinction."[2] Amazed and elated, many observers in the West then began thinking in terms of world history's cartwheeling smartly into a brand new "post-communist" era – an era of comprehensive transition toward democratic systems of governance in countries all

---

[2] Jowitt, *New World Disorder: The Leninist Extinction.*

around the globe, including China. Hopes were high then, in the West, for a rather speedy Chinese transition to democracy, through one scenario or another. As Andrew Nathan was retrospectively to acknowledge, in the wake of the 1989 Tiananmen crisis "many China specialists and democracy theorists – myself among them – expected the regime to fall to democratization's 'third wave.' [But] instead, the regime has reconsolidated itself."[3] Recognizing then that the "causes of its resilience are complex," Nathan nonetheless went on to single out the degree and nature of the Chinese regime's institutionalization – which he defined in terms of the "adaptability, complexity, autonomy, and coherence of state organizations" – as playing the determinative role in ensuring its suppleness and survival through the Deng Xiaoping era, and beyond.

Nathan's 2003 observations about Chinese party-state institutions were in keeping with the findings of a growing number of other studies within the broader field of comparative governance. Scholars of politics in other contemporary settings had by then begun documenting the dynamics of an "undemocratic undertow" detected in the wake of democracy's "third wave." Certain authoritarian regimes were found to be stubbornly "resilient" or "durable" in face both of internal and external challenges. As Snyder was to note, the final ebbing of the third wave saw entrenched totalitarian and post-totalitarian party-states maintain their grip on power not only in the People's Republic of China (PRC), but also in North Korea, Cuba, Laos, and Vietnam; autocratic monarchies persisted in Saudi Arabia, Morocco, and Jordan; dictatorships, theocracies, ethnocracies, and military regimes continued to survive across the globe.[4] Thus, by the dawn of the twenty-first century "transitology," and what Carothers had famously called the "transition paradigm,"[5] were already showing signs of having exhausted their usefulness –particularly as "hybrid" political regimes (partly authoritarian and partly democratic) were perceived to be proliferating.

Without missing a beat then, a new generation of Western scholarship began probing the characteristics and dynamics of these more obstinate authoritarian regimes, mapping out broader taxonomies to include newly recognized categories as well, such as "competitive autocracies" and "defective democracies."[6] In contrast to an earlier scholarly literature on non-democracies, which had posited that it was the defective design of state institutions that would ultimately undermine the hold of elites on

---

[3] Nathan, "Authoritarian Resilience," 6.
[4] Snyder, "Beyond Electoral Authoritarianism."
[5] Carothers, "The End of the Transitions Paradigm."
[6] Levitsky and Way, *Competitive Authoritarianism*; Merkel, "Embedded and Defective Democracies"; Bogaards, "How to Classify Hybrid Regimes?"

power in authoritarian regimes,[7] a growing number of studies in the emerging field of "comparative authoritarianism" argued instead that autocratic elites were becoming adept at creating modern political institutions that would consolidate their hold on power and, in so doing, successfully foster more durable forms of authoritarian rule. Increasingly, this newer scholarship regards the existence of liberalizing and democratic institutions, such as political parties and legislatures in autocracies, no longer as mere fig leaves thinly disguising the exercise of coercive and repressive power. Instead, it links the structures and functions of such institutions to popular quiescence, social stability, and regime survival, significantly altering our understanding of how authoritarianism actually works, on the inside.[8] This rapidly developing literature not only posits that institutions and organizations "matter" in non-democracies, it employs functionalist models[9] to demonstrate that political institutions are in fact *the critical causal variables* in the survival of authoritarian regimes.

This so-called "institutional turn" in the comparative study of authoritarianism[10] has already had a significant impact on scholarship in the China field. Nathan's influential article coining the term "authoritarian resilience" in reference to the post-Mao party-state argued that sustained popular support for the government was owed in large part to the skillful deployment of a variety of "input institutions" that worked to siphon off popular discontent without destabilizing the system as a whole.[11] Dali Yang's *Remaking the Chinese Leviathan* argued, in a similar vein, that since the late 1980s the post-Deng leadership had responded to periodic crises by rebuilding the "institutional sinews of the central state," undertaking costly but necessary administrative restructuring which, in turn, improved governance.[12] Several recent studies point to the functional adaptability of the CCP itself in ensuring system survival, highlighting the regularization and upgrading of internal party procedures governing cadre appointments, promotions, and management,[13] including leadership training and education.[14] The considerable malleability of

---

[7] Bunce, *Subversive Institutions*.

[8] Key works in this vein include Brownlee's *Authoritarianism in an Age of Democratization*; Gandhi's *Political Institutions under Dictatorship*; Levitsky and Way's *Competitive Authoritarianism*; Magaloni's *Voting for Autocracy*; and Slater's *Ordering Power*. For a fine review of some of this literature, see Art, "What Do We Know about Authoritarianism after Ten Years?"

[9] Jones, "Seeing like an Autocrat," 26; Blaydes, *Elections and Distributive Politics in Mubarak's Egypt*, 2–3.

[10] Pepinsky, "The Institutional Turn in Comparative Authoritarianism."

[11] Nathan, "Authoritarian Resilience," 6.   [12] Yang, *Remaking the Chinese Leviathan*.

[13] Landry, *Decentralized Authoritarianism*; Edin, "State Capacity and Local Agent Control."

[14] Tsai and Dean, "The CCP's Learning System"; Pieke, *The Good Communist*.

party ideology, further, is cited by some as an important contributor to its longevity;[15] while others put more emphasis on the important role of *informal* institutions in ensuring party-state survival. Kellee Tsai, for example, singles out the role of informal coping strategies deployed by actors working in local settings to expand the range of allowable activities and responses within preexisting institutions. These "informal adaptive institutions" in her view, which range from the quasi-legalization of private enterprise to the calculated expansion of the party's ranks to embrace private entrepreneurs, and even the amendment of the state constitution to sanction private sector development, all worked, without ever subverting the prevailing political system, to adjust and enlarge existing institutions of state power and address new challenges.[16] Likewise, in her work on public goods provision in rural China, Lily Tsai highlights the roles of "informal institutions of accountability" in bolstering the resilience of the system. Looking at local solidary groups – chiefly village temple associations whose activities foster a sense of shared moral obligation between local officials and rural residents – she documents how extra-bureaucratic, extra-legal forms of community accountability can supplement the perceived legitimacy, and increase the responsiveness, of a multi-tiered governing apparatus otherwise acutely prone to remoteness and rigidity.[17]

Even as these new studies helped to deepen our understanding of the workings of "authoritarian resilience," however, they also revealed a wide and partly conflicting range of opinions coexisting within the Chinese elite regarding the ultimate rationales and longer-term goals of political reform, as well as its optimal timing and sequencing.[18] These internal debates were protracted, and frequently fierce. With so much intense elite contestation about *how to reform and reinvigorate the party-state system* going on inside China itself, a few unflinching scholars, like Jean-Pierre Cabestan, were moved to question the necessary inevitability of Western-style liberalization and raise instead the possibility "that China will once again innovate and manage its retreat from communism through a movement towards a softer but stabilized authoritarianism." Cabestan envisioned evolution into a system "that is consultative yet also elitist and corporatist"; one "equipped with a certain legal modernity but not with the rule of law, and only partly institutionalized."[19] Most scholars in the

[15] Shambaugh, *China's Communist Party: Atrophy and Adaptation*; Holbig, *Ideological Reform and Regime Legitimacy*; Dickson, *Wealth into Power*.
[16] Tsai, "Adaptive Informal Institutions." [17] Tsai, *Accountability without Democracy*.
[18] See, e.g., Dittmer, "Three Visions"; Heberer and Schubert, "Political Reform and Regime Legitimacy."
[19] Cabestan, "Is China Moving?," 21.

field, however, like John Lewis and Litai Xue, remained inclined to rule out any satisfactory middle way or "soft authoritarian" solution in the longer run. Either simply overlooking or thoroughly discounting many of the actual reforms that were then ongoing within the party, as well as the lively internal contestation over the very meaning of "political system reform" itself, they concluded instead that "one party rule in China" is still just "living on borrowed time."[20] A *clear choice* against authoritarianism and in favor of democracy would still, one day, have to be made, they argued, on the grounds that, "More challenging forms of political competition will sooner or later emerge as divergent interests further fracture party unity and as the disfranchised and disconnected elements of society seek political justice and coalesce into a viable opposition."[21]

Much of the most sophisticated scholarship in the China studies field of late has, thus, still left us juggling uncomfortably with an antinomy. The mounting evidence does seem to show that, over the years, the CCP has, on the one hand, learned how to rule more subtly and astutely than before. And yet, many have predicted that the "reform-authoritarian" learning curve of the party-state will not extend indefinitely, particularly in light of continuously rising levels of social protest and rampantly festering official corruption. As Andrew Nathan once again, embracing the "performance legitimacy" approach to analyzing the party-state's longevity, has more recently observed, the presumed durability of China's authoritarian pact remains contingent upon the party's ability to deliver consistently high rates of economic growth and deflect internal challenges. But, in order to do so, the "regime must perform constantly like a team of acrobats on a high wire, staving off all crises while keeping its act flawlessly together." Under such tenuous conditions, rather than as a display of "resilience," he suggests that the state of affairs in China now might better be characterized as one of "authoritarian impermanence."[22] Pei Minxin and Cheng Li have likewise sounded speculative early warning bells on the continued longevity of China's ostensibly resilient authoritarian regime, citing a decline in the CCP's capacity to coopt new elites, the crystallization of increasingly activist oppositional forces within Chinese society, and persistent schisms within the upper echelons of the party.[23] Writing on the eve of the world

---

[20] Dickson, *Red Capitalists*; Cabestan, "Is China Moving?"; Yang, *Remaking the Chinese Leviathan*; Schubert, "Reforming Authoritarianism"; and Tsai, *Capitalism without Democracy*.

[21] Lewis and Xue, "Social Change and Political Reform," 942.

[22] Nathan, "Authoritarian Impermanence."

[23] Li, "The End of the CCP's Resilient Authoritarianism?"; Pei, "Is CCP Rule Fragile or Resilient?"

financial crisis and drawing attention to what some continued to treat as a puzzling contrast between the PRC's remarkably positive economic performance and its autocratic political vulnerabilities, Susan Shirk similarly went so far as to tag China as the "fragile superpower."[24]

Among prominent scholars based within the PRC itself, Sun Liping has drawn attention to the ways in which the "phantom of instability" (不稳定幻像) continues to drive a vicious circle of repression that he predicts will likely produce large-scale social unrest in the future.[25] Yu Jianrong has criticized the Hu-Wen government's pursuit of a "socialist harmonious society" as having generated instead a form of "rigid stability" (刚性稳定) that may easily be broken, because it is based on the coercive power of the state to suppress social interests. The only way to reduce the mounting pressure on the system as a whole, Yu argues, is through a combination of "fundamental institutional change and institution-building" and construction of "a robustly institutionalized mechanism for the protection of rights."[26] Sooner or later – or so the evidence seems to indicate to many experts, both in and outside of China, "authoritarian resilience" must somehow be supplanted by genuinely liberal, more democratic, political institutions to avert the potential future crisis of state collapse.

The Limits of the Authoritarian Resilience Paradigm

Thus, at its core, notwithstanding Carothers' hasty proclamation of the end of transitology and the "transition paradigm," this newer scholarly literature on comparative authoritarianism continues to be driven – either explicitly or implicitly – by a conspicuous intellectual yearning to explain the incomplete, partial, and failed "third wave" of democratization. As Howard and Walters point out in a recent critique, the continued reliance upon "[t]erms such as 'authoritarian persistence' and 'authoritarian resilience' ... imply that authoritarianism is somehow unnatural or unsustainable under normal circumstances, thus unintentionally bringing back some of the assumptions of 'transitology' that were supposedly rejected" by the initial champions of the concept. The failure of political scientists to predict first the Soviet collapse in the aftermath of the 1989 Eastern European revolutions, and then the cascading effects of social mobilization during the 2011 Arab Spring, they reason, is the result of analysts' having overemphasized in their models "the prospects for or barriers to democratic reform," thus

[24] Shirk, *China: Fragile Superpower.*   [25] Sun Liping, "The 'Phantom of Instability'."
[26] Yu Jianrong, "From Rigid Stability to Resilient Stability"; Yu Jianrong, "The Present Predicament of Stability Maintenance," 6.

limiting "the purview of what political developments are seen as relevant and important objects of study."[27]

Sensing, as an abiding imperative, a need to *explain* the persistent non-transition of stable autocracies and probe the reasons for the incomplete transition of a range of functional hybrid political regimes then, contemporary scholars of comparative authoritarianism have crafted painstaking, and undoubtedly insightful, accounts that center on the institutions – formal, informal, and adaptive – upon which non-democracies rely in consolidating and perpetuating their rule. In this work, however, the precise connection between particular institutions and overall regime resilience remains, as Karen Orren and Steven Skowronek have observed, still more often presumed than conclusively demonstrated. As they see it, what the neo-institutionalist turn in political science has produced, in large part due to its undergirding assumptions about how institutions operate within political systems, is "an increasingly elaborate iconography of order." Whether institutions are taken to be the crystallization of a political culture's fundamental value orientations, or as the "rules of the game" that shape behavior within a political order, or as the structures and procedures that determine the strategic context within which individuals calculate their self-interest, Orren and Skowronek argue that institutions have long been equated with homeostatic equilibria in political regimes. The enduring focus on institutions as "pillars of order in politics" frequently serves to exaggerate the fixity of political institutions, while eliding the inherent systemic fragilities, maladaptive responses, and "patterned anarchy" that actually comprise the core of much of political life. They conclude that the near-exclusive focus in much institutional analysis on explaining stability, order, and regularity "has obscured a good deal of what is characteristic about institutions in politics and what they have to teach us about political change."[28]

Arguably also, with respect to the study of non-democracies, a neo-institutionalist "iconography of order" may potentially be especially misleading, because institutions in authoritarian regimes commonly exist and operate at the discretion of rulers and their supporting elites.[29] Whereas political institutions in democratic systems are generally interpreted to represent the equilibria of a game among open competitors that is stable, durable, and robust, in authoritarian political contexts, institutions are particularly susceptible to strategic manipulation by powerful elites. As Thomas Pepinsky points out, despite its use of sophisticated

---

[27] Howard and Walters, "Explaining the Unexpected."
[28] Orren and Skowronek, "Beyond the Iconography of Order."
[29] Lagacé and Gandhi, "Authoritarian Institutions."

qualitative and quantitative research designs, the existing "state-of-the-art" in empirical research on comparative authoritarianism has failed to demonstrate the causal effects of institutions on regime durability and resilience.[30] Non-democratic regimes and the institutions that sustain them *may* persist over long periods of time, appearing to weather shocks and challenges, but may *also* – as was the case with the collapse of communist party-states across Eastern Europe and the Soviet Union – suddenly and quite unexpectedly melt away, despite the persistence of adequately functioning institutions.[31] As Andrew Walder acknowledged in retrospect about the wave that brought down single-party-states beginning in 1989: "While today we can look back upon an inexorable cumulative crisis, a few years ago one could just as easily be struck by how little ... deeply rooted problems seemed to shake these stable and stagnant regimes ... [these] regimes [had] appeared [then] to be tougher, more resilient than other varieties of authoritarian rule – and in fact they *were*."[32] *Ex post facto* explanations of collapse that centered primarily on institutional factors, as Stathis Kalyvas argues, failed to differentiate between the relative impacts of institutional decline over the longer term, and the more immediate precipitants of institutional breakdown, and therefore ultimately could not provide a conclusive and robust answer to the question, "Why 1989?"[33] Indeed, with the benefit of hindsight, we can now see that institutionally grounded arguments stressing systemic exhaustion can be interpreted as predicting *both* path-dependent self-perpetuation *and* sudden self-destruction in equal measure and, for that reason, lack real explanatory power.[34]

Not all researchers working within an institutionalist paradigm, of course, were contributing to quite such a static iconography. Those, especially, who were keenly involved in developing alternative modes of *comparative-historical* analysis had begun tackling questions about how institutions can and do change; thus moving away from older-style institutionalist exercises in "comparative statics," to generate something of a "burst of interest in institutional change."[35] New concepts such as "bounded innovation" and "gradual transformative change" – concepts aiming explicitly to conjoin *structure* with *process* as observed over time – gained currency,[36] especially in the study of advanced capitalism's

---

[30] Pepinsky, "The Institutional Turn," 633–635.   [31] Yurchak, *Everything Was Forever.*
[32] Walder, "The Decline of Communist Power," 297–298; See also Dimitrov, "Understanding Communist Collapse and Resilience."
[33] Kalyvas, "The Decay and Breakdown," 334.
[34] Walder, "The Decline of Communist Power," 297.
[35] Hacker, Pierson and Thelen, "Drift and Conversion," 203.
[36] As, e.g., in Streeck and Thelen, *Beyond Continuity.*

morphing economic institutions. To a degree, this newer, more evolutionary, strain in comparative-historical thinking also informed the recent spate of work analyzing, comparatively, the conditions and dynamics of durable authoritarianism.[37] Little of this explicitly more process-oriented or "evolutionary" historical institutionalism, however, seems to have made its way into the literature on China.[38]

More widely noted, within the subfield of Chinese politics, has been some interesting work done lately by Elizabeth Perry, Sebastian Heilmann, and others, aimed at broadening our working concepts concerning adaptive authoritarianism. Rejecting excessively static or linear path-dependency perspectives on "resilience" in favor of an *agency-centered* definition of adaptability, Perry and Heilmann find that it is "the capacity of actors in a system to further resilience" through a *process of continual adjustment* that generally outweighs the importance of institutional mechanisms per se in securing regime persistence. In their reading, regime resilience depends on the ability and willingness of individual and collective *actors* either to innovate or to break from the "rules of the game," and to engage in "maximum tinkering" that may produce new discoveries and novel solutions to existing problems. Inasmuch as the CCP's "guerrilla policy style," as Perry and Heilmann identify and define it, is experimentalist and non-repetitive, they decline to characterize or classify it as an "informal institution." In their 2011 volume instead, through a series of retrospective studies, they trace this distinctive practice of policy generation permitting maximal flexibility as it was in operation *from the Mao era forward* across a broad range of policy areas, and down to the present day.[39]

Yet, despite the salutary theoretical efforts of scholars to leaven institutionalist linearity with considerations of "process" and "agency," the very concepts of adaptation and resilience, which have been imported into comparative governance studies from the ecological and engineering sciences, each carry core assumptions of their own that are problematic

---

[37] Levitsky and Way, "Not Just What, but When (and How)."

[38] For one very recent exception, however, see Ang, *How China Escaped the Poverty Trap*.

[39] Perry and Heilmann, eds., *Mao's Invisible Hand*. Even more recently, Martin Dimitrov and his collaborators have attempted a reprise of the institutionalist framework in synthesis with the continuous adjustment approach as it was articulated by Perry and Heilmann. Their research, which centers on adaptations within consolidated communist states in the realms of economy, ideology, party inclusiveness, and those institutions that promote official accountability, leads them to formulate a theory-straddling contention that the resilience of mature communist party-states "is a function of *continuous adaptive institutional change*," and ultimately to draw the spin-off conclusion that whereas the resilience of mature communist party-states "depends on the ability of [these] regimes to adapt, collapse is more likely when the regimes are no longer capable of implementing adaptive change." Dimitrov, ed., *Why Communism Did Not Collapse*, 3–4 (italics added), 16.

in modeling political affairs. Assertions of the resilience or durability of a particular political system implicitly project assessments of that system's demonstrated capacity to weather previous crises and shocks into the future. Such rectilinear reasoning, however, is tenuous at best. As ecologist C. S. Holling – a leading critic of the concept of stable equilibria – explains, "what a complex system is *doing* seldom gives any indication of what it *would do* under changed conditions."[40] And as Lewis and Steinmo have observed, whereas some colleagues in the social sciences continue reflexively to embrace an oversimplified version of "generalized Darwinism," modern evolutionary biologists are careful to avoid predicting future trends and outcomes in the systems they study. The most sophisticated contemporary advances in natural-world evolutionary theory recognize that random variations within complex systems can and very frequently do set development along totally new and unpredictable paths, not all of which contribute to or ultimately result in overall system survival.[41] Or, as Anthony Giddens long ago perceptively tried to warn us, the concept of adaptation, when transposed from a natural world into a social context, is "irremediably amorphous": either applied so broadly that it is "vacuous," or supportive of "specious and logically deficient claim[s] to functionalist explanation."[42]

Others too have cautioned that since complex non-linear systems are constantly evolving, lessons once learned in the past may no longer retain validity in the present, even amid circumstances that appear to have changed only slightly; and the nature of systems and systems equilibria also can and do change, often unpredictably. In other words, in both the natural world and the human one, behaviors and practices that appear *merely* adaptive may in fact, either incrementally or more rapidly, be shifting the mainstream of change, or even the system *as a whole*, in new and unanticipated directions.[43] Then, too, accommodations in one realm of activity that appear positively adaptive in response to pressures or shifts in the short term may prove maladaptive over a longer time frame, generating path-dependent patterns or feedback loops that undermine the longer-term resilience of a system.[44]

In sum, current concepts of authoritarian resilience and adaptive change have, to be sure, proved useful in challenging the underlying but often implicit teleological assumptions of transitology. They have also offered us some new tools for analyzing how non-democracies may not

[40] Holling, *Adaptive Environmental Assessment and Management.*
[41] Lewis and Steinmo, "Taking Evolution Seriously in Political Science," 238–239.
[42] Giddens, *The Constitution of Society*, 233–234.
[43] Nadasdy, "Adaptive Co-Management and the Gospel of Resilience."
[44] Pierson, *Politics in Time.*

only survive but succeed over time. Nonetheless, researchers in our China studies subfield must confront the fact that more critical imagination is urgently called for if we are to move beyond "authoritarian resilience" and what remain its rather artificially narrowed conceptual frames. If genuinely non-linear paradigms and research questions and hypotheses not still heavily inflected by teleology and false dichotomy are ever to be achieved, then one of our most pressing tasks must be to capture better vantage points from which to survey the full field upon which the political action plays out. Our next step, that is, must be to seek new perspectives from which to apprehend the broader panorama of multivalent practices and processes that are all simultaneously present, exerting influences and energies, and needing to be traced out as contributors to the flow of China's swiftly ongoing political evolution.

Although, arguably, the literature we have been reviewing so far has constituted the mainstream of analysis, especially within the American academy and in the discipline of political science, not by any means all scholars in the China studies field in the West have followed precisely the sort of pathway from transitology to authoritarian resilience that we have sketched. Nor have all been as intent on privileging the study of institutions. Those especially who have been more deeply influenced by the Foucauldian turn in modern social theory have, in their own efforts to move away from the banal either/or choice between liberalism and authoritarianism, been offering us, instead, some interestingly different vantage points on these problems. Gary Sigley, for example, in his introduction to a special issue of *Economy and Society* on Chinese governmentalities, begins with the observation that "China's transition from 'plan' to 'market' has been accompanied by significant shifts in how the practice and objects of government are understood, calculated and acted upon." He speculates that we are witnessing the emergence of a "hybrid socialist-neoliberal (or perhaps "neoleninist') form of political rationality that is at once authoritarian in a familiar political and technocratic sense yet, at the same time, seeks to govern certain subjects, but not all, through their own autonomy."[45] In contrast to Foucault's original conception of governmentality, developed in the context of Western liberal societies, Sigley situates his discussion within a more comprehensive consideration of "non-Western governmentalities." He underscores the disparateness of the elements that can go into the making of such modern yet non-Western governing apparatuses, as well as the opportunism and historical conditionality of their formation. "There is no single hand, invisible or otherwise, projecting its will upon the population," he asserts, "on the

[45] Sigley, "Chinese Governmentalities," 489.

contrary ... government is a much more decentred, ad hoc and contingent affair."[46] Most revealingly in this vein, perhaps, the fascinating proliferation of novel "techniques of the self" and of other powerful forms of governmentality now emerging in China's rapidly re-stratifying, urbanizing, and globalizing society, has been well documented by contemporary China scholars, especially those working in the disciplines of sociology, anthropology, and cultural studies.[47] And this too has alerted at least *some* students of politics to the imperative of expanding their analyses to accommodate those dimensions and practices of "governing" and of "governance" that lie beyond the reach of conventional political institutions and earlier twentieth-century models of "progress" toward political modernity.

For all these reasons, each one of the contributors to this volume may be read as striving, similarly, to move away from the dreary dichotomy of liberalism and authoritarianism to offer different vantage points on the problems of governing and being governed in China. We have shared a working orientation toward the understanding of governance today as full of countervailing pressures, moving in more than one direction at any one time, thus potentially full of paradox; as a *hybrid* or an *amalgam*, made up of rather widely differing purposes and praxes, not all of a piece; and as a complex of shifting forces, one most definitely with "no single hand" in control.

What we believe is required is an approach capable of accommodating, if not "patterned anarchy," then at the very least the mixed-effects *multi-directionality* observable within processes of political change; an approach attuned to recognizing the internal strains of criss-crossed and intersecting trends within political systems. We require a new metaphor, or frame for analysis capable of capturing incremental factors and processes, including those (both great and small, both institutional and otherwise) that can be regarded as contributing to form a "mainstream" of evolutionary change, along with those that may wander off into other channels, drawing strength *away* from the main, and complicating the interplay of political energies and forces. As elaborated further in the sections to come, striving for such a broader panorama – both of converging tributaries and of dead-ended or debilitating offshoot channels of change, such an interlaced modeling of the multiple directions of flow in patterns of

[46] Ibid.
[47] For readers not already entirely familiar with the concept, "techniques of the self" were defined by Foucault as: "those reflective and voluntary practices by which men not only set themselves rules of conduct, but seek to transform themselves, to change themselves in their singular being, and to make of their life an *oeuvre* that carries certain aesthetic values and meets certain stylistic criteria." Foucault, *The Use of Pleasure*, 10–11.

political evolution over long periods of time – is the kind of approach we seek to assist in advancing in the research reported here.

Reframing our Analyses: A Repertoire or a River?

As noted here at the outset, therefore, our initial expectation for our 2012 conference was that, by displaying the illustrative variety of the authors' ongoing research and their findings, we would enable readers of this collection to perceive more vividly the very richness and expansiveness of the *repertoire* of diverse practices enmeshed in different dimensions of governing China today. Our starting point was, then, to acknowledge that whenever we look seriously at political life in China these days, we do find change and evolution continually taking place, but almost never change in just one direction. We believed that only by tacking back and forth – not just *between* different levels of institutions and groups of social actors, but *also across* the full panorama of quite different spheres of political and social encounter – would we begin to apprehend the criss-crossing pressures driving and reshaping patterns of governance, and of power, in China today. Our aim was to conduct a preliminary scan, as it were, of the operative range of governing practices open to careful study in the contemporary Chinese context.

This volume, accordingly, presents the findings of a rich array of up-to-date research investigations, consciously ordered and juxtaposed so as to highlight and illuminate the distinct types of governing practices they examine, and how these are currently at work in the contemporary Chinese polity. Our first three essays explore strategic practices at the level of national political leadership. Elizabeth Perry scrutinizes processes of **manipulating political symbols and sentiments** in hopes of generating authority and emotional support for the party's leadership. Looking at today's "public sentiment" offices and at new digital networks designed to access and assess popular mentalities, she explores the party-state's capacities to transform its vast propaganda apparatus from the forbidding echo chamber of the high-socialist past into more interactive platforms for sustaining mass engagement and persuasion. Sebastian Heilmann next traces distinctive practices of linkage and coordination which have been carried out over time at highest government levels in China, on a professed vital mission to rectify economic distortions and reconcile conflicting interests, while balancing and comprehensively **steering the national economy** and guiding its development. Vivienne Shue then explores contemporary, state-of-the-art practices of mapping, land use planning, and spatial redesign on a grand scale, as these are deployed now by an ever-more technocratically inclined Chinese political leadership seeking to manage the many unwieldy present-day social issues and obstacles it confronts partly through pictorial and cartographic exercises in **envisioning the future**. In these painstakingly mapped visions, we observe the totality of the Chinese nation-space now imagined as one of comprehensively ordered, thoroughly harmonized ultra-productive efficiency, with ecological sustainability and strict preservation guaranteed both for China's priceless natural resources and its prized cultural heritage.

In the following two essays, the spotlight shifts from governance practices at the highest levels of political leadership to sites part the way down the governance hierarchy, where state agents and citizens encounter one another more directly. In this realm – the realm of "people's government" in CCP parlance – we can better observe governing practices now deployed for the monitoring of popular dissatisfactions and the proper regulation of relations between agents of the state and an increasingly critical and demanding public. Here, Joel Andreas and Yige Dong reveal both interesting continuities and significant alterations over time in Chinese practices of "mass supervision," that longstanding CCP technique for eliciting public input and **citizens' oversight** of lower-level power holders within their single-party system. In this middling realm of governance also, Robert Weller considers and dissects state administrators' practices of **overlooking**, or "turning a blind eye" in the face of certain types of transgressive social behavior, episodes of popular noncompliance, even insubordination. Pretending not to notice can be a valuable option in the toolkits of mid-level officials tasked by their superiors to get many, many things done at once, especially when feigned ignorance of what is really going on amongst the people can work to harness extra popular energies to those tasks. Weller here invites us to look at some of the ways in which more ad hoc or informal political arrangements, encounters, and accommodations can prove both reasonably effective in achieving satisfactory social governance and even more enduring than outcomes attainable either through enforcement of formal rules or through repeated acts of resistance against those rules. He argues that "shared fictions" and "lies not intended to deceive" can serve as vital mechanisms for governing, especially in the quickly changing Chinese context, precisely because they are more amenable to improvisation, reinterpretation, and annulments as required.

Our next two essays are devoted to carefully unpacking some aspects of governance as it is currently practiced by agents of the "local state" in China's surging urban and urbanizing settings. Nothing has been more consequential for the trajectory of China's transformation over the last three decades than the calculated expansion of market and market-like relations and transactions throughout all aspects of human interaction – economic, social, and governmental. And these two essays shed much fascinating light on the contemporary application of market-like exchange relationships to newly arising challenges in grassroots-level governance. Both essays focus on the hard-headed **bargaining** and **deal-making** techniques now commonly adopted by local-state actors to settle obstructive conflicts and disputes amid a vocal throng of newly empowered interested parties. As Ching Kwan Lee and Yong Hong Zhang make disturbingly clear in their study, the stakes are high for those who find themselves squatting in the path of urban progress. As protest actions by aggrieved citizens in China's cities have proliferated, local authorities have developed tactics for "buying order" or social stability, thereby turning social instability itself into a medium of exchange at the urban grassroots. Similarly, as Luigi Tomba details, for "rural" villagers anticipating the incorporation of their communities and properties into new urban spaces, the precise terms of exchange on which they will trade away their old collective entitlements in return for urban benefits are stubbornly negotiated. These often protracted tests of will embroil village elites, mid-level authority holders, and agents of the local state in ferocious contests for the best terms and conditions, and the sweetest deals. Through such local-state practices of buying and selling, the outcomes of the bargained settlements reached have varied significantly, yielding only greater fragmentation in what were already uneven patterns of grassroots governance practices.

In the final three essays, our contributors turn to consideration of contemporary Chinese practices of governing the individual, and to the widening exercise of "techniques of the self." Here, the emphasis is on a more subversive realm of governing practices – the making of new classes, the labeling of problematic social categories, and the setting of new individual standards of conduct and quality as measures of personal attainment. Jean-Louis Rocca first dissects the intertwined and cross-cutting processes entailed in the making of China's new middle classes. **Idealizing**, even lionizing, these classes and their habits to celebrate and represent modernity's social "winners" has been and remains a contested process in itself, as he reveals, but one with profound implications for how the contemporary "Chinese urban" is now designed and managed, as well as for how a contemporary "Chinese-style urbanity" is being imagined and enacted, before both domestic and global audiences. Patricia Thornton examines the party-state's multi-stranded governing strategies for simultaneously **patronizing** and policing the new urban underclass, by conjoining the goals of party-building, public service, and social welfare management at the grassroots in China's fast-growing cities. She finds that, alongside new discourses both of salutary self-help and of solicitous charitable assistance to those at the bottom of the social hierarchy, the party now combines "party-building" and "mass work" techniques inherited from the past with newer modes of recruiting, surveiling, and subduing members of the urban poor and the "at-risk" populations, in its quest to guarantee social harmony and stability in urban neighborhoods.

In our final study of **haunting** – a disciplining of the modern self that internalizes within the person a determined, ever-restless "will to improve" – Christian Göbel and Thomas Heberer delve most deeply of all into the ways by which new "techniques of the self" are being applied to the governing of China's governors. Their analysis explores how the imperative pressures brought to bear on party-state officials prompt them to seek ways of raising their game and of improving their performance, particularly through acts of demonstrable, practical problem-solving, policy innovation. They show how this micro-technique of power, although it is applied at the level of the individual official, can be multiplied to produce far-reaching results in redistributing power and responsibility across the entire governing apparatus. If Chinese mid- and low-level officials are increasingly "haunted" by a felt need to improve themselves, as Göbel and Heberer argue, will society and economy be better governed? (Such is the positive, calculated hope of the leadership in Beijing, of course.) Or will other social and economic actors, beyond the bureaucracy, not be swept up and "haunted" too, in the pulsating imperative to keep up? Read together, these three final essays map out several intriguingly fresh territories in Chinese politics and society where what it now means to govern, and to be governed, are still to be explored.

Nurturing self-disciplining state officials possessed of an obsessional "will to improve"; idealizing and celebrating the socio-economy's new classes of "winners"; patronizing and policing its potentially troublesome "losers"; mixing threats with monetary inducements to strike hard political bargains at local levels; disregarding legal violations and overlooking certain political transgressions when convenient; renewing and updating routinized systems for the public oversight of officials; emphatically envisioning glowing futures for the nation, mediated through the magic of super-sophisticated high-tech tools and computer projections, while holding out a dream of sublime balance and bounty; determinedly steering the national economy "rationally," comprehensively and from the top; and assiduously manipulating public sentiment through the repackaging of key historical and cultural symbols – these are some of the most salient and intriguing practices of governing in China today that our contributors have uncovered and chosen to highlight. But is a "repertoire" the most appropriate frame or metaphor to use, we must now pause to reconsider, in characterizing such an interesting tangle of techniques?

Two important observations can be made about the practices our contributors have elucidated here. First, and in all cases, the practices we have drawn attention to in this volume do *not* conform to fixed scripts; they are not static, but are in themselves continually undergoing renewal, revision, and reform. Such governing practices as these are, in themselves, and as a collection or constellation of governing techniques, forever fluid; continuously "in the making." Second, these practices are never performed singly; they overlap each other in time, inhabiting different spaces or dimensions, so to speak, of the larger overall process of governing, intersecting with one another at intervals, but with no one set of practices ever dominating all the action on the political stage. The political stage itself, in fact, does not seem very much to resemble the single platform, artfully set and suitably illuminated, situated at the front of a theater designed to hold the spellbound gaze of an audience. The stage on which the performance of governing proceeds appears more akin to that of a carnival or circus with multiple rings, stalls, and tents all simultaneously offering separate juggling or gymnastic acts, trained animal tricks, popular attractions, games and amusements, some of which the circus-goer is intended only to watch and applaud, but others where the public can join in and try, perhaps, to win a prize.

These two important features of the governance practices explored here – their kinetic fluidity and the simultaneity of their performance – are perhaps not, after all, best captured conceptually as choices made from a pre-set menu or from a pre-rehearsed theatrical repertoire. It was of course Charles Tilly who, most recently and influentially all across the social sciences, deployed the notion of a "repertoire" in his towering studies of collective action. Adapting, as we set out to do, this metaphor of a repertoire to express the availability of a range of political options, from the study of *protest* to the study of issues and tactics in *governing* can also, we do still believe, be useful as an initial orientation to analysis. But if we are to be faithful to Tilly's concept, and avoid stretching it unduly when applying it in the contemporary Chinese context, then we are bound to be attentive to the points where it is discovered to be ill-fitting.

Tilly used the term "repertoire" to describe "a limited set of routines that are learned, shared and acted out through a relatively deliberate process of choice. Repertoires are learned cultural creations, but they do not descend from abstract philosophy or take shape as a result of political propaganda; they emerge from struggle." Rooted in the everyday lived experience of a population, repertoires arise from the practices of "daily social life, existing social relations, shared memories and the logistics of social settings."

By the same token, individuals "experiment constantly with new forms in the search for tactical advantage, but do so in small ways, at the edge of well-established actions." Thus, Tilly understood the "repertoire" as channeling and constraining people's actions along certain well-established pathways, "even when in principle some unfamiliar form of action would serve their interests much better."[48] As on Tilly's conception, our contributors do clearly understand contemporary Chinese *repertoires of governing practices* as, to a degree, both channeling and constraining the work of party-state agents through familiarly patterned sequences and along certain well-worn tracks, to be sure. But the emphasis in these studies is far more, we would have to say, on reinvention; on disrupting prior sequences, departing from previous practices, and deliberately creating new conduits of political interchange if, despite their unfamiliarity, these can be crafted, by governors and governed alike, to "serve their interests much better." And here it is, or so it seems to us now, that the conceptual framework of the *repertoire* reaches certain limits, and does not fit the dynamically unfolding facts on the ground in China quite as well as we had foreseen.

Is there a more fluid metaphor, a better-fitting heuristic to be conjured for our conceptual purposes and tasks, then? Heeding the injunction of Lewis and Steinmo[49] about "taking evolution seriously in political science," the findings of our contributors have stimulated us to turn our attention to some of the revisionist theorizing now taking shape in the fields of evolutionary ecology, including research in macro-evolutionary processes. We have been curious to consider, in particular, some of the very latest and very inspiring work being done by paleo-anthropologists investigating the evolutionary histories of primates, including early hominins such as Australopithecus, and the emergence of the genus *Homo*. Propelled by advances in DNA analysis, and by some extraordinary fossil finds made in recent years over different parts of the globe, these sciences have been going through an especially rich period of theoretical questioning and rethinking. With working assumptions rooted in the Darwinian model of evolution, scientists in these fields once sketched their images of evolutionary change (including primate evolution) in a straight, linear, ever upwardly ascending design; a convention that was later replaced by a conception which came to be represented in the form of a branching tree, and then a bush. But the branches (differing species) on such trees and bushes, still familiar to every school child just a generation ago, were imagined as discrete ones, growing off and away from each other, never to interconnect again in space or time.

---

[48] Tilly, *Popular Contention in Great Britain, 1758–1834*, 42; Tilly, "How to Detect, Describe and Explain Repertoires of Contention," 7.

[49] Lewis and Steinmo, "Taking Evolution Seriously in Political Science."

With the lately mounting genetic and fossil evidence of early hominin population flows and intersections (even inter-breeding), however, many today have concluded that "It is now time to replace" the representation of a tree "with that of an interwoven plexus of genetic lineages that branch out and fuse once again with the passage of time."[50] A new impetus has emerged lately in evolutionary science circles in favor of substituting a more liquid, watery image – and specifically, that of a "braided stream" – for the familiar, but stiff and twiggy tree. The "braided stream" looks now to be a leading candidate for representing some of these empirical researchers' fresh under-standings of the processes they have uncovered through empirical research.[51]

It is worth noting that this concept of a "braided stream" was not invented by the paleo-anthropologists, but rather borrowed by them from the science of physical geography, as a metaphor to better capture the overall patterns of flow and change that they have been observing and seeking to describe. Braided rivers frequently form when glacial ice melts (Figure I.1). Water moves away from the source in fast-flowing streams and rivers, sometimes (depending on the nature of the underlying substrate) transporting great quantities of sediment and larger debris. If the sediment load is very large in relation to the velocity of the stream, coarser material may begin blocking the stream, diverting it and forcing it, often repeatedly, to change course.

Such rivers consist of multiple, smaller channels that divide and recombine, forming an intertwining pattern resembling a braid. A dynamic and fluid model like this may also be appropriately employed to express over-all patterns encountered in other evolutionary processes, including political evolutions, such as those captured in the work of our contributors. A dynamic and fluid model, postulating an ornate tracery of interlacing flows, traveling at differing speeds over uneven spaces and across time could, we think, be fruitfully adapted as a guide to future research in comparative politics as well; as a supplement to some of our more familiar linear (tree-like) and performative (repertoire-like) heuristics.

---

[50] Non-scientists, see Finlayson, "Viewpoint." For a more technical report on some of the science leading up to this change in view, see Hawks and Cochran, "Dynamics of Adaptive Introgression."

[51] For a discussion of the concept aimed at a public policy audience, see Chatterjee, "The River of Life." The stunning and much publicized 2015 report on fossil finds at the Rising Star cave site in South Africa, which documented a previously unknown extinct species of the genus *Homo*, has only added greater persuasive power to such calls for a more riverine model of evolutionary change over extremely long periods of time. The full technical report on these finds can be found at Berger et al., "*Homo naledi*." One non-specialist account is Shreeve, "This Face Changes the Human Story." On the virtues of more woody and more watery metaphors, see Van Arsdale, "Moving beyond Trees."

Figure I.1 Meandering Hopkins River, South Island, New Zealand
Credit: Danita Delimont.

Each of the essays in this volume explores a different dimension of governing as it is being practiced in China today; an analytically distinguishable tributary in the tangled currents of political change. Each is presented below on its own terms and in its own scholarly voice. There has been no attempt to impose a unified view or judgment in the studies collected here. When read together, however, we believe these essays can serve to point our field on to some new conceptual starting points, and fresh research directions. While none of the scholars writing here would ever suggest that institutions, as such, either can or should be overlooked or neglected when studying political and social change, their essays have focused less on governing institutions per se, and more on processes animating, supplementing (or sidestepping) those institutions. As a collection, therefore, they do highlight the harvest to be gleaned by a deliberate broadening of our empirical and analytical concerns beyond the familiar boundaries of a "system reform" approach to our studies, to discern what can be learned as well from explicit observations of governing in practice, and the consequences of those practices for the overall patterning of power processes.

Read and considered together, the essays here also make it apparent that processes of governing and being governed are enacted not as a single, all-absorbing theatrical repertoire. They may be better approached as a circus, staged in different rings and under many tents at once, with performers and audiences intermingling and band music and crowd noises carrying from one space to the next. Under such performing conditions, improvisation can count for as much, or even more, than pre-rehearsals. The model these collected essays suggest, for approaching the study of governance in the Chinese context today therefore, is that of a work (always) "in progress": a work in perpetual if uneven flow, sometimes interrupted, winding and backtracking around obstructions, sometimes even splitting or parting ways to head off in divergent directions from a single juncture. This would be a model of evolutionary change, as it is now being theorized in some of the biological sciences, rather than a model of either linear transition or of orbiting involution and reprise.

To govern China now, these essays suggest, is to *meander*: a multi-stranded process which privileges nimbleness, mutability, and an openness to institutional invention and procedural change, both proactive and reactive. Such protean qualities as these are *not* ones most political scientists associate *either* with the functioning of routinized, elite-managed authoritarian political systems *or* with the prevailing political rhythms that characterize institutionalized, electoral and rule-of-law based democratic systems. Yet they seem to us to capture well that condition of unceasing restlessness so characteristic both of those striving to govern, and of those being governed, in China today.

References

Ang, Yuen Yuen. *How China Escaped the Poverty Trap*. Ithaca, NY: Cornell University Press, 2016.

Armitage, Derek, Berkes, Fikret, and Doubleday, Nancy, eds. *Adaptive Co-management: Collaboration, Learning and Multi-level Governance*. Vancouver: University of British Columbia Press, 2007.

Art, David. "What Do We Know about Authoritarianism after Ten Years?," *Comparative Politics*: (April) 2012, 351–373.

Berger, Lee R., Hawks, John, de Ruiter, Darryl J., Churchill, Steven E. et al. "*Homo naledi*, a New Species of the Genus *Homo*, from the Dinaledi Chamber, South Africa," *eLife* 2015, at elifesciences.org/content/4/e09560.

Blaydes, Lisa. *Elections and Distributive Politics in Mubarak's Egypt*. Cambridge: Cambridge University Press, 2011.

Bogaards, Matthijs. "How to Classify Hybrid Regimes? Defective Democracy and Electoral Authoritarianism," *Democratization*, 16, 2: 2009, 399–423.

Brownlee, Jason. *Authoritarianism in an Age of Democratization*. Cambridge: Cambridge University Press, 2007.

Bunce, Valerie. *Subversive Institutions: The Design and the Destruction of Socialism and the State*. New York: Cambridge University Press, 1999.

Cabestan, Jean-Pierre. "Is China Moving Towards 'Enlightened' but Plutocratic Authoritarianism?," *China Perspectives*, 55 (September – October): 2004, at chinaperspectives.revues.org/412.

Carothers, Thomas. "The End of the Transitions Paradigm," *Journal of Democracy*, 13, 1: 2002, 5–21.

Chatterjee, Sankar. "The River of Life: A Genetic Perspective on Macroevolution," Forum on Public Policy, 2009, at forumonpublicpolicy .com/summer09/archivesummer09/chatterjee.pdf.

Dickson, Bruce. *Red Capitalists in China: The Party, Private Entrepreneurs and Prospects for Political Change*. Cambridge: Cambridge University Press, 2003.

Dimitrov, Martin K. "Understanding Communist Collapse and Resilience," in Dimitrov, ed., *Why Communism Did Not Collapse*, 3–39.

Dimitrov, Martin K., ed. *Why Communism Did Not Collapse: Understanding Authoritarian Regime Resilience in Asia and Europe*. Cambridge: Cambridge University Press, 2013.

Dittmer, Lowell. "Three Visions of Chinese Political Reform," *Journal of Asian and African Studies*, 38, 4–5: 2003, 347–376.

Dodd, Lawrence C. and Jilson, Calvin, eds. *The Dynamics of American Politics: Approaches and Interpretations*. Armonk, NY: Westview Press, 1994.

Edin, Maria. "State Capacity and Local Agent Control in China: CCP Cadre Management from a Township Perspective," *China Quarterly*, 173: 2003, 35–52.

Finlayson, Clive. "Viewpoint: From Tree to Braid." BBC Science and Environment, December 31, 2013, at www.bbc.co.uk/news/science-environment-25559172.

Foucault, Michel. *The Use of Pleasure. The History of Sexuality: Volume Two*. Trans. R. Hurley. Harmondsworth: Penguin (1992) [1984].

Gandhi, Jennifer. *Political Institutions under Dictatorship*. Cambridge: Cambridge University Press, 2010.

Giddens, Anthony. *The Constitution of Society: Outline of the Theory of Structuration*. Cambridge: Polity Press, 1984.

Hacker, Jacob S., Pierson, Paul, and Thelen, Kathleen. "Drift and Conversion: Hidden Faces of Institutional Change," in Mahoney and Thelen, eds., *Advances in Comparative-Historical Analysis*, 180–208.

Hawks, John and Cochran, Gregory. "Dynamics of Adaptive Introgression from Archaic to Modern Humans," *PaleoAnthropology*: 2006, 101–115, at webpages. icav.up.pt/ptdc/CVT/105223/2008/References%20for%20BigBos%20proposal %20[PTDC-CVT-105223-2008]/PDF%20files%20of%20references_ max30%20[BigBos]/Hawks%202006_Review%20on%20human%20introgres sion.pdf.

Heberer, Thomas and Schubert, Gunter. "Political Reform and Regime Legitimacy in Contemporary China," *ASIEN*, 99: 2006, 9–28.

Heilmann, Sebastian and Perry, Elizabeth J., eds. *Mao's Invisible Hand: The Political Foundations of Adaptive Governance in China*. Cambridge, MA: Harvard University Asia Center, 2011.

Holling, C. S. *Adaptive Environmental Assessment and Management*. London: John Wiley and Sons, 1978.

Howard, Marc Morjé and Walters, Meir R. "Explaining the Unexpected: Political Science and the Surprises of 1989 and 2011," *Perspectives on Politics* 12, 2: (June) 2014, 394–408.

Jones, Calvert W. "Seeing like an Autocrat: Liberal Social Engineering in an Illiberal State," *Perspectives on Politics*, 13, 1: (March) 2015, 26.

Jowitt, Ken. *New World Disorder: The Leninist Extinction*. Berkeley: University of California Press, 1992.

Kalyvas, Stathis N. "The Decay and Breakdown of Communist One-Party Systems," *Annual Review of Political Science* 2: 1999, 323–343.

Lagacé, Clara Boulianne and Gandhi, Jennifer. "Authoritarian Institutions," in Dimitrov, ed., *Why Communism Did Not Collapse*, 278–291.

Landry, Pierre. *Decentralized Authoritarianism in China: The Communist Party's Control of Local Elites in the Post-Mao Era*. Cambridge and New York: Cambridge University Press, 2008.

Levitsky, Steven and Way, Lucan A. *Competitive Authoritarianism: Hybrid Regimes after the Cold War*. Cambridge: Cambridge University Press, 2010.

Levitsky, Steven and Way, Lucan A. "Not Just What, but When (and How): Comparative-Historical Approaches to Authoritarian Durability," in Mahoney and Thelen, eds., *Advances in Comparative-Historical Analysis*, 97–120.

Lewis, John and Xue Litai. "Social Change and Political Reform in China: Meeting the Challenge of Success," *China Quarterly*, 176: 2003, 926–942.

Lewis, Orion and Steinmo, Sven. "Taking Evolution Seriously in Political Science," *Theory in Biosciences*, 129: 2010, 235–245.

Li, Cheng. "The End of the CCP's Resilient Authoritarianism? A Tripartite Assessment of Shifting Power in China," *China Quarterly*, 211: 2012, 595–623.

Magaloni, Beatriz. *Voting for Autocracy: Hegemonic Party Survival and its Demise in Mexico. New York*, Cambridge: Cambridge University Press, 2008.

Mahoney, James and Thelen, Kathleen, eds. *Advances in Comparative-Historical Analysis*. Cambridge: Cambridge University Press, 2015.

Merkel, Wolfgang. "Embedded and Defective Democracies," *Democratization*, 11, 5: 2004, 33–58.

Nadasdy, Paul. "Adaptive Co-management and the Gospel of Resilience," in Armitage, Berkes, and Doubleday, eds., *Adaptive Co-management*, 208–227.

Nathan, Andrew J. "Authoritarian Impermanence," *Journal of Democracy*, 20, 3: 2009, 37–40.

Nathan, Andrew J. "Authoritarian Resilience," *Journal of Democracy*, 14, 1: 2003, 6–17.

Orren, Karen and Skowronek, Steven. "Beyond the Iconography of Order: Notes for a 'New Institutionalism'," in Dodd and Jilson, eds., *The Dynamics of American Politics*, 311–330.

Pei, Minxin. "Is CCP Rule Fragile or Resilient?" *Journal of Democracy*, 23, 1: 2012, 27–41.

Pepinsky, Thomas. "The Institutional Turn in Comparative Authoritarianism," *British Journal of Political Science*, 44: 2013, 631–653.

Pieke, Frank N. *The Good Communist: Elite Training and State Building in Today's China*. Cambridge: Cambridge University Press, 2009.

Pierson, Paul. *Politics in Time: History, Institutions, and Social Analysis*. Princeton: Princeton University Press, 2004.

Schedler, Andreas, ed. *Electoral Authoritarianism: The Dynamics of Unfree Competition*. Colorado: Lynn Rienner, 2006.

Schubert, Gunter. "Reforming Authoritarianism in Contemporary China: Reflections on Pan Wei's Consultative Rule of Law Regime," *ASIEN*, 94: 2005, 7–24.

Shambaugh, David. *China's Communist Party: Atrophy and Adaptation*. Berkeley: University of California Press, 2008.

Shirk, Susan L. *China: Fragile Superpower*. Oxford: Oxford University Press, 2008.

Shreeve, Jamie. "This Face Changes the Human Story. But How?," *National Geographic*, September 10, 2015, at http://news.nationalgeographic.com/2015/09/150910-human-evolution-change/.

Snyder, Richard. "Beyond Electoral Authoritarianism: The Spectrum of Nondemocratic Regimes," in Schedler, ed., *Electoral Authoritarianism*, 219–232.

Streeck, Wolfgang and Thelen, Kathleen, eds. *Beyond Continuity: Institutional Change in Advanced Economies*. Oxford: Oxford University Press, 2005.

Sun Liping (孙立平). ("The 'Phantom of Instability' and the Vicious Cycle of Stability Maintenance"). "'不稳定幻像'与维稳怪圈," 人民论坛, 7: 2010, 23–4.

Tilly, Charles. "How to Detect, Describe and Explain Repertoires of Contention," Working Paper No. 150, Center for Studies of Social Change, The New School for Social Research, New York, 1992.

Tilly, Charles. *Popular Contention in Great Britain, 1758–1834*. Cambridge, MA: Harvard University Press, 1995.

Tsai, Kellee. "Adaptive Informal Institutions and Endogenous Institutional Change in China," *World Politics*, 59: 2006, 116–141.

Tsai, Kellee. *Capitalism without Democracy: The Private Sector in Contemporary China*. Ithaca, NY: Cornell University Press, 2007.

Tsai, Lily L. *Accountability without Democracy: Solidary Groups and Public Goods Provision in Rural China*. New York: Cambridge University Press, 2007.

Tsai, Wen-Hsuan and Dean, Nicola. "The CCP's Learning System: Thought Unification and Regime Adaptation," *China Journal*, 69: 2013, 87–107.

Van Arsdale, Adam. "Moving beyond Trees: Metaphors for Evolution," *The Pleistocene Scene – A.P. Van Arsdale Blog*, September 10, 2015, at blogs .wellesley.edu/vanarsdale/2015/09/29/fossils/moving-beyond-trees-metaphors -for-evolution/.

Walder, Andrew G. "The Decline of Communist Power: Elements of a Theory of Institutional Change," *Theory and Society*, 23, 2: 1994, 297–323.

Yang, Dali L., *Remaking the Chinese Leviathan: Market Transition and the Politics of Governance in China*. Stanford: Stanford University Press, 2004.

Yu Jianrong (于建嵘). ("From Rigid Stability to Resilient Stability: An Analytical Framework for China's Social Order"). "从刚性稳定到韧性稳定 – 关于中国社会秩序的一个分析框架," 学习与探索, 184: 2009, 113–118.

Yu Jianrong (于建嵘). ("The Present Predicament of Stability Maintenance Pressure and the Way Forward"). "当前压力维稳的困境与出路," 探索与争鸣, 9: 2012, 6.

Yurchak, Alexei. *Everything Was Forever, Until It Was No More: The Last Soviet Generation*. Princeton: Princeton University Press, 2006.

Zheng, Yongnian. *Will China Become Democratic? Elite, Class and Regime Transition*. Singapore: Eastern Universities Press, 2004.

I

Leadership Practices

Manipulating Symbols and Sentiments

1   Cultural Governance in Contemporary China: "Re-Orienting" Party Propaganda

Elizabeth J. Perry

In explaining the surprising staying power of the Chinese communist regime, analysts point to a number of critical factors: the party-state's ability to recruit, monitor, and hold accountable government officials; to grow and guide the economy via flexible policy levers; to invest in valued public goods; to enlist the active support of entrepreneurs and other key social groups; and to keep the lid on popular protest through a clever combination of coercion, censorship, cooptation, and conciliation.[1] There is, however, a more elusive, yet no less critical, element of regime endurance: the facility of the party-state to justify its rule in terms that resonate both at home and abroad. For this task, the People's Republic of China (PRC) leans heavily upon *cultural governance*, or the deployment of symbolic resources as an instrument of political authority. It does so, moreover, in a manner that underscores the distinctively "Chinese" character of the political system. A state whose ideology and institutions were imported almost wholesale from the Soviet Union is represented in party propaganda as part and parcel of a glorious "Chinese tradition." Over the years, the CCP has "re-Oriented" its message so as to come across as culturally congruent with its principal target audience. The process bespeaks a dynamic and diversified propaganda operation that is as attentive to popular emotions as to party ideology.

Cultural Governance

Cultural governance figures in the legitimation and perpetuation of any enduring state system.[2] When practiced by critics of the system (whether from inside or outside the state apparatus), cultural governance may serve

---

[1] Tsai, *Accountability without Democracy*; Tsai, *Capitalism without Democracy*; Naughton and Yang, eds., *Holding China Together*; Heilmann and Perry, eds., *Mao's Invisible Hand*; Chen, *Social Protest*.
[2] Edelman, *The Symbolic Uses*; Shapiro, *Methods and Nations*.

to question – or even to resist – state power.[3] Controlling and channeling symbolic political expression so that it strengthens rather than challenges regime legitimacy is a concern for all states, but perhaps especially so for those which lack robust and respected electoral and legal institutions capable of conferring procedural legitimacy on state leaders.[4] In the absence of firmly established democratic institutions, leaders may find historical and cultural assertions of particular value in staking a claim to legitimacy.

China's rulers today are explicit in the high value they place on cultural governance. They are almost equally explicit in their instrumental use of cultural governance for nationalistic ends. In an address to the 18th Party Congress in November 2012, retiring CCP General-Secretary Hu Jintao declared that "culture is the life blood of the nation." He emphasized that "the strength and international competitiveness of Chinese culture is an important indicator of China's power and prosperity and the revival of the Chinese nation." Hu called for promoting "traditional" Chinese culture and made multiple references to the "great revival of the Chinese nation" (中华民族伟大复兴), a phrase repeated by incoming CCP General-Secretary Xi Jinping in his own remarks to the Party Congress. Standing in front of a monumental painting of the Great Wall, Xi proudly referenced China's 5,000-year-old civilization, proclaiming that "the great revival of the Chinese nation is the greatest dream of the Chinese nation in modern history."[5] Immediately after the Congress, to hammer home his "China Dream" Xi led the Politburo Standing Committee on a well-publicized visit to the National Museum to view an exhibition entitled *The Road to Revival* which featured the heroic role of the Communist Party in spearheading nationalist struggles. Opening with China's humiliation in the Opium Wars, the exhibit sounded a triumphal note with its declaration that "today the Chinese nation towers majestically in the Orient; the brilliant prospect of the great revival is already unfolding before us. The dream and quest of China's sons and daughters can definitely be realized!"[6] The CCP was re-Orienting its propaganda to showcase the glories of the ancient civilization that it claims to be representing and reviving.

That this line of cultural-cum-nationalist propaganda enjoys considerable currency in the contemporary PRC had been demonstrated two years earlier when the CCP celebrated its 90th anniversary with a blockbuster movie entitled *Beginning of the Great Revival*. Featuring a star-studded cast of Chinese and Overseas Chinese actors, the film

---

[3] Callahan, *Cultural Governance and Resistance*.   [4] Wedeen, *Ambiguities of Domination*.
[5] "New Party Leadership"; "Xi Jinping Pledges."   [6] fuxing.chnmuseum.cn/intro.php.

conflated the birth of the Communist Party with the great revival of the Chinese nation and portrayed the young Mao Zedong as a central figure in that national renaissance. While some of its popularity can be ascribed to the large number of complimentary tickets issued by government agencies, *Beginning of the Great Revival* was reportedly the top-selling Chinese movie in the PRC in 2011, outranking even *Harry Potter* and *Spiderman* in ticket sales.[7]

Cultural Nationalism

The current prominence of cultural nationalism in PRC governance is often interpreted as a recent development, traceable to the suppression of the Tiananmen Uprising of 1989 and subsequent Patriotic Education Campaign. Faced with the discrediting of Marxism-Leninism in the post-Cold War era, so the argument goes, the Chinese state cast about for a new framework of legitimation, settling upon a formula intended to derive strength from popular pride in the glories of Chinese civilization (as well as the gains of the communist revolution).[8] The state-sponsored Patriotic Education Campaign, launched with much fanfare in the 1990s, sought to inoculate the younger generation against the temptations of "bourgeois liberalism" by a dual focus on the cultural splendors of the Chinese past and the heroic sacrifices of the CCP in rebuilding the Chinese nation.[9]

There is definite merit in this argument, as long as it does not obscure the importance of cultural governance with nationalist objectives as an instrument of mobilization and rule (played in different keys and at different decibel levels) throughout the ninety-plus-year history of Chinese communism. As Mao proclaimed during the war with Japan:

Our national history goes back several thousand years and has its own characteristics and innumerable treasures ... We should sum up our history from Confucius to Sun Yat-sen and take over this valuable legacy ... [W]e can put Marxism into practice only when it is integrated with the specific characteristics of our country and acquires a definite national form ... Foreign stereotypes must be abolished, there must be less singing of empty, abstract tunes, and dogmatism must be laid to rest; they must be replaced by the fresh, lively Chinese style and spirit which the common people of China love.[10]

The contemporary emphasis on cultural nationalism, rather than a sharp break with an earlier reliance on Marxism-Leninism-Mao Zedong

---

[7] "Historic Rankings."   [8] Guo, *Cultural Nationalism*, 1–2.
[9] Zhao, *A Nation-State by Construction*, 219.
[10] Mao, "The Role of the Chinese Communist Party," 155–156.

thought as the ideological foundation of Chinese communism, marks yet another turn in a tortuous legitimation project that has frequently (if fitfully) drawn upon a wide range of resonant symbols from the Chinese past – elite and folk culture alike – to buttress the standing of the CCP. Today's Patriotic Education Campaign is a recent expression of an impulse with deep roots in the experience of the Chinese Communist Party.[11]

Mao Zedong drew the connection between the victory of his revolution and the revival of the Chinese nation ten days before the official founding of the PRC, when he declared dramatically that China had at last "stood up" to reclaim its historical birthright:

the Chinese people, comprising one quarter of humanity, have now stood up. The Chinese have always been a great, courageous and industrious nation; it is only in modern times that they have fallen behind ... From now on our nation will ... work courageously and industriously to foster its own civilization ... Ours will no longer be a nation subject to insult and humiliation. We have stood up.[12]

A focus on patriotic mobilization, intended to reclaim China's rightful place in the world order, marked PRC governance practices from the outset. With the outbreak of the Korean War in 1950, Chinese citizens were encouraged to sign "patriotic pledges" (爱国公约) guaranteeing their commitment to the nationalist cause. That period also saw the beginning of a series of impressive "Patriotic Health Campaigns" which framed mass public health and sanitation programs as "patriotic" actions to restore the Chinese nation to good health in order to combat American imperialism.[13] In the Great Leap Forward and Cultural Revolution, Chinese nationalism was reframed in opposition to Soviet revisionism. Mao Zedong was now revered as a leader who had not only rescued the Chinese nation from the threat of Western imperialism and Japanese militarism; he was also touted as the global guru of revolutionary ideology. Henceforth, political correctness would be decided not in Moscow but in Beijing.

In the early post-Mao era, when "reform and opening" encouraged criticism of Mao Zedong and his radical policies, CCP leaders debated how to deal with the Maoist legacy.[14] Deng Xiaoping's decision to stem the rising tide of de-Maoification by affirming commitment to "Socialism with Chinese Characteristics" was critical in facilitating a formidable

---

[11] Perry, *Anyuan*.   [12] Mao, "The Chinese People Have Stood Up!"
[13] Rawnsley, "The Great Movement," 303ff. The anti-SARS campaign of 2003 was also presented as a "patriotic health campaign," but without the anti-Americanism of earlier days.
[14] Baum, *Burying Mao*.

blend of "traditional" and "revolutionary" sources of symbolic authority to serve a nationalist end. Although the practice of cultural nationalism gained further attention and momentum after the suppression of the 1989 Tiananmen Uprising, it was already a pillar of CCP propaganda prior to June Fourth.

Internal circulation publications of the Central Propaganda Department (CPD) show that the project of re-Orienting its message to make the communist system appear more "Chinese" is not a post-June Fourth development. In 1983–1984, for example, the CPD issued a series of directives that called for strengthening both "patriotic educa-tion" in Chinese history and "education in the revolutionary tradition."[15] On April 19, 1989, only a few days after the Tiananmen protests had begun and almost two months before the suppression of June Fourth, the CPD communicated a new policy on the hanging of portraits in Tiananmen Square that revealed central leaders' commit-ment to the indigenization of their revolutionary tradition. Whereas past practice had called for the portraits of Marx, Engels, Lenin, and Stalin to be hung alongside Mao's portrait on the two major national holidays of May 1 and October 1, the new policy mandated that henceforth no foreign luminaries would be displayed on these occasions. On May 1 (International Labor Day), Mao's portrait would hang in solitary splen-dor atop the Gate of Heavenly Peace. On October 1 (National Day), Mao would be joined by Sun Yat-sen. The CPD circular explained that most countries display portraits of their national heroes on national holidays and that it was therefore appropriate that Sun Yat-sen, as forefather of China's modern revolution, should hang alongside Chairman Mao, who had led the Communist Party and the Chinese people in a revolution that overthrew the "three big mountains" (imperi-alism, feudalism, and bureaucratic capitalism) to establish the People's Republic of China.[16]

The project of indigenizing the regime's claim to legitimacy was thus well underway prior to June Fourth, but the official verdict on the Tiananmen Uprising reinforced the trend. In the immediate aftermath of the crackdown, party leaders charged that the student protest had been a product of the neglect of propaganda and "thought work" on the part of the now disgraced former General-Secretary of the CCP, Zhao Ziyang. Zhao's lax attitude, it was alleged, had allowed proponents of wholesale Westernization to debase China's traditional culture and revolutionary tradition, thereby permitting "Western bourgeois" notions of democracy,

[15] CPD, ed., "Utilize Revolutionary Relics," 73.
[16] CPD, ed., "Conditions for Hanging Portraits," 1867.

freedom, and human rights to gain hold among the young.[17] To rid the nation of such pernicious ideas, the CPD (assisted by the iron fist of public security) spearheaded a massive censorship sweep in which thirty-eight publishing houses were closed down, more than 700 periodicals were discontinued, and some 32 million books and magazines were confiscated.[18]

Censorship has been an essential tool of party control over the ideological arena, but of greater significance in the long run would be a proactive effort to re-Orient the terms of public discourse. Quoting Chairman Mao's warning that "if the East wind does not prevail over the West wind, then the West wind will prevail over the East wind," the new General-Secretary of the CCP, Jiang Zemin, called for an acceleration of ideological work intended to showcase China's "dazzling material and spiritual civilization."[19] In response, a central party directive of July 1989 enjoined propaganda departments and social science academies across the country to undertake systematic research into Chinese history, culture, society, and economy to serve as the foundation for a propaganda initiative that would demonstrate the Chinese people's "creativity, fighting capacity, and commitment to national unification."[20]

The concern for cultural governance has grown steadily in recent years. Although the budget of the CPD is not publicly accessible, figures for government spending on "cultural undertakings" (文化事业) give a rough idea of the general trend. In the years immediately following the Tiananmen Uprising, these expenditures increased by over 200 million yuan per year (from RMB 1,357,000,000 in 1989 to RMB 1,946,000,000 in 1992). With the launching of the Patriotic Education Campaign, spending on cultural initiatives took another major leap (from RMB 2,237,000,000 in 1993 to RMB 3,425,000,000 in 1994). It has continued to climb ever since. In 2010, the official figure stood at RMB 52,952,000,000 – a fifty fold increase in twenty years.[21]

Internal bulletins from the CPD, intended for the use of cadres in the cultural, propaganda, and education fields, stress that the CCP is to be depicted as the chief custodian of Chinese civilization, credited with perpetuating an uninterrupted party tradition of protecting ancient cultural relics as national treasures. Even under the duress of war, it is

[17] Jiang Zemin, "Talk at the National Conference," 916–918; CPD, ed., "Utilize Revolutionary Relics," 72–74.
[18] Wang Renzhi, "Stick to Correct Policy," 964.
[19] Jiang Zemin, "Talk at the National Conference," 915.
[20] Party Central Notice, 938–949.
[21] *Statistical Yearbook of Cultural Initiatives*; Editorial Committee of the Chinese Financial Yearbook, ed., *Chinese Financial Yearbook*.

alleged, the party ordered the military to go to great lengths to safeguard China's cultural heritage. In order to preserve priceless artifacts such as those contained in the Forbidden City, for example, the CCP supposedly took every possible measure to ensure the peaceful liberation of the city of Beijing. In the forty years thereafter, the importance of cultural preservation was reflected in the establishment of a special government agency and the promulgation of numerous national laws, policies, and directives for this purpose.[22]

The CPD emphasizes that schools, family, and society all bear responsibility for instructing the younger generation in the protection and promotion of cultural relics, which is considered beneficial for cultivating allegiance to one's hometown as well as fostering patriotism.[23] National holidays, anniversaries of important historical events (including those causing national humiliation), and major athletic competitions are singled out as excellent opportunities for disseminating propaganda capable of stirring strongly patriotic feelings. The collective participation and mass enthusiasm exhibited on such occasions, it is explained, permits a deep and abiding educational impact.[24] These bulletins make no mention of the destructive episodes in CCP history when party leaders actively encouraged vicious attacks on elements of Chinese tradition: the Red Terror of the 1920s, the Destroy the Four Olds of the 1960s, and the Criticize Lin Biao Criticize Confucius Campaign of the 1970s, for example.[25] Rather, the re-Orientation of the CPD calls for the recognition, protection, and preservation of revolutionary and pre-revolutionary relics alike, as though they are all an integral part of a unitary and uninterrupted glorious "Chinese tradition."[26]

As part of the post-Tiananmen Patriotic Education Campaign, propaganda departments at all levels of the system are encouraged to identify familiar local sites to serve as "educational bases" where instruction in the history of China and the indispensable role of the CCP in unifying and modernizing the nation can be effectively conducted.[27] Such education, it is stressed, should encourage young people to nurture fervent feelings for the motherland.[28] "Patriotism," the CPD explains, "is the powerful emotion ... of deeply loving the motherland ... The children of China, having been raised in the bosom of the motherland, should harbor

---

[22] CPD, ed., "Notice of CPD, Ministry of Culture, and National Relics Bureau concerning Publication of 'Everyone Loves and Protects the Relics of the Motherland'," 1875.
[23] Ibid., 1876.   [24] Wang Renzhi, "Stick to Correct Policy," 964–965.
[25] Some CCP leaders did, however, make an effort to protect certain cultural treasures from Red Guard rampages in the Cultural Revolution. See Ho, "To Protect and Preserve."
[26] CPD, ed., "Important Points from the Conference," 1949–1951.
[27] CPD, ed., *Raise High the Banner*, 152.   [28] Party Central Notice, 938–949.

profound sentiments toward the motherland akin to what they feel toward their own mother."[29] The key to instilling these feelings is said to be a proper appreciation of China's unique "national character" (国情).[30]

Reeducating Chinese youth so as to prevent another student uprising was a top priority in the aftermath of June Fourth, but party leaders also recognized a pressing need to counteract the hostility of the international community. At a July 1989 meeting of provincial propaganda directors from around the country, Premier Li Peng blamed reporting by American and Hong Kong journalists for having fanned the flames of insurgency prior to the imposition of martial law. Li went on to reveal that he had recently floated with Chinese diplomats posted overseas his own suggestion that the CPD produce a video sympathetic to the June Fourth crackdown and pay for it to be broadcast on television networks around the world. Having been rebuffed on grounds that his scheme would be unacceptable to the foreign media, Li Peng remarked sarcastically that although the Western media claimed to have a free press, it was obviously highly restricted and rigid! He bemoaned China's having failed to seize the propaganda initiative while the Tiananmen protests were still underway, and concluded that the PRC must redouble its international propaganda efforts in future.[31]

The dismantling of the Soviet Union in 1991 further convinced the Chinese leaders of the need for an international propaganda initiative that would distinguish its own "national character" from that of its erstwhile communist "Big Brother." The CPD called for drawing a sharp contrast between China's political stability and the existential crisis unfolding in the former USSR.[32] Post mortems on the Soviet collapse highlighted the issue of cultural governance, noting the significance of ethnic and cultural identity in sustaining or subverting a communist system.[33] As one analyst put it,

The survival of the Soviet Union as a sovereign state was due to the eleven minorities who allied in support of the socialist system and Marxist ideology. It was precisely this cultural identity that constituted the national interest of the Soviet Union. As soon as this cultural identity was no longer recognized, the national unity of the USSR disintegrated. From this we can see that cultural identity [文化认同] is the precondition for national interest.[34]

---

[29] CPD, ed., *Raise High the Banner*, 217.   [30] Party Central Notice, 945.
[31] Li Peng, "Talk at the National Conference," 926.
[32] Wang Renzhi, "Stick to Correct Policy," 966.
[33] See, for example, the internal circulation video on lessons from the Soviet collapse produced for party cadres by the Central Discipline Commission in 2006, *Thinking of Danger*.
[34] Tao Xiuao, "The Advent of an Era," 13.

Overseas Chinese, especially those residing in Taiwan, Hong Kong, and Macau, are a major focus of international propaganda efforts aimed at solidifying national identity and interest. The selection of sites for patriotic education that would appeal to this critical constituency is particularly encouraged. For example, in 1994–1995, Shaoxing's Propaganda Department was praised for having identified and publicized (with the assistance of academic expertise) more than twenty sites in the city that could be associated with Yu the Great, a legendary ruler who is respected along with Yao and Shun as one of the three major sages of ancient China and to whom prayers were traditionally offered for purposes of flood prevention. Noting that Overseas Chinese continue to pay homage to Yu, the Zhejiang government approved a recommendation by the Shaoxing Propaganda Department to promote the public worship of Yu the Great by refurbishing his tomb so that tourists and pilgrims could congregate there for collective observances. In connection with the city's initiative, dubbed the "Number One Construction Project for Worshiping Yu," donations were sought from both domestic and overseas organizations and individuals. The Shaoxing native-place association of Hong Kong explained its sizable donation to the project by noting that public worship of Yu "promotes our Chinese national spirit, perpetuates our excellent historical and cultural traditions ... and strengthens national cohesion." To publicize the initiative, the Shaoxing Propaganda Department convened several international academic conferences and sponsored the publication of a series of scholarly monographs on the subject of Yu the Great. It also fed favorable reports about the project to domestic and international newspapers, magazines, radio, and television. At a ceremony to mark the first public commemoration of Yu at his refurbished tomb on April 20, 1995, more than a thousand representatives of the PRC's people's political consultative conference, central ministries, and provincial and city governments were joined by delegates from Taiwan, Hong Kong, Macau, and even a number of Western countries.[35]

As the Shaoxing case suggests, propaganda departments often enlist professional academic talent in the effort to uncover and exploit appropriate cultural resources. This is not a new practice; establishment intellectuals have long played a critical role in promoting the party-state's agenda.[36] Grants from the Ministry of Education and other government agencies are frequently tied to projects that reflect propaganda priorities. Academies of social sciences at all levels and departments of social

---

[35] CPD, ed., *Raise High the Banner*, 119–122.
[36] Hamrin and Cheek, eds., *China's Establishment Intellectuals*.

sciences and humanities in the major universities depend heavily upon such funding and routinely reshape research programs to align with the party's changing priorities as announced by the CPD.[37] Today, for example, researchers across the country are scrambling to put some flesh on the barebones of Xi Jinping's call for a "China Dream."[38] But this work is not left entirely to academics. Cadres are also supposed to devote serious attention to investigation and study. According to an internal directive of the CPD, propaganda cadres are expected as a rule of thumb to spend 90 percent of their workday engaged in research and only 10 percent in formulating propaganda materials and policy recommendations.[39] The CPD by no means sees its primary mission as an academic one, however. It is much more concerned about the emotional and political than the cerebral or scholarly impact of its efforts.

Emotion Work

The importance of gauging and guiding public emotions, both domestic and international, is emphasized repeatedly in CPD teaching materials developed for party cadre schools at all levels of the system. The overriding goal is to make people *feel* sympathetic to the party's agenda. Central to this goal is a concern for "public sentiment" (舆情) – an umbrella concept that refers to the cumulative emotional and cognitive impact on ordinary people (Chinese and foreigners alike) of party and government actions. In contrast to the more familiar phrase "public opinion" (舆论), the term "public sentiment" highlights the emotional – as opposed to rational – underpinnings of public discourse. It is the responsibility of party cadres to assess and interpret public sentiment so that policies can be fine-tuned in response.[40]

Under the principle that "internal and external are different" (内外有别), the CPD recommends discrimination in choosing appropriate symbols to appeal to different audiences. When the target audience is international rather than domestic, Chairman Mao and the revolutionary origins of the PRC usually go unmentioned in favor of concentrating on the splendors of the "Chinese cultural tradition." Within this "tradition," moreover, international propaganda may be further differentiated according to the

[37] Brady, *Marketing Dictatorship*; Sleeboom-Faulkner, *The Chinese Academy of Social Sciences*, 19–22.
[38] Propaganda chief Liu Yunshan also ordered that the concept of the Chinese dream be written into school textbooks so that it "enters students' brains." "Chasing the Chinese Dream."
[39] Wang Renzhi, "Stick to Correct Policy," 978.
[40] Fan Hongyi, ed., *The Latest in Party Propaganda Work*, 182–183.

particular country toward which it is directed. A recent cadre handbook notes that propaganda aimed at the United States should emphasize the contributions of individual heroes in Chinese history because Americans admire individuals; propaganda targeting Japan should emphasize China's beautiful natural scenery and colorful folk customs because these appeal to Japanese sensibilities; propaganda directed at Europe should highlight China's love of the environment and its inherent pacifism in order to satisfy the Green and anti-war sympathies of Europeans, and so on.[41]

CPD directives often begin with a familiar quote from Chairman Mao: "Without investigation, no one has a right to speak." The main purpose of investigation, today as in the past, is to understand the attitudes and outlook of the intended audience so as to formulate effective tactics and strategies to advance Communist Party priorities. The CPD still points to Mao's 1927 *Report on an Investigation of the Peasant Movement in Hunan*, which extolled revolutionary violence in the Chinese countryside, as setting the standard for gauging public emotions in accordance with "mass line" principles. Cadres are urged to approach their work as an art form as well as a science; propaganda should appeal as strongly to ordinary people's aesthetic and emotional awareness as to their reason. At the same time, propaganda work must be continuously upgraded and updated to suit the ever-evolving inclinations of a wide variety of contemporary audiences.[42]

As the reference to Mao's *Hunan Report* indicates, serious attention to mass emotions is nothing new for the Chinese Communist Party. From its revolutionary days, the CCP systematized "emotion work" as part of a conscious strategy of psychological engineering. After 1949, patterns of emotion work developed during the wartime years lived on in a series of highly charged mass campaigns that stretched from Land Reform and the Suppression of Counter-Revolutionaries through the Great Leap Forward and the Cultural Revolution.[43]

Mao Zedong himself was keenly attuned to the importance of emotions in mass mobilization, and devoted significant attention in his writings to a discussion of the role of human feelings in revolutionary transformation.[44] But Mao was not alone among the Chinese communist revolutionaries in this recognition. As early as the Anyuan workers' club of 1922–1925, CCP propaganda cadres made a conscious and concerted effort to enlist mass emotions to serve the revolutionary cause. Cultural activities such as drama and cinema were seen as especially effective

[41] Ibid., 163–164. [42] *Pragmatics of Propaganda Work*, 59–67.
[43] Perry, "Moving the Masses," 111–128; Perry, "From Mass Campaigns to Managed Campaigns," 30–61.
[44] See, for example, Mao, "Talks at the Yenan Forum."

mobilizing vehicles because of their ability to tug at people's heartstrings.[45] The process of cultural governance with an eye toward its emotional effect was further systematized after the establishment of the Jiangxi Soviet in the early 1930s. A CCP propagandist recalled of the make-shift theatrical performances staged in Ruijin to generate support for the Red Army: "When the audience watched the comic scenes they laughed loudly; when they watched tragic scenes they lowered their heads and wept or angrily denounced the landlords. Thus we knew that the drama had deeply stirred the audience, achieving propaganda results. How happy we were then!"[46] Once moved by such cultural performances, peasant recruits were encouraged to articulate their own accusations against their former oppressors. As a propaganda worker in the northeast noted, "We felt that speaking bitterness was extremely effective in stimulating class hatreds and heightening feelings of vengeance ... The purpose of war became clear, and the emotions of the troops were raised."[47]

The origins of the Chinese communist revolutionaries' unusual aptitude for emotion work are obscure, but presumably traceable to a number of sources. China's rich history of peasant rebellion, which Mao Zedong so admired, offered ample evidence of the ingenious use of local opera, folk religion, and other elements of popular culture for purposes of mass mobilization.[48] The Bolshevik practice of "agitprop," communicated by Soviet advisors, was certainly another important inspiration. But both of these sources were also available to the Guomindang (GMD), or Chinese Nationalist Party, which despite its own persistent efforts at mass mobilization fell far short of the accomplishments of the CCP. The difference between the two revolutionary parties in this respect may have stemmed from the contrasting social backgrounds of their leaders. Whereas most of the early GMD leaders hailed from the coastal cities of China, their CCP counterparts had generally grown up in villages located deep in the interior of the country.[49] The Chinese communists' greater familiarity with rural customs probably afforded an advantage in deploying cultural symbols with an earthy flair that resonated emotionally with their target audience. Ultimately, however, much of the credit for the CCP's comparative success surely lies with the temperament and talent of individual leaders such as Mao Zedong, Peng Pai, and Li Lisan, who brought to the task of revolutionary mobilization an exceptional level of both empathy and creativity.

---

[45] Perry, *Anyuan*, chs. 2–3.
[46] Pan Zhenwu, "Remembering the Propaganda Team," 146.
[47] Mo Wenhua, "Political Work," 194.
[48] See, for example, Esherick, *The Origins of the Boxer Uprising*.
[49] North, *Kuomintang and Chinese Communist Elites*.

Modernization and Improvisation

The tradition of revolutionary "emotion work," modernized to take advantage of advances in communications technology, lives on in post-Mao China. A telling example was the suppression campaign that party leaders launched against Falun Gong in the summer of 1999. Television and radio broadcasts flooded the air waves with highly charged testimonials by bereaved relatives of Falun Gong victims who railed against the "evil cult" that had led their loved ones astray. Although television and radio had supplanted the community theater as the favored venue for carefully orchestrated emotional performances, the CPD's methods bore more than a passing resemblance to previous mass campaign tactics.[50]

Less than a decade after the anti-Falun Gong campaign, the CPD embarked on another technological upgrade, this time graduating from radio and television to internet and cell phone as more effective means of reaching a population that relies increasingly on these new modes of communication. Impressive as such modernization efforts are, they constitute but the latest chapter in a long history of governance practices designed to resonate emotionally with their target audience so as to win popular acceptance for the party's political agenda.

To note such continuities is certainly not to suggest that nothing has changed in recent years. In sharp contrast to Mao's day, when propaganda was intended to move the masses to revolutionary action, today the point is to dampen any sparks of protest in order to stabilize party rule. Yet the importance of engineering popular emotions in service to party concerns remains a central focus, and "emotion work" creatively combines cutting-edge technology with older mobilization practices. In a recent CPD teaching manual, for example, Hebei Province is commended for establishing an effective "public sentiment office" (舆情办) in response to the infamous tainted milk scandal that beset that province in 2008. With an estimated 300,000 victims of adulterated milk, including six infants who died of kidney failure, the incident triggered impassioned protests by distraught parents seeking redress. The public sentiment office, led by ten cadres from the Hebei Propaganda Department, initially focused on internet communications as a guide to popular feelings. It analyzed tens of thousands of web postings by Hebei netizens, on the basis of which the office issued instructions to internet control agencies (网管部门) on how to manage digital portals, chat rooms, and bulletin boards so as to defuse public outrage. The sentiment office also proactively manufactured internet discussions in order to seize control of the

[50] Perry, "Reinventing the Wheel?"

public discourse. Once the office had dealt with the internet threat, it undertook a more familiar form of investigation and mobilization. A ten-person survey research team, assisted by seventy investigators, visited every town and neighborhood in Shijiazhuang (where the milk powder scandal had originated) over a one-month period in order to gauge the feelings of various social groups in the affected area. The public sentiment office provided daily updates in a special bulletin for cadres entitled *Daily Trends in Public Sentiment*, and compiled executive summaries with proposals for new government policies – e.g. low-interest loans to dairy farmers for the purchase of high-quality fertilizer – based on the survey findings. This coordinated effort was credited with forestalling mass protest in response to the deadly breach of food safety.[51]

Governance under the PRC bespeaks an inventiveness born of decades of experimentation. In a co-edited volume with Sebastian Heilmann, *Mao's Invisible Hand*, we propose that the revolutionary past of the CCP continues to exert a significant influence on contemporary policies. The achievements of the post-Mao economic reforms, we suggest, are due not only to Adam Smith's invisible hand of market forces, but also to Mao's invisible hand of "guerrilla policy-making": a pragmatic, trial and error method of handling crisis and uncertainty that characterized the communist wartime base areas. Thanks to its unusual revolutionary origins, the Chinese communist political system allows for more diverse and flexible input and response than would be predicted from its formal political structures, which remain for the most part standard Leninist institutions.[52]

The CCP operates according to classic Soviet principles of so-called "democratic centralism," and exercises control over the bureaucracy through standard Soviet Nomenklatura procedures (with the Organization Department assigning party and government officials to their posts). Anyone familiar with the political institutions of the former USSR or the communist countries of Eastern Europe would have little difficulty grasping an organization chart of the PRC.[53] But despite this institutional similarity, the operations of the Chinese system are distinctive in ways that reflect China's unusual revolutionary history and that have bequeathed a surprisingly adaptive and responsive policy approach. In reaction to massive tax riots that erupted across the Chinese countryside in the 1990s, for instance, the government in 2005 took the

---

[51] *Propaganda, Thought and Cultural Work*, 279–289.

[52] Heilmann and Perry, "Embracing Uncertainty," 1–29.

[53] To be sure, there are some differences: the top policy-making group of the CCP, the Standing Committee of the Politburo, was not part of the Communist Party of the Soviet Union's institutional make-up, for instance.

extraordinary step of abolishing the centuries-old agricultural tax. In response to widespread internet complaints about abusive treatment of migrant workers at the hands of the police, China substantially revised its repressive vagrancy laws. Such instances by no means imply that the political system is democratic, but they do suggest that there is more policy responsiveness and flexibility than one would expect on the basis of China's communist institutions per se.[54]

China's propaganda czar Liu Yunshan, one of the Standing Committee members of the Politburo elected at the 18th Party Congress, gave an instructive account of this adaptive policy style in a speech entitled "Being Good at Summing up Experience is Our Party's Excellent Tradition." Liu opened his speech with a quote from Mao: "We depend for a living on summing up experience." He proceeded to explain that "propaganda, thought and cultural work" today, as in the revolutionary past, must operate as a pragmatic response to crisis and uncertainty. Liu cited the 2008 Sichuan earthquake, the unrest in Tibet and Xinjiang, and the international financial crisis as examples of recent battles during the course of which the CPD learned to adapt to new challenges with the aid of new tools – cellular technology, the internet, and new social media in particular.[55]

Liu Yunshan's speech was reprinted as the preface to a series of case studies published as teaching materials at the National Academy for Propaganda Cadres in Beijing. The case studies, based on recent incidents, were chosen to illustrate "breakthroughs" (突破) in propaganda work – some due to planned experiments and others to improvisations "in the midst of battle." According to Liu, the period in the run up to the Beijing Olympics saw a major shift in propaganda work, from a reactive toward a more proactive approach, as cadres turned to the aggressive use of new communications technology to gain the upper hand in dealing with potentially unsettling issues. In Guangdong, for example, in 2009 the provincial Propaganda Department partnered with the local branch of China Mobile, the largest cell phone and internet provider in the province, to develop an attractive and interactive webpage complete with video games and animated cartoons intended to convey in easily digestible form the official line on a range of sensitive international and domestic questions. Within a few months, the website was being visited regularly by more than half a million netizens.[56] Another case singled out for praise and emulation was the Jincheng Coal Group in Shanxi Province. An old

[54] Perry, "The Illiberal Challenge of Authoritarian China," 3–15.
[55] Liu Yunshan, "To be Good at Summing up Experience," 1–7.
[56] *Propaganda, Thought and Cultural Work*, 47–53.

state-owned enterprise burdened by a large number of disgruntled employees when it embarked on privatization, Jincheng's Propaganda Department contracted with IT specialists at Shanghai's Jiaotong University to construct a multi-tiered digital network aimed at assessing the mentality (思想动态) of all 60,000 members of its workforce. Workers were encouraged to share their concerns and complaints through emails and blogs. As the Jincheng Party Secretary instructed his propaganda cadres, "In this network, information about employees' thoughts are 'letters' that circulate freely. You are the postmen responsible for handling the mail." The more than 10,000 messages received from Jincheng workers provided a treasure trove of information that the enterprise leadership credited with permitting a smooth privatization process, free from the vociferous demonstrations and sit-ins that plagued the privatization of many other state-owned enterprises.[57]

In the above cases, protests may have been averted thanks to the preemptive use of high-tech communications, but in other instances propaganda methods are honed in the actual process of managing protests. On June 1, 2007, thousands of residents of the city of Xiamen took to the streets for what they euphemistically called a "stroll" (散步) to register opposition to the construction of a PX chemical factory in the area. To determine the level of dissatisfaction, Xiamen authorities conducted an online poll that revealed widespread and deep discontent. As a result, provincial officials agreed to relocate the plant to a desolate piece of land in Zhangzhou municipality, a safe distance from Xiamen. When journalists and bloggers encouraged Zhangzhou residents to emulate the Xiamen "strollers," the municipal Propaganda Department engaged experts from the Chinese Academy of Sciences and Xiamen University to attest to the appropriateness of the new site in internet postings and other media. The Propaganda Department also came up with a catchy and widely publicized slogan intended to foster collective pride in Zhangzhou's acceptance of the chemical plant: "Maritime development begins with Zhangzhou; Loving Zhangzhou begins with us!" The propaganda cadres realized the need to dispense with their usual practice of responding to protest by censoring the media, in favor of an alternative approach that actively enlisted the participation of the media (state and private alike) in a propaganda blitz intended to "guide public sentiment" along lines congruent with state policy. Hundreds of radio and television broadcasts publicized the remarks of leading officials and academic authorities in support of the factory relocation; newspapers and other periodicals were instructed to print favorable stories; prime-time

[57] Ibid., 57–61.

news reports were preempted to announce new developments and work plans for the PX project; countless cellular and computer messages transmitted a stern public security warning against illegal mass disturbances. The city of Zhangzhou employed a group of over 120 distinguished "experts" drawn from propaganda, media, and academia to serve as internet monitors and commentators (网络阅评员) to respond to netizen complaints with blogs and microblogs that defended the government's position. More than 500 college student volunteers were also dispatched to surrounding villages to educate rural dwellers in the official line through "heart-to-heart" chats with individual families. On the basis of these household visits, influential villagers were selected to participate in state-sponsored visits to Nanjing and other cities where PX factories were already operating without incident so that they could spread the good word to skeptical neighbors. In short, a range of mobilizing techniques – some drawn from decades-old mass campaigns and others from recent technological advances – were deployed in service to the cause.[58] As the Zhangzhou case indicates, PRC governance is not simply a matter of the state imposing its will on an otherwise inert and uninvolved society. Both in Mao's day and today, society itself (in the person of journalists, professors, students, villagers, and others) plays a critical role in constructing and communicating state policy.

Another contentious incident that the CPD credited with generating new approaches to collective protest was the notorious Weng'an riot, which erupted in Guizhou Province in June of 2008 after a middle-school girl drowned under suspicious circumstances that her family believed involved police culpability. Crowds broke through public security cordons and set fire to government buildings and police vehicles. Although the rampage was triggered by the girl's death, it reflected deep-seated anger toward the Weng'an authorities, who for some years had employed heavy-handed tactics to forcibly relocate residents to make way for lucrative development projects. News of the riot went viral on Chinese social media, and by the time the Guizhou authorities intervened the situation was dire. The Guizhou Propaganda Department reported the circumstances to the State Council News Office (新闻办), which gave permission to censor both public and commercial press and internet to eliminate stories deemed harmful to the restoration of order. But provincial authorities soon realized that, with the information having already been so widely disseminated, censorship alone would prove inadequate. Rather than simply silence the discussion, therefore, they decided actively to "shape public sentiment" by commissioning and publishing

[58] Ibid., 126–135.

information intended to mobilize citizen support for the provincial response to the crisis (which included three contrite public apologies by the provincial governor to the people of Weng'an for the poor performance of their local county authorities). For a time, one third of *Guizhou Daily*, the official newspaper for the province, was dedicated to government-sponsored reporting on the Weng'an incident. The provincial Propaganda Department also recruited dozens of "internet critics" to compose and post hundreds of upbeat essays intended to change the tone of electronic discussions. Having carefully prepared the ground, the provincial Propaganda Department proceeded to invite reporters from all the major national print and digital media outlets to visit Weng'an to conduct prearranged interviews with the victim's parents, relatives, eye-witnesses, and local residents. Within the space of two weeks, nearly 150 reporters from more than thirty media outlets had traveled to Weng'an at the invitation of the provincial Propaganda Department to hear its side of the story, which blamed the incident entirely on the county government.[59]

Symbolic Resources

Propaganda departments at all levels make liberal use of both revolutionary and pre-revolutionary material to project a persuasive message. The particular issues and instruments vary from one incident to another, but underpinning these diverse efforts is a consistent aim to foster a powerful collective identity that will contribute to the legitimacy and stability of the communist party-state. Prior to the precipitous demise of Chongqing Party Secretary Bo Xilai, the CPD gave high marks to his "singing Red" campaign to revive the Maoist revolutionary spirit, citing surveys which indicated that 97.25 percent of the city's residents had participated in the campaign with 96.51 percent of the participants reporting a high degree of satisfaction with the initiative. Improbably, the CPD credited the campaign with having restored popular faith in Marxism among the younger generation of Chongqing, noting that by the end of 2010 nearly 80 percent of those surveyed responded that they believed in Marxism, an increase of more than 10 percent over the previous year.[60] An examination of the lyrics of the thirty-six approved "red songs" featured in the campaign reveals, however, that the songs make little if any mention of Marxism. Instead, the dominant themes are patriotism, national unification, and the splendors of Chinese tradition. The top song on the list, entitled *Toward Revival (走向复兴)*, includes the

[59] Ibid., 150–157.   [60] Ibid., 237–245.

lyrics "We are the heroic sons and daughters of China, whose ancient civilization sparkles anew. To revive the Chinese nation is our ideal ... China towers majestically in the Orient; march onward, onward toward revival."[61] The symbolic correspondence with Xi Jinping's "China Dream" is clear.

A continuing commitment to honoring the legacy of Mao Zedong's revolution as an integral part of "Socialism with Chinese Characteristics" has not diminished the party-state's interest in claiming much older foundations of legitimacy. In response to a "national learning craze" (国学热) focused on the Confucian classics, which swept the country at the turn of the twenty-first century, the symbol of Confucius was deemed especially useful as a vehicle for cultural governance, both externally and internally.[62] In 2004, a government-sponsored program for a global network of Confucius institutes was launched in Beijing. Eight years later, more than 350 Confucius institutes and 500 Confucius classrooms had been established in over 100 countries around the world.[63]

Evidently encouraged by this trend, the CPD took the unusual step in January 2011 of installing without prior announcement a large bronze statue of Confucius in the center of Tiananmen Square, directly in front of the National Museum (formerly the Museum of Revolutionary History) and just beside Mao's mausoleum. The move generated an online outcry from disapproving netizens, however, who drew attention to the jarring impropriety of situating the ancient sage amidst all the monuments to the revolution, and the statue was removed (unannounced and overnight) three months later, just as suddenly and surreptitiously as it had been installed. As the bungled Confucius statue incident shows, efforts at cultural governance – even by as seasoned a practitioner as the CPD – may be ill-considered and unsuccessful. Another example of a failed initiative was the attempt to resuscitate that quintessential exemplar of the Maoist spirit, Lei Feng, through a series of melodramatic movies released in the spring of 2013. The films proved to be a box office disaster, much to the chagrin of responsible officials in the CPD and Ministry of Culture.[64]

Party propaganda does not always strike a chord with its intended audience. Even worse, from the party's perspective, officially approved symbols and slogans can be hijacked for alternative purposes. The state's

---

[61] baike.baidu.com/view/2861610.htm.

[62] Within China, the popularization of the Confucian classics among college-age youths has been a notable trend. Tellingly, Yu Dan's accessibly written *Notes on Reading the Analects* sold three million copies in four months in 2006–2007. Guo, *Repackaging Confucius*, 41.

[63] Zhou and Mo, "How 21st-Century China Sees Public Diplomacy," 19.

[64] Levin, "Cinematic Flops."

own rhetoric may backfire when, for example, cynics assign unauthorized meanings to Jiang Zemin's Three Represents or workers march behind portraits of Chairman Mao to protest lay-offs at state enterprises. Cultural governance, in other words, is a *variable* – the effects of which will fluctuate depending not only upon the symbols themselves, but also upon the venue, format, timing, and audience. Indeed, it is the CPD's recognition that not all of its projects resonate with the public which explains its close attention to such matters as attitudinal investigation, technological innovation, and emotional impact.

Conclusion

Current efforts to commingle revolutionary and pre-revolutionary symbolic resources, as though there were no inherent contradiction between the two, are but the latest twist in a complicated and circuitous process aimed at justifying the Communist Party's right to rule. The imaginative application of cultural appeals to augment the CCP's moral and political authority by presenting itself as the savior of the nation has played a crucial – albeit ever changing – role since the very inception of the party. Xi Jinping's allusions to a "China Dream" of a strong nation led by a protective Communist Party fits comfortably within this familiar frame of reference.

These days, the CCP makes no apology for the denunciation and devastation that it unleashed on remnants of China's so-called "feudal" culture at various junctures in its tumultuous history. In fact, it makes no mention of these sorry episodes. At the sixth plenum of the 17th Party Congress in October 2011, a central party decision on deepening cultural reform unabashedly asserted that "the 5,000 years of our national cultural development has been a major spiritual force for the Chinese nation and a major contributor to the civilization of all humanity. From the day of its founding, the Chinese Communist Party has been the faithful heir and advocate of this outstanding traditional Chinese culture."[65] The infamous Document 9, issued secretly in the spring of 2013, prohibits teaching about the party's historical mistakes (along with six other "speak-nots"), suggesting that the CCP's record of cultural destruction is unlikely to emerge as a topic of public debate in the near future.[66] Xi Jinping recently proffered a blunt warning against any such criticism: "Never allow eating the Communist Party's food and then smashing the Communist Party's cooking pots."[67]

[65] Quoted in Zhang Chuanjia, *Promote the Great Development*, 1.
[66] "Chinese Government Bans."   [67] Buckley and Jacobs, "Maoists in China."

As one of the most imaginative chefs of CCP cuisine, the CPD does not hold an unblemished record of success in cultural governance, yet its cumulative achievement – especially in light of the collapse of most other communist systems – is remarkable nonetheless. The endurance of the Chinese communist party-state must be attributed to many factors, including brute coercion and bald censorship. But not to be discounted in explaining the regime's persistence are the kindred feelings that many Chinese evidently harbor toward their political system. The party-state by most accounts enjoys a surprising degree of acceptability in the eyes of its own citizens.[68] As Andrew Nathan summarizes the findings of empirical research on post-Tiananmen Chinese political attitudes, "There is much evidence from both quantitative and qualitative studies to suggest that ... the regime as a whole continues to enjoy high levels of acceptance."[69] One reason for this popular support, it would seem, has been a re-Orientation of party propaganda to present the CCP as the acknowledged leader of a national revival that lays claim not only to the legacy of modern revolution but also to much older symbols of cultural splendor and power.[70]

The current brand of Chinese cultural nationalism cooked up by the CPD is not without intrinsic limitations. The prospect of reviving the "Chinese nation" is surely more appetizing to those who self-identify as Han Chinese (wherever they may reside) than, for example, to Uighurs or Tibetans living within the territorial borders of the PRC. Secessionist sympathies among the minority populations of Xinjiang and Tibet suggests that state-sponsored efforts to celebrate the "Chinese nation" are seen as unwelcome expressions of Han chauvinism by some citizens of the PRC who do not identify as Han. This is obviously worrisome to a Chinese leadership mindful that the collapse of the Soviet Union was propelled in part by the defection of non-Russian minorities. Nevertheless, the PRC's accomplishment in fostering a sense of shared cultural identity and national unity among the Han – whose "dialects" of Chinese are linguistically as diverse as the various Romance languages – is no small achievement. The fact that over 90 percent of the population of the PRC identifies as Han Chinese (and, thanks to state-supported migrations, that even Tibet and Xinjiang are now heavily populated by Han) renders this feat of considerable political significance.

Even among the Han, however, cultural nationalism can be a double-edged sword. On the one hand, nationalist sentiment encourages popular support for a strong Chinese state. On the other hand, perceived signs of

---

[68] Holbig and Gilley, "Reclaiming Legitimacy," 395–422.
[69] Nathan, "Authoritarian Resilience," 6–17.
[70] Guo, "Political Legitimacy and China's Transition," 21–22.

weakness or incompetence on the part of Chinese government officials are liable to generate criticisms of the regime by those same nationalistic citizens. The chance of a nationalist movement turning into an anti-government protest is always a possibility.

The Communist Party over which Xi Jinping currently presides faces a host of extremely serious governance challenges. Many of these difficulties stem directly from the basically unreformed Leninist political institutions that persist in contemporary China. Shortcomings inherent in these types of institutions, after all, have been proposed as a key explanation for the collapse of communism across Eastern Europe and the former Soviet Union.[71] The Chinese leadership is well aware of the vulnerabilities of its Leninist institutions. Behind closed doors, Xi Jinping warns his fellow Communist Party leaders that unless they manage to combat corruption, the PRC will suffer the same fate as the former Soviet Union.[72] But publicly, Xi seldom likens his regime to other communist systems. Rather, he portrays the PRC as an essentially Chinese system, fully in keeping with China's own national character. His attack on official corruption, associated in Chinese political culture with extravagant banqueting, calls for the exercise of culinary restraint with the folksy slogan: "Four Dishes and One Soup."[73]

A public opinion poll conducted recently among residents in seven major Chinese cities suggests the degree to which China's communist system has been successfully indigenized. When asked to name their twelve favorite countries, respondents failed to include any other communist or formerly communist country. China was the overwhelming favorite, followed at a considerable distance by the United States.[74] When queried as to whether the collapse of the Soviet Union had been more helpful or harmful to China, only 12 percent considered the Soviet collapse harmful to China's interests.[75] A strong majority (nearly 70 percent) responded affirmatively to the question: "Influenced by domestic and international factors, contemporary young people have less knowledge of traditional Chinese culture. Do you have confidence in the continuation and flourishing of traditional Chinese culture?"[76]

Skillful as the PRC's leadership has been in re-Orienting its propaganda to both suit and shape public sentiment, it has not managed to eliminate political dissatisfaction among the populace. These days, many Chinese citizens (Han and non-Han alike) readily voice severe criticisms of their political system – from rampant corruption to ruthless coercion.

---

[71] Solnick, *Stealing the State*; Bunce, *Subversive Institutions*.
[72] Buckley, "Vows of Change."   [73] "Four Dishes."
[74] Global Sentiment Survey Center, ed., *Survey of Chinese Public Opinion*, 27.
[75] Ibid., 326.   [76] Ibid., 176.

But very seldom do they complain that the system is in any way *un-Chinese.*[77] Rather than attribute such problems to the shortcomings of an unreformed Soviet system, disgruntled citizens are apt to ascribe the faults of their polity to unjust tendencies rooted deep within the soil of Chinese political culture – nepotism, bureaucratism, preference for rule by man over rule of law, feudal remnants. Those who feel aggrieved at the hands of unscrupulous officials rarely point the finger of blame at the communist system itself. Instead, like their ancestors in bygone centuries, demonstrators often kneel beneath banners emblazoned with the age-old cry of protest in imperial China: "Wronged" (冤枉)![78] The implication is that "if the emperor only knew" of the offenses being committed by corrupt officials at the grassroots level, justice would be served. Even liberal critics of the political system, who advocate democratic reforms, depict the root of the governance problem as residing with a CCP leadership that remains "essentially" Chinese in its thought and practice.[79] Decades of inventive and intensive cultural positioning and patronage on the part of the CCP have paid off handsomely. A political system alien in its institutional and ideological origins has been made to feel indigenous. The foreign has been rendered familiar; a Russian recipe has been cooked so as to taste authentically Chinese.

References

Baum, Richard. *Burying Mao: Chinese Politics in the Age of Deng Xiaoping.* Princeton: Princeton University Press, 1994.

Brady, Anne-Marie. *Marketing Dictatorship: Propaganda and Thought Work in Contemporary China.* Lanham, MD: Rowman and Littlefield, 2008.

Buckley, Chris. "Vows of Change in China Belie Private Warning," *New York Times,* February 14, 2013.

Buckley, Chris and Jacobs, Andrew. "Maoists in China, Given New Life, Attack Dissent," *New York Times,* January 4, 2015.

---

[77] Among the innumerable ironies of "Chinese" cultural governance is the fact that the country's current territorial boundaries were established in the eighteenth century as part of the (non-Han) Manchu conquest. Perdue, *China's March West.*

[78] See, for example, images from the Wukan protests of December 2011. www.bbc.co.uk /news/world-asia-china-17821844.

[79] The prominent liberal critic Xu Youyu, while praising Chinese society for supposedly embracing universal human rights after the trauma of Tiananmen, nevertheless characterizes the CCP leadership as continuing to operate in the imperial mold: "In several thousand years of Chinese history, the unchanging rule was that of one tyranny replacing another. Among ordinary people, the idea of 'preparing the way for Heaven' was very deeply rooted as well ... From 1989 to 2009, the face and social psychology of Chinese society has undergone enormous change. Yet ... the mentality of the leaders who took the political stage after '89 did not change." Xu Youyu, "From 1989 to 2009."

Bunce, Valerie. *Subversive Institutions: The Design and the Destruction of Socialism and the State*. New York: Cambridge University Press, 1999.

Callahan, William A. *Cultural Governance and Resistance in Pacific Asia*. New York: Routledge, 2006.

Central Discipline Commission, ed. (*Thinking of Danger in the Midst of Peace: Historical Lessons from the Collapse of the Soviet Union*). 居安思危 – 苏联亡党的历史教训. Internal circulation video.

"Chasing the Chinese Dream," *The Economist*, May 4, 2013.

Chen, Xi. *Social Protest and Contentious Authoritarianism in China*. New York: Cambridge University Press, 2012.

"Chinese Government Bans Seven 'Speak-Not' Subjects," *Global Voices Online*, May 16, 2013.

CPD, ed. (中央宣传部办公厅). ("CPD Notice concerning Conditions for Hanging Portraits of Famous Figures at Tiananmen Square during Holidays"). "中央宣传部关于节日期间天安门广场悬挂伟人像的情况通知," 党的宣传工作文件选编, *1988–1992*. 北京: 中共中央党校出版社, 1994, 1867. Internal circulation publication.

CPD, ed. ("CPD Office and National Relics Bureau Notice concerning Publication of 'Important Points from the Conference on Revolutionary Relics Propaganda Work'"). "中央宣传部办公厅国家文物局关于印发'革命文物宣传工作座谈会会议纪要' 的通知," 党的宣传工作文件选编, *1988–1992*. 北京: 中共中央党校出版社, 1994, 1948–1954.

CPD, ed. ("Notice of CPD, Ministry of Culture, and National Relics Bureau concerning Publication of 'Everyone Loves and Protects the Relics of the Motherland Propaganda Outline'"). "中央宣传部，文化部，国家文物局关于印发'人人爱护祖国文物宣传提纲'的通知," 党的宣传工作文件选编. *1988–1992*. 北京: 中共中央党校出版社, 1994, 1872–1877.

CPD, ed. (*Raise High the Banner of Patriotism*). 高举爱国主义旗帜. 北京: 学习出版社, 1997.

CPD, ed. ("Utilize Revolutionary Relics, Strengthen Traditional Education"). "运用革命文物加强传统教育," 宣传动态, *1990*. 北京: 人民日报出版社, 1991), 71–79. Internal circulation publication.

Edelman, Murray. *The Symbolic Uses of Politics*. Chicago and Urbana: University of Illinois Press, 1964.

Editorial Committee of the Chinese Financial Yearbook (中国财务年鉴编辑委员会), ed. (*Chinese Financial Yearbook*). 中国财政年鉴, 北京: 中国财政杂志社, 1992– .

Esherick, Joseph W. *The Origins of the Boxer Uprising*. Berkeley and Los Angeles: University of California Press, 1987.

Fan Hongyi (范虹轶), ed. (*The Latest in Party Propaganda Work*). 最新党的宣传工作. 北京: 人民出版社, 2010.

"Four Dishes and One Soup," *China Economic Review*, January 22, 2013.

Global Sentiment Survey Center (环球舆情调查中心), ed. (*Survey of Chinese Public Opinion*). 中国民意调查. 北京: 人民日报出版社, 2012.

Guo, Baogang. "Political Legitimacy and China's Transition," *Journal of Chinese Political Science*, 8, 1–2: (Fall) 2003, 1–25.

Guo, Xiaolin. *Repackaging Confucius: PRC Public Diplomacy and the Rise of Soft Power*. Stockholm: Institute for Security and Development Policy, 2008.

Guo, Yingjie. *Cultural Nationalism in Contemporary China*. New York: Routledge, 2004.

Hamrin, Carol Lee and Cheek, Timothy, eds. *China's Establishment Intellectuals*. Armonk, NY: M. E. Sharpe, 1986.

Heilmann, Sebastian and Perry, Elizabeth J. "Embracing Uncertainty: Guerrilla Policy Style and Adaptive Governance in China," in Heilmann and Perry, eds., *Mao's Invisible Hand*, 1–29.

Heilmann, Sebastian and Perry, Elizabeth J., eds. *Mao's Invisible Hand: The Foundations of Adaptive Governance in China*. Cambridge, MA: Harvard University Asia Center, 2011.

"Historic Rankings of China's Domestic Movie Ticket Sales." "中国内地电影票房历史排行" *Mtime*, group.mtime.com/12781/discussion/253526/. Accessed March 10, 2013.

Ho, Dahpon David. "To Protect and Preserve: Resisting the Destroy the Four Olds Campaign," in Joseph W. Esherick, Paul G. Pickowicz, and Andrew G. Walder, eds., *The Chinese Cultural Revolution as History*. Stanford: Stanford University Press, 2006, 64–95.

Holbig, Heike and Gilley, Bruce. "Reclaiming Legitimacy in China," *Politics and Policy*, 38, 3: 2010, 395–422.

Jiang Zemin (江泽民). ("Talk at the National Conference of Propaganda Department Directors, July 20, 1989"). "在全国宣传部长会议上的讲话," 党的宣传工作会议概况和文献, *1951–1992*. 北京: 中共中央党校出版社, 1994, 914–922. Internal circulation publication.

Levin, Dan. "In China, Cinematic Flops Suggest Fading of an Icon," *New York Times*, March 11, 2013.

Li Peng (李鹏). ("Talk at the National Conference of Propaganda Department Directors, July 20, 1989"). "在全国宣传部长会议上的讲话," 党的宣传工作会议概况和文献, *1951–1992*.北京: 中共中央党校出版社, 1994, 923–928.

Liu Yunshan (刘云山). ("To be Good at Summing Up Experience is Our Party's Excellent Tradition"). "善于总结经验是我们党非常好的传统," 宣传思想文化工作: 案例选编. 北京: 学习出版社, 2010–2011, 1–7.

Mao, Zedong. "The Chinese People Have Stood Up!" in *Selected Readings from the Works of Mao Tse-tung*, vol. V (September 21, 1949). Beijing: Foreign Languages Press, 1977, 15–18.

Mao, Zedong. "The Role of the Chinese Communist Party in the National War," in *Selected Readings from the Works of Mao Tse-tung* (October 1938). Beijing: Foreign Languages Press, 1971, 138–159.

Mao, Zedong. "Talks at the Yenan Forum on Art and Literature," in *Selected Readings from the Works of Mao Tse-tung*. Beijing: Foreign Languages Press, 1971, 250–86.

Mo Wenhua (莫文骅). ("Political Work in the Liaodong Military Zone during the War of Liberation"). "解放战争时期辽东军区的政治工作," 中国党史资料, 39: 1991, 193–205.

Nathan, Andrew J. "Authoritarian Resilience," *Journal of Democracy*, 14, 1: 2003, 6–17.

National Academy for Propaganda Cadres (全国宣传干部学院), ed. (*Propaganda, Thought and Cultural Work: Selected Cases*). 宣传思想文化工作: 案例选编. 北京: 学习出版社, 2011.

Naughton, Barry J. and Yang, Dali L., eds. *Holding China Together*. New York: Cambridge University Press, 2004.

"New Party Leadership Gains Limelight," *Xinhua*, November 15, 2012.

North, Robert C. *Kuomintang and Chinese Communist Elites*. Stanford: Stanford University Press, 1952.

Pan Zhenwu (潘振武). ("Remembering the Propaganda Team of the Red Number One Military Troupe"). "忆红一军团宣传队," 星火燎原, 2. 北京: 人民文学出版社, 1962, 145–151.

Party Central Notice ("Concerning Strengthening of Propaganda, Thought Work, July 28, 1989"). "中共中央, 关于加强宣传,思想工作的通知," 党的宣传工作会议概况和文献, *1951–1992*. 北京:中共中央党校出版社, 1994, 938–949.

Perdue, Peter. *China's March West: The Qing Conquest of Central Eurasia*. Cambridge, MA: Harvard University Press, 2005.

Perry, Elizabeth J. *Anyuan: Mining China's Revolutionary Tradition*. Berkeley: University of California Press, 2012.

Perry, Elizabeth J. "From Mass Campaigns to Managed Campaigns: 'Constructing a New Socialist Countryside,'" in Heilmann and Perry, eds., *Mao's Invisible Hand*, 30–61.

Perry, Elizabeth J. "Moving the Masses: Emotion Work in the Chinese Revolution." *Mobilization: An International Journal*, 7, 2: 2002, 111–128.

Perry, Elizabeth J. "Reinventing the Wheel? The Suppression Campaign against Falun Gong." *Harvard China Review* (2000).

Perry, Elizabeth J. "The Illiberal Challenge of Authoritarian China," *Taiwan Journal of Democracy*, 8, 2: (December) 2010, 3–15.

Pragmatics of Propaganda Work. 宣传工作实务. 北京: 红旗出版社, 2012.

Rawnsley, Gary D. "'The Great Movement to Resist America and Assist Korea': How Beijing Sold the Korean War," *Media, War, and Conflict*, 2, 3: 2009, 285–315.

Shapiro, Michael J. *Methods and Nations: Cultural Governance and the Indigenous Subject*. New York: Routledge, 2004.

Sleeboom-Faulkner, Margaret. *The Chinese Academy of Social Sciences*. Leiden: Brill, 2007.

Solnick, Steven Lee. *Stealing the State: Control and Collapse in Soviet Institutions*. Cambridge, MA: Harvard University Press, 1998.

Statistical Yearbook of Cultural Initiatives. 文化事业统计年鉴. 北京: 文化艺术出版社, 1993–1995.

Tao Xiuao (陶秀璈). ("The Advent of an Era of Cultural Diplomacy"). "文化外交时代的来临."陈文力, 陶秀璈 编, 中国文化对外传播战略研究. 北京: 九州出版社, 2012, 3–22.

Tsai, Kellee S. *Capitalism without Democracy: The Private Sector in Contemporary China*. Ithaca, NY: Cornell University Press, 2007.

Tsai, Lily L. *Accountability without Democracy: Solidary Groups and Public Goods Provision in Rural China*. New York: Cambridge University Press, 2007.

Wang Renzhi (王忍之). ("Stick to Correct Policy, Carry out Work Deeply, Meticulously and Accurately"). "坚持正确方针，把工作做深做细做实 (1991 年1月16日)," 党的宣传工作会议概况和文献, *1951–1992*. 北京:中共中央党校 出版社, 1994, 960–980.

Wedeen, Lisa. *Ambiguities of Domination: Politics, Rhetoric and Symbols in Contemporary Syria*. Chicago: University of Chicago Press, 1999.

"Xi Jinping Pledges 'Great Renewal of Chinese Nation,'" *Global Times*, November 30, 2012.

Xu Youyu (徐友渔). ("From 1989 to 2009: Twenty Years of Evolution in Chinese Thought"). "从1989到2009 – 中国20年思想演进", online edition in 博讯热点：六四.

Zhang Chuanjia (章传家). (*Promote the Great Development and Great Flourishing of Socialist Culture*). 推动社会主义文化大发展大繁荣. 北京：人民日报出版社, 2011.

Zhao, Suisheng. *A Nation-State by Construction: Dynamics of Modern Chinese Nationalism*. Stanford: Stanford University Press, 2004.

Zhou, Qingan and Mo Jinwei. "How 21st-Century China Sees Public Diplomacy as a Path to Soft Power," *Global Asia*, 7, 3: (Fall) 2012, 18–23.

Steering

2 China's Core Executive: Pursuing National Agendas in a Fragmented Polity

Sebastian Heilmann

What normative, institutional, or leadership mechanisms help to explain why the Chinese government is so ambitious (and often regarded as superior to other emerging and developing countries) in providing essential public and social goods (such as poverty alleviation, universal education, basic health care, and physical infrastructure) and in pursuing long-term development objectives (such as sustained economic growth, industrial diversification, technological upgrading, and global economic expansion), in spite of ample evidence of bureaucratic fragmentation and short-term rent-seeking by state officials and their entourages?

This essay aims at a deeper diachronic understanding of the rationale and the mechanisms that guide top-level, supra-ministerial accommodation on development strategies and multi-year programs. To explain the encompassing and long-term goals that can be found in the developmental strategies of the Chinese government, I employ an analytical perspective that draws on comparative studies of national *core executives*. This approach focuses on the shifting functions and resources of "all those organizations and structures which primarily serve to pull together and integrate central government policies, or act as final arbiters within the executive of conflicts between different elements of the government machine."[1]

The core executive in this study comprises the supra-ministerial web of formal bodies, leadership Staff Offices, policy task forces, and their interactions in the government executive that serve to coordinate deliberation and accommodation on cross-sectoral, long-term policy priorities and programs that transcend the remit of lower-ranked, specialized government bodies.[2] Core executive policy-making thus poses a counterweight

---

[1] Dunleavy and Rhodes, "Core Executive Studies in Britain," 4.
[2] This modified definition is based on Rhodes, "Introducing the Core Executive," 12; Smith, *The Core Executive in Britain*, 1–4.

against the bureaucratic bargaining, particularistic interests and centrifugal forces inherent in China's "fragmented authoritarianism."[3]

The core executive concept was explicitly designed by Rhodes and his collaborators to provide a neutral, non-normative analysis of decision processes at the center of governments in radically different political systems.[4] According to Rhodes, the distribution of resources and the division of labor among multiple actors within core executives, rather than being fixed, vary over time along with the change of leaders, situational pressures, shifts in the larger socio-economic context, and policy outcomes that are claimed as successes by, or ascribed as failures to, certain actors even if originally unintended. Functions (who does what?) and resources (who can impose or exchange what in initiating, supporting, bargaining over, or opposing certain policies?) are at the center of core executive studies.[5]

The study undertaken here will focus on relations *within* the supraministerial core executive (rather than on relations between the core executive and other actors). It is the search for the recurrent rules of the game that will provide insights into how core executive bodies attempt to tackle the challenge of determining national policy agendas across sectoral and jurisdictional demarcations. This kind of supra-ministerial policy-making requires not only aggregating, but rather *overriding* the inputs and interests of ministerial, regional, or industrial lobbies. Consequently, processes and institutions that enable the core executive to assert or reassert central decisiveness (the ability to make authoritative decisions and pursue a set of interlinked policies, i.e. comprehensive multi-year action programs) are at the heart of this contribution.

The essay hypothesizes that it is the entrenched policy mission and resilient institutional configuration of the core executive that help explain China's unusual record of broad-based and long-term development strategies. China's core executive has been shaped by a trajectory of norms and organs that can be traced back to a comprehensive "Finance and Economics" (财政经济; shorthand: 财经 FinEcon) mission, first defined by the Communist Party leadership in the late 1940s. Despite periodically severe disruptions, we find a striking resilience (after recurring but temporary periods of dismantling) from 1948 to 2012 of supra-ministerial institutions that are charged with pursuing and defending the Party Center's FinEcon mission: FinEcon Leading Small Groups with their high-level strategy units (FinEcon Staff Offices), the Prime Ministerial

---

[3] Cf. Lieberthal and Oksenberg, *Policy Making in China*; Lieberthal and Lampton, eds., *Bureaucracy, Politics and Decision Making.*
[4] Elgie, "Core Executive Studies," 72.   [5] Cf. Smith, *The Core Executive in Britain*, 7.

Inner Cabinet, and cross-sectoral planning bodies. These guardians of central developmental power, however, have had to face recurrent challenges from among top party leaders, centrifugal forces in the administrative system, as well as severe cycles and shocks in the domestic and external economy.

The research presented in this essay is based on diachronic Chinese sources and publications as well as on a series of interviews with senior economic officials, mostly belonging to the National Development and Reform Commission (NDRC) cluster and central leadership Staff Offices, held between 2007 and 2015. In June 2015, an officially approved visit to the Central FinEcon Leading Small Group's Staff Office at Zhongnanhai and to several high-level NDRC units facilitated access to nine Vice-Ministerial and bureau-level officials actively involved in core executive work.

The approach focuses on supra-ministerial policy interactions but it is close to the institutionalist explanations pioneered by Lieberthal and Oksenberg in their work on China's national economic administration.[6] Lieberthal differentiates between "key generalists" at the very top of the system (GenSec, Premier) and "bridge leaders" (Vice-Premiers, State Councillors) who are responsible for coordinating policy and resolving differences that crop up within and between specialized bureaucracies in the policy process.[7]

The supra-ministerial staff units, organs, and task forces that surround and serve the key generalists and the bridge leaders are at the center of the following analysis. They constitute China's core executive which works as a powerful counterweight against the routine mode of "fragmented authoritarianism" and bureaucratic bargaining. By demonstrating how the party leadership manages to assert, or periodically reassert, its authority over fragmented, or corrupted, bureaucracies and sectoral interests, the findings presented here enrich and qualify widely held characterizations and understandings of China's political-administrative system.

The heuristic of "fragmented authoritarianism," in particular, does not explain the governance mechanisms that China's central leadership can draw on to restore central decisiveness and override administrative fragmentation. The reorganization of the central policy-making system under Xi Jinping from 2012 to 2017 revealed the limits and vulnerability of bureaucratic and interest group politics. Xi Jinping relied not just on his personal leadership ambitions and skills, but rather on an extension of traditional core executive mechanisms: reorganizing and reinforcing

---

[6] Lieberthal and Oksenberg, *Policy Making in China*, 22, 35–62.
[7] Lieberthal, *Governing China*, 212.

Central Leading Small Groups and their staff units as drivers of top-priority policy agendas so as to concentrate policy-making authority, arrest the breakdown of party hierarchies and disrupt entrenched bureaucratic, regional, and industrial interest group interaction and corruption.

This essay is structured as follows. The next section presents a brief account of the FinEcon mission's foundations and objectives. We then turn to the institutional arrangements supporting the guardians of "encompassing interests" within the core executive, and their changing approaches to planning and guiding economic and social development. The tensions between central technocrats and particularistic interests, and how dependent the technocrats are on top-level initiative, are addressed in the penultimate section. The conclusion points to the importance of understanding policy-making dynamics within the core executive to explain how long-term development agendas have been pursued by the Chinese government in a comparatively effective way.

The FinEcon Mission

From 1949 to the present, it has been a conspicuous and unusual feature of developmental policy-making in China to treat FinEcon as a policy arena that requires comprehensive, integrated top-level political supervision. This stands in contrast to the necessities of administrative specialization and the realities of administrative fragmentation in modern polities. From the central government perspective, treating FinEcon as an interconnected whole entails particular normative assumptions and organizational conditions.

The origins of the FinEcon mission can be traced back to the formative experiences that shaped the Chinese Communist Party's approach to economic construction. A homegrown, down-to-earth experience with a unified economic administration can be found in the coarse, yet integrated, management of finance and economics in the scattered communist base areas and during the civil war prior to 1949. Beginning in 1948, concrete plans and preparations were made that aimed to unify FinEcon work and economic administration beyond the autarkic communist-controlled areas.[8] An external influence that worked for an encompassing approach to FinEcon was the Soviet model and Soviet advice on how to establish a Communist Party-controlled socialist economy. Soviet attempts at unified developmental coordination through the government

---

[8] Kim, *The Politics of Chinese Communism*, 92–95; Xue Muqiao, *Xue Muqiao's Memoirs*, 184–187; Xue Muqiao, ed., *Summing up FinEcon Work*; Li et al., eds., *Unifying Finance and Economics*.

executive (Council of Ministers) and the central planning commission (Gosplan) were closely emulated during the formative period of the Chinese communists' administration.[9]

After the founding of the People's Republic of China (PRC), unified FinEcon headquarters materialized in the establishment of the Central FinEcon Commission (CFEC, 1949–1954) whose mission and name would resurface throughout PRC history during intermittent efforts to coordinate the economy as an integrated whole. The CFEC was seen as the "strategic headquarters" for China's economy,[10] or even as a separate "economic government."[11] From 1949 through 1954, economic policy coordination powers were concentrated in one all-embracing party-state organ through the CFEC. Despite temporary individual demotions, a core circle of nine policy-makers was in charge of supervising the operation of the Chinese economy. Throughout the 1949–1966 period, this circle functioned as an economic "high command."[12]

What policy arena does the FinEcon concept define? Foundational leaders defined it as an integrated understanding of "socialist construction," with a clear focus on state-led industrialization, driven by administrative resource allocation and centralized planning, yet held in check by "planned proportional development" and "comprehensive balancing" (based on material input-output balances) and recurrent administrative "readjustments" (ad hoc interventions and recentralization in investment activity and material allocation to counter cyclical ups and downs).[13] After the provision of basic goods and the containment of inflation were unexpectedly realized by 1951–1952, the FinEcon arena was extended to include the socialist transformation of private business and the establishment of the complex mechanisms of a Soviet-type planned economy.[14]

The trajectory of unified FinEcon coordination became manifest in a set of distinctive normative, organizational, and procedural patterns that continue to exert a decisive influence on the Chinese party-state's mid- to long-term policy-making to the present. For China's planning officials, the 1949–1954 Central FinEcon Commission became a model

[9] "Proposals Raised by Soviet Advisors"; Xue Muqiao, *Xue Muqiao's Memoirs*, 230–231; Shen Zhihua, *Soviet Experts*.

[10] Yao Yilin, "Yao Yilin's Evening Chats," 23; Zou Ximing, *A Chronicle of the Evolution*, 73, 77.

[11] Huang, *Factionalism in Chinese Communist Politics*, 157.

[12] Cf. Bo Yibo, *Reflections on Certain Major Decisions*; Diao and Zagoria, *The Nature of Mainland Chinese Economic Structure*, 62, 183.

[13] For authoritative statements, see the chapters on the early 1950s in Jin and Chen, *Biography of Chen Yun*; Fang and Jin, *Biography of Li Fuchun*; Bo Yibo, *Reflections on Certain Major Decisions*.

[14] On these formative experiences, see Wu Li, "Foundations and Conditions for Implementing"; Wu Li, "Formulation and Implementation."

of comprehensive centralized coordination and oversight, and from the mid-1950s through the 1980s, this model was held in high regard as the benchmark of FinEcon work.[15] Through these formative experiences, the FinEcon tasks, programs, interventions, and reviews that were undertaken by the party leadership became standard mechanisms to cope with recurring perceived losses of central control over the economy.

The center's FinEcon mission, which was originally conceived in the late 1940s and expanded after the founding of the PRC, seeks to unify China's fragmented economy, "concentrate forces" on top-priority projects and the most pressing bottlenecks, promote industrial expansion, and correct destabilizing imbalances, while safeguarding party control over the economy's "commanding heights" and multiplying the financial resources in the hands of the party-state. Pursuing this FinEcon mission requires overriding regional, sectoral, and bureaucratic interests to define development priorities that fortify central political and financial power, thereby also supporting the central leadership's capability to strengthen China's international security and status.

A determining feature of China's FinEcon arena are the *comprehensive policy reviews* that have been undertaken since 1953 either as part of the annual and Five Year Planning rhythm or for extraordinary policy initiatives. Year-end national planning conferences have been broadened into Central Economic Work Conferences since 1994.[16] The regularized top-level reviews that are an unusual feature of China's policy process in international comparison are supposed to serve as a counterweight to the increasing specialization and narrow horizon of economic bureaucracies (see Table 1).

In pursuit of the FinEcon mission throughout PRC history, plan or market coordination, state or collective or private firms, competition or industrial policy came to be seen, depending on the shifting political "line" and development strategy, as exchangeable instruments in a variable mix of useable governance mechanisms – as long as the Party Center's power was not compromised. The FinEcon mission rules out a sweeping privatization of core state assets (though it does not preclude the selective privatization of firms or assets in sectors that are seen as non-strategic), a dominant role of foreign or private enterprises in sectors that are politically defined as strategic, protracted dependence on imported technologies, uncontrolled exposure to the volatilities of global capital markets, or a wholesale liberalization of the political order.

[15] Cf. Cao Yingwang, *Assessments by Mao Zedong.*
[16] See the extensive documentation in *People's Daily*, "A Retrospective."

Table 1: *Annual rhythm of economic policy review (post-1994)*

	Top-level policy review	Working-level policy input
Nov.–Dec.	CCP Politburo special meeting on economic work in preparation of Annual Central Economic Work Conference (top-level policy review and adjustment; defines key policy tasks for next year).	Top-level decision-making prepared by CFELSG Staff Office in collaboration with NDRC after broad-based consultations in economic bureaucracies and research communities.
Dec.	Year-end State Council meeting assigns policy tasks for next year.	Separate annual National Work Conferences on development planning
Jan.	Provincial governors' meetings with central government leaders.	(NDRC), public finance (MoF), banking (PBoC, CBRC) etc.
Mar.	Government work report presented to National People's Congress with focus on policy review and new policy tasks.	Separate reports by NDRC and MoF to the National People's Congress on goal fulfilment in past year and policy goals for current year.
Apr.–June	Central and regional gov. bodies hold meetings to coordinate implementation of new policy tasks.	
July–Aug.	Mid-year Politburo and State Council meetings, assessing current situation and deciding on policy responses.	CFELSG Staff Office and NDRC undertake mid-year policy review; solicit feedback from central and regional gov. bodies; start preparing next year's policy plan.
Nov.–Dec.	[relaunch of policy coordination cycle as outlined above]	

CFELSG: Central FinEcon Leading Small Group; NDRC: National Development and Reform Commission; MoF: Ministry of Finance; PBoC: People's Bank of China; CBRC: China Banking Regulatory Commission.

FinEcon Guardians

This section deals with the particular institutional setup of China's core economic policy executive. Its workings are not yet well understood in Western research and therefore require a detailed analysis based on findings from our interviews with senior officials and researchers who have operated within and around the core executive bodies.[17]

At the center of the FinEcon mission, we find a triangle of policy coordination that can be traced back throughout PRC history (see Figure 2.1): first, the Party Center with the GenSec and the Politburo Standing Committee as the top-level decision-makers; second, the Prime

---

[17] The information and assessments presented in the following sections are based on visits to the CFELSG Staff Office at Zhongnanhai (June 2015) and the NDRC (five visits in the 2007–2015 period) that facilitated access to vice-ministerial and bureau-level officials involved in economic strategy and policy work for the core executive.

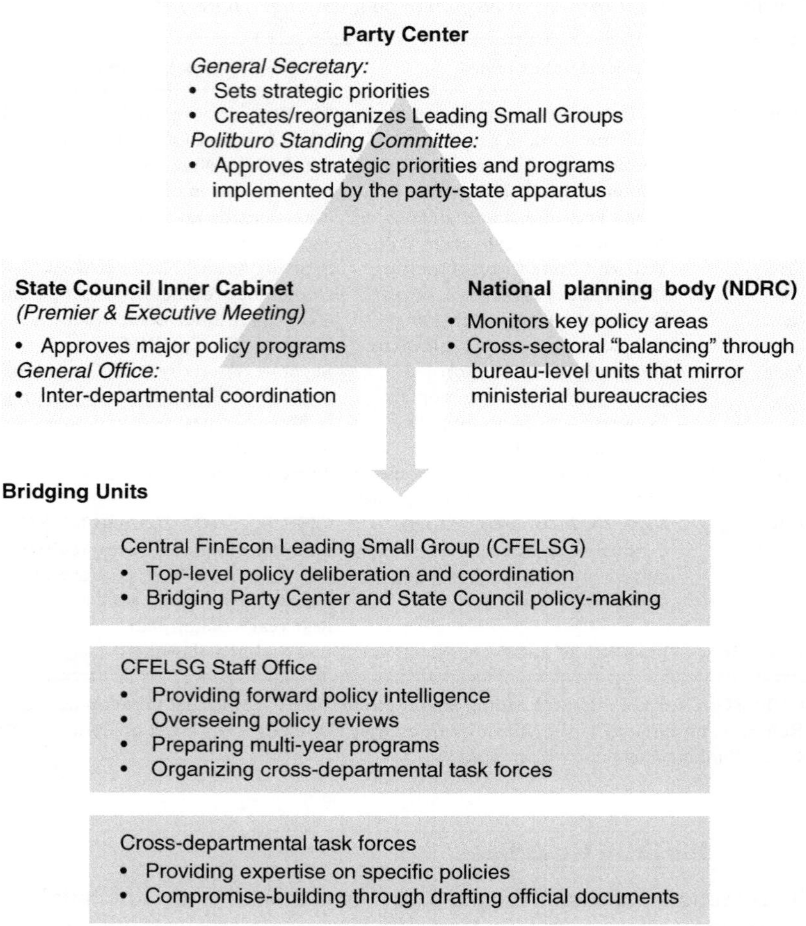

Party Center

General Secretary:
- Sets strategic priorities
- Creates/reorganizes Leading Small Groups
Politburo Standing Committee:
- Approves strategic priorities and programs implemented by the party-state apparatus

State Council Inner Cabinet
(Premier & Executive Meeting)

- Approves major policy programs
General Office:
- Inter-departmental coordination

National planning body (NDRC)
- Monitors key policy areas
- Cross-sectoral "balancing" through bureau-level units that mirror ministerial bureaucracies

Bridging Units

Central FinEcon Leading Small Group (CFELSG)
- Top-level policy deliberation and coordination
- Bridging Party Center and State Council policy-making

CFELSG Staff Office
- Providing forward policy intelligence
- Overseeing policy reviews
- Preparing multi-year programs
- Organizing cross-departmental task forces

Cross-departmental task forces
- Providing expertise on specific policies
- Compromise-building through drafting official documents

Figure 2.1 The core executive triangle: policy functions and bridging units

Ministerial Inner Cabinet (i.e. the regular "Executive Meeting" of the State Council including the Premier, Vice-Premiers, State Councillors and the head of the State Council's General Office); third, the national planning body (formerly the State Planning Commission, SPC; today the National Development and Reform Commission, NDRC) with its powerful policy bureaus. Within this triangle, the Central FinEcon Leading Small Group (CFELSG) serves as the pivotal party-state bridging body. It is provided with policy input by its attached FinEcon Staff

Office that in turn organizes cross-departmental task forces to obtain broad-based policy intelligence for the core executive.[18]

For most of the time in PRC history, the CCP paramount leaders and GenSecs have had a rather detached position in economic policy-making since the government executive (Premiers, Vice-Premiers, and State Councillors at the top of the State Council) has been at the center of policy coordination. Party leaders could have easily claimed regular decision-making power. But for most of the time, they chose to stay away from day-to-day policy-making and concentrated on setting strategic priorities, launching broad policy campaigns, and reorganizing the central leadership system so as to maintain control over the direction, not the details, of the national developmental agenda.

Top party leaders delegate to specialized bodies the authority to make and implement policy not only "because the bureaucrats have more expert and specialized information than party leaders have,"[19] but also to avoid the risks of being blamed for policy failures. In spite of continuous delegation, party leaders have always been suspicious of the authority exercised by officials and bureaucracies that worked as economic policy specialists.[20]

The function of the *Premier and Vice-Premiers with their secretarial office staff* as the permanent liaison hub in the national policy process has remained a continual feature of policy-making in the core executive since the founding of the PRC. The prime minister functions as the chief administrator who regularly has to report to the party's top leader and the Politburo Standing Committee on the state of economic affairs.[21] Inside the State Council General Office, economic policy issues have always been a core component of regular work.[22] Staff members are meant to take a strategic, non-departmental perspective and to work as neutral policy generalists rather than as sectoral experts. Specialized expertise in the General Office is thus purposely limited.

The State Council and, to a lesser and contested extent, the national planning body (NDRC) are the only government organs whose documents have a supra-ministerial status. A deeply hierarchical understanding of policy authority is at the heart of this: documents that are issued only in the name of ministries are regarded as less authoritative, binding,

[18] For details on these bodies with their diachronic trajectories and striking resilience, see Heilmann, "China's Economic Policy Core Executive."
[19] Shirk, *The Political Logic*, 57.
[20] Cf. Teiwes, "A Critique of Western Studies"; Teiwes, "Politics at the 'Core'"; MacFarquhar, *The Origins of the Cultural Revolution*; Shih, *Factions and Finance*.
[21] Huang, *Factionalism in Chinese Communist Politics*, 183, 201–202; Cheng Hua, *Zhou Enlai and his Secretaries*.
[22] State Council General Office, *Organizational Structure of the Central Government*; Wang Jingsong, *Government and Politics*, 79–80, 85.

and credible by other government bodies than documents issued in the name of the State Council.

In the Chinese polity, the functional equivalents to cabinet committees and interministerial committees in parliamentary systems are the so-called Leading Small Groups (LSGs) that assemble those decision-makers whose participation is essential to coordinate a particular and usually broad policy mission (such as dealing with cross-sectoral adjustments necessitated by WTO accession, promoting homegrown technological innovation across industries, or implementing the ambitious agenda of organizational, economic, and legal restructuring that was issued after Xi Jinping took over as GenSec). Comprehensive LSGs are created to propel top-priority agendas. They include top party and government leaders and therefore have considerable clout.[23]

The most secretive organ of China's economic core executive is the Central FinEcon Leading Small Group (CFELSG) with its affiliated Staff Office. It has served as a peculiar "amphibious" leadership body straddling party and government.[24] After the Central FinEcon Commission's dissolution in 1954, the top-level FinEcon unit was no longer constituted as a full-blown bureaucracy but rather as a leader-driven, variable body of policy assistance. CFELSG was activated as a top-level policy unit whenever the party's leaders felt the need to exercise closer oversight over economic affairs. In periods of economic distress, CFELSG has recurrently proved indispensable for supra-ministerial crisis management.[25]

The extra-constitutional character of the CFELSG (which is not mentioned in either the party or the state constitution) is made clear by the fact that it cannot issue formal party or government documents in its own name. Instead, it has to borrow the authority of either the Politburo or the State Council to participate in rule-making. As a variable policy-making vehicle, the CFELSG has taken on diverse functions: as a top-level deliberation body on economic strategy and major policy initiatives; as a decision-making body authorized to formulate economic policy on behalf of the State Council and the Politburo; as a top-level principal of government-linked think-tank research; as a crisis management body organizing broad-based "readjustments" and re-balancing during severe economic cycles; and as a crisis anticipation and early warning body.[26]

---

[23] Yang Shengchun, *The Assistants to the CCP's Top Leadership*, 33–34; Hamrin and Zhao, eds., *Decision-Making in Deng's China*; Lieberthal, *Governing China*, 215–218.

[24] Shirk, *The Political Logic*, 61–62.

[25] Bo Yibo, *Reflections on Certain Major Decisions*, 1086–1087; Zou Ximing, *A Chronicle of the Evolution*, 188–191, 206.

[26] In two crucial instances, 1996 and 2007, the CFELSG crisis meetings were convened at an early stage to prepare counter-measures against external shocks to the Chinese

Since the 1980s, CFELSG's *FinEcon Staff Office* has served as the most influential "meta-think-tank" and as a forward-thinking strategy unit for top-level policy-makers. It functions as the central gatekeeper and interface for economic advice, information, and initiative between the top leadership and China's policy research community. Key functions of the FinEcon Staff Office include preparing mid-year and year-end policy reviews and proposals for the Politburo (including the year-end Central Economic Work Conference that defines the policy tasks for the following year), contributing to the Premier's annual government work report and coordinating the preparatory work for China's Five Year Plans that are traditionally conceived of as the Communist Party's programs for national development.[27]

Since the 1990s, it has been one of the most important functions of the FinEcon Staff Office to assemble comprehensive task forces that represent a broad spectrum of policy positions and help to formulate the "encompassing interests" of the Party Center, in contrast to narrow ministerial or sectoral interests. The Staff Office coordinates policy research, filters information, selects and revises proposals provided by research groups, drafts policy papers and, with regard to annual and five-year programs, proposes the division of labor among government bodies for implementation work.[28] The involvement of a diversity of think-tanks helps to break the specialized ministries' conventional monopoly on information, thereby providing a more integrated, cross-departmental perspective on policy problems, which is precisely what is required at the level of the core executive.[29]

Since the senior officials of the FinEcon Staff Office have direct and regular access to the top leadership, they constitute a pivotal component of the core executive. The FinEcon Staff Office's small permanent staff of only about twenty officials is regularly augmented by outside experts who are invited to contribute to specific policy proposals. A wide and flexible range of researchers and officials from diverse bodies and fields are pulled in for temporary task forces and to participate in drafting groups that fulfill a crucial function in Chinese-style consensus-building (unity of thinking 统一思想) through document drafting.[30]

China's Central FinEcon Staff Office clearly does not constitute a formalized and prominent top-level "pilot agency" of the type that has

---

economy. See Li Peng, *Markets and [Governmental] Regulation*, 1296–1299; Xinhuanet, "700 Days of Macro-Control."

[27] Zou Ximing, *A Chronicle of the Evolution*, 206.

[28] See also Hamrin and Zhao, eds., *Decision-Making in Deng's China*, 103.

[29] Halpern, "Information Flows and Policy Coordination," 130–131.

[30] Wu Li, "Foundations and Conditions for Implementing."

been seen during certain periods of other East Asian developmental states. Chalmers Johnson and many other scholars pointed to the important role of powerful and professional executive agencies as centers of economic guidance and regulation in the initial decades of industrialization in Japan, South Korea, and Taiwan.[31] Whereas core executive agencies in these cases became prominent government units that initiated and implemented widely influential public policies, China's Central FinEcon Staff Office has remained a mostly invisible policy unit that is designed to organize, process, and compress policy input for top leaders, but does not issue or implement national policy itself. The FinEcon Staff Office is designed to mobilize informational and analytical resources from a broad set of bureaucratic and research units, in an effort to make the core executive less dependent on the expertise of specialized and self-interested bureaucracies that try to shape policy formulation from their narrow agency point of view.[32] Overall, the FinEcon Staff Office pursues the type of broadened, yet tightly controlled, consultation that has become a constituent element of Chinese policy-making since the 1990s.[33]

Among the regular government bureaucracies, planning bodies traditionally are meant to serve as the guardians of the FinEcon mission. They have been charged with transforming China into a mighty industrial power, preventing economic destabilization, and asserting the strategic goals set forth by the Party Center for national development. When the *State Planning Commission* (SPC) was founded in 1952, it was given an elevated status and reported directly to the top party and state leaders. Yet the authority of the SPC was frequently challenged and its prerogative in supra-ministerial coordination remained precarious. Ever since 1954, beginning only two years after its institution, the SPC has gone through frequent reorganizations and functional splits into two or three commissions which, in 2003, were eventually again merged into only one

---

[31] Johnson, *MITI and the Japanese Miracle*; Woo-Cumings, *The Developmental State*. While core executive agencies in Japan and South Korea displayed a much stronger policy effectiveness than comparable economic bureaucracies in most other developing (or newly industrializing) economies, striking recent research work (e.g. Steffensen, "The Weak State of Japan"; and Kang, "Bad Loans to Good Friends") produced strong evidence that East Asian pilot agencies were involved in regular exchanges with industrial lobbies (including cases of outright corruption) and subject to severe conflicts of political and business interests within the administration. The image of executive agencies that were "insulated" from interest group pressures appears untenable in the light of these research findings.

[32] For a comparative perspective from the UK context, see Smith, *The Core Executive in Britain*, 171–177.

[33] Cf. Naughton "The New Common Economic Program."

planning body. Planning was designed to serve, not to determine, the Party Center's developmental strategies.[34]

The power and status of the planning bodies were boosted and moved to the foreground of the policy process in times of economic emergency: curtailing investment excesses and boom-bust cycles or, in CCP terminology, "readjusting," "rectifying," and "rebalancing" the often wild swings in investment, growth, and inflation in an economy that repeatedly seemed to be on the verge of spiraling out of control.[35] "Readjustments" have always been a golden time for the planners who obtained additional powers in the context of centralized crisis management.[36]

With the advent of the "socialist market economy" agenda in 1992–1993, imperative planning appeared to have become useless, and a dismantling of the planning bureaucracy was discussed among top policy-makers.[37] Yet SPC planners gradually managed to reinvent themselves from a guardian of material balances and investment quotas into a macro-economic watchdog. The planners adapted their traditional FinEcon mission of "comprehensive balancing" (based on material balances, input-output tables, etc.) to a new mission of market-oriented "aggregate balancing," "macro-control," and "rebalancing" with the aim of macro-economic stabilization through cross-sectoral policy analysis, coordination, and programs. As a result, senior SPC/NDRC officials continued to define themselves as the guardians of national development. They gained new traction through ambitious multi-year industrial policy programs launched during the 2000s. Then they came under pressure to curtail their industrial policy ambitions when the Xi/Li administration launched its restructuring and deregulation agenda. However, the NDRC in turn tried to reinvent itself as an anti-monopoly regulator targeting large foreign companies in the mid-2010s. In retrospect, through constant mission-seeking in the new economic environment, the national planning body has demonstrated a remarkable resilience as an indispensable bureaucratic hub and guardian for shifting national agendas.[38]

In sum, despite recurrent institutional and personnel disruptions, the core organs tasked with defending the FinEcon mission have remained in place, or have been resurrected repeatedly by Communist Party leaders to

---

[34] See Liu Rixin, *A Brief History of Economic Construction*, 137–139, 211–213; Bo Yibo, *Reflections on Certain Major Decisions*, 73–74; Teiwes, *Politics at Mao's Court*, 29; Diao and Zagoria, *The Nature of Mainland Chinese Economic Structure*, 2, 19.

[35] Bo Yibo, *Reflections on Certain Major Decisions*, 1086–1087.

[36] Cf. Wang and Fewsmith, "Bulwark of the Planned Economy."

[37] Chen Jinhua, *Recollections on State Affairs*, 257–277.

[38] See Heilmann and Shih, "The Rise of Industrial Policy."

claim or reassert an encompassing approach to economic development, growth, and stability. The strategists, planners, brokers, and balancers who work in the FinEcon organs see themselves as those who are keeping China's national development on track while containing severe economic cycles and acute crises.

For the top leaders, the FinEcon bodies serve to deal with the challenges of obtaining non-particularistic input and forging compromises on top-priority policy adjustments and initiatives. Recognizing and brokering the trade-offs among interests and goals in overarching, multi-year programs is one of the most demanding elements of policy-making. In managing this task, the FinEcon bodies are obviously regarded as very useful by top leaders who have retained the basic institutional arrangements of FinEcon work to the present day.

The resilient patterns of interaction in the FinEcon triangle, boosted by the build-up of Leading Small Groups as enforcers of the Party Center's priority agendas under Xi Jinping, attest to the functional indispensability of supra-ministerial core executive organs in China's fragmented administrative system.

FinEcon in Action: Transmutations of the Planning Ambition

Historically, the FinEcon mission has been closely bound to the ambitions of centralized state planning. Since the 2000s, the communist leadership, while dismantling many typical features of socialist industrial planning and resource management, has reinvigorated its ambitions in terms of long-term, cross-sectoral coordination of economic, social, technological, and environmental development. The Chinese government has drafted long-term policy agendas that attempt to anticipate, utilize, and shape domestic and global market trends so as to promote China's economic, technological, and social developments. Regarding the comprehensiveness and intended domestic and global impacts of long-term policy programs, China has arguably become the most ambitious planning polity of our times. We find multi-year policy programs with binding and indicative targets in virtually every sector, from space programs and infrastructural construction through human resources and education to public services, health care, and cultural life.[39]

---

[39] For documentation on the diverse programs, see the planning section on the NDRC's website (ndrc.gov.cn). The following paragraphs draw on Heilmann and Melton, "The Reinvention."

From 1993 on, development planning has been reorganized funda-mentally in terms of function, content, process, and methods to allow room for market coordination while still preserving overall state control. Whereas planning had once been seen and used as a *substitute for markets* in line with Soviet conceptions, Chinese administrators were now charged with "taking markets as the foundation," that is, to *plan with and for markets*, and to absorb major trends in domestic and global markets into multi-year government programs. Planning was redefined as one of three key mechanisms of "macro-control," along with fiscal and monetary policy, that were supposed to facilitate the "comprehensive coordination" and "aggregate balancing" of economic activity. Instead of fixing a huge number of quantitative targets and control figures, plan-ners were ordered to focus on macro-, strategic, and policy issues and to refrain from giving orders to ministries, regions, and enterprises. Plan functions were curtailed and redirected to give "overall guidance" for the transformation of the economic structure along with the market-oriented industrial policies.[40] The "ex ante coordination" through plans was sup-posed to be made compatible with the ad hoc coordination through markets.[41]

China's post-1993 "new-style development planning" moved farther and farther away from Soviet-style administrative resource management. Yet, the very essence of state development planning has been preserved in China as a governmental effort at *strategic policy coordination* (prioritizing and coordinating state policies from an anticipatory, long-term, cross-sectoral perspective); *resource mobilization* (mobilizing and pooling resources to bring about structural changes identified by policy-makers as necessary to achieve sustained economic and social development); *macro-economic control* (controlling the level and growth of principal eco-nomic variables to achieve a predetermined set of development objec-tives, prevent severe cyclical fluctuations, and contain the effects of external shocks).[42] In this sense, China clearly still is a *planning polity* committed to guiding development through state coordination from a long-term, strategic perspective.

To improve formulation and implementation, Chinese planners have tried to combine multi-year plans with a multitude of consultative and corrective mechanisms that are intended to make planning more respon-sive to unanticipated contextual changes, more open to operative

[40] CCP Central Committee, "Decision of the CCP Central Committee on Some Issues"; Li and Li, "A Retrospective on Planning System Reform."
[41] Gui et al., *China's Planning System Reform*, 72–76.
[42] Cf. Todaro and Smith, *Economic Development*, 518; Xiang Wei, "Reflections on Drafting," 40.

adjustments, and more conducive to producing and using new policy instruments. Anticipatory economic policy coordination in China thus moved from the early reform-era mode of *centralized, closed, intra-state bargaining, and coordination* (often punctuated by interference from top policy-makers until the early 1990s) to *controlled multiple advocacy* that is based on carefully orchestrated consultation of state, non-state, and even foreign, economic actors and on much more regularized administrative procedures that are supposed to support "scientific" policy-making.[43]

Post-1993 Chinese development planning and sustained government intervention so far have succeeded in boosting investment- and export-driven growth, infrastructural buildup, and industrial diversification, while keeping basic macro-economic indicators and balances (inflation, foreign debt, foreign exchange, the capital account, and the current account) under national governmental control. Planned and ad hoc interventions have so far preserved a remarkable degree of macro-economic stability and crisis resilience despite major external shocks that hit the Chinese political economy in 1997 and 2008. Development planning and administrative interference were employed as a means to benefit from, and at the same time control, domestic and transnational market dynamics and market participants.

Goals and targets stated in Chinese development programs were implemented most effectively in those policy fields in which government programs managed to align political cadre career incentives (and therefore administrative action) with domestic and transnational market opportunities. Despite a comparatively successful macro-economic record in stabilizing high growth rates while curtailing inflation, there are obvious and hard limits to the planning ambition with regard to fundamental economic restructuring and the transition toward an efficiency-, innovation-, and domestic consumption-driven mode of development. The growth imperative and the adjacent fixation with industrial investment and expansion (this fixation was seen by many planning officials interviewed for this study as traditionally "socialistic" but no longer tenable) tended to override any efforts by comprehensive and environmental planners to guide China's economy in a more sustainable direction. In contrast to the record of extensive growth, government programs and interventions have proven largely ineffective in guiding macro-structural shifts, i.e. the "transformation of the growth and development

---

[43] See the programmatic volume on up-to-date planning approaches edited by Yang Weimin, who has been one of the most influential program drafters and coordinators in the core executive from the late 1990s to 2017: Yang Weimin, chief ed., *The Theory and Practice*.

mode" that has been defined as a core mission with changing formulas in all five-year programs from the mid-1990s on.[44]

Fundamentally, the FinEcon mission aims to impose political priorities upon economic markets. Along with the post-2008 global financial crisis, this ambition has been bolstered by a growing distrust and critique of policy-making in Western democracies. In the opinion of Chinese planners, policy-making in democratic systems is limited to compensatory ad hoc interventions and leaves control over the direction of social development to "blind" market forces, even though long-term strategies are required to cope with challenges such as capital market dysfunctions, environmental degradation, or demographic change. To put it in social science terminology, China's FinEcon guardians aim at *long-wave policy-making*, as opposed to *short-cycle policy-making*, that characterizes the policy process with its frequent ad hoc reprioritizations in most political economies.

Yet, the effectiveness and far-sightedness of the FinEcon mission must not be overstated. While planners, in China as elsewhere, like to present themselves as protagonists of "scientific planning," the making of comprehensive strategies and programs clearly is not a supra-political activity.[45] Even if sectoral or regional lobbying cannot exert a determining influence on cross-sectoral, multi-year macro-plans, plan-making per se is an intensely politicized process, since strategic decisions about the distribution and redistribution of resources have to be made. A government can try to frame this as "scientific" prioritization and coordination. But, in effect, making plans cannot be detached from struggles about prioritizing certain objectives, sectors, regions, or groups at the expense of others. And this is the very essence of politics.

Despite their continued planning ambition, Chinese FinEcon guardians have come to accept that the future of economies and societies is characterized by many unknowns and uncertainties that cannot be anticipated through planning. One top-level FinEcon official interviewed for this study conceded that even the most careful planning cannot prevent the occurrence of disastrous events, economic downturns, or external shocks, since far too many variables are outside of the planners' control. But in his view, foresighted planning can provide a strong foundation to deal with the impact of such events in a swift and coordinated manner, and thereby will greatly help to contain the societal damage.

Chinese policy-makers try to keep key variables that they identify to be crucial to China's current and future development trajectory (Communist

---

[44] This criticism was widely shared by planning officials in interviews.

[45] On planners' aspirations to frame planning as a supra-political activity, see Friedmann, *Planning in the Public Domain*; Rutland, *The Myth of the Plan*.

Party rule and executive leadership; political control over economic sectors and corporations identified as strategic; macro-economic variables such as growth, inflation, fiscal deficits, credit volume, current and capital accounts, currency exchange rates, etc.) under tight control and as steady as possible.

Core Executive Technocrats and Particularistic Interests

The policy communities that are knit around the core FinEcon bodies fit the standards of informed technocratic insulation since they are detached from sectoral vested interests, yet open to absorb information through regularized, broad-based, though non-public, policy consultation and debate. The policy brokers and scholars-turned-bureaucrats of the core executive organs are constantly exposed to political pressures and tactical expediencies. But due to non-industrial career patterns and encompassing planning tasks, they mostly remain aloof from the interest networks and bargaining over resources and investments that govern ministerial and regional policy-making. Under the Hu/Wen (2003–2012) and Xi/Li (2013–) administrations, top leaders have privileged technocratic staff with a background in policy research and planning that is committed to "top-level design" in national policy-making.[46] These technocrats serve as senior policy brokers for the core executive. Maintaining broad contacts across different functional organs and elites is at the heart of their daily tasks and capabilities. It is a major qualification for senior staff in the core executive bodies that they are acceptable to a broad spectrum of leaders and ministries as neutral brokers.[47]

The policy units and networks that support China's core executive are held together not only by personal loyalties, professional expertise, or thirst for power and status, but also by shared beliefs, similar career patterns, and formative experiences, as well as a unifying work style. Whereas hard-core socialist ideology has been diluted among today's FinEcon guardians, patriotism (making China strong and modern), social concerns (eliminating poverty and pursuing more equitable growth), "statist" orientations (the indispensability of state control over the direction of economic and social development) as well as attitudinal ideals (the "upright official" as role model) are commonly stated beliefs

---

[46] Cf. Liu He, "The Basic Logic of the Proposal." Liu was a core FinEcon policy broker and economic advisor under the Hu/Wen administration and continues to serve in a pivotal advisory position under the new GenSec Xi Jinping.

[47] On this, see the rules of the game in General Office work as pointed out by an insider: Li, *The Chinese Staff System.*

and objectives among the central technocrats who make up the policy-shaping second and third tiers of China's core executive.[48]

Chinese efforts at developmental policy coordination entail a multitude of comprehensive, spatial, sectoral, and regional multi-year programs whose political constraints appear analogous to past Japanese efforts that, according to Okimoto, formed "a motley assortment of policy measures" besieged by a multitude of special-interest groups, inter-agency rivalries, and unavoidable contradictions.[49] Whereas cross-sectoral national planning is built on a serious effort at broad-based consultation and consistency, the sectoral programs, industrial policies, and investment projects that are purportedly designed to put the mid- and long-term plans into practice are shaped by massive bargaining among the bureaucratic and business interests that are affected by government regulation and funding schemes.[50]

As Rodrik states, it is a critical challenge for developmental policies "to find an intermediate position between full autonomy" (exercised by all-powerful policy-makers and bureaucrats) and "full embeddedness" (pursued by corruption-prone policy-makers and bureaucrats).[51] Chinese FinEcon guardians do not offer consistent management of, or institutionalized solutions to, this dilemma.

Since the start of market-oriented reforms, China's core executive has been under constant challenge not only by sectoral and bureaucratic interests, princeling and cadre family networks and corrupt local cadres, state managers, and property dealers but also by an extremely fast-changing socio-economic, technological, and international environment. Such a volatile environment has made forward-looking policy intelligence and purposive cross-sectoral coordination for the longer term extremely difficult.

The emphasis on multi-year, centrally sponsored national programs for "indigenous innovation" (launched in 2006), "industrial revitalization" (2008), or institutional restructuring ("comprehensively deepening reform," 2013) is conceived by leading technocrats as a response to centrifugal forces that are evading, and thereby undermining, the national FinEcon mission. The pressures of particularist interests, from oligopolistic state industries to regional property-cum-finance operations and

---

[48] See in detail Heilmann and Shih, "The Rise of Industrial Policy."

[49] Okimoto, *Between MITI and the Market*, 3–4.

[50] See the studies on government–business interactions in, for instance, the steel industry (Taube and in der Heiden, *The State-Business Nexus*) or the automobile industry (Thun, *Changing Lanes in China*). For a broader perspective on business lobbying in China, see Kennedy, *The Business of Lobbying*.

[51] Cf. Rodrik, *One Economics, Many Recipes*, 111–112.

multi-functional princeling networks, are recognized as a serious challenge to central power. Yet the core executive has potent means at its
disposal to enforce its authority. The defense of the FinEcon mission
became tangible in the anti-corruption campaign that was targeted
against entrenched rent-seeking in the party-state apparatus and in state-
owned enterprises under Xi Jinping's leadership. While the campaign
served the broader objective to restore organizational discipline and
central authority within the party-state, massive regulatory and campaign-style interventions were directed at financially overstretched and
corruption-prone sectors that were clear cases for centrally sponsored
"rectification" in line with the FinEcon mission.

The swift restoration of central policy decisiveness under Xi Jinping
required a high degree of autocratic aggressiveness and ruthlessness on
the part of the new central leadership. And it made clear the essential
precondition for pursuing the FinEcon mission: the technocrats working
for the core executive can try to promote a broader and longer view of
economic and social development only if their plans and policies are
backed and adopted by a self-confident and authoritative leadership.

In contrast, macro-economic rebalancing (which in the Chinese context implies transiting from an investment- and export-driven economy to
an economy driven by domestic demand, technological innovation, and
productivity gains) and ambitious institutional restructuring (which is at
the heart of the "comprehensively deepening reform" agenda launched
under Xi Jinping in 2013) are problematic enterprises that in effect may
run counter to the FinEcon mission eventually. A massive transfer of
financial resources from party-state coffers to private households and
non-state market participants would threaten a central plank of the
FinEcon mission, that is, concentrating funds in the hands of the central
party-state. Rebalancing and deregulation would in effect curtail central
power and control. This conflict with the FinEcon mission may explain
why the rebalancing agenda (that had been addressed with differing
terminology in all Five Year Plans since the mid-1990s) has made only
slow and limited progress.

Conclusion

In studies of China's economic transformation, decentralized reform
initiative and local policy experimentation are widely accepted as having
facilitated marketization, entrepreneurialism, and policy innovation.
The contribution of the national core executive to pursuing long-term
agendas and providing public goods tends to be underrated in most
studies. Conceptual frameworks such as "playing to the provinces"

(Shirk), "fragmented authoritarianism" (Lieberthal and Oksenberg), "market-preserving federalism" (Montinola et al.), or "experimentation under hierarchy" do not explain the multi-year national programs that were launched by the central leadership with clearly varying, but in important areas (e.g. infrastructure, technology, social security) cumulatively remarkable effects. Central guidance and priorities, even though challenged and diluted by centrifugal forces, have made a difference in crucial areas of national development.

It is thus the key proposition of this essay that China's core executive, in spite of recurrent setbacks and temporarily weakened authority, has served as an effective counterweight against centrifugal forces and particularistic interests in the political-administrative system.

Central decisiveness, that was forcefully reasserted under Xi Jinping's reign, is founded on autocratic policy pushes and leader-driven agendas that are transformed into comprehensive long-term programs within the core executive triangle. The reorganization and reinforcement of Central Leading Small Groups is crucial to signal top-level determination and formulate top-priority agendas. The enforcement of such ambitious agendas, however, is inconceivable without additional governance mechanisms controlled by the Party Center, such as campaign-style mobilization and discipline inspection as well as reevaluation of performance criteria in the cadre hierarchy. These governance mechanisms enable the core executive to launch top-down policy pushes and override bureaucratic, sectoral and regional interests while still facing silent evasion, resistance, or paralysis in policy implementation on the ground.

Overall, central leadership in China is not about being "benign" or "benevolent" to as many people as possible. If the core executive pursues long-term developmental goals and provides public goods to a large segment of the population, it undertakes this to defend the Party Center's interest in containing centrifugal forces, controlling financial resource flows, preventing popular revolt, and making the nation-state strong and safe in a world that does not necessarily welcome the rise of new powers.

References

Brødsgaard, Kjeld Erik and Young, Susan, eds. *State Capacity in East Asia: Japan, Taiwan, China, Vietnam*. Oxford: Oxford University Press, 2000.

Bo Yibo (薄一波). (*Reflections on Certain Major Decisions and Events*). 若干重大决策与事件的回顾. 2 vols. 北京: 中共党史出版社, 2008.

Cao Yingwang (曹应旺). ("Assessments by Mao Zedong, Zhou Enlai, Liu Shaoqi, and Deng Xiaoping of Chen Yun's FinEcon Work"). "毛泽东, 周恩来, 刘少奇, 邓小平对陈云财经工作的评价," 党的文献, 4: 2005, 54–9.

CCP Central Committee. "Decision of the CCP Central Committee on Some Issues concerning the Establishment of a Socialist Market Economic Structure" (official translation). Xinhua News Agency News Bulletin, No. 16388, Nov. 17, 1993.

Chen Jinhua(陈锦华). (*Recollections on State Affairs*). 国事忆述. 北京: 中共党史出版社, 2005.

Cheng Hua (程华). (*Zhou Enlai and his Secretaries*). 周恩来和他的秘书们. 北京: 中国广播电视出版社, 1992.

Diao, Richard and Zagoria, Donald. *The Nature of Mainland Chinese Economic Structure, Leadership and Policy (1949–1969) and Prospects for Arms Control and Disarmament: Final Report.* Report prepared for the US Arms Control and Disarmament Agency. 2 vols. Feb. 1972.

Dunleavy, P. and Rhodes, R. A. W. "Core Executive Studies in Britain," *Public Administration*, 68, 1: 1990, 3–28.

Elgie, Robert. "Core Executive Studies Two Decades On," *Public Administration*, 89, 1: 2011, 64–77.

Fang Weizhong (房维中) and Jin Chongji (金冲及). (*Biography of Li Fuchun*). 李富春传. 北京: 中央文献出版社, 2001.

Friedmann, John. *Planning in the Public Domain: From Knowledge to Action.* Princeton: Princeton University Press, 1987.

Gui Shiyong (桂世镛), Wei Liqun (魏礼群), and Zheng Xinli (郑新立), eds. (*China's Planning System Reform*). 中国计划体制改革. 北京: 中国财政经济出版社, 1994.

Halpern, Nina. "Information Flows and Policy Coordination in the Chinese Bureaucracy," in Lieberthal and Lampton, eds., *Bureaucracy, Politics and Decision Making in Post-Mao China*, 125–148.

Hamrin, Carol Lee and Zhao, Suisheng, eds. *Decision-Making in Deng's China: Perspectives from Insiders.* Armonk, NY: M. E. Sharpe, 1995.

Heilmann, Sebastian. "China's Economic Policy Core Executive: A Diachronic Study." Paper (much longer version) prepared for the international conference "Power in the Making: Governing and Being Governed in Contemporary China," Oxford University, March 30 – April 1, 2012.

Heilmann, Sebastian and Melton, Oliver. "The Reinvention of Development Planning in China, 1993–2012," *Modern China*, 39, 6: 2013, 580–628.

Heilmann, Sebastian and Shih, Lea. "The Rise of Industrial Policy in China, 1978–2012." Harvard-Yenching Working Paper, 2013.

Huang, Jing. *Factionalism in Chinese Communist Politics.* New York: Cambridge University Press, 2000.

Jin Chongji (金冲及) and Chen Qun (陈群). (*Biography of Chen Yun*). 陈云传. 2 vols. 北京: 中央文献出版社, 2005.

Johnson, Chalmers A. *MITI and the Japanese Miracle: The Growth of Industrial Policy, 1925–1975.* Stanford: Stanford University Press, 1982.

Kang, David C. "Bad Loans to Good Friends: Money Politics and the Developmental State in South Korea," *International Organization*, 56, 1: 2002, 177–207.

Kim, Ilpyong J. *The Politics of Chinese Communism: Kiangsi under the Soviets.* Berkeley: University of California Press, 1973.

Li Hai (李海) et al., eds. (*Unifying Finance and Economics: Laying the Foundation for a New China*). 统一财经: 为新中国奠基立业. 北京: 当代中国出版社, 2008.

Li Peng (李鹏). (*Markets and [Governmental] Regulation: Li Peng's Economic Diaries*). 市场与调控: 李鹏经济日记. 3 vols. 北京: 新华出版社, 2007.

Li Pumin (李朴民) and Li Bing (李冰). ("A Retrospective on Planning System Reform in China during the 9th Five Year Plan Period"). "九五 时期我国计划体制改革回顾," 宏观经济研究, 2: 2001, 24–6.

Li, Wei. *The Chinese Staff System: A Mechanism for Bureaucratic Control and Integration*. Berkeley: Institute of East Asian Studies, University of California, 1994.

Lieberthal, Kenneth G. *Governing China: From Revolution through Reform*. 2nd edn. New York: Norton, 2004.

Lieberthal, Kenneth G. and Lampton, David M., eds. *Bureaucracy, Politics and Decision Making in Post-Mao China*. Berkeley: University of California Press, 1992.

Lieberthal, Kenneth G. and Oksenberg, Michel. *Policy Making in China: Leaders, Structures, and Processes*. Princeton: Princeton University Press, 1988.

Liu Guoguang (刘国光), ed. (*Research Report on Ten Chinese Five Year Plans*). 中国十个五年计划研究报告. 北京: 人民出版社, 2006.

Liu He (刘鹤). ("The Basic Logic of the Proposal for the 12th Five Year Plan"). "'十二五' 规划建议的基本逻辑," 中国民营科技与经济, 4: 2011, 82–90.

Liu Rixin (刘日新). (*A Brief History of Economic Construction in New China*). 新中国经济建设简史. 北京: 中央文献出版社, 2006.

MacFarquhar, Roderick. *The Origins of the Cultural Revolution: The Coming of the Cataclysm 1961–1966*. New York: Columbia University Press, 1997.

Montinola, Gabriella, Qian, Yingyi and Weingast, Barry. "Federalism, Chinese Style: The Political Basis for Economic Success in China," *World Politics*, 48: 1995, 50–81.

Naughton, Barry. "The New Common Economic Program: China's Eleventh Five Year Plan and What it Means," *China Leadership Monitor*, 16: 2006.

Okimoto, Daniel I. *Between MITI and the Market: Japanese Industrial Policy for High Technology*. Stanford: Stanford University Press, 1989.

People's Daily (人民日报), ed. ("A Retrospective on the Central Economic Work Conferences, 1994–2005"). "中央经济工作会议回顾, 1994–2005," 12 月 6 日 2005. Available at finance.people.com.cn/GB/1045/3917584.html.

"Proposals Raised by Soviet Advisors on the Initial Drafts of China's Five Year Plan, May 1954." "苏联顾问对我国五年计划纲要 (初稿) 的建议 (1954年5月)," 中共党史资料, 78: (June) 2001.

Rhodes, R. A. W. "Introducing the Core Executive," in Rhodes and Dunleavy, eds., *Prime Minister, Cabinet and Core Executive*, 1–8.

Rhodes, R. A. W. and Dunleavy, P., eds. *Prime Minister, Cabinet and Core Executive*. London: Macmillan, 1995.

Rodrik, Dani. *One Economics, Many Recipes: Globalization, Institutions, and Economic Growth*. Princeton: Princeton University Press, 2007.

Rutland, Peter. *The Myth of the Plan: Lessons of Soviet Planning Experience*. La Salle, IL: Open Court, 1985.

Shen Zhihua (沈志华). (*Soviet Experts in China, 1948–1960*). 苏联专家在中国: 1948–1960. 北京: 中国国际广播出版社, 2003.

Shih, Victor C. *Factions and Finance in China: Elite Conflict and Inflation.* Cambridge: Cambridge University Press, 2008.

Shirk, Susan L. *The Political Logic of Economic Reform in China.* Berkeley: University of California Press, 1993.

Smith, Martin J. *The Core Executive in Britain.* London: Macmillan, 1999.

State Council General Office (国务院办公厅), ed. (*Organizational Structure of the Central Government*). 中央政府组织机构. 北京: 党建读物出版社, 2008.

Steffensen, Sam K. "The Weak State of Japan," in Brødsgaard and Young, eds., *State Capacity in East Asia*, 17–36.

Taube, Markus and in der Heiden, Peter. *The State-Business Nexus in China's Steel Industry.* Munich: Thinkdesk Research, 2009.

Teiwes, Frederick C. "A Critique of Western Studies of CCP Elite Politics," *IIAS Newsletter*, 9: 1996, 37.

Teiwes, Frederick C. "Politics at the 'Core': The Political Circumstances of Mao Zedong, Deng Xiaoping and Jiang Zemin," *China Information*, 15, 1: 2001, 1–66.

Teiwes, Frederick C. *Politics at Mao's Court: Gao Gang and Party Factionalism in the Early 1950s.* Armonk, NY: M. E. Sharpe, 1990.

Thun, Eric. *Changing Lanes in China: Foreign Direct Investment, Local Governments, and Auto Sector Development.* New York: Cambridge University Press, 2006.

Todaro, Michael P. and Smith, Stephen C. *Economic Development.* 9th edn. Harlow/London: Pearson, 2006.

Wang Jingsong (王敬松). (*Government and Politics in the PRC, Oct. 1949–1992*). 中华人民共和国政府与政治, 1949.10–1992. 北京: 中共中央党校出版社, 1995.

Wang, Lixin and Fewsmith, Joseph. "Bulwark of the Planned Economy: The Structure and Role of the State Planning Commission," in Hamrin and Zhao, eds., *Decision-Making in Deng's China*, 51–65.

Woo-Cumings, Meredith, ed. *The Developmental State.* Ithaca, NY: Cornell University Press, 1999.

Wu Li (武力). ("Formulation and Implementation of the First Five Year Plan, 1953–1957"). "第一个五年计划的制定和实施 (1953–1957)," in Liu Guoguang, ed., *Research Report on Ten Chinese Five Year Plans*, 52–113.

Wu Li (武力). ("*Foundations and Conditions for Implementing Administrative Planning in the PRC*"). "中华人民共和国实施计划管理的基础和条件," in Liu Guoguang, ed., *Research Report on Ten Chinese Five Year Plans*, 1–51.

Xiang Wei (相伟). ("Reflections on Drafting the 12th Five Year Plan"). "对十二五规划 编制的思考," 宏观经济管理, 1: 2009, 38–40.

Xinhuanet (新华网). ("700 Days of Macro-Control Decision-Making under Crisis"). "危机下的宏调决策700天," 6 月 8 日 2009. Available at http://news.xinhuanet.com/fortune/2009–06/08/content_11507575.htm.

Xue Muqiao (薛⊠桥). (*Xue Muqiao's Memoirs*). 薛暮桥回忆录. 天津: 天津人民出版社, 1996.

Xue Muqiao (薛⊠桥), ed. (*Summing up FinEcon Work, Welcoming National Victory: Documenting Two Important FinEcon Conferences on the Eve of National Liberation*). 总结财经工作, 迎接全国耗利 – 记全国解放前夕两次重要的财经会议. 北京: 中国财政经济出版社, 1996.

Yang Shengchun (杨耘春). (*The Assistants to the CCP's Top Leadership Group*). 中国最高领导班子的左右手. 台北: 永業出版社, 2000.

Yang Weimin (杨伟民), chief ed. (*The Theory and Practice of Development Planning*). 发展规划的理论和实践. 北京: 清华大学出版社, 2010.

Yao Yilin (姚依林). ("Yao Yilin's Evening Chats"). "姚依林白夕谈," III, 传记文学, 12: 1995, 23–44.

Zou Ximing (邹锡明). (*A Chronicle of the Evolution of CCP Central Organs July 1921 – September 1997*). 中共中央机构沿革实录, 1921.7–1997.9. 北京: 中国档案出版社, 1998.

Envisioning

3   Maps, Dreams, and Trails to Heaven: Envisioning a Future Chinese Nation-Space

Vivienne Shue *

Trails to Heaven

The modern anthropology of indigenous peoples teaches us that, even before there were states, before settled agriculture and "civilization," human beings surviving in groups – hunters and gatherers – were making maps, out of dreams about the future, and associating their maps with power. In Hugh Brody's classic study of Canadian Subarctic Indian cultures and practices for example, a small band of modern-day hunter-trappers, recalling some of their people's old ways for the ethnographer, endeavor to explain the enigmatic powers to foretell the future here on earth, and even to point the way toward paradise, that some good maps could hold

Some old-timers, men who became famous for their powers and skills, had been great dreamers. Hunters and dreamers ... They did not seek uncertainly for the trails of animals whose movements we can only guess at. No, they located their prey in dreams, found their trails, and made dream-kills. Then, the next day ... they could go out, find the trail, re-encounter the animal, and collect the kill. Maybe ... you think this is all nonsense, just so much bullshit. Maybe you don't think this power is possible. Few people understand ... The Indians around this country know a lot about power. In fact, everyone has had some experience of it. The fact that dream-hunting works has been proved many times ... Today it is hard to find men who can dream this way. There are too many problems ... Maybe there will again be strong dreamers when these problems are overcome. Then more maps will be made. New maps.

Oh, yes, Indians made maps. You would not take any notice of them. You might say such maps are crazy ... Old-timers made maps of trails, ornamented them with lots of fancy. The good people.

* My thanks go to Chen Fan, Wei Xing, and Xu Xibai for unstinting assistance in collecting and sorting the documentary, oral, and visual materials on which this essay is based.

None of this is easy to understand. But good men, the really good men, could dream of more than animals. Sometimes they saw heaven and its trails ... You may laugh at these maps of the trails to heaven, but they were done by the good men who had the heaven dream, who wanted to tell the truth. They worked hard on their truth.[1]

In this essay, we take a close look at mapping and dreaming – techniques of political leadership and governance still interestingly practiced in China today, albeit in suitably updated forms – as the twenty-first-century party-state grapples with all the cross-cutting dilemmas generated by its headlong pursuit of development, prosperity, and modernization in these postmodern times. We examine the strategy recently adopted by Chinese leaders to cope with one set of the most crucial challenges their country faces; that of regulating land use for national sustainability, under conditions of global climate change, across a vast terrain of diverse ecologies, amid non-stop demands for rapid economic growth and pressures for accelerated rates of social transformation, toward greater equity, and better guarantees of public welfare, safety, and security.

Our first section considers the general design of China's new national land use Master Plan and the key concepts that inform it, reviewing a small sample of the astonishing national maps that accompanied the Master Plan's launch at the outset of the 12th Five Year Plan. The section that follows then sets the making of this highly ambitious central land use plan within its broader political-historical context: those eternal tensions between upper and lower levels of the state – between central authority and local discretion – that imbue the Chinese governing system. The third section moves on to discuss in greater detail how the development of a national Master Plan for the regulation of land use was orchestrated from the center over the course of this century's first decade, highlighting the phased mobilizations of technical experts and researchers from multiple disciplines and from around the country, repeated rounds of investigation, consultation, and localized experimentation. This is followed by a brief review of certain techniques central leaders have elected to utilize in subsequent efforts to implement and enforce the stricter land use regulations of the Master Plan in localities around the country. To conclude, we return to our initial observations about the dynamic relationships among maps, dreams, and concepts of good and virtuous leadership to explore further how *the very acts* of mapping out a way through a threatening environment, and envisioning an eventual, safe arrival at a plentiful future – even if such visions nowadays may be accessed more through painstaking statistical data collection and

[1] Brody, *Maps and Dreams*, 44–46.

computer modeling projections than through *dreams* per se – can remain familiarly vital tools of authority; necessary performances of power, obligatory tasks of political leadership, and telling responses to elemental human cravings for the solace of hope and for a semblance of control in the face of uncertainty.

Zoning the Nation

As "Document No. 46" – after more than four years in preparation and with text, maps, and tables running to a total of more than 170 pages – China's national spatial Master Plan was officially promulgated by the State Council in the closing days of December 2010.[2] For those who did not already know much about this document with the clumsy title "National Principal Function Zoning Plan" (全国主体功能区规划) – the People's Republic of China's (PRC) first-ever strategic plan intended to govern the development and use of the *whole* of the national territory, *all* its land, and *all* its waters – the immensity of its objectives and the sheer ambition of it must have been startling. Even some months after its formal promulgation, at the rather animated briefing and press conference introducing the Master Plan to the public, the questions posed by some journalists who gathered for the event, and the intensity with which they could be seen reading and studying the briefing document they had been handed, revealed the difficulty they were still having in getting their minds round several of its basic goals and concepts.[3]

The Principal Function Zoning (PFZ) Plan stipulated that all China's land and all its territorial waters would be classified into categories, according to the main "function" each area is deemed to perform. These categorical zoning assignments are, in turn, to determine the speed, the extent to which, and the guidelines according to which each zoned space, and any of the valuable resources that lie within it, may (or may not) be utilized for future development. The basic framework upon

---

[2] "State Council Communiqué on Issuing."

[3] Video coverage of that June 8, 2011 public briefing is at www.china.com.cn/zhibo/ 2011–06/08/content_22712930.htm. The Master Plan had been ratified as a component in the nation's 12th Five Year Plan, released in March 2011, after which there was a concerted effort to feature news of the Plan in the media. See, e.g., "NDRC Detailed Briefing"; "Deciphering the National Principal Function Zoning Plan"; "PFZ Strategy"; Xie Qing, "Implement the 'Principal Function Zoning' Strategy"; and Ma Kai, "Implementing the Principal Function Strategy." In earlier years, as the Master Plan was evolving, interim research reports and other background materials on it had been published and circulated to many in government and to policy and planning experts. For example, Chen Youshan and Zhang Ruo, "Principal Function Zoning"; "State Council Opinions regarding the Making"; *The National PFZ Program: Reference Materials*; and Tsinghua University, *Policy Research*.

which the PFZ Plan rests posits just three types of "principal functions" to which territorial space can be devoted in furthering national development: urban/industrial functions, rural/agricultural functions (including animal husbandry and fisheries), and ecological functions (conceived as the generation of essential "ecological products" such as clean water, fresh air, and sufficient biodiversity to sustain a tolerable climate and an environment in which human life can survive and flourish).[4]

According to the Master Plan, zones designated as having principally urban/industrial functions must be *intensively* built up to include a sufficient mix of residential, production, public service, and commercial spaces. Zones designated as having principally rural/agricultural functions can and should be less thickly settled, but must also contain sufficient built-up sections to provide efficiently designed residential accommodation, agricultural processing industries, and continuously improving agricultural-technical and public services. Zones designated as having principally ecological functions should be as lightly settled as possible, consistent with the goals of conserving and protecting natural habitats and resources. But even these critical zones, sometimes referred to as "environmental security areas," are to be allowed some mixed uses, including mining and other forms of resource extraction utilizing cleaner technologies. Thus, principal functional zoning, while it is meant to be strictly monitored and enforced, is not expected to create spaces necessarily performing a single function only, to the exclusion of auxiliary functions.[5]

The national PFZ Master Plan is premised on a sober assessment of China's existing pattern of spatial development as one already dangerously out of balance. The nation's natural geographic endowment – with its vast stretches of mountainous terrain, arid deserts, and high-altitude plateaux – confronts its leaders and its still-growing population with a comparatively severe shortage of space remaining suitable for development. And that

---

[4] Several key concepts used in the PFZ Master Plan – such as "intensity of development," "ecological products," and "ecological function zones" – are briefly defined in *The National PFZ Program: Reference Materials*, 117–123. The fundamental background thinking informing the Plan, concerning the natural limits China faces in charting a sustainable development course, is explained succinctly in Yang Weimin, "Implement the Principal Function Zoning Strategy." The broader thinking behind national- and local-level planning is summarized in the Institute of Geographic Sciences' research report on spatial master planning and demarcating zones, in Zhang Ping, chief ed., *The Twelfth Five Year Plan*, vol. I, 396–418.

[5] Yang Weimin, "Implement the Principal Function Zoning Strategy," section 2.1, notes the unavoidable need there will always also be for certain additional spaces, not comprised under *any* of these three broad categories, performing "miscellaneous" functions – such as transport (railways, highways, airports, seaports, pipelines) and water management networks or facilities required for sustaining the overall economy; as well as certain spaces that must be devoted to "special uses" such as religious sites and national defense installations.

already challenging natural endowment has been further compromised by sprawling urban growth, destruction of farmland, and uncontrolled exploitation of natural resources in recent decades, as well as by numerous misguided earlier attempts at "development" that proved damaging, especially during the latter half of the twentieth century. Many of the country's once-vital water basins in particular – its lakes, swamps, and wetlands – have already been drained or dried up as a result of misconceived or improperly executed development projects. Still others, along with the wildlife that depended upon them, have been heavily affected by pollution. Land resources, likewise, have been squandered in overly extensive, irrationally planned, wastefully fragmented, uncoordinated, and duplicative construction projects. The result of all this has been to worsen what was already a precariously unbalanced distribution of population and natural resources, as well as an unbalanced distribution of income, and an unbalanced pattern of access to public services, modern infrastructure, transport, and information facilities.

On this rather ominous general assessment put forward by China's central planners, the challenges to development the nation faces are posed as largely spatial ones. In rural areas, over the past half century, proportionally too much land had been brought under cultivation, leaving far too little natural green space. In urban areas, especially during the first three to four decades following the establishment of the PRC in 1949, proportionally too much space had been occupied by industrial production facilities, and too little developed for residential use and community services. The urgent need to begin redressing such macro-spatial imbalances as these, while *at the same time* persevering in the country's program of rapid urbanization and infrastructure development, was judged to have necessitated the adoption of a comprehensive, strategic approach to national spatial planning.[6]

---

[6] PF zones designated by *national*-level planners, as illustrated in the first of several maps of the nation reproduced here, may span as many as several dozen counties and be measured in tens of thousands of square kilometers, with boundaries generally not drawn to split a single county in two. All *future* local development planning is meant to be designed in strict conformity with these broadly drawn national-level zoning boundaries, and only then ratified by the provincial and lower-level jurisdictions concerned. To be approved, provincial and local plans for the zone-by-zone development (or conservation) of land and other resources will ultimately need to be traced out in far finer – kilometer by kilometer, hectare by hectare, and (in towns and cities) block by block – detail. For fuller discussions, see Du Ping, "Regional Planning" and Li Shouxin, "Principal Function Zoning Programs" (I am grateful to Sebastian Heilmann for sharing his copy of this source with me). To sample the technical complexity now entailed in generating and selecting computer models for achieving efficiency with sustainability in China's ecologically more sensitive environments, and especially in those requiring that a unified approach be taken across large areas and different governmental jurisdictions, see the recent evaluation of alternative designs for the future of the Poyang Lake region in Chen et al., "A Spatial Optimization Model."

Once the principal function of a zone is set, it can be further categorized into one of just four spatial development groupings. Zones where, in accord with the national Master Plan, future development is to be:

- **optimized:** for areas that have already undergone extensive development and where the carrying capacity of the land and other resources is already approaching its limits
- **prioritized:** for areas where the carrying capacity of the local environment and its resource endowment are relatively strong, and where conditions are favorable for creating new, greatly expanded urban population concentrations
- **restricted:** for areas where environmental carrying capacity and resources are weak, where conditions for establishing urbanized concentrations of population are poor, or for areas where maintaining the security of the ecology and environment are crucial to the well-being of other parts of the country and
- **prohibited**: for areas containing protected forests, parks and natural reserve lands of all kinds, as established by law.

(1) Those zones where future development is to be **optimized** are the ones already most heavily developed and urbanized. These are arrayed along the coast and encompass, from north to south, the Bohai Gulf, the Yangzi River Delta, and the Pearl River Delta – booming macro-regional economies that are planned to continue to urbanize and grow rapidly, but in future must be made to do so in ways that are more space intensive and will optimize consumption of land, energy, and resources using high-efficiency technologies.

These three colossal coastal zones are envisioned to rank among the most densely populated and highest value-producing regions on the planet, and the more efficient, rational, resource conserving modes of development they are tasked by the Master Plan to achieve are expected not only to continue anchoring China's global competitiveness and spurring faster growth around the rest of the country, but also to generate new scientific knowledge, new talent, and innovative engineering technologies that will contribute to reversing ecological damage already done, and to cleaning up the nation's environment.

(2) Those zones where future development is to be **prioritized** are the ones with already comparatively strong economic underpinnings and capacities for innovation and modernization, that are expected to succeed in turning themselves into *new* growth poles for the national economy as a whole (see Figure 3.1). These are areas, primarily in the middle regions of the country, which have lagged behind the coast on

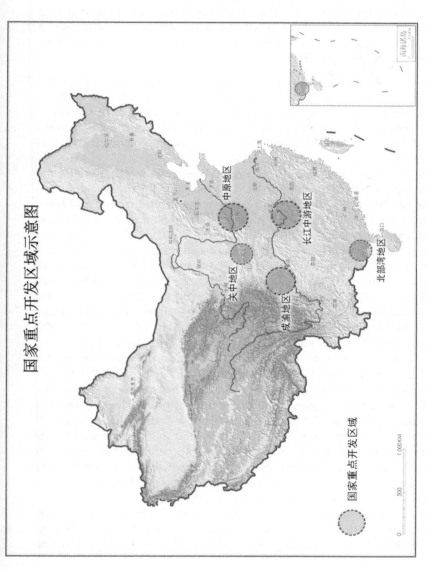

Figure 3.1 Prioritized development zones. *Source:* This and the maps to follow are drawn from "State Council Communiqué on Issuing." They form parts of the PFZ Master Plan itself.

The maps printed here are greyscale adaptations from color slides. Readers wishing to view them in color may find them under the Resources tab at www.cambridge.org/9781107193529.

almost all economic and social indicators, but where a good start has already been made in spurring the growth of new urban clusters and integrated regional economies that should permit them to evolve into metropolitan regions. As these prioritized zones take off, their growth is expected to contribute greatly to narrowing the yawning gaps in income, public services, and life chances that have widened so alarmingly in recent years.

As the optimized and prioritized zones all continue to develop and grow, becoming better linked together via enhanced networks of high-speed transport and communication, they are envisioned to be key nodes in an urban-modern integrated economy extending, along "two horizontal and three vertical belts" across the entire national territory, from north to south and east to west (Figure 3.2).

On this overall plan for national urban development, according to the Chinese Academy of Sciences' (CAS) "Roadmap" for the decades leading up to 2050, stretching broadly along these two horizontal and three vertical territorial bands, China is anticipated to have created 3 "mega-urban agglomerations" (Pearl River Delta, Yangzi River Delta, and Greater Beijing area); 20 "large urban agglomerations" including 5 "ultra-mega-cities" with populations over 10 million (Beijing, Shanghai, Tianjin, Guangzhou, Nanjing); 10 "mega-cities" with populations over 5 million (Wuhan, Chongqing, Chengdu, Shenyang, Zhengzhou, Xi'an, Shenzhen, Jinan, Qingdao, Harbin); 50 "major cities" with populations over 1 million; 150 "large cities" with populations of 0.5 million; 200 "medium-sized cities"; and 250 "small cities." Total urban population, was then projected to reach 775 million (for an overall urbanization rate of 54.45 percent) by 2020; 888 million (61.63 percent) in 2030; and 940 million (67.98 percent) in 2050. Through the "optimizing" strategy, the 3 "mega-urban" agglomerations are rather rapturously envisioned as becoming "innovative," "ecology-based," "low-carbon," and "digital." And "urban agglomeration" itself is anticipated to "become a new geographical unit participating in the global competition and international division of labor," a "dynamic core strategic growth pole ... profoundly affect[ing] the international competitiveness of China, and ... determining ... [its overall] strategic situation."[7]

Following the earnest announcement of the PFZ Master Plan however, much anxious attention was understandably focused on the less blissful fates of those zones where large-scale urbanization will henceforward be

---

[7] Lu and Fan, eds., *Regional Development Research ... A Roadmap*, 112–113; Hu et al., *China in 2030*.

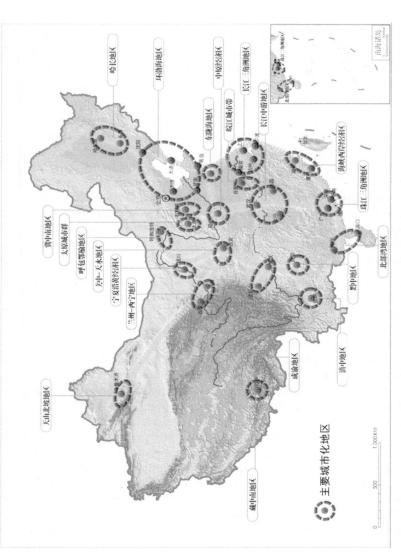

哈长地区

环渤海地区

中原经济区

长江三角洲地区

海峡西岸经济区

珠江三角洲地区

北部湾地区

滇中地区

黔中地区

成渝地区

天山北坡地区

宁夏沿黄经济区

兰州—西宁地区

呼包鄂榆地区

太原城市群

关中地区

江淮城市带

呼和浩特

银川

大连

北京

南海诸岛

主要城市化地区

0   500   1,000 KM

Figure 3.2 Key urbanized areas: two horizontal and three vertical belts. As the map indicates, not all prioritized development zones are in the Central region: in the East, parts of central-southern Hebei, central Jiangsu, and northern Anhui and Henan, as well as the Fujian coast across the strait from Taiwan, are included; in the West, prioritized zones include not only Hohhot–Baotou–Yulin, and the whole of the Chengdu–Chongqing region, but also parts of coastal Guangxi, central Guizhou, central Yunnan, areas in central-southern Tibet, southern Shaanxi, the Yellow River basin in Ningxia, the Lanzhou–Xining region, and portions of the northern Tianshan Mountain area.

restricted, or even prohibited. If "development" as such is understood to rest squarely on planned, rapid, and intensive urban growth as the main path to global competitiveness and accelerated capital accumulation, what then would be the future for those regions *not* selected for continued urban growth? These are the districts that will feel the pinch; the regions where everyone expects that central-level spatial planning will inevitably conflict with the felt needs, aspirations, and demands of local people, and of local officials who, for many years, have been incentivized to measure their own, and their jurisdiction's, success through the maximization, above all, of local GDP.

(3) Those zones where future development is to be **restricted** are broken into two groups in the Master Plan. First, there are the regions where agriculture, fisheries, and allied technical support, service, food processing, and distribution industries are to be concentrated (see Figure 3.3). Here, the national goals are cast somewhat starkly in terms of taking all steps to assure the nation's *food security* by protecting farmland and modernizing agriculture in the key river-fed plains regions of northern and southern China, and over the more reliably arable areas of the drier northwest, as well as the Hetao irrigated zone in Ningxia.[8]

The second group of **restricted** development zones comprises several areas of critical importance to the nation's *environmental security*. Sometimes referred to as the "two shields and three belts," these areas encompass significant expanses of forested land vital to the protection of the country's major water sources, as well as grasslands and environmental control projects or installations essential for soil conservation and anti-desertification efforts. Also included are certain areas deemed to need protection for the value of their still-remaining relatively rich levels of biodiversity (see Figure 3.4). In these zones, future goals include permitting only environmentally friendly industrial development and reducing human populations where they have reached levels putting dangerous pressures on natural resources, in part by engineering planned migrations of excess populations *out* of these regions and into other areas zoned for urban development.

Demarcation (if not de facto protection) of China's environmentally critical areas is already well advanced, as indicated on the more detailed map of "Keypoint Ecological Function Zones" (Figure 3.5). As early as 2008, areas slated eventually to be protected in this category totalled some

---

[8] This scheme, sometimes referred to as the "seven regions, twenty-three belts" plan, demarcates twenty-three farming areas vital to secure national supplies of rice, maize, and twenty-one other staple agricultural commodities. See "State Council Communiqué on Issuing," 57.

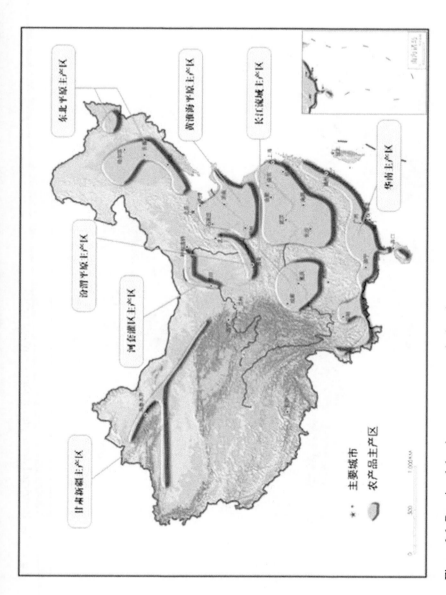

Figure 3.3 Restricted development zones: agricultural

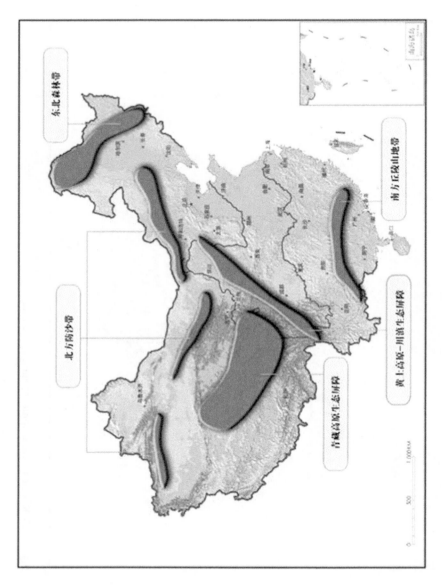

东北森林带

南方丘陵山地带

黄土高原—川滇生态屏障

北方防沙带

青藏高原生态屏障

Figure 3.4 Restricted development zones: environmental

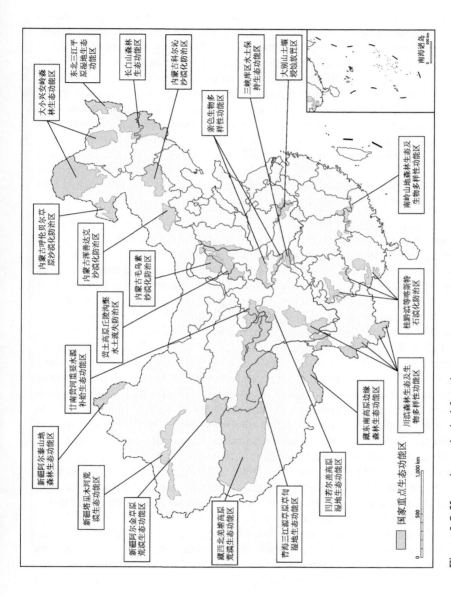

大小兴安岭森林生态功能区

东北三江平原湿地生态功能区

长白山森林生态功能区

内蒙古科尔沁沙漠化防治区

三峡库区水土保持生态功能区

大别山水土保持生态功能区

黄色生物多样性功能区

南岭山地森林生态及生物多样性生态功能区

内蒙古呼伦贝尔草原沙漠化防治区

内蒙古浑善达克沙漠化防治区

内蒙古毛乌素沙漠化防治区

黄土高原丘陵沟壑水土流失防治区

桂黔滇喀斯特石漠化防治区

甘南黄河重要水源补给生态功能区

新疆阿尔泰山地森林生态功能区

川滇森林生态及生物多样性生态功能区

藏东南高原边缘森林生态功能区

新疆塔里木河荒漠生态功能区

新疆阿尔金草原荒漠生态功能区

藏西北羌塘高原荒漠生态功能区

若尔盖草原湿地生态功能区

四川若尔盖高原湿地生态功能区

国家重点生态功能区

南海诸岛

500 km

0   500   1,000 km

Figure 3.5 Keypoint ecological function zones

3.86 million square kilometers or just over 40 percent of the entire national land area – then home, however, to just 8.5 percent of the total population.[9]

(4) Those zones where future development is to be entirely **prohibited** are also already quite clearly marked out, and again they are extensive (Figure 3.6). According to the Master Plan, they amount to a total of 1,443 zones in all, including national reserves (319), UN World Heritage sites (40), nationally protected natural scenery and tourism zones (208), national forests (738), and national geological parks (138). These all together comprise another 1.2 million square kilometers, or 12.5 percent of total national land area. The names, locations, and spatial dimensions of *all* the designated Keypoint Ecological Function Zones and *all* the Prohibited Development National Parks and Forests are spelled out in lengthy appendices to the Master Plan document, along with a list of China's approved and anticipated UN World Heritage Sites. These too have already been mapped.

In interpreting this graphic, as in reading all the national-level PFZ maps here, it is important to remind ourselves that what we are looking at is *a map of a plan* – a long-term spatial plan. Some of what is represented on the map accords with a certain reality already existing on the ground and with actual governance structures and practices, or at least with structures and practices now in formation. But much else that appears on the map is not yet real.

Some may be inclined to dismiss such maps as "just" a dream. Others will be content to accept them as charting out a vision for the future, or as goals to be realized. Among the scientific experts, technicians, and map-makers, and the solemnly resolute senior central planners who have promoted such maps and the meanings that lie behind them in recent years, it may be more accurate to say that these digitized spatial imaginings are conceived more as elegant sketches of what remain long, hard roads ahead. For China's leading development planners, these maps are the tracings of cold and treacherous trails that needs must be trodden by all, and in double quick time; in real fear of ecological collapses, thirsty calamities, social disorientations, even nationwide privation; and in hungry pursuit of the comforting promise, instead, that at the end of the trail will be found a latter-day, urban-modern, higher-tech version of a kind of heaven on earth for the nation and its people.

Now, anyone who possesses even a superficial familiarity with Chinese political realities will be aware that central plan target setting, as a standard tool of governance, is one thing; and implementation (or non-implementation) of planned targets on the ground is something else

[9] Ibid., 59.

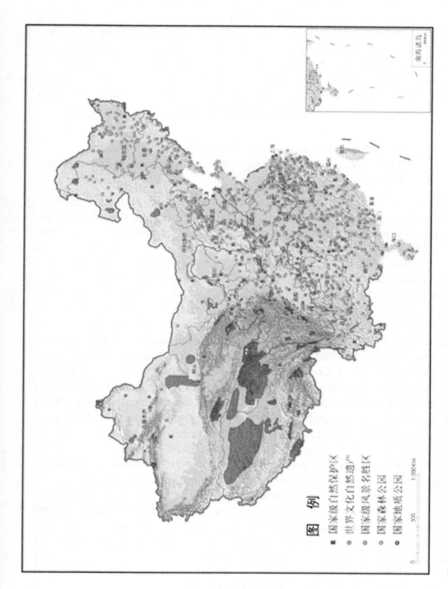

图 例

■ 国家级自然保护区
◎ 世界文化自然遗产
⊙ 国家级风景名胜区
○ 国家森林公园
◉ 国家地质公园

0   500   1 000KM

Figure 3.6 National-level prohibited development zones

entirely. Several interesting approaches crafted for this Master Plan's implementation and enforcement are briefly summarized below. But before moving on to that set of practical matters, in order to gain a fuller understanding of the special salience of each of these measures, it is important to recall some of the larger political-economic trends and conditions that had unfolded through the 1980s and 1990s, prompting central leaders to conclude, at the beginning of the twenty-first century, that they would need to draw up and devise ways to implement such a national land use Master Plan in the first place.

Prelude to National Spatial Regulation in China: The Strategic Withdrawal and Redeployment of Central Planning

The much-discussed "retreat of the state," to make way for "the market," that was widely thought to be occurring in the early phases of the post-Mao reform process was, as we now more clearly understand, a far more complicated affair than the binary language of state vs. market permits us to capture. What happened under Deng may more accurately be described as a "strategic withdrawal" by the state; a maneuver that would (predictably enough) be followed by a "regrouping" of state forces and a readying for future strategic redeployment.[10] Still, it would not be correct to suggest with this simile of "strategic withdrawal," that *all* elements of the state – central, local, and in-between – so simply or so evenly pulled back from the mounting market fray. On the contrary, most serious observers of Chinese domestic political economy would now be more likely to argue that while the organs of the central state and of central planning did without a doubt conduct a conscious, staged, stepping back from *direct* control over the economy, central planning, as such, was never completely dismantled. Planning at the center was, rather, gradually "redefined as one of three key mechanisms of 'macro-control' along with fiscal and monetary policy, that were supposed to facilitate 'comprehensive coordination' and 'aggregate balancing' of economic activity."[11] Meanwhile, it was local-state actors (in cities, towns, and counties all over the country) who most vigorously seized the field, firmly embracing the market and calculatedly intervening in it, to produce China's trademark hybrid "local-state-led/market driven" pattern of seemingly irrepressible development through the 1980s and 1990s.

---

[10] As argued by Sigley, "Chinese Governmentalities," 497.

[11] Heilmann and Melton, "The Reinvention." On the continuity of central planning in China under reform, see also Liu Guoguang, chief ed., *Research Reports*; Yan Yilong, "China's Five Year Plans"; and Yang Weimin, chief ed., *The Theory and Practice*, ch. 1.

Rather than state self-disempowerment or disengagement from the market, what we witnessed, during that earlier phase, was a dramatic decentralization of fiscal resources, authority, and discretion *from higher to lower levels of the state*, enabling local-state agents to enter the market in pursuit of particularistic (public and private) local benefits. As Pierre Landry concluded, referring to the resulting Chinese pattern of political economy as one of "decentralized authoritarianism," the PRC rapidly became "one of the most decentralized countries in the world" as its "sustained economic decentralization ... led to a variety of reform outcomes [in dissimilar administrative districts and regions], rising inequalities, and increased competition between localities."[12] So much so that, as George C. S. Lin has observed: "With the retreat of the central state from local developmental affairs, the imperative for the mobilization and primitive accumulation of capital [became preeminent]. Moreover, decentralization and globalization of the political economy ... placed all localities in a new battlefield competing with each other for foreign capital investment and export facilities from overseas."[13] As the central state took a step back, then, and local-state officials came to the forefront in the fray, the key lines of competitive administrative/economic battle were redrawn more obliquely, and intensely fragmented skirmishes broke out all across the field of engagement.[14]

At the same time, lower-level officials, pressured by the demands of the still-centralized cadre evaluation systems, regularly strove to maximize local capital accumulation by making local-state appropriations of *land* for conversion to urban-industrial, luxury consumption, and speculative uses. Such uncoordinated, hasty, and over-heatedly competition-driven local-state urban development projects and investments yielded not only far too many gross misappropriations of public and collectively owned assets, for high profit-earning but (at best) semi-public, corporate ventures. It also led to widespread sacrifice and waste of land and water, despoliation of the natural environment, and misuse of other scarce resources.[15]

---

[12] Landry, *Decentralized Authoritarianism*, 3, 258. Hu and Ma, "Government Power and its Impact," 181, characterize this inter-local governmental competition as "the emergence of local economic dukedoms." On worsening inequalities over this period and their interrelationships with fiscal and administrative decentralization and local cadre incentive systems, see also Shue and Wong, eds., *Paying for Progress*.

[13] Lin, *Developing China*, 61.

[14] Readers seeking a primer on just how dramatically these competitive "battle lines" were redrawn, even within a single province, may consult *OECD Territorial Reviews: Guangdong*, chs. 2, 3 and *passim.*

[15] For fuller elaboration of the links between decentralized economic growth, the lack of a rigorous national land monitoring system, and environmental degradation in China during this period, see again, *OECD Territorial Reviews: Guangdong*, ch. 4, which concludes: "A major factor in urban sprawl and unmanaged spatial growth is that a large part

Central party-state planners and decision-makers – who during the 1980s had so momentously resolved to step back and to concede more space to competitive local forces in navigating a new course for national economic development – had already by the early 1990s clearly made a mixed (in some ways positive, in others very critical) assessment of the ensuing trends. In response, rather than seeking indiscriminately to recontain or crush all those newly released but unruly local capacities, upon which continued rapid development of the economy had so evidently come to depend, they moved tactically, adjusting their institutions and rhetoric to the novel political environment. They began what was to become more than a decade-long, staged campaign gradually to claw back greater capacity, initiative, support, and influence at the center; to harness the tools – more ample revenues, more inclusive institutions, better-trained personnel – and to sharpen the administrative mechanisms central leaders required to contribute more credibly and authoritatively to charting and guiding what they judged to be a safer, and more salutary, direction of travel for economy, polity, and the nation's natural ecology.

With hindsight, it is not hard to see that the 1994 fiscal recentralization was but a first crucial step in this campaign, returning to the center the necessary wherewithal to plan and act, as national GDP continued leaping forward and the strictures of the old economy of *shortage* gave way to *surplus*. The calculated attraction *back* to China of trained academic and technical specialists with experience of study abroad; the well-choreographed wooing also of foreign investments that brought state-of-the-art technologies with them; the dramatic improvement of salaries and benefits offered to staff working in China's own research and higher education infrastructure; the deliberate engagement with international development institutions and the effort to synthesize and draw lessons from the successes and failures of other developing and developed economies; the resolute maintenance of tight central controls over key political-administrative personnel appointments; the return of a general civil service examination system to China with associated ideals of technical meritocracy; the coordinated drive to upgrade the formal credentials and the overall "quality" of cadres high and low; along with the cultivation of a popular political rhetoric of mistrust and blame for "bad local officials" (who were ever more commonly figured discursively as selfish

---

of Chinese cities' revenue ... depends on land-related income, such as land leases, land auctions and land development rights ... Although these can be valuable instruments to capture land value increases and to finance infrastructure, in practice local governments in China have been so motivated to generate revenues from land sales and leasing that they have generated an oversupply of land for construction. This has stimulated sprawled development and loss of cultivated land."

betrayers of the progressive "public interest" ideals articulated by the center) – all these and many more such techniques and tactics were deployed, incrementally, in an extended crusade aimed at restoring greater capacity to *lead* the nation's economic development, once again, from the center. And this time, it would be with the benefit of a loftier, "scientific" perspective and with technically superior, country-wide Master Plans.[16]

This extended effort reached a certain consummation, with the 11th Five Year Plan, the first one over the conception and development of which the Hu-Wen government presided. That document was notable for its insistence on comprehensive (or holistic) planning rooted in a more "scientific" concept of the meaning of development – 全面贯彻落实科学发展观.[17] It was at that point that the term *guihua* (规划), connoting something more like an overall blueprint or a comprehensive Master Plan, was selected for use, in place of the socialist-era term *jihua* (计划). The character for *ji* refers to calculating, and calls to mind the kind of plan put together primarily by counting; a summing up of discrete tasks, best represented perhaps in tabular, or list, form. This was a term well-suited to describe the tasks involved in the materials balance planning of the earlier socialist era. *Guihua*, by contrast, suggests the type of plan that is made by smoothing out and aligning a pattern; a project often best represented in graphic or map form. (The character for *gui* contains a root element relating to the eye, the sense of sight, or *vision*.) With the appropriation of this rather magisterial term, China's central planners – who had indeed "stepped back" but never abandoned the struggle for (or the onus for) guidance control entirely – were making a bold move at the beginning of the twenty-first century, to reclaim for themselves, and the technical experts who served them, the capacity and the ultimate responsibility for *envisioning* and mapping the nation's future.[18]

---

[16] Key dimensions in this protracted process are well analyzed in Heilmann and Melton, "The Reinvention." For an earlier-formulated account, see Yang, *Remaking the Chinese Leviathan*. On the roles of experts and academics in recasting "the ecological or natural environment ... as a site of governmental action and intervention in the PRC," see Hoffman, "Governmental Rationalities"; and on expertise more generally, statistics, mapmaking, the command of space, and the concentration of power and authority in modern states pursuing "development," see the seminal discussion in Mitchell, *Rule of Experts*.

[17] US–China Economic and Security Review Commission, *Backgrounder*, 18.

[18] On the change from 计划 to 规划, see Heilmann and Melton, "The Reinvention"; on how national plans and planning have been evaluated for effectiveness over the years, Hu and Yan, *China: Onward Toward 2015*, Appendix 1 and *passim*; and on the perceived advantages of combining long-term macro-planning with market forces, Hu Angang, "Understanding the Twelfth Five Year Plan."

In the 11th Five Year Plan, this aspiration to *envision* and comprehensively *project*, or map forward, was still primarily applied only to dynamic economic and social relationships, and to problems of achieving and maintaining "orderly" growth and development through planned intersectoral balancing – balancing of the overall supply and demand of goods and services in economy and society. In the 12th Five Year Plan, however, this scientific ambition came to be extended – 深入贯彻落实科学发展观 – as illustrated by the maps reproduced here, to long-term, comprehensive *spatial planning* as well, and to problems of achieving not only "orderly" but also "dynamic" yet "sustainable" growth and development through a comprehensively planned reengineering of the nation-scape, its territory, population, and environment.

The PFZ Planning Process: Expertise and Experiments

According to Yang Weimin,[19] the PFZ approach to spatial planning was first raised as early as 2002 in a document entitled "Opinions on Several Issues regarding the Reform of the Planning System," where it was argued that the making of plans, in pursuit of macro-economic balancing, should also be governed by the principle of "spatial balance and coordination" and the "need to strengthen the spatially guiding and binding function of planning."[20] At that time, strategic thinking about differential regional development across the national territory was still quite crude, with the country only very roughly segmented by planners into eastern, western, and central regions, each with particular paces and patterns of progress. Yang and others then raised the concept of functional zoning with leaders at the Chinese Academy of Engineering in 2003, when briefing them on the key background research projects needing to be carried out in preparation for generating the 11th Five Year Plan. Following that briefing, numerous engineers and technical experts were recruited by the Academy and the National Development and Reform Commission (NDRC) to investigate the topic of functional zoning, after which the general idea of demarcating just four types of PFZs emerged and was proposed to the State Council. Still, at that time, it was not yet contemplated that PFZs could or would cover the *whole* of the national territory. In the "Outline"

---

[19] In June 2011, just six months after the PFZ Master Plan had been approved, Yang Weimin assumed the duties of Vice-Minister, Office of the Central Leading Group on Finance and Economic Affairs, which carries responsibilities for national development strategy making, mid- and long-term planning, and economic structure policy design. Before that, he worked in the NDRC for twenty-two years, rising from Director of the Department of Development Planning to Vice-Secretary General, and then Secretary General.

[20] "Deciphering the National Principal Function Zoning Plan."

document released pending approval of the 11th Five Year Plan (eventually passed in March 2006), just 2,200 words were devoted to the PFZ concept, and a total of only twenty-two "restricted development" zones were specified.

Once the "Outline" was approved, however, Ma Kai, the NDRC's Chairman at the time, launched the substantive process of drawing up a workable PF zoning plan. Further general background research was done and, informed by that, in July 2007 the State Council issued a new document, "Opinions regarding the Making of the PFZ Plan," setting out the basic principles and objectives of the exercise and stipulating that, initially, integrated plans would be made, for just *two* administrative levels – central and provincial. It was only at that juncture that the NDRC, working with the CAS Institute of Geographic Sciences and Natural Resources, commenced the detailed work of creating a Master Plan.

With the help of the CAS Institute, a comprehensive technical evaluation of the carrying capacity of *the entire national territory* was carried out, making extensive use of satellite imaging and GIS science to collect, analyze, and present what would become immense amounts of geographically referenced data. While numerous teams of natural and environmental scientists and technicians were at work gathering, collating, and analyzing the empirical measurements and the images, teams of social scientists were also commissioned to carry out preparatory "policy research" relating to the Plan's ultimate implementation.[21] As part of the background policy research, information was gathered about regimes of spatial planning and environmental protection as these have evolved in other nations. Few other countries in the world – and none even approaching the territorial scale of China – have developed comprehensive *national* land use plans. But the experiences of Germany, Japan, and the Netherlands were found to be ones with useful lessons for China.[22]

Simultaneously with this extended background research and report-writing, eight different provinces were tapped to carry out PF zoning on an *experimental* basis over portions of their territories.[23] Liaoning had actually been selected as early as October 2006 to conduct preliminary

[21] Tsinghua University's China Development Planning Research Center formed a twenty-one-member Project Study Group under the leadership of Li Shantong that became especially influential in this sphere of preparatory research. A collection of the Tsinghua Study Group's detailed policy reports was published in mid-2009 as *Policy Research on Principal Function Zoning in China*.
[22] Some aspects of US environmental regulation were also flagged as noteworthy. See *The National PFZ Program: Reference Materials*, 99–114.
[23] Liaoning, Hubei, Jiangsu, Zhejiang, Henan, Chongqing, Yunnan and Xinjiang, "NDRC Report Suggests."

research on technical standards and measures, database construction, and to carry out some trial partitioning of provincial territory into PFZs. The Liaoning work, where Liaoyang and Panjin were selected as sites for the trials, yielded seven major research reports and a geographic database framework for application in PFZ planning.[24] In Zhejiang, thirteen counties were selected for preliminary experimentation, and trial partitioning was prepared for the designation of "prohibited" development zones and "prioritized" development zones – selected because the boundaries delimiting these two types of zones were anticipated to be the *most difficult* to agree.[25] And as expected, numerous political-administrative difficulties did arise clearly to the surface in the Zhejiang trials.

As Yang Qingyu details, some districts dragged their feet and were very slow to respond to the project once launched, hoping to extract financial concessions from provincial authorities in return for compliance. Other districts were at a loss to find ways of reconciling the goals of PF zoning with preexisting local spatial plans and projects which had already received upper-level approval, and were thus viewed by local actors as fully authorized, fixed, and not subject to revocation. In Zhejiang, as well, the earliest experiments plainly flagged numerous remaining uncertainties and disagreements about the most effective administrative format for spearheading the PFZ effort. Some local officials favored putting territorial zoning tasks under the leadership of the Development and Reform Commission's office at the county level. Others considered this too weak a political instrument to lead such a self-evidently contentious program locally, arguing instead for setting up special county-level cross-ministerial task forces, chaired by the county head (or at least by one of the vice-county heads) to press it forward.[26]

Based on the initial research and the results of local zoning experiments then, a first draft of the PFZ proposal was drawn up in February 2008. The NDRC convened a major meeting to discuss and critique it, and further meetings were held with local officials once again to gather additional feedback and opinions, after which some major revisions were made to the draft plan. Starting from 2008, in fact, and running right up to the final release of the Master Plan in December 2010, the NDRC went through repeated cycles of internal discussion and critique, wider

---

[24] The reference to these reports consulted has been taken down from the Liaoning government site. But for a synthesis of viewpoints on goals and procedures from the same period, see Gao Guoli, "Characteristics, Principles and Basic Concepts." According to Yang Qingyu, "Vigorously Promote Construction," Chongqing also began conducting comprehensive PFZ planning in 2007.

[25] "On Zhejiang's Early Experimental Testing."

[26] Yang Qingyu, "Vigorously Promote Construction."

opinion gathering, and further revision.[27] A final draft of the Master Plan had originally been scheduled for completion by November 2008.[28] But in the event, that target was missed. One factor slowing completion was the catastrophic earthquake, and the many aftershocks, in Sichuan in the spring of 2008.[29]

Furthermore, as one report published five months after the Plan's approval and release made clear, during the planning process *strong opposition* had been voiced by many localities to any new land use regime that could serve to restrict development in parts of their territory. These objections had necessitated protracted further discussions and negotiations before consensus on the Master Plan could be achieved.[30] Reportedly, local-level officials harbored *three main fears* about macro-spatial planning: fear that economic development in their districts (measured by local GDP) would suffer; fear that living standards for people in their localities would suffer (in comparison with other districts); and fear that their own performance evaluations and political careers would suffer too, as a consequence. If these trepidations were to be allayed sufficiently to allow the Master Plan to win their support and go forward, *major commitments to compensate affected localities with cash and other inducements* would clearly be necessary. And the sums required to purchase cooperation from all the affected localities, it gradually emerged, were going to be truly tremendous. In a conversation with Yang Weimin in the autumn of 2011, when asked what he thought the most difficult aspect of actually implementing the PFZ Master Plan was going to be, he did not hesitate to say that the biggest problem would be "finding the money" – finding sufficient funds at the center to, in effect, *purchase compliance* from both local officials and the general population living and working in areas where unfettered (ecologically unsustainable) "development" was to be impeded by the Plan.[31]

Governing the Governors: Approaches to On-the-Ground Implementation

At the conclusion of a lengthy lecture buttressed by an impressive power point presentation introducing the PFZ Master Plan to a packed lecture hall at the Tsinghua School of Public Policy and Management

---

[27] "Deciphering the National Principal Function Zoning Plan."
[28] "State Council Opinions regarding the Making."
[29] Many members of the research staff in the Institute of Geographic Sciences were unable to give attention to the Master Plan for several months because they were seconded to other urgent work in the aftermath of the terrible quake. Interview with Li Shantong, August 2, 2011.
[30] "PFZ Strategy: A Look behind the Scenes."
[31] Interview with Yang Weimin, Beijing, October 28, 2011.

in October 2011, Yang Weimin was asked by one of his student listeners if he did not think local officials would surely be able to find ways to subvert the Plan, continuing to pursue recklessly unsustainable development projects if those projects offered good short-term payoffs, despite dangers to the local environment. Comfortable and at ease in a room full of younger friends and admirers at his home university, Yang's reply, though inflected with humor, was a sardonic one. There were going to have to be long-drawn-out, locality by locality negotiations. No getting around it he said, with a weary sigh. Local officials could be depended upon to hem and haw and much liquor would have to be drunk together with them before they would finally give in and accept the best deals they were offered. But like it or not, they would not be able to resist forever. Sooner or later they were going to have to come to terms, he said, because the Master Plan had set out "binding targets."[32] Such targets cannot simply be ignored, he insisted. And if obstinate local officials should, after a time, try to break any agreements duly negotiated with province and center – or if they should attempt by stealth to continue with construction or resource extraction in areas off limits – they would be found out, investigated, and held to account. Satellite imaging and modern GIS technologies – the central state's eyes in the sky – are extremely sensitive, he stressed. Illicit development projects *will* be spotted, and local officials who are complicit in allowing proscribed activities to go forward *would* find themselves in serious trouble.[33]

In the event, it was the NDRC which was given overall responsibility for executing the Master Plan, but that agency often lacked the administrative apparatus and personnel at local levels of the state actually to enforce its targets. Through the subsequent period of the 12th Five Year Plan, gradual progress did take place in establishing a stronger legal basis for environmental protection in China.[34] Notably also, with effect from January 2015, a new national environmental protection law has started to be implemented. This law represents the first comprehensive revision and updating of China's original basic environmental protection statute (dating from 1989), and it features far tougher accountability measures aimed now

[32] On "binding targets" and why they were reintroduced along with the 11th Five Year Plan, see Heilmann and Melton, "The Reinvention." Such targets – regarded as "government promises" – were set not for enterprises or corporations to meet, but to discipline officials; and specifically lower-level state officials.

[33] In the West, spatial planning is generally enforced through law, but as of 2011 it was estimated it would take at least another decade just to debate, design, and enact the comprehensive legislation required, and buttress the Chinese court system sufficiently to handle such prosecutions. So it was agreed that, in the interim, binding targets negotiated with local authorities would be a better expedient than a law-based approach to enforcement. Interview with Li Shantong, August 2, 2011.

[34] Wang, "The Search for Sustainable Legitimacy"; Brettell, "A Survey of Environmental Deterrence."

both at polluters and at government officials charged with responsibilities for keeping lawbreakers in check.[35]

From the outset, nonetheless, much more attention was given to crafting central policies in ways that would incentivize localities to comply with land use zoning regulations, rather than punish them in cases of noncompliance. At first glance, the complementary constellation of fiscal, investment, sectoral, land, population, environmental, and other "policies" that were rolled out may appear excessively intricate. But there is little that is subtle about them. One way or another, these were intended to neutralize opposition by buying off local people, local corporations, and local officials with promises of subsidies and transfers, compensatory payments and rewards, preferential investments and tax breaks, buyouts, land-swaps, and other managed incentive schemes.[36] The relevant policies were broken down into categories.

- **fiscal policies**: such as (1) raising the levels of "equalizing transfer payments" (均衡性转移支付) allocated to districts in restricted and prohibited development zones, so as to bring their standards of public service provision more quickly up to those in zones where development is being prioritized; (2) establishing horizontal fair exchange mechanisms by which zones that benefit from the "ecological products" generated in conservation areas make direct compensation payments to people living and working in those zones; and (3) significantly increasing budgetary expenditures in natural reserve zones.
- **investment policies**: such as (1) changing the apportionment of state budgetary investments, formerly allocated on an economic sector by sector basis, to include both sectoral allocations and allocations for support and development of PFZs – using the PFZ factor in the allocation formula to promote acceptable modes of modern development in restricted development zones; (2) making targeted investments on a five-yearly basis to clean up and restore the environment in areas where the ecology was already damaged and people's livelihoods had suffered.
- **industrial policies**: such as (1) amending local policy documents and regulations to clarify for the public where, precisely, development would be promoted, or restricted or prohibited; (2) drawing up new provincial and local-level development plans to comply with the Master Plan; and (3) specifying "market exit mechanisms" to accelerate closure

---

[35] For a brief summary of key measures, see Falk and Wee, "China's New Environmental Protection Law."

[36] Ma Kai, "Implementing the Principal Function Strategy"; Tsinghua University, *Policy Research*.

and removal of unacceptable industries operating in fragile local ecologies by giving them subsidies for leaving the area; to include land exchanges, loan guarantees, compensation for equipment depreciation and purchases of new equipment etc.

- **land policies**: such as tightening enforcement of existing controls on land use and reevaluating previously approved local development plans not conforming to new land use efficiency standards.
- **population policies**: such as (1) loosening residential registration (户口) restrictions, actively encouraging immigration to cities and smaller towns, and equalizing the entitlements of rural migrants living in cities with stable jobs and residences there; (2) drawing up and actively promoting plans for emigration from restricted and prohibited development zones, "helping" people find work and move to new homes in prioritized and optimized development zones instead; and (3) gradually revising the registration system to equalize entitlements for those residing in rural and in urban areas.
- **environmental protection policies**: such as (1) instituting emissions permit systems to enforce differentiated levels of emissions and environmental pollution in different PFZs – to achieve lower emissions in prioritized and optimized development zones, steadily declining levels in restricted development zones, and zero emissions of pollutants in prohibited development zones; (2) establishing differentiated market entry standards for industries – requiring new enterprises to meet best international environmental protection standards in optimized development zones, and levels in line with best domestic standards in prioritized development zones, etc.
- **cadre performance evaluation policies**: such as instituting differentially weighted evaluation criteria for officials posted in different types of zones rewarding: good performance in moving to more efficient, innovative development models and standards in optimized development zones; in promoting local industrialization and urbanization in prioritized development zones; in raising agricultural output and modernizing production, food processing and distribution systems in agricultural zones; and demonstrated conservation achievements in environmental protection in prohibited development zones.

Such zone-differentiated responsibilities, tasks, and priorities were to be made to serve as key criteria for local cadres' selection, promotion, training, reward, and punishment. And in subsequent policy discussions on motivating compliance, ways to hold accountable mid- and higher-level officials, who are typically rotated through posts in numerous different localities over the course of a career, have become more prominent, with greater emphasis put on keeping track of each individual official's cumulative record in promoting or hindering environmental goals.[37]

To achieve the fullest possible implementation of the Master Plan, it was acknowledged, much effort over the longer term would also need to be expended along other dimensions, such as educating party-state officials intensively about the importance and the worth of environmental protection work – so as to raise their levels of technical understanding and change their appreciation for living and working in a healthier and developmentally sustainable environment. And by 2014, there was even official talk of striving to raise broader *public consciousness* of the struggle for sustainability; promoting "green lifestyles" and working to make ecological progress into a "mainstream value ... spread to all corners of our society." The goal must be "to foster a stronger social consensus around the idea that living economically is a virtue while being wasteful is shameful." Once public environmental awareness was raised, then "public oversight" could be expected to become "the most direct and effective means of monitoring ecological environments."[38]

Still, most emphasis in public discussions about implementing the Master Plan to date has been put on material and career incentives – on huge downward fiscal transfers from provincial and central budgets, and on devising and enforcing differentially weighted cadre evaluation formulas. The foundational assumption on which all these approaches rest, plainly, is that the target group needing to be motivated and monitored through the modulation and manipulation of these various policy tools is, first and foremost, local-level party and state officials. The political problematic, as seen from the center, is one of finding ways and means of governing the governors. And those ways and means that have been accentuated so far will have to make simply enormous financial drains, especially on central and provincial budgets.

In some of the more probing published interviews with Yang Weimin, he has likened "ecological products" such as clean air and fresh water to goods that everyone needs, but no one can afford to buy. It is the role and responsibility of government, he argues, to put enough money on the table, in effect, "to purchase" these goods for the people and for the nation. It is the underlying ecosystem that generates the natural resources and the other "products" essential for primitive capital accumulation to take place. And *only if* that ecosystem is kept intact can China hope to

---

[37] An authoritative 2014 report, "Vigorously Promoting Ecological Progress," offered this opinion on new measures needing to be put in place to guarantee high-level cadre accountability: "Leading cadres should be subject to natural resource asset audits before they leave office. Also, *a lifelong accountability system for ecological damage* should be put in place."

[38] "Vigorously Promoting Ecological Progress."

perform the colossal feats of accumulation still required to reach a reasonably comfortable socio-economic equilibrium. For technocrats and planners like Yang, clearly, making every effort to raise the "environmental consciousness" of the Chinese people is all to the good. But just waiting around for the sincere impetus to conserve to arise from other levels of the system, or from the population at large, is not an option. Only the center can bear the price – both economic and political – of leading the coming crusade to reengineer the nation-space.

Maps and Dreams: Chinese Techno-visions and Political Leadership

"Maybe ... you think this is all nonsense," the North American Indian hunters hastened to say, anticipating a sceptical reception for their beliefs about the power in dreams, and in maps. But envisioning the future, mapping it out to inspire or enlighten others, can be at once a summoning of authority and a projection of it. The recent extension of the scope of Chinese central planning to include now comprehensive national *spatial planning* therefore – this brashly ambitious, high-tech reenvisioning and remapping of the nation-space that came along with the 12th Five Year Plan – deserves to be read by us as much more than merry fantasy. These national maps are well worth a second look, in fact, and not only for what they *want* to tell, but for their "silences."[39]

Many standard maps of contemporary China we encounter display its division into different provinces – marked off from each other by heavy boundary lines or even juxtaposed, one with another, by the use of contrasting colors. But on the maps of China in the Master Plan, the only borders we see are those of its national territorial boundaries. No domestic political-administrative divisions appear at all. The names of a very few major cities are indicated in such neutral colors that they all but fade into the background. Only Beijing is shown in red, and marked with a star to indicate its status as the national capital. Missing also from these maps are any indications whatsoever of China's relationships or connections to other national territories – no neighboring nations are included, and no hints of any possible wider links to global flows (economic, hydrological, meteorological, or otherwise) are represented. The nation is depicted as an isolate, a territorial unity with only the most gently shaded hues added to suggest the diversity of its

---

[39] "The concept of 'silences' on maps is central to any argument about the influence of their hidden political messages ... [M]aps ... exert a social influence through their omissions as much as by the features they depict and emphasize." Harley, "Maps, Knowledge and Power," 136.

topographical features, and with its two main river systems traced out prominently in blue. Upon this seemingly undivided expanse, great nodes of planned human interaction, networks of interconnection, and zones of special importance and sensitivity to the national development project are superimposed without any indication of geophysical or political administrative impediment to their realization.

If the creation of these maps is, in itself, a performance of power, then the power they represent is, and can only be, that of the nation, and of the party-state "center" that presides over it. Yet, those in Beijing who are responsible for these maps are, we know, only too aware that the image of splendid isolation and unity they project is a mirage. The PFZ Master Plan will get nowhere without disciplined compliance and cooperation from the provinces. And then too, the course of China's future development and the actual consequences of that development for the environment are precariously contingent on the effects of international and global forces over which Chinese leaders will have only marginal influence, at best.

For these good reasons, the maps reproduced here may well still be dismissed out of hand by many as mere fantasy. Some truly good men in Beijing may have dreamed a fine vision of the future and "worked hard on their truth," just as the Athapaskan Indian hunters said their own map-making visionary-artist ancestors had worked hard on theirs. But setting out together to do the actual trekking and hauling over those steep trails to heaven in the icy Canadian Subarctic must have been much harder work still. And so, we know, it also is in China today. So much of what cannot but be a protracted, taxing, and painfully contentious struggle to bring the situation on the ground into conformity with the techno-visions of China's well-meaning mapmakers still lies ahead. In 2010, it was expected to take the whole of the 12th Five Year Plan period, for example, just to drink all that liquor with local party-state officials, bargain them down to each and every one of the necessary agreements needing to be made countrywide, and get to the point of unambiguously demarcating every single PFZ, large and small. The making of the national maps, they recognized full well in Beijing, constituted only the very first step.

As of this writing, the 12th Five Year Plan is already history, but no comprehensive evaluation of progress achieved, or setbacks encountered, in the numerous provincial and local PFZ planning exercises launched around the country has yet been released. Early indications, nonetheless, are that the wheels under this general policy thrust have been continuing to turn. Billions of dollars have been allocated from the central budget to compensate jurisdictions designated as ecological function zones, and in mid-2014, an additional new central outlay of $7.8bn on such subsidies was announced.[40] Starting from 2012 also, functional zoning was extended beyond land to the sustainable management of China's *coastal and marine territories* as well.[41] Then, in the spring of 2014, came two further significant developments. China's long awaited new environmental protection law was approved, and a new Master Plan setting comprehensive goals and guidelines for urban development to 2020 was announced.[42] From the outset, this so-called "new-type" national urbanization plan situates itself firmly within the context of the general goals laid out in the 12th Five Year Plan, and references the spatial regulations and restrictions on land use of the PFZ Master Plan. The Master Plan for the zoning of land and for national spatial development, this updated urbanization Master Plan makes clear, forms a key part of the fundamental framework within which all future development, across the country, is to be conceived and carried out.

Once the national Master Plan was ratified, the next phase of (even more detailed) work envisioned was that each and every provincial-level government readjust its own spatial development plans to conform with the national maps, standards, and requirements. Reports indicate that some reasonable progress on this was also made during the 12th Five Year Plan. By early 2013, fourteen provinces and autonomous regions (plus the Xinjiang Construction Corps) had drawn up final agreed PFZ master plans for their entire jurisdictions, submitted them to the NDRC, and had them approved.[43] Still, sounding somewhat impatient in his speech at a Politburo study group session to review "ecological progress" in May 2013, Xi Jinping declared, "We will accelerate the work of functional zoning," and "Any violations regarding environmental protection will be punished."[44]

Guangdong's fully approved PFZ Master Plan was released by provincial authorities in September 2012. The necessary readjustments to this

---

[40] See "China Spends Billions"; and Chen Youshan and Zhang Ruo, "China Sets Fresh Funds." Signs are that the NDRC, during this first phase, gave priority to the application of spatial master planning aimed at protecting regions in the far west of the country, such as in Sichuan and Tibet – where there are a number of especially fragile ecosystems – backing these with particularly large budgetary allocations. See further "Methods for Making Transfer Payments"; and "Master Plan for Eco-Region Protection."

[41] Fang et al., "Marine Functional Zoning"; Chen Youshan and Zhang Ruo, "China Approves Marine Functional Zoning."

[42] An English translation of the 2014 Law is at www.chinadialogue.net/Environmental-Protection-Law-2014-eversion.pdf. The new urban Master Plan is in "Official Release." See "Transcript: Press Conference" for a summary.

[43] Heilongjiang was first, followed by Gansu, Inner Mongolia, Xinjiang, Guangdong, Guangxi, Hunan, Fujian, Hubei, Shandong, and Jiangxi, as well as the provincial-level municipalities of Beijing, Tianjin, and Shanghai. Interview with a Tsinghua University economist close to the project, Beijing, March 15, 2013.

[44] Xi Jinping, *The Governance of China*, 231.

province Plan must have been relatively easy to agree, since so many portions of Guangdong were slated for continuing very high levels of investment and future development. If we take it as an example, then we see that many maps were generated, like the two here, *very* closely paralleling those that *had already been incorporated* into the national Master Plan. The first of these Guangdong maps (Figure 3.7) gives a schematic representation of the overall pattern of urbanization intended for the province, featuring at its heart the booming Pearl River Delta. The second (Figure 3.8) charts the entire territory of the province with *all* principal function zones specified, and clear indications of which level of government – central or provincial – will be taking responsibility for administering and protecting them.[45]

For other provinces, where the national Master Plan calls for restrictions and prohibitions to be applied over much *more* of their territory, the trails to negotiated agreement and final approval of an acceptable province-wide plan are surely proving to be slower, steeper, and more slippery ones to traverse. And today, of course, all such maps as these, national or provincial, remain only dreams – maps of dreams. Yet our central purpose here has simply been to remind us all that the mapping of dreams – *envisioning* the future – has long been an indispensable first step in the practice of power; a reflective/creative performance through which leaders (actual and potential) of human groups, from hunting and fishing communities to modern-day national political leaders, exercise both cognitive and practical influence over the world today, and the world to come. To envision the future, to map it, has regularly served as an instrument of leadership; one technique for agenda setting, for striving to move all concerned parties onto the same page, and for pointing the way forward. As Thongchai Winichakul expressed it some two decades ago, "[A] map not only represents or abstracts spatial objects. Perhaps the most fascinating novelty of this technology is its predictive capacity . . . A map may not just function as a medium; it could well be the creator of the supposed reality."[46]

All these maps, we must realize further, have been generated in response to an environmental crisis that many, in China and around the world, regard as already desperate. Yet their clear aim is to convey to any who chance to glance at them, at home or abroad, a deep sense of confident national calm, energy, order, and command. And that truly

---

[45] Guangdong's complete PFZ Plan, 168 pages long with appendices and many detailed statistics, target figures, tables, lists, and maps, is at http://zwgk.gd.gov.cn/006939748/201211/t20121107_352873.html. Anticipated impacts of global climate change, and steps to be taken to prepare for the more frequent, violent climate-related natural disasters to be expected in Guangdong, are also discussed in its updated Master Plan.

[46] Winichakul, *Siam Mapped*, 54, 56.

图3 广东省城市化战略格局示意图

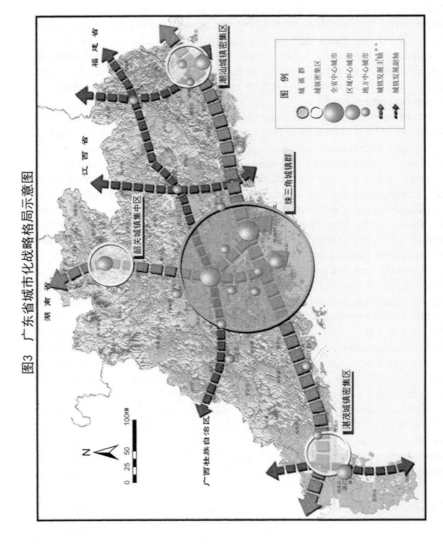

Figure 3.7 Guangdong Province: intended pattern of urbanization

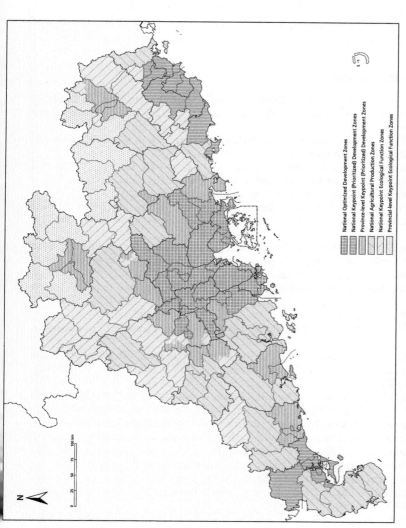

National Optimized Development Zones

National Keypoint (Prioritized) Development Zones

Province-level Keypoint (Prioritized) Development Zones

National Agricultural Production Zones

National Keypoint Ecological Function Zones

Provincial-level Keypoint Ecological Function Zones

Figure 3.8 Guangdong Province: map of all principal functional zones. Note that the term "restricted development" used in the national Master Plan has been dropped here, no doubt to facilitate acceptance of the Plan by local officials and people. We find now only urbanizing areas, agricultural development zones, and ecological development zones; and in all three, certain "restrictions" on development are to apply. There are other maps and lists in the provincial plan, however, that stipulate in detail those sites and locations all over Guangdong that are to be protected parks, forests, and nature reserves where further development is to be "prohibited."

is, we might well say, *the main point*. These maps *are* for show, after all then, yes; but not *only* for show. They are the graphic artifacts of a particular style of political leadership; one that has evolved out of past governance achievements, lapses, and missteps, and in response to challenges presenting themselves on a scale and at a level of complexity never imagined or grappled with before. They illustrate handsomely a distinct style of leadership that has become one of the trademark characteristics of twenty-first century Chinese governing practice.

References

Brettell, Anna. "A Survey of Environmental Deterrence in China's Evolving Regulatory Framework," in Ren and Shou, eds., *Chinese Environmental Governance*, 21–82.

Brody, Hugh. *Maps and Dreams: Indians and the British Columbia Frontier.* London: Faber and Faber, 2002.

Chen, Wenbo, Carsjens, Gerrit J., Zhao, Lihong, and Li, Haifeng, "A Spatial Optimization Model for Sustainable Land Use at Regional Level in China: A Case Study for Poyang Lake Region," *Sustainability*, 7: 2015, 35–55.

Chen Youshan (陈秀山) and Zhang Ruo(张若). "China Approves Marine Functional Zoning of Coastal Regions." *Xinhua, English.news.cn*, October 16, 2012.

Chen Youshan (陈秀山) and Zhang Ruo(张若). "China Sets Fresh Funds of $7.8 bn for Ecological Zones," *The Brics Post*, July 1, 2014, at thebricspost.com/china-sets-fresh-funds-of-7-8-bn-for-ecological-zones/.

Chen Youshan (陈秀山) and Zhang Ruo(张若). ("Principal Function Zoning from Conceptualization to Operationalization"). "主体功能区`从构想向操作," 决策杂志, 12: 2006.

"China Spends Billions to Subsidize Ecological Zones." *Xinhua, English.news.cn*, July 1, 2014.

"Deciphering the National Principal Function Zoning Plan: Interview with Yang Weimin." "解读全国主体功能区规划: 专访国家发展改革委秘书长杨伟民," 中国投资, 4: 2011.

Du Ping (杜平). ("Regional Planning: Progress and Prospects"). "区域规划的演变与展望," in Yang Weimin, chief ed., *The Theory and Practice*, 79–97.

Falk, Robert and Wee, Jasmine. "China's New Environmental Protection Law: Implications for Overseas Investors, Joint Ventures and Trading Partners," *Morrison/Foerster Client Alert*, September 30, 2014, at www.mondaq.com/x/345 932/Environmental+Law/Chinas+New+Environmental+Protection+Law.

Fang, Qinhua, Zhang, Ran, Zhang, Luoping, and Hong, Huasheng. "Marine Functional Zoning in China: Experience and Prospects," *Coastal Management*, 39: 2011, 656–667.

Gao Guoli (高国力). ("Characteristics, Principles and Basic Concepts of the National PFZ Plan"). "我国主体功能区规划 的特征，原则与基本思路," 中国农业资源与区划, 28, 6: 2007, 8–13, at www.cjarrp.com/zgnyzyyqh/ch/reader/create_pdf.aspx?file_no=20070696.

Harley, J. Brian. "Maps, Knowledge and Power," in Henderson and Waterstone, eds., *Geographic Thought*, 129–148.

Heilmann, Sebastian and Melton, Oliver. "The Reinvention of Development Planning in China, 1993–2012," *Modern China*, 39, 6: 2013, 580–628.

Henderson, George and Waterstone, Marvin, eds. *Geographic Thought: A Praxis Perspective*. London and New York: Routledge, 2009.

Hoffman, Lisa. "Governmental Rationalities of Environmental City-Building in Contemporary China," in Jeffreys, ed., *China's Governmentalities*, 107–124.

Hu Angang (胡鞍钢). ("Understanding the Twelfth Five Year Plan, Part 1"). "十二五规划决策与解读, 上," Lecture at Tsinghua University School of Public Policy and Management, March 16, 2011 [power point presentation].

Hu Angang (胡鞍钢), Yan Yilong (鄢一龙), and Wei Xing (魏星). (*China in 2030: Toward Common Prosperity*). *2030 中国：迈向共同富裕*. 北京：中国人民大学出版社, 2011.

Hu Angang (胡鞍钢) and Yan Yilong (鄢一龙). (*China: Onward Toward 2015*). *中国走向 2015*. 杭州：浙江人民出版社, 2010.

Hu, De and Ma, Hailong. "Government Power and its Impact on Pan-Pearl River Delta Regional Cooperation: Cooperative Networks and Regional Governance," in Yeh and Xu, eds., *China's Pan-Pearl River Delta*, 181–190.

Jeffreys, Elaine, ed. *China's Governmentalities: Governing Change, Changing Government*. London and New York: Routledge, 2009.

Landry, Pierre F. *Decentralized Authoritarianism in China: The Communist Party's Control of Local Elites in the Post-Mao Era*. Cambridge and New York: Cambridge University Press, 2008.

Li Shouxin (李守信). ("Principal Function Zoning Programs"). "主体功能区规划," in Yang Weimin, chief ed., *The Theory and Practice*, 65–78.

Lin, George C. S. *Developing China: Land, Politics and Social Conditions*. London and New York: Routledge, 2009.

Liu Guoguang (刘国光), ed. (*Research Reports on Ten Chinese Five Year Plans*). *中国十个五年计划研究报告*. 北京人民出版社, 2006.

Lu, Dadao and Fan, Jie, eds. *Regional Development Research in China: A Roadmap to 2050*. Dordrecht: Springer Berlin Heidelberg, 2010.

Ma Kai (马凯). ("Implementing the Principal Function Strategy, Scientifically Developing Our Homeland"). "实施主体功能区战略科学开发我们的家园," 求是杂志, 17: 2011, 9–14.

"Master Plan for Eco-Region Protection and Development in Sichuan and Tibet." "川西藏区生态保护与建设规划", at www.gov.cn/gzdt/2013–03/25/content_2361425.htm.

"Methods for Making Transfer Payments to National Keypoint Ecological Zones." "关于印发《国家重点生态功能区转移支付办法》的通知," 财预, 428: 2011, full text at www.gov.cn/gzdt/2011–07/28/content_1915488.htm.

Mitchell, Timothy. *Rule of Experts: Egypt, Techno-Politics, Modernity*. Berkeley: University of California Press, 2002.

The National PFZ Program: Reference Materials. 全国主体功能区规划：参考资料, 全国主题功能区规划领导小组办公室，北京, 2008.

"NDRC Detailed Briefing on the National Principal Function Zoning Plan: Complete Transcript." "发改委详释：全国主体功能区规划 [实录]," *财经*, 6: 2011.

"NDRC Report Suggests Dividing the Entire Country into Four Principal Functional Zones." "发改委报告建议全国划分四大主体功能区," February 28, 2007, at www.sc.gov.cn/tzsc1/wmyhz/zwxx/200702/t20070228_175371.shtml.

OECD Territorial Reviews: Guangdong, China. OECD Publishing, 2010.

"Official Release: National New-Type Urbanization Master Plan (2014–2020)." "授权发布:国家新型城镇化规划 (2014－2020年)," 新华，2014年3月16日, at http://news.xinhuanet.com/politics/2014–03/16/c_119791251_6.htm.

"On Zhejiang's Early Experimental Testing of the Principal Function Zone Plan." "浙江：主题功能区规划先行先试的探索与实现," April 3, 2008, at http://blog.sina.com.cn/s/blog_51839217010097r8.html.

"PFZ Strategy: A Look behind the Scenes." "主体功能区战略台前幕后," 瞭望, May 16, 2011.

Ren, Bingqiang and Shou, Huisheng, eds., *Chinese Environmental Governance: Dynamics, Challenges and Prospects in a Changing Society*. New York: Palgrave Macmillan, 2013.

Shue, Vivienne and Wong, Christine, eds., *Paying for Progress in China: Public Finance, Human Welfare and Changing Patterns of Inequality*. London and New York: Routledge, 2007.

Sigley, Gary. "Chinese Governmentalities: Government, Governance and the Socialist Market Economy," *Economy and Society*, 35, 4: 2006, 487–508.

"State Council Communiqué on Issuing of the National Principal Function Zoning Plan." "国务院关于印发全国主体功能区规划的通知," Document No. 46, December 21, 2010, at www.gov.cn/gongbao/content/2011/content_1884884 .htm.

"State Council Opinions regarding the Making of the Principal Function Zoning Plan." "国务院关于编制全国主体功能区规划的意见," Document No. 21, July 2007.

"Transcript: Press Conference on New Urbanization Plan." March 19, 2014, at china.org.cn/china/2014–03/19/content_31836248_11.htm.

Tsinghua University, China Development Planning Research Center Study Group （清华大学中国发展规划研究中心课题组）. (*Policy Research on Principal Function Zoning in China*). 中国主体功能区`政策研究. 北京：经济科学出版社, 2009.

US–China Economic and Security Review Commission. *Backgrounder: China's 12th Five Year Plan*. June 24, 2011, at origin.www.uscc.gov/sites/default/files/ Research/12th-FiveYearPlan_062811.pdf.

"Vigorously Promoting Ecological Progress to Build a Beautiful China," updated English translation from *Qiushi* (求是), May 20, 2014, at english.qstheory.cn/ 2014–05/20/c_1110774279.htm.

Wang, Alex. "The Search for Sustainable Legitimacy: Environmental Law and Bureaucracy in China," *UCLA Public Law & Legal Theory Series*, September 5, 2013, 365–440, at escholarship.org/uc/item/8hc948zx.

Winichakul, Thongchai. *Siam Mapped: A History of the Geo-Body of a Nation*. Honolulu: University of Hawai'i Press, 1994.

Xi Jinping. *The Governance of China*. Beijing: Foreign Languages Press, 2014.

Xie Qing (谢庆). ("Implement the 'Principal Function Zoning' Strategy to Create a Highly Efficient, Well-Coordinated, and Sustainably Beautiful Homeland: Interview with NDRC Secretary General Yang Weimin"). "实施主体功能区战略, 构建高效, 协调, 可持续美好家园: 专访国家发展和改革委员会秘书长杨伟民," *行政管理改革*, 5: 2011, 10–16.

Yan Yilong (鄢一龙). ("China's Five Year Plans: Transformation and Performance 1953–2010"). "中国五年计划转型之路: 绩效与经验解释　1953–2010," Ph.D. dissertation, Tsinghua University, School of Public Administration, 2010.

Yang, Dali L. *Remaking the Chinese Leviathan: Market Transition and the Politics of Governance in China*. Stanford: Stanford University Press, 2004.

Yang Qingyu (杨庆育). ("Vigorously Promote Construction of Principal Function Zones"). "着力推进主体功能区建设," *求是, 2011 年12 月1 日*, at www.qstheory.cn/zxdk/2011/201123/201111/t20111129_126527.htm.

Yang Weimin (杨伟民), chief ed. (*The Theory and Practice of Development Planning*). *发展规划的理论和实现*. 北京: 清华大学出版社, 2010.

Yang Weimin (杨伟民). ("Implement the Principal Function Zoning Strategy to Create a Highly Efficient, Well-Coordinated, and Sustainably Beautiful Homeland"). "实施主体功能区战略, 构建高效, 协调, 可持续美好家园," 中央财经领导办公室, 2011 年10 月28 日 [power point presentation].

Yeh, Anthony G. O. and Xu, Jiang, eds., *China's Pan-Pearl River Delta: Regional Cooperation and Development*. Hong Kong: Hong Kong University Press, 2011.

Zhang Ping (张平), chief ed. (*The Twelfth Five Year Plan: Strategic Research*). "十二五" 规划: 战略研究. 2 vols. 全国发改委, 北京: 人民出版社, 2010.

II

People's Government
Overseeing

4 "Mass Supervision" and the Bureaucratization of Governance in China

Joel Andreas and Yige Dong

Supervising Cadres

In the summer of 2013, only months after he took over leadership of the Chinese Communist Party, Xi Jinping launched a widely publicized campaign to mobilize the populace to criticize the behavior of party and state officials. "We must . . . lead the masses to carry out their supervision responsibilities, raise more complaints and suggestions, so as to sincerely help leading cadres reform and improve themselves," Xi declared. "Party members and cadres have to let the masses see clearly what they are changing and how they are changing, they have to accept the supervision of the masses."[1] The campaign, part of the major anti-corruption drive launched that year, was promoted by the Chinese press under the banner of the party's "mass line" tradition, and Western commentators debated whether the campaign heralded a return to practices of the Mao Zedong era.[2]

In fact, from its earliest days in power until the present, the Chinese CCP has consistently encouraged the Chinese populace to monitor and criticize party and government officials. In the party's lexicon, these efforts are known as "mass supervision" (群众监督).[3] Conventionally translated as "supervision," 监督 might also be rendered as "monitoring" or "holding accountable." Although this term seems to belong to the Mao era, it remains ubiquitous in party publications and in the Chinese press today. Figure 4.1 displays the proportion of articles published in *People's Daily* every year between 1949 and 2008 that mention mass supervision. The proportion reached a highpoint that has never been surpassed during

---

[1] Xi Jinping, "Mobilize the Enthusiasm of the Cadres and the Masses."

[2] See, for instance, Miller, "Road to the Third Plenum"; Moses, "Xi Jinping's Maoist Turn"; and Roney, "Xi's Mass Line Campaign."

[3] The meaning of 监督 does not include supervision in the sense of directing the work of subordinates. In CCP publications, the term 群众 (masses) is typically used to refer to people who are not cadres or party members. In common usage, it is often interchangeable with 老百姓 (the common people).

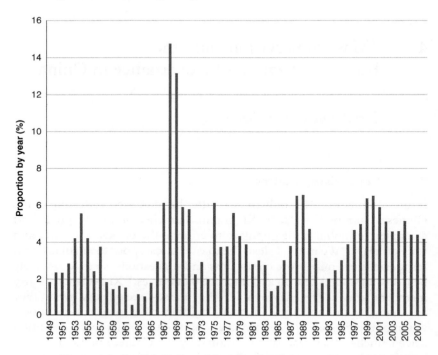

Figure 4.1 *People's Daily* articles about mass supervision, 1949–2008

the Cultural Revolution years, but it remains a recurring theme in the pages of the CCP's flagship periodical.

Mass supervision is one aspect of efforts by the CCP to control corruption and abuse of power by party and government officials. These efforts also include top-down methods, which have involved monitoring and investigation by party and state organizations, including most prominently the Ministry of Supervision and the Party's Central Commission for Discipline Inspection.[4] Party leaders, however, have long recognized that top-down controls are insufficient, and so they have endeavored to develop bottom-up controls as well. These have taken a wide variety of forms, from mass political movements to complaints offices. Although all of these forms of mass supervision have depended on the active

---

[4] On the CCP's top-down means of controlling cadre behavior, see Edin, "State Capacity"; Gong, "The Party Discipline Inspection"; Huang, "Administrative Monitoring"; Lü, *Cadres and Corruption*; Schurmann, *Ideology and Organization*, 309–364; Sullivan, "Role of the Control Organs"; Wedeman, "Intensification of Corruption"; Young, "Control and Style."

participation of common people, the project is designed to meet party goals. The underlying political dynamic can be described as *top-and-bottom-versus-the-middle*. In this pattern, to which Max Weber drew attention, central authorities act in concert with groups at lower echelons of the social hierarchy against local officials and local elites. Central authorities, Weber pointed out, must constantly struggle to monitor and control their local agents and they often enlist the help of subordinate groups for this purpose. Mark Lupher has argued that this kind of top-and-bottom-versus-the-middle logic was at work when Mao Zedong mobilized students, workers, and peasants to attack party cadres during the Cultural Revolution.[5] The same logic has underpinned all forms of mass supervision, even in less turbulent times.

Our aim in this essay is to compare mass supervision today with mass supervision during the Mao era. For this purpose, we have conducted a content analysis of the *People's Daily*, making use of a searchable digital database of articles published from 1949 to 2008. We find that although mass supervision retains the same general function – enlisting the masses to help monitor and criticize local party leaders – there have been major changes in both form and content. Two of these changes stand out and will be the focus of this essay. In terms of the shift in form, mass supervision has moved away from collective, face-to-face methods toward individualized, technical methods. During the Mao era, it was carried out mainly through political movements, typically took place in meetings of different types, and was based in villages, factories, schools, military units, and urban neighborhoods. These collective methods have subsequently disappeared, and mass supervision now takes place largely in the form of individual reporting through hotlines and offices of the State Bureau for Letters and Visits, internet sites, and so on. The shift in content has been just as dramatic. During the Mao era, the behavior that was criticized most often in articles about mass supervision was 官僚主义, typically translated as "bureaucratism." In the post-Mao era, official concern about bureaucratism has waned, while corruption has become the dominant theme.

Many scholars have noted the striking change in the form of mass supervision, observing that the tumultuous campaigns of the Mao era have given way to more orderly and institutionalized methods.[6] In

---

[5] Lupher, *Power Restructuring*.

[6] See, for instance, He Qin, "Mass Supervision"; Huang and Hu, "The Party's Theory"; Ji Yaguang, "An Experiment in Institutionalizing Mass Supervision"; Luehrmann, "Citizen Complaints"; O'Brien and Li, "Lodging Complaints"; Manion, *Corruption by Design*; Mo Jiwu, *Political Supervision System*; Shi, *Political Participation*; Yang Rong, "A Comparative Study"; and Zhang and Wang, "Mass Supervision."

contrast, the change in content has received much less attention. Scholars have, of course, been cognizant of the chief target at the moment. For instance, in 1967 when A. Doak Barnett wrote *Cadres, Bureaucracy, and Political Power in Communist China* and in 1981 when Harry Harding wrote *Organizing China: The Problem of Bureaucracy, 1949–1976*, it was self-evident that the main target of mass supervision was bureaucratic behavior. On the other hand, more recent works, such as Xiaobo Lü's *Cadres and Corruption: The Organizational Involution of the Chinese Communist Party* (2000) and Melanie Manning's *Corruption by Design: Building Clean Government in Mainland China and Hong Kong* (2004), have discussed mass supervision as if its main target has *always* been corruption. The underlying shift in content has largely escaped notice. As a result, no one has analyzed the causes or consequences of this shift, or considered the relationship between the change in content and the change in form. These are the main concerns of this essay.

The shifts in the form and content of mass supervision, we will argue, are closely related and they reflect a fundamental change in the way the CCP governs China. On the one hand, this change has entailed the *bureaucratization* of governance, in the sense in which Max Weber used the term. For Weber, bureaucratization entailed administrative centralization and the rationalization of human interaction, which resulted in impersonalization and the dissolution of communal ties. Weberian-type bureaucratization has been accompanied by a growing distance between state officials and the population, which is the essential meaning of bureaucratism in Chinese communist discourse. Before detailing the results of our analysis, we will first discuss these two concepts in more detail, identifying their similarities and differences.

Overlapping Concepts: Bureaucratization and Bureaucratism

Although Weber's concept of bureaucratization coincides in some ways with the CCP's concept of bureaucratism, the two are fundamentally different. Recognizing the similarities, scholars have often failed to differentiate between them. For instance, in what is probably the most thorough effort to analyze the CCP's endeavors to combat bureaucratism during the Mao era, Harry Harding used the two concepts interchangeably.[7] It is worthwhile, however, to first carefully distinguish the two before identifying areas in which they correspond.

For Weber, bureaucratization is the defining feature of modernity and it involves transforming relations of authority by replacing traditional

---

[7] Harding, *Organizing China*.

relationships and charismatic inspiration with rationalized, centralized, rule-based organizations. We will briefly discuss these transformations, focusing on those elements of Weber's ideas that involve relations between basic-level authorities and the populace.

Under traditional political arrangements, local power holders were largely autonomous from the central state and were usually members of the community they governed; their authority was based on longstanding, multi-faceted personal relations with community members that involved mutual obligations. Bureaucratization breaks down these communities, turning their erstwhile members into individual citizens of the state. It replaces the particular rights and responsibilities entailed by communal membership with universal individual rights and responsibilities determined by the state. Traditional local leaders, whose authority was derived from their positions in the community, are replaced by government officials, whose authority is derived from their positions in the state bureaucracy. Governance becomes increasingly professionalized, with less and less room for non-specialists. This bureaucratic reorganization of political authority is part of a broader rationalization and impersonalization of human relations, which involve the replacement of strong communal ties with weaker associational ties and the reorientation of social interaction so that it is based on the formal rationality of market exchange and standardized rules.

Bureaucratization can also involve what Weber called the "routinization of charisma." Charismatic authority, for Weber, is the inspiration for revolutionary change, as it mobilizes people to break the rules that underpin the status quo, whether traditional or bureaucratic. Leaders of charismatic movements inspire their followers to abandon mundane pursuits and dedicate themselves instead to a transcendent mission, demanding great commitment and self-sacrifice. Charismatic authority, however, is fleeting; it cannot withstand the normality that sets in once a new order is established, in which regular rules and mundane calculation of interests reassert themselves.[8]

In the CCP's conceptual universe, bureaucratism is not a principle of modern organization, but rather a malady afflicting those who have power. The concept was shaped by Bolshevik usage as well as the CCP's experience governing its revolutionary base areas in rural China. In base-area villages, the party recruited local activists to administer village affairs and mobilize peasants to carry out the party's revolutionary

---

[8] A number of scholars have applied Weber's concepts of bureaucratic and charismatic authority to analyzing politics in Mao-era China. See, for instance, Andreas, "Charismatic Mobilization," and Dittmer, *China's Continuous Revolution*.

agenda, and it insisted that these basic-level cadres maintain close ties to the villagers. While the Party Center depended on its local agents to implement its policies, it was constantly concerned about them becoming local tyrants, abusing their power, and antagonizing the local population. The watchword of communist governance in its base areas was maintaining good "cadres–masses relations" (干群关系). Communist cadres were exhorted to be honest and comport themselves according to the party's harshly ascetic norms of "plain living and hard work" (艰苦奋斗). They were also expected to abide by the party's "mass line" (群众路线), maintaining close ties with the populace, treating villagers with respect, listening to their opinions, and keeping them content (even when party policies made this difficult).

Bureaucratism was understood to be styles of work that undermined the relations between communist cadres and the masses. As noted above, the most important meaning was the separation of cadres from the masses. The party demanded that its cadres "live, eat, and work" (同住同吃同劳动) with the peasants; they were required to lead them, but at the same time they were expected to listen to their criticisms and suggestions, attend to their concerns, and involve them in local governance. "Isolation from the masses" (脱离群众), "commandism" (命令主义), stifling of criticism from below, arrogance, and failing to adhere to a "democratic work style" (民主作风) were denounced as bureaucratic behaviors, which party leaders feared would alienate the masses and threaten the party's ability to govern its base areas and mobilize peasants behind its revolutionary agenda.

After 1949, bureaucratism remained a persistent concern of the CCP. A 1957 *People's Daily* commentary defined the term this way:

What is bureaucratism? It is hard to define, but it is reflected in the following aspects. First, not following the "mass line," that is, not relating to the masses, not trusting the masses, and not relying on the masses; only thinking about being responsible to those above you and not attending to voices from below, so that you get isolated from the masses and become more and more distant from them both psychologically and in terms of daily life.[9]

Bureaucratism was also seen to be a product of communist cadres losing their revolutionary commitment and orientation. During the early years of the People's Republic, the party was engaged in radically transforming Chinese society, tearing down existing institutions and building new ones. If an official neglected ideology and revolutionary values and goals and was preoccupied with his/her own powers and

---

[9] Wang Zaoshi, "Our Democratic Life."

prerogatives, that was, at the time, regarded as showing symptoms of succumbing to an undesirable tendency toward bureaucratism.

Mass supervision was understood to be an essential antidote for bureaucratism. The tendency of cadres to listen only to those above them and not those below them could not be effectively counteracted by top-down methods. During the Mao era, the two phenomena were constantly linked; a typical rendition was included in a 1950 *People's Daily* commentary: "Mass supervision and criticism is the most effective weapon for fighting against bureaucratism."[10] Supervision from below was seen as crucial in order to prevent cadres from becoming aloof from the masses. In fact, a parsimonious definition of bureaucratism might simply be lack of effective mass supervision.

While Weber's bureaucratization and the CCP's bureaucratism are very different concepts, they overlap in important ways. In the main terrain of our concern – authority relations between basic-level leaders and the populace – they both involve the concentration of authority in the hands of officials and the weakening of communal ties and obligations. From a different angle, they also both involve the abandoning of revolutionary orientations. Although they should not be conflated, both concepts are useful when interpreting changes in the CCP's mode of governance over the last six decades.

Methods[11]

Because this essay grew out of a project that initially focused on governance during the first two decades of communist power the bulk of our research has been on that period. We read every *People's Daily* article that mentioned mass supervision published during the 1949–1968 period (957 articles). For the present essay, in order to compare the Mao era and the most recent period, we read every article that mentioned mass supervision published during the 2007–2008 period (298 articles).[12]

In analyzing the articles, we focused on five aspects of mass supervision, two of which concern content – the groups and behaviors that became targets – and three of which concern form – the methods, sites, and agents of supervision. Initially, we also intended to analyze the results of mass

[10] Hou Yong, "Weapon against Bureaucratism."

[11] Because of space constraints, we are only able to briefly explain the methods used in the content analysis on which this essay is based. For a more detailed explanation and a list of the codes used, please contact Joel Andreas, jandreas@jhu.edu.

[12] There are several databases that have digitized all *People's Daily* articles from 1946 to 2013. We chose to use "人民日报图文电子版" ("Digitized graphics and texts of the *People's Daily*") provided by Beijing University Library because it is the most accurate and best organized. When we conducted this research, it only included articles to 2008.

supervision, but we found that *People's Daily* articles generally failed to report results. Through an inductive process, for each of the five aspects we developed a list of types to which articles frequently referred, combining these types into a smaller set of categories with which to code the articles. For instance, for targeted groups we created the codes "cadres," "rank-and-file party members," "intellectuals," "capitalists," etc. (a list of the codes we developed is available on request). In analyzing each article, for each of our five aspects we recorded all of the categories mentioned and then determined which category was discussed most prominently.

It must be stressed that because the content we are analyzing comes exclusively from an official organ of the CCP, we can only draw conclusions about how the party has *presented* mass supervision, rather than about how it has actually been carried out in practice and the way people actually experienced it. Any journalistic source has biases and limitations, and this is particularly true of the *People's Daily*, the content of which has always been tightly controlled by central party officials. The differences between presentation and practice are significant, and we will note some of them. In this essay, however, our central concern is analyzing changes over time in the official presentation of mass supervision. There is much we can learn from these changes; the striking differences in the form and content of mass supervision, as presented in the pages of the *People's Daily*, tell us a great deal about fundamental shifts in the CCP's mode of governance.

We will place our quantitative analysis of the content of *People's Daily* articles in historical and institutional context, drawing on a range of other sources, including interviews with well over one hundred cadres and workers employed in Chinese factories at some point between 1949 and the present.

Mass Supervision during the Mao Era

Mass supervision, as it was practiced in China after 1949, had three important roots. The first was the imperial grievance (告状) tradition, in which people were encouraged to report the malfeasance of "corrupt officials" and "evil gentry" to higher authorities through petitions that ultimately might reach the emperor.[13] The second was Soviet traditions, many of which – including the conception of bureaucratism and the practice of organizing criticism of communist officials from below – were

---

[13] See Fang, *Chinese Complaint Systems*; Ocko, "I'll Take It"; and Perry, "Chinese Conceptions."

borrowed directly by the Chinese party.[14] The third was the "mass line" tradition developed by the CCP during its early years as an insurgent organization ensconced in remote villages; mass supervision was understood to be an essential element of the party's mass line approach. The manner in which mass supervision was implemented in base-area villages was vividly described in William Hinton's ethnographic account of meetings in which villagers were urged to criticize the shortcomings of local communist cadres, each of whom had to "pass the gate" in order to continue in his position of authority.[15] During its insurgent years, the CCP was a remarkably disciplined organization and its capacity to compel its cadres to carry out its policies and comply with its norms was due in large part to the cadres' ideological indoctrination and political commitment, as well as the party's formidable system of internal controls, including its grueling practice of "criticism and self-criticism." The mechanisms of mass supervision developed in communist base areas, however, undoubtedly also contributed to this discipline.

After 1949, the CCP brought the mode of governance it had developed in its revolutionary base areas, including the tradition of mass supervision, to the rest of China. During its first decade in power, it reorganized the entire country so it could govern the way it had in base-area villages. Virtually the entire population was organized into collective units – production brigades in the countryside and work units in cities – each of which was administered by a small group of party cadres. Workers and peasants were permanent members of these collectivities, as were cadres (although top cadres were subject to transfer). Vivienne Shue has described rural China during the Mao era as a cellular, honeycomb-like structure of relatively insular villages.[16] The same image fits urban China during this period, with its honeycomb of work units enclosed by protective walls, although in cities there was far greater exchange and interdependence. This cellular organization was reminiscent of traditional societies, but it was tied together by a centralized political party, which ran a state that was far more ambitious and capable than its imperial predecessors, and its agents were expected to be firmly in charge of each cell.

The CCP governed China's population largely through these production brigades and work units, which became the primary sites of social control. Governance took place through constant personal interaction

---

[14] On Soviet practices, see Andrle, *Workers in Stalin's Russia*; Chase, *Workers*; Fitzpatrick, "Workers against Bosses"; Granick, *Management of the Industrial Firm*; and Lupher, *Power Restructuring*.

[15] Hinton, *Fanshen*, 319–364, 449–472, and 568–569. Also see Li, "Mass Democracy."

[16] Shue, *Reach of the State*.

between communist cadres and rank-and-file villagers and workers, and – with the curtailment of market mechanisms – economic activity also required mobilization of the populace by cadres. Village and factory life was marked by an endless stream of meetings. In factories, for instance, every worker was a member of a small group that met daily before and after work, workshops held monthly meetings, and the entire workforce was convened to announce the arrival of a new production campaign or political movement. The Party Secretary and other local cadres enjoyed tremendous authority over the lives of villagers and work unit members.[17]

While communist cadres were expected to monitor and supervise the members of production brigades and work units, members were also expected to monitor and supervise the cadres. This kind of mutual supervision was facilitated by the fact that basic-level cadres did, indeed, live, eat, and work with the masses. This was true not only in villages, but also in factories, which resembled urban villages. The factory Party Secretary typically lived in the same apartment blocks as the workers, rode his bicycle to work down the same lanes, shopped in the same stores, got his hair cut by the same barber, was seen by the same clinic doctor, and sent his children to the same childcare center and the same schools. The party continued to impose its harshly ascetic norms on the populace, including its own cadres, keeping wages low, and demanding simple living and hard work. Everybody knew exactly how much everyone else – including the Party Secretary – was paid and where they lived, and the lives of all members of these relatively insular communities were subject to mutual scrutiny.

The conditions created under the production brigade and work unit systems continued to nourish the CCP's preoccupation with bureaucratism – and with mass supervision. In the following sections, we will analyze how mass supervision was presented in the pages of the *People's Daily* during the Mao era, first looking at its content and then at its form.

Content of Mass Supervision

Targeted Groups   The groups targeted for mass supervision during the Mao era, as described in the pages of the *People's Daily*, can be divided into two camps, which from the CCP's point of view might be called "insiders" and "outsiders." Among the first camp were the new cadres (political leaders, administrators, and managers) appointed by the

---

[17] Classic Western ethnographic accounts of power relations in Chinese villages and urban work units have stressed the power of leadership cadres; see, for instance, Chan et al., *Chen Village*; and Walder, *Communist Neo-Traditionalism*.

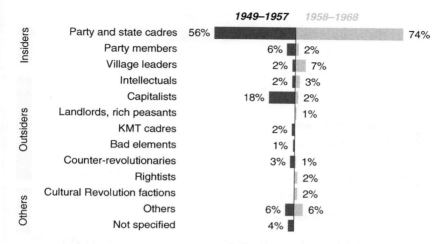

Figure 4.2 *People's Daily* articles about mass supervision, 1949–1957 vs. 1958–1968: targeted groups

communist regime, as well as village leaders and accountants (who were not paid by the state and did not have formal cadre status), and rank-and-file party members. Among the second camp were members of the old elite classes (capitalists, landlords, and rich peasants), old regime cadres and intellectuals (including many teachers and technical and professional staff), who were generally distrusted by the new regime because of their old elite origins, and those judged to be "bad elements" (criminals) or politically hostile. A small number of articles also encouraged the masses to monitor individuals of more ordinary stature, including workers, peasants, soldiers, and small entrepreneurs (all of which we included in the "other" category).

During all periods we analyzed, the great majority of the articles about mass supervision targeted communist cadres and other "insiders," and this proportion increased over time (see Figures 4.2 and 4.3). During the first decade of communist power (1949–1957), about 64 percent of the articles were directed against insiders, while over 26 percent targeted outsiders. Almost all of the latter articles involved the party mobilizing workers and peasants to monitor and criticize members of the old elites, and many featured reports about workers denouncing malfeasance by capitalists and old regime managers, as the CCP sought to gain control over and socialize industrial and commercial enterprises.

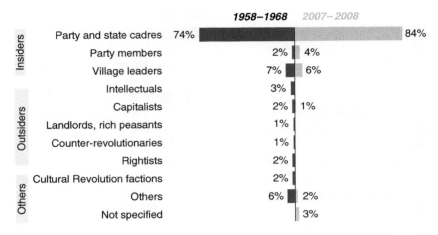

Figure 4.3 *People's Daily* articles about mass supervision, 1958–1968 vs. 2007–2008: targeted groups

The groups targeted shifted abruptly after 1957, when the socialist conversion of private enterprises and rural collectivization were completed. From that point on, the rubric of mass supervision, as it was used in the *People's Daily*, was reserved almost entirely for insiders. During the 1958–1968 period, the party's own cadres and other insiders were the target of 83 percent of the articles about mass supervision, while only 9 percent were directed against members of the old elite classes and other suspect outsiders. This does not mean members of the old elites were immune from attack during this period; on the contrary, they were subject to particularly harsh assaults during the Four Cleans movement and the Cultural Revolution. It simply means that once the old elites were no longer in positions of power, the *People's Daily* generally did not use the language of mass supervision when referring to them.

Targeted Behaviors   *People's Daily* articles about mass supervision targeted a wide variety of behaviors (see Figure 4.4).[18] Most of these were specific to cadres, including conduct associated with bureaucratism (isolation from the masses, commandism, subjectivism, arrogance, suppression of criticism, etc.), inefficiency (waste, incompetence, poor

---

[18] In our quantitative analyses of targeted behaviors, we eliminated 432 articles (about 30 percent of the total) that did not mention a specific behavior.

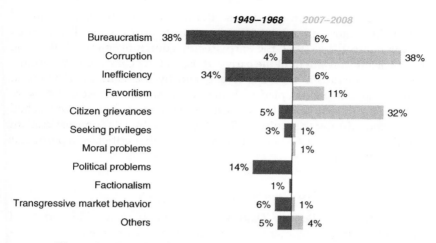

Figure 4.4 *People's Daily* articles about mass supervision, 1949–1968 vs. 2007–2008: targeted behaviors

quality output or service, etc.), corruption (illegal economic activities by officials, including accepting bribes, embezzlement, using public resources for private benefit, and theft of public property), favoritism (promoting people improperly and providing people with special access), and official conduct that led to citizen or employee grievances (unsafe work, unsafe products, unfair distribution of goods and services, wrongful punishment, etc.). Other articles were specific to entrepreneurs and involved various kinds of transgressive market behaviors (profiteering, failure to pay taxes, cheating on contracts, bribery, etc.). Still others focused on political offenses ranging in gravity from counterrevolutionary behavior, Rightism, and carrying out revisionist policies to placing too much emphasis on expertise and too little on politics. Finally, many articles urged vigilance against privilege-seeking (特殊化) and selfishness (私心).

Throughout the first two decades of CCP power, bureaucratism among communist cadres was clearly of great concern to the party leadership. From 1949 to 1968, 38 percent of *People's Daily* articles about mass supervision focused on this problem, making it far and away the most prevalent topic. "Our method," a 1950 *People's Daily* article declared, "is to organize mass supervision and criticism, to combine bottom-up mass

criticism and top-down criticism so that we root out bureaucratism."[19]
All of the major campaigns directed against cadres – the Three Antis
movement in 1951–1952, the Party Rectification movement of 1957, the
Four Cleans movement of the early 1960s, and the Cultural Revolution –
made bureaucratism a central target, and by the Cultural Revolution
years, Mao was preoccupied with the idea that communist cadres were
becoming a "bureaucratic class." Articles about mass supervision reached
a crescendo during the Cultural Revolution and by 1968, bureaucratism
was the focus of over 60 percent of the articles that criticized a particular
type of behavior.

Forms of Mass Supervision

Methods   People's Daily articles pointed to a wide variety of
methods used to implement mass supervision. We grouped these disparate methods into fourteen categories and, following our theoretical interest, divided these categories into two groups – methods that were
primarily individual and/or technical and methods that involved collective, face-to-face activities.

Individual and technical methods, including many that would become
the mainstay of mass supervision in the reform era, also existed during
the Mao era, but were clearly secondary. Altogether, about 25 percent
of the People's Daily articles about mass supervision published from
1949 to 1968 reported mainly on individual and technical methods (see
Figure 4.5).[20] The methods that got most attention were reporting
systems (including anonymous letter boxes) and petition and grievance
systems (including "letters and visits" offices). A number of articles also
promoted use of the mass media and many of these reported on the work
of "worker correspondents," who contacted media outlets to report
abuses and air grievances. We included in this category articles that did
not indicate any specific method of denunciation, but simply promoted
efforts to make the party and state administration more open in order to
facilitate public monitoring (including public display of party and administrative policies, decisions, personnel, and promotions).

During the Mao era, however, the stress was clearly on collective and
face-to-face methods. In 72 percent of the People's Daily articles about
mass supervision published during the 1949–1968 period, the main
method discussed was collective; an additional 8 percent mentioned a

[19] Teng Daiyuan, "Root out Bureaucratic Work Styles."
[20] Following the same procedure as we did with targeted behaviors, in our quantitative
analyses of methods we eliminated 481 articles (about 33 percent of the total) that did not
mention a specific method.

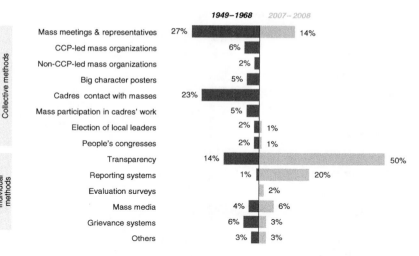

Figure 4.5 *People's Daily* articles about mass supervision, 1949–1968 vs. 2007–2008: methods

collective method, even though the article focused on individual methods. The most important category on the collective side involved meetings of one kind or another. These included the election of rank-and-file representatives to monitor leaders (such as staff and workers representative congresses in urban workplaces and poor and lower-middle peasants associations in villages), the participation of rank-and-file representatives in leadership meetings, leaders reporting to mass meetings, the participation of rank-and-file party members in party branch and party committee meetings, discussion of leadership performance in the regular basic level groups (such as village production teams and small groups in factory workshops), as well as special mass meetings convened to criticize leaders.

People's Daily articles also assigned mass supervision responsibilities to "mass organizations," including those controlled by the CCP (the union, women's federation, youth league, and militia) and others that were somewhat more autonomous (the "democratic parties" of the 1950s and Cultural Revolution "rebel" organizations). Many articles suggested that mass supervision could be accomplished through cadres spending more time with the masses; examples included requiring factory leaders to spend one day a week doing productive labor or county leaders to spend

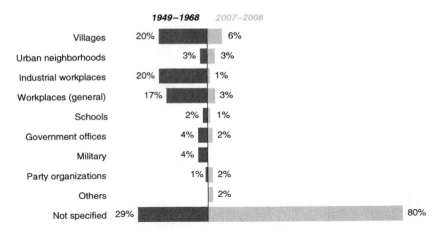

Figure 4.6 *People's Daily* articles about mass supervision, 1949–1968 vs. 2007–2008: sites

one month a year living and working in a village. We have also included among collective methods big character posters and open forum discussions on workplace blackboards because they were designed to promote debate within a work unit.

Other collective methods included intermittent popular elections of basic level leaders (in villages and enterprises) and local people's congresses (which were formally tasked with monitoring government agencies). The fact that these potentially important forms were only mentioned in connection with mass supervision in a relatively small number of articles, however, seems to indicate that the CCP leadership was not very committed to using them for this purpose.

Sites   The collective nature of mass supervision during the Mao era was further indicated by press reports about it taking place inside work units, with members expected to directly monitor and criticize unit leaders. Figure 4.6 shows the distribution of *People's Daily* articles about mass supervision from 1949 through 1968 according to the type of site in which it was reported as occurring. Over two-thirds of the articles were about mass supervision taking place in a particular site or a particular kind of site – workers were described carrying out mass supervision in their factories, peasants in their villages, urban residents in their neighborhoods, soldiers in their military units, party members in their party organizations, etc. Only 29 percent of the articles failed to mention a specific site or type of site.

Agents We also tracked how *People's Daily* articles portrayed the agents of mass supervision. Once again, our categories are largely inductive; we simply grouped the many descriptive terms used in the articles into a smaller number of broader categories. The pattern we observed for agents was similar to those we observed with regard to methods and sites. During the 1949–1968 period, more than 60 percent of the articles about mass supervision highlighted the role of specific groups – workers, employees (职工, which refers not only to workers, but also to technical staff and cadres), peasants, soldiers, students, or party members (see Figure 4.6). Reflecting the CCP's ideological agenda during this period (when it was continuing to mobilize the lower classes against the old elites and educated classes), workers and peasants were the groups most often identified as the agents of mass supervision.

Mass Supervision Campaigns In practice, mass supervision was hampered by the danger of retaliation, which was strictly prohibited in principle, but was difficult to prevent. This was not as much of a concern with individual methods designed to protect confidentiality, but it was particularly problematic for the collective, face-to-face methods favored during the Mao era. The CCP endeavored to solve this problem by organizing periodic large-scale campaigns, which punctuated the Mao era. The ebb and flow of these campaigns can be roughly traced in the number of articles about mass supervision published in the *People's Daily*, presented in Figure 4.1. The quantity of articles surged in during the extended campaign to nationalize private enterprises in the mid-1950s (which was accompanied by many articles promoting mass supervision over capitalists), the Party Rectification campaign in 1957, the initial upheavals of the Cultural Revolution, and the 1975 campaign against Right deviationism (the chief target of which became Deng Xiaoping).

It is evident that mass supervision during the Mao era relied largely on these campaigns. We have interviewed over eighty workers and cadres who were employed in industrial workplaces during this period and they generally concurred that between campaigns people were relatively reticent about criticizing factory leaders; it was only during campaigns – when criticism of local leaders was not only authorized by central party authorities, but was mandated – that large numbers of people dared speak up. Typically, higher levels of the party organization sent work teams to villages and factories to lead these campaigns; these teams set aside the local leadership and mobilized peasants and workers to investigate and denounce wrongdoing by cadres in big character posters and meetings. During the Cultural Revolution, the work teams were withdrawn and workers and peasants were encouraged to organize "rebel" groups, which – on Mao's authority – hauled local leaders before mass meetings to be questioned, criticized, and humiliated. During this period, when local party organizations were paralyzed, mass supervision escaped from party control and attacks on local leaders led to sharp, often violent, factional conflict. Both the unrestrained mass supervision of the Cultural Revolution and the more regimented forms employed in previous mass movements provoked great fear among local cadres, who were subjected to cruel and degrading treatment by their subordinates. Cadres ultimately faced demotion, transfer, and punishment, and suicides were tragically common.[21]

Mass Supervision during the Post-Mao Era

Market reforms carried out during the post-Mao era have dissolved the collective entities through which the CCP had governed China. In the early 1980s, the rural production brigades were broken up and in the early 1990s, the CCP began dismantling the urban work unit system. Work units were converted into profit-oriented enterprises – most were privatized, while some remained state property – and new private enterprises proliferated. Most important for workers, permanent job tenure was eliminated and work unit members were converted into contract employees who could be hired and fired as dictated by managerial requirements, technical needs, and market conditions. As a result, workers' relationship to workplaces became much more tenuous and Chinese society became much less cellular and much more mobile.

Class differences have grown exponentially. Already by the 1980s, CCP leaders had decisively rejected the radical egalitarianism and asceticism of the Mao era. Cadres were encouraged to wear shirts with ties rather than work clothes, and they were given significantly higher wages and bonuses; today, the compensation of top managers dwarfs that of ordinary workers. Without the collective forms of organization that once bound cadres to workers (and vice versa), cadres are no longer expected to live, eat, and work with the masses; indeed, they have moved out of work unit apartment blocks and into exclusive high-rise condominiums

---

[21] Among the many works on political campaigns during the Mao era, the following include a significant focus on mass supervision of cadres: Andreas, *Rise of the Red Engineers*; Baum, *Prelude to Revolution*; Dittmer, *China's Continuous Revolution*; Lieberthal, *Revolution and Tradition*; Lupher, *Power Restructuring*; MacFarquhar, *The Hundred Flowers*; Perry and Li, *Proletarian Power*; and Teiwes, *Politics and Purges*.

and gated communities. Moreover, managers are no longer recruited from among workers, but rather from among university graduates. The CCP, which once strived to maintain a membership base among the masses, now has much less interest in recruiting ordinary workers and peasants.[22]

Under these conditions, mass supervision has also changed. The CCP still endeavors to enlist the masses to monitor its cadres and report transgressions, but both the content and the form have changed dramatically.

Changing Content of Mass Supervision

Targeted Groups   Mass supervision today continues to be an instrument used by the CCP almost exclusively to clean up its own house, rather than to monitor and criticize other sectors of the population. Of articles about mass supervision published in *People's Daily* during the 2007–2008 period, virtually all focused on "insiders" – 84 percent on party and state cadres, 6 percent on village leaders, and 4 percent on rank-and-file party members (see Figure 4.3). This continued the pattern that had been evident since private enterprise was eliminated in the late 1950s, after which communist cadres became the focus of the overwhelming majority of articles about mass supervision. Of course, by 2007–2008, most of the Chinese economy was once again in the hands of private owners, including very large capitalists. The CCP, however, did not make them the target of mass supervision, as it had done with capitalists in the early and mid-1950s. Only a handful of articles targeted private entrepreneurs; these typically called on the masses to report venders who sold fake or substandard goods or failed to display their names and registration numbers on market stalls. The CCP was no longer in the business of populist mobilization against capital.

Targeted Behaviors   While cadres remain the main objects of mass supervision, there has been a sea change in the behaviors targeted. Bureaucratism, which had been by far the most common target of articles about mass supervision during the Mao era, has almost entirely disappeared from the radar screen. While the problems associated with the term – isolation from the masses, commandism, subjectivism, arrogance, suppression of criticism, and so forth – have certainly not disappeared, these problems were featured in only 6 percent of articles about mass supervision published in *People's Daily* during the 2007–2008 period (see

---

[22] Dickson, "Dilemmas of Party Adaptation," 37–38.

Figure 4.4).[23] The Mao-era preoccupation with political transgressions has also faded. Instead, official corruption had become the most pressing concern. Of the articles in our sample, 38 percent targeted cadre corruption, while another 11 percent targeted favoritism (including nepotism).

In addition to cadre corruption, the issues highlighted in *People's Daily* articles about mass supervision included cadre privileges. Over the last two decades, the wages, bonuses, and perks received by state and party cadres have skyrocketed causing tremendous popular resentment, so it is no surprise that cadre privileges have become a more important topic. A large number of articles also featured specific popular grievances, such as unsafe products, environmental harm, unsafe working conditions, high taxes and fees, and land seizures, all of which were also presented as problems to be tackled by mass supervision.

Changing Forms of Mass Supervision

Methods   Since the end of the Mao era, the methods of mass supervision have changed dramatically. Of the *People's Daily* articles from 2007–2008, only 16 percent focused on any kind of collective method, in sharp contrast to the Mao era, when 72 percent of articles highlighted collective methods, most commonly mass meetings of one kind or another, often carried out in the course of mass movements (see Figure 4.5). Articles in the latter period, in contrast, tended to highlight individual actions. Citizens were encouraged to fill out surveys and make use of grievance procedures, media outlets, and various reporting systems to denounce official misdeeds. Among the reporting systems promoted were telephone hotlines, mobile reporting stations, government websites, and officially sponsored online discussion boards. These methods are not only individual, but they are increasingly technical, as much of a citizen's monitoring duties can now be done through the internet, which has been acclaimed as a "barometer of public opinion."[24] The mass media has also been given a longer leash and individuals continue to be encouraged to provide information to journalists in order to facilitate "media supervision" of cadres. Channels for individuals to submit grievances – which have existed since the CCP took power – have also been enhanced, particularly with the further institutionalization of the petition system.[25]

---

[23] Following the same procedure as we did for the Mao-era articles, in this figure we eliminated 148 articles (about 50 percent of the total) that did not mention a specific behavior.

[24] He Guanghua, "Liberation of Thinking."

[25] China's petition system has been the topic of a number of articles, including Chen, *Social Protest*; Luehrmann, "Citizen Complaints"; and O'Brien and Li, "Lodging Complaints."

Although individuals can collaborate in making claims, the petition system is designed to limit such collaboration.[26]

Most of the recent articles about mass supervision did not actually focus on concrete methods of denunciation, but rather on the duty of officials to carry out their activities transparently so they could be subject to mass supervision. Among the articles published in 2007–2008, 50 percent focused on making the party and the government more open. Among the forms promoted were broadcasting new policies and regulations through the mass media, printing citizen handbooks to explain municipal affairs, creating public project information stations, listing publicly the names and responsibilities of cadres, posting promotion decisions, and the allocation of jobs, family planning quotas, and changes in household registrations. These forms, of course, are not mass supervision per se, but they facilitate monitoring by giving the public access to information so they can report violations and inconsistencies.

The post-Mao approach to mass supervision was summed up concisely by General-Secretary Zhao Ziyang in 1989. "To solve the problem of corruption, we should not rely on movements, but rather on building institutions," he declared.

We should make our institutions and outcomes transparent, and we also need supervision. Reporting is a crucial form of supervision. Transparency itself is a method of supervision. Once we carry out our business in an open fashion, we become supervised. Therefore, I think it is a wise approach to promote transparency, rely on mass supervision, and build mechanisms both within the party and in society to curb corruption.[27]

Sites   The shift from collective to individual forms is also clearly indicated by the fact that few reform-era reports about mass supervision mention specific sites. While 71 percent of *People's Daily* articles from our Mao-era sample discussed mass supervision taking place in villages, factories, schools, and so forth, only 20 percent of the articles from the 2007–2008 period mentioned any kind of site (see Figure 4.6). With this decline in geographical specificity, mass supervision has become a much more diffuse affair, with articles simply asking the citizenry in general to participate.

The sharp decline in reports about mass supervision in villages and urban workplaces is clearly connected to the dismantling of the rural production brigade and urban work unit systems. Today, little remains

[26] Collective petitions, for instance, are formally limited to five people, although this limit is routinely ignored in practice.
[27] Zhao Ziyang, "A Clean Political System."

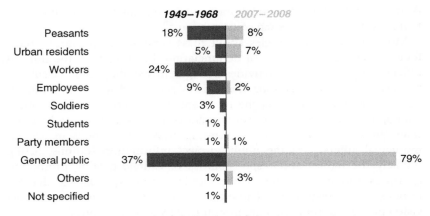

Figure 4.7 *People's Daily* articles about mass supervision, 1949–1968 vs. 2007–2008: agents

of the collective entities that had once served as the most important sites of mass supervision. The drop in reports about mass supervision in factories and other urban workplaces has been particularly pronounced; by 2007–2008, only 4 percent of articles about mass supervision featured urban workplaces, compared with 37 percent of articles from our Mao-era sample, when factories in particular were highlighted. Today, when both public and private enterprises are compelled to maximize profits, the *People's Daily* no longer encourages workers to monitor and criticize their bosses.

Agents   In the pages of the *People's Daily*, the agents of mass supervision have also become less distinct over time. While during the Mao era, more than 60 percent of the articles about mass supervision referred to workers, peasants, or other specific groups as agents, by 2007–2008, nearly 80 percent of the articles failed to specify an agent. Only 8 percent mentioned peasants, 2 percent mentioned urban employees, and none mentioned workers (see Figure 4.7). The respective figures for the Mao era had been 18 percent, 9 percent, and 24 percent.

The growing indefiniteness of the agents of mass supervision is another indication of the shift from collective to individual methods. We can, however, also discern a class twist. The CCP came to power as a revolutionary party, which claimed to be the vanguard of the workers and peasants. Today, the party has largely abandoned any pretense of being the champion of the workers and peasants, and the writing staff of the *People's Daily* clearly feels uncomfortable even pronouncing the names of these lower echelon classes in connection with mass supervision. "Workers," it seems, is a particularly sensitive term, as it never appears in this context. Instead, it is probably not too much of a stretch to think that the typical protagonist in most of today's articles about mass supervision is imagined by the authors to be a middle-class citizen adept at both reading information posted on the internet by party and state agencies and at using technical reporting channels to expose malfeasance.

Mass Supervision outside Official Channels The *People's Daily* articles examined above describe the official channels created to facilitate popular monitoring and criticism of cadres. The dynamics of mass supervision, however, extend beyond official channels. A wide variety of other avenues for grassroots complaints about cadre behavior have emerged, particularly in recent years. Among the most important are unofficial websites on which the masses vent frustration and anger about cadre corruption and abuse of power. One of these sites, 人民监督 (People's supervision), has become a particularly prominent magnet for exposing official misdeeds (and has recently been accused of blackmailing cadres).[28] The so-called 人肉搜索 (human-flesh search) campaigns, in which cyberactivists collectively dig up information about suspected wrongdoers, are part of this online trend.[29] The resulting scandals have become a highlight of Chinese political life. One indication of the extent to which the concept of the mass supervision continues to inform popular political thinking in China can be found in a manifesto issued by organizers of 'Jasmine' pro-democracy rallies in 2011, which featured as its main demand that the government 'genuinely fight corruption and accept the supervision of the people'.[30]

For the party leadership, unsanctioned mass supervision efforts are certainly a cause of concern, as they operate outside of party control and can easily get out of hand or become instruments of opposition and subversion. Nevertheless, they are tolerated to a certain extent because they perform an important function in controlling cadre behavior. It is clear that the CCP treats online denunciations of cadre transgressions as well as popular street protests (which have become a regular feature of Chinese life) as unofficial forms of mass supervision. Online denunciations often result in punishment, and in China's all-important cadre

[28] Jacobs, "Chinese Blogger." Also see Xinhua Net, "Zhu Ruifeng."
[29] Wang et al., "Human Flesh Search Engine."
[30] Organizers of the Jasmine Rallies, "Letter to the Chinese People."

evaluation system – which links career trajectories to quantifiable measures of success and failure – the number of 'mass incidents' (protests) in a cadre's jurisdiction is among the key criteria used to assess his or her performance.[31]

Bureaucratization of Mass Supervision and Governance

Mass supervision of cadres continues to be an important element in the CCP's model of governance, but it has changed dramatically since the Mao era. This change has been evident in the anti-corruption campaign launched by Xi Jinping in 2013. Although Xi has heightened the drama by bringing back rhetoric from the Mao years, both the form and the content of the campaign belong wholly to the current era. The masses have been called upon to participate, but there is little semblance of the mass movements of the past, when the entire population was mobilized and cadres were hauled before mass meetings in every village and factory. In contrast, the current campaign has been carried out largely by the Central Commission for Discipline and Inspection and supervision from below has mainly taken the form of individuals reporting abuses. Moreover, as in all recent campaigns that have targeted cadres, the focus is on corruption. The main preoccupation of the Mao era – the abuses of power identified as bureaucratism – are of little concern in the current campaign.

Thus, the nature of Xi's anti-corruption campaign exemplifies the two key shifts in mass supervision that we have documented in this essay. In terms of the form of mass participation, there has been a shift from face-to-face, collectivist methods to individual, technical methods; in terms of content, corruption has replaced bureaucratism as the leading target. The two shifts are connected and they both reflect a profound transformation in the way the CCP governs China. This transformation can be described as bureaucratization, in both the Weberian and the Chinese communist understandings of this term.

The changes in mass supervision have followed structural changes that have altered the social context in which it takes place. During the Mao era, the entire population was organized into rural production brigades and urban work units, which served as the main interface between state and society. These were strong communities based on permanent membership, and they fostered close personal ties between leaders and members that entailed mutual obligations. Governance took place through constant interaction between local party cadres and villagers or work unit members. The CCP endeavored to exercise control over the

---

[31] Minzer, "Riots and Cover-Ups."

members of production brigades and work units through its local agents, and at the same time the party sought to mobilize members of these communities to help it control these agents. Brigades and work units were tight-knit settings in which party cadres could monitor the populace, and by the same token these settings facilitated collective monitoring of cadres by their subordinates. Although nepotism and favoritism were among the targets of mass supervision, the overall aim was not to break down collective ties, but to strengthen them. The party employed collective forms of mass supervision – especially mass campaigns – based in production brigades and work units, because it wanted to strengthen these collective structures and make local cadres more accountable to the communities they were governing. Communist leaders were hardly Weber's rationalizing state elites intent on governing through impersonalized structures and cultivating agents without local entanglements and personal ties.

In contrast, since Mao died, the CCP has moved decisively in the direction that Weber would expect of modern state elites. The village production brigades and urban work units that had served as the interface between the state and the populace have been dismantled. Individuals are no longer members of government-organized collective entities and Chinese society is much more mobile. With regard to the CCP's conception of bureaucratism, the party's mode of governance has become far more distant. The ties between local leaders and their subordinates have become – for better or worse – much looser, more ephemeral, and more impersonal. Cadres and workers no longer live in work unit housing, but in scattered residences divided by income. Party cadres no longer lead semi-permanent collectivities, they administer enterprises and offices made up of individuals, and they are no longer expected to govern through face-to-face interaction and collective mobilization, but through enforcing rules by means of market-based and bureaucratic incentives and deterrents.

Separation has reduced the scope for mutual surveillance, giving both the masses and the cadres greater freedom. In the absence of production brigades and work units, social control has become more diffuse. Citizens are expected to comply with the country's laws, but although these laws multiply by the year, as does the police force, both are much thinner than the work unit-based norms and enforcement mechanisms of the past. And while the CCP is no longer as exacting in the demands it imposes on the masses, the same is true of its own cadres. Like ordinary citizens, cadres are expected to comply with the law (at least those laws that are enforced), but they are no longer burdened by the ascetic, egalitarian, and "mass line" norms of the past.

As the physical and social distance between the populace and government cadres has grown and the mechanisms of social control from above have become more bureaucratic and technical, the forms of mass supervision have followed pace. With the dissolution of government-organized collective entities, methods of mass supervision have of necessity become more individual and technical. The CCP no longer has the capacity to mobilize collective supervision over its cadres and does not attempt to do so. Endless meetings and disruptive mass movements are distant memories. Encouraging official transparency and individual reporting now seem more feasible and appropriate.

Nevertheless, the CCP continues to confront the same fundamental conundrum: to be effective, mass supervision requires a certain degree of autonomy. On the one hand, trying to maintain too much control stifles initiative from below; on the other hand, loosening the reins carries its own risks, which have been dramatically evidenced in different ways by the activities of rebel factions of the Cultural Revolution and today's cyberactivists.

In terms of the content of mass supervision, the party's previous preoccupation with bureaucratism has faded to the extent that it barely registers as an issue in the official press, while corruption has become the main target. This shift has in part been a response to growing opportunities for official malfeasance, but it also reflects the more distant mode of governance adopted by the CCP. The problems associated with bureaucratism – cadre arrogance, authoritarian behavior, and isolation from the masses – certainly have not disappeared, but because the CCP has adopted methods of governance that do not depend as much on "cadres–masses relations," these are no longer seen as pressing issues. With the shift to bureaucratic methods of governance, bureaucratism is no longer considered to be a cause of great concern.

While this essay has focused exclusively on efforts to enlist supervision of cadres from below, a broader investigation into the evolution of CCP endeavors to monitor and control its cadres would undoubtedly reinforce our main conclusions. In the party's overall cadre supervision scheme, the relative weight of supervision from below has certainly declined, while the importance of supervision from above – as embodied in the Ministry of Supervision, the Central Commission for Discipline Inspection, and other organs of bureaucratic control – has greatly increased. The overall picture is of a governing party that is increasingly bureaucratic, in the Weberian sense of centralization, rationalization, individualization, and professionalization, as well as in the communist sense of isolation from the masses. A profound irony contained in the evolution of mass supervision is that a practice originally designed to combat bureaucratism has by now been transformed into a rationalized instrument of a highly bureaucratic regime.

References

Andreas, Joel. *Rise of the Red Engineers: The Cultural Revolution and the Origins of China's New Class.* Stanford: Stanford University Press, 2009.

Andreas, Joel. "The Structure of Charismatic Mobilization: A Case Study of Rebellion during the Chinese Cultural Revolution," *American Sociological Review*, 72, 3: 2007, 434–458.

Andrle, Vladimir. *Workers in Stalin's Russia: Industrialization and Social Change in a Planned Economy.* New York: St. Martin's Press, 1988.

Baum, Richard. *Prelude to Revolution: Mao, the Party, and the Peasant Question, 1962–1966.* New York: Columbia University Press, 1975.

Chan, Anita, Madsen, Richard, and Unger, Jonathan. *Chen Village: Revolution and Globalization.* Berkeley: University of California Press, 2009.

Chase, William. *Workers, Society, and the Soviet State: Labor and Life in Moscow, 1918–1929.* Urbana: University of Illinois Press, 1987.

Chen, Xi. *Social Protest and Contentious Authoritarianism in China.* Cambridge: Cambridge University Press, 2012.

Dickson, Bruce. "Dilemmas of Party Adaptation: The CCP's Strategies for Survival," in Gries and Rosen, eds., *Chinese Politics*, 22–40.

Dittmer, Lowell. *China's Continuous Revolution: The Post-Liberation Epoch 1949–1981.* Berkeley: University of California Press, 1987.

Edin, Maria. "State Capacity and Local Agent Control in China: CCP Cadre Management from a Township Perspective," *China Quarterly*, 173: 2003, 35–52.

Fang, Qiang. *Chinese Complaint Systems: Natural Resistance.* New York: Routledge, 2013.

Fitzpatrick, Sheila. "Workers against Bosses: The Impact of the Great Purges on Labor-Management Relations," in Siegelbaum and Suny, eds., *Making Workers Soviet*, 311–340.

Gong, Ting. "The Party Discipline Inspection in China: Its Evolving Trajectory and Embodied Dilemmas," *Crime, Law and Social Change*, 49: 2008, 139–152.

Granick, David. *Management of the Industrial Firm in the USSR: A Study in Soviet Economic Planning.* New York: Columbia University Press, 1954.

Gries, Peter Hays and Rosen, Stanley, eds. *Chinese Politics: State, Society, and the Market.* New York and London: Routledge, 2010.

Harding, Harry. *Organizing China: The Problem of Bureaucracy, 1949–1976.* Stanford: Stanford University Press, 1981.

He Guanghua (贺广华). ("An Example of Liberation of Thinking in a Central Province: Emerging from Administrative Change in Hunan"). "一个中部省份的思想解放样本–湖南，从行政方式改起," 人民日报, 11月14日: 2008.

He Qin (何芹). ("The Processes, Patterns, and Experiences of Mass Supervision during the Past Six Decades of New China"). "新中国60年来群众监督的历程、趋势和经验," 探索, 5: 2009, 66–71.

Hinton, William. *Fanshen: A Documentary of Revolution in a Chinese Village*. New York: Vintage Books, 1966.

Hou Yong (侯永). ("Weapon against Bureaucratism"). "克服'官僚主义'的武器," 人民日报, 8月20日: 1950.

Huang, Yasheng. "Administrative Monitoring in China," *China Quarterly*, 143: 1995, 828–843.

Huang Yihua (黄义华) and Hu Shuyan (胡淑燕). ("The Party's Theory on Mass Supervision since the Establishment of New China"). "试论新中国成立以来党的群众监督思想," *中共南昌市委党校学报*, 8, 3: 2010, 23–26.

Jacobs, Andrew. "Chinese Blogger Thrives as Muckraker," *New York Times*, February 5, 2013, at www.nytimes.com/2013/02/06/world/asia/chinese-blogger-thrives-in-role-of-muckraker.html?pagewanted=all&_r=0.

Ji Yaguang (纪亚光). ("An Experiment in Institutionalizing Mass Supervision: The People's Inspector in the 1950s"). "群众监督的制度化尝试 – 20世纪50年代人民监察通讯员制度探析," *理论学刊*, 188: 2009, 85–89.

Li, Fangchun. "Mass Democracy, Class Struggle, and Remolding the Party and Government during the Land Reform Movement in North China," *Modern China*, 38, 4: 2012, 411–445.

Lieberthal, Kenneth. *Revolution and Tradition in Tientsin, 1949–1952*. Stanford: Stanford University Press, 1980.

Lü, Xiaobo. *Cadres and Corruption: The Organizational Involution of the Chinese Communist Party*. Stanford: Stanford University Press, 2000.

Luehrmann, Laura. "Facing Citizen Complaints in China, 1951–1996," *Asian Survey*, 43, 5: 2003, 845–866.

Lupher, Mark. *Power Restructuring in China and Russia*. Boulder: Westview Press, 1996.

MacFarquhar, Roderick. *The Hundred Flowers*. London: Stevens and Sons, 1960.

Manion, Melanie. *Corruption by Design: Building Clean Government in Mainland China and Hong Kong*. Cambridge, MA: Harvard University Press, 2004.

Miller, Alice. "The Road to the Third Plenum," *China Leadership Monitor*, 42: 2013, at www.hoover.org/sites/default/files/research/docs/clm42am-2013.pdf.

Minzer, Carl. "Riots and Cover-Ups: Counterproductive Control of Local Agents in China," *University of Pennsylvania Journal of International Law*, 53: 2009, at http://scholarship.law.upenn.edu/jil/vol31/iss1/2.

Mo Jiwu (莫吉武). (*The Political Supervision System in Contemporary China*). 当代中国政治监督体制研究. 北京：中国社会科学出版社, 2002.

Moses, Russell Leigh. "What to Make of Xi Jinping's Maoist Turn," *Wall Street Journal*, June 21, 2013, at http://blogs.wsj.com/chinarealtime/2013/06/21/what-to-make-of-xi-jinpings-maoist-turn/.

O'Brien, Kevin and Li, Lianjiang. "Campaign Nostalgia in the Chinese Countryside," *Asian Survey*, 39, 3: 1999, 375–393.

Ocko, Jonathan. "I'll Take It All the Way to Beijing: Capital Appeals in the *Qing*," *Journal of Asian Studies*, 47, 2: 1988, 291–315.

Organizers of the Jasmine Rallies. ("Open Letter to the Chinese People from the Organizers of the Chinese Jasmine Rallies.") "中国茉莉花集会组织者 致全国人民公开信," *博讯网*, 2月23日 2011. Available at www.boxun.com/news/gb/china/2011/02/201102230351.shtml.

Perry, Elizabeth. "Chinese Conceptions of "Rights': From Mencius to Mao – and Now," *Perspectives on Politics*, 1: 2008, 37–50.

Perry, Elizabeth and Li, Xun. *Proletarian Power: Shanghai in the Cultural Revolution*. Boulder: Westview Press, 1997.

Roney, Tyler. "Xi's Mass Line Campaign Casts a Dark Shadow over China," *The Diplomat*, October 2, 2013, at thediplomat.com/china-power/xis-mass-line-ca mpaign-casts-a-dark-shadow-over-china/.

Schurmann, Franz. *Ideology and Organization in Communist China*. Berkeley: University of California Press, 1968.

Shi, Tianjian. *Political Participation in Beijing*. Cambridge, MA: Harvard University Press, 1997.

Shue, Vivienne. *The Reach of the State: Sketches of the Chinese Body Politic*. Stanford: Stanford University Press, 1988.

Siegelbaum, Lewis and Suny, Ronald Grigor, eds. *Making Workers Soviet: Power, Class and Identity*. Ithaca, NY: Cornell University Press, 1994.

Sullivan, Lawrence. "The Role of the Control Organs in the Chinese Communist Party, 1977–1983," *Asian Survey*, 24, 6: 1984, 597–617.

Teiwes, Frederick. *Politics and Purges in China: Rectification and the Decline of Party Norms, 1950–1965*. Armonk: M. E. Sharpe, 1993.

Teng Daiyuan (滕代远). ("Root out Bureaucratic Work Styles in the Railroad System"). "铲除铁路系统中的官僚主义作风," 人民日报, 5月6日: 1950.

Walder, Andrew. *Communist Neo-Traditionalism: Work and Authority in Chinese Industry*. Berkeley: University of California Press, 1986.

Wang, Fei-Yue, Zeng, Daniel, Hendler, James, Zhang, Qingpeng, Feng, Zhuo, Gao, Yanqing, Wang, Hui, and Lai, Guanpi. "A Study of the Human Flesh Search Engine: Crowd-Powered Expansion of Online Knowledge," *Computer*, 43, 8: 2010, 45–53.

Wang Zaoshi (王造时). ("Our Democratic Life Will Be Better and Happier: On Anti-bureaucratism, Mutual Supervision, and Expanding Democratic Life"). "我们的民主生活一定日趋丰富美满: 王造时谈克服官僚主义、进行互相监督与扩大民主生活的问题," 人民日报, 3月20日: 1957.

Wedeman, Andrew. "The Intensification of Corruption in China," *China Quarterly*, 180: 2004, 895–921.

Xi Jinping (习近平). ("Xi Jinping: Fully Mobilize the Enthusiasm of the Cadres and the Masses; Ensure that Education, Practices, and Activities Are Carried out in a Sound Way"). "习近平: 充分调动干部和群众积极性保证教育实践活动善做善成," 新华网, 7月15日 2013. Available at www.gs.xinhuanet.com/zuz hibu/2013–07/15/c_116542725.htm.

Yang Rong (杨荣). ("A Comparative Study about Thoughts on Mass Supervision of the Three Generations of Chinese Leadership"). "中国三代领导人群众监督思想的比较研究," 科学社会主义, 5: 2010, 139–141.

Young, Graham. "Control and Style: Discipline Inspection Commissions since the 11th Congress," *China Quarterly*, 97: 1984, 24–52.

Zhang Hua (张华) and Wang Nengchang (王能昌). ("Mass Supervision during China's Social Transformation"). "论我国转型社会中的群众监督," 求实, 1: 2004, 57–58.

Zhao Ziyang (赵紫阳). ("How Do We Begin Building a Clean Political System? Transparent Institutions, Transparent Results, Relying on Mass Supervision: At a Conference Zhao Ziyang and Others Affirm the Experience of Pilot Site Work Units"). "廉政制度建设从何入手？公开办事制度、公开办事结果、依靠群众监督: 赵紫阳等在座谈会上肯定试点单位经验," 人民日报, 2月17日: 1989.

"Zhu Ruifeng: Six Out of Seven of the Sex Videos Were from the Chongqing Police." "朱瑞峰: 7段不雅视频中6段由重庆警方内部线人提供," 新华网, 1月30日 2013. Available at news.xinhuanet.com/local/2013–01/30/c_124296437.htm.

Overlooking

5 Shared Fictions and Informal Politics in China

Robert P. Weller

There is an old saying in Chinese: "hanging up a sheep's head but selling dog meat" (挂羊头卖狗肉). It describes a butcher's shop that advertises high-quality mutton by displaying the sheep's head, but customers actually get only dog, a much less respectable meat. It most commonly simply refers to false advertising, but a more interesting reading recognizes that this is an unusual kind of falsehood because the customer must know as well as the butcher that the meat is only dog. Why would the customer go to such a shop? It appeals because consumers do not want to be seen buying dog, even though it may be just what they hunger for, or perhaps all they can afford.[1] Both butcher and buyer gain by sharing the fiction of the sheep's head.

I will argue here that similar subjunctive worlds – shared fictions, lies not intended to deceive – constitute an important mechanism of governance, one which currently plays a large role in China's informal politics. I will draw examples from many aspects of contemporary Chinese life to try to clarify how this works, but let me begin with just a single anecdote. I visited the Longquan Monastery in suburban Beijing in 2009 and spoke to one of the senior monks about the activities of their charitable non-governmental organization (NGO), the Ren Ai Charitable Foundation (仁爱慈善基金会), during the 2008 Wenchuan earthquake.[2] Like many religious groups, they had been quick to mobilize money and manpower, and he said they had a strong presence during the relief effort. I asked how this was possible, because as a religious group they are not legally permitted to run an NGO.[3] The answer was simple, he explained. They just asked some lay followers to register directly with the Civil Affairs Bureau, so that on paper there was no religious connection at all. In the eyes of the

---

[1] I am by no means the first to offer this reading of the phrase. See, for instance, Hu Ping, "Absurd China."

[2] I am grateful to Sun Yanfei, who joined me on this interview.

[3] The relevant regulations changed, to some extent, three years after this interview, in 2012.

officials this was a purely lay organization. He said this with a bit of a grin at the cleverness of the strategy. He added that when the NGO's volunteers were in Sichuan, none of them could legally wear Buddhist dress, but that they made sure some monks were always right beside them so that everyone could recognize their affiliation.

Surely no one at all was duped by this.[4] The Longquan Monastery is controlled by the Venerable Xuecheng, a Vice-President of the official Buddhist Association. There are very few Buddhist leaders more closely tied to the state. The monastery's website (www.longquanzs.org) and that of the NGO (www.chrenai.com) make extensive reference to each other and to Ven. Xuecheng, making the connection as obvious as when robed monks walked next to volunteers from an allegedly non-religious NGO. This example has the three primary markers of sheep's-head governance:

1. There is a clearly stated rule, in this case the regulation that religious organizations can only carry out religious activities and cannot create NGOs.
2. The state (in this case the Beijing Civil Affairs office) turns a blind eye as the law is ignored.
3. In exchange, the local people (in this case the followers of Ven. Xuecheng) agree to maintain the fiction that they are acting within the law. They do not, for example, challenge state authority by trying to register directly as a religious NGO.

Such things have long been noted in a scattered way in the literature on China. When they are taken seriously, authors usually discuss them within a discourse of resistance and accommodation or in the related Chinese terms of every official policy being met by counter-strategies from below (上有政策, 下有对策). Such things are undoubtedly important in China, as elsewhere, but neither resistance nor accommodation captures the dynamic of these interactions very well. Establishing a misleading registration for an NGO is not resistance in the sense of attempting to change the system or challenging its rules. Yet it is also no simple accommodation because it undercuts the very rules that it claims to accept.

Guosheng Deng, who has written on exactly this kind of misleading NGO registration practice, interprets it as obedience to a set of "hidden rules" that differ from the open rules of laws and regulations, but which are just as widely shared and known and which allow the state informal

---

[4] This is the same group discussed in McCarthy, "Serving Society, Repurposing the State." Note, however, that my interpretation is not the same as hers, which views this group as offering a form of resistance through "repurposing." The vocabulary of resistance, as discussed below, is too dichotomous to capture the complex relationship I see evolving.

influence over the NGOs.[5] My approach is close to his, but recognizes that these sorts of informal political arrangements are much more open to improvisation, reinterpretation, and abrogation than any set of rules, hidden or not. If there is a rule of any kind here, it is something like the ruler that Aristotle describes being used by builders in Lesbos. It was made of lead, which the carpenters could bend and flex to match their needs of the moment.[6] That is, I see this form of governing by turning a blind eye as fundamentally contextual rather than rule-governed.

Rather than turn to either the idea of resistance/accommodation or of rules, it may be more useful to think of these techniques as a sort of shared subjunctive world.[7] I am thinking primarily of some anthropological discussions of other arenas in which we lie with no intention to deceive. At the simplest level, we can see this in much of everyday etiquette. In the United States, for instance, we always answer a colleague's "How are you?" with "I'm fine." It makes no difference if you have a headache or just had a fight with your daughter. You are always "fine" because any other response breaches the etiquette. It may be a literal lie, but no one is deceived because the intent of the question was never to determine your internal state, but instead just to recognize a social relationship. In the very different etiquette of rural Taiwan, the standard greeting to a neighbor is "Have you eaten?" and the response is always "Yes, I'm full." This is also often false, but dismissing it as a lie fails to recognize its crucial social function. Truth and falsehood are not particularly important in such interactions. Instead, they reflect shared social conventions that allow us to recognize each other as colleagues and neighbors. When I ask my son "please" to clean his room, I also create a shared social world in which he is imagined as a socially autonomous equal who has the right to say no. Much American etiquette reinforces this logic even though it may also be false – my child is not an autonomous equal, and as subsequent yelling will establish, does not really have the right to say no. Courtesies like this create a subjunctive world whose existence depends on our joint willingness to keep the fiction alive.

Most ritual works in just the same way.[8] Taking part in it need not imply anything about accepting truth or even believing in anything (although such things are quite important in some traditions). We never in fact know what people believe. By taking part in such actions, however,

[5] Deng, "The Hidden Rules."
[6] Aristotle, *Nichomachean Ethics*, book 5, chapter 10, 1137b27–31.
[7] For a recent consideration of similar issues, but which looks instead from the angle of signalling, see Stern and O'Brien, "Politics at the Boundary."
[8] This idea of subjunctive worlds, especially in the context of ritual, is developed much further in Seligman et al., *Ritual and Its Consequences*.

people are accepting the conventions that establish those rituals – that is the key to creating subjunctive worlds, which exist only "as if" they were true. Hanging up a sheep's head and selling dog meat is just such a subjunctive, one that lets everyone act "as if" they were buying and selling mutton, just as etiquette allows everyone to imagine themselves as if they were fine, or equal, or full. Something similar, I hope to suggest, occurs when religious NGOs register as if they were secular. Everyone accepts the fiction of a corporatist management system where social needs are tuned to harmonize with the one-party-state while at the same time getting on with a much more complex and pragmatic process on the ground. This is something like what Lisa Wedeen observed about the Hafiz al-Asad regime in Syria, which she describes as orienting Syrians "by providing guidelines for proper public speech and conduct. People are not required to believe the cult's fictions, and they do not, but they are required to act as if they did ... [T]he cult's 'politics of as if' enforces obedience, induces complicity, and structures the terms of both compliance and resistance."[9] The key is not belief or sincerity, but instead nominal acceptance of convention.

My approach here is similar to Hans Steinmüller's recent discussion of what he calls "communities of complicity" – networks that tie local people and officials together in activity that they all recognize as appropriate but that flies in the face of national pronouncements.[10] He argues that there is thus a large gap separating the world of national regulation and media statements from the intimacies of local life. He is drawing here on the influential work of the anthropologist Michael Herzfeld, whose idea of "cultural intimacy" gets at just these areas where everyone knows their behavior is somehow inappropriate by national or international or just public standards, but everyone accepts it anyway.[11] As Steinmüller describes it, "the boundaries between state and society are made by exposing and hiding spaces of cultural intimacy; and this everyday practice reproduces both local sociality and the state itself."[12] I would differ from him only in suggesting that such techniques are by no means limited to the local, but can have powerful effects even at the level of the nation.

Some Examples

Let me run briefly through a range of examples that might usefully be seen as forms of governing by turning a blind eye in contemporary China. I will

[9] Wedeen, *Ambiguities of Domination*, 30.
[10] Steinmüller, "Communities of Complicity."   [11] Herzfeld, *Cultural Intimacy*.
[12] Steinmüller, "Communities of Complicity," 548.

begin with some resources provided directly by the state, and move on to issues of the management of social institutions, especially NGOs and religious groups. In addition to some of my own work, I will draw on a wide range of secondary sources, because this kind of arrangement has frequently been noticed, although scholars have been less quick to generalize about it.

I will start with a story from rural Guizhou, where I was consulting on poverty relief for the World Bank in 1999. I was looking, among other things, at educational opportunities for minority students. I had just spent a warm morning in a Miao village high in the hills listening to people complain about schools that were far away and whose fees were impossibly high.[13] Several families expressed particular frustration over one bright child, an excellent student they all said, who had to drop out of high school because no one had the few hundred RMB that he needed to continue. My Chinese counterpart and I then headed down into the valley to interview the principal of the elementary school. Given how few Miao children were in school, I started by asking him the percentage of school-age students who were actually enrolled, and was surprised when he told me it was about 98 percent. This was indeed the figure reflected in the statistical information posted on his office wall, and represented what he reported to his superiors. My Chinese counterpart was angry, though, saying: "Tell the truth! This is important. Millions of dollars are at stake; Guizhou's development is at stake."

The principal was flustered, but he explained that 98 percent was not exactly untrue. Nearly every school-age child comes to school on the first day of class – everyone knows that the law requires their children to enroll. After a few days, however, when the school starts collecting fees, many children stop coming. The children's families enroll them to be in nominal accord with the law, and the school has little to gain from trying to force regular attendance. Everyone is thus happy enough with the fiction that coming to the first few days of class counts as if they were in school.

Something similar was occurring with the odd gender ratios I noticed in the school's official data. First grade was fairly balanced and so was fifth grade (the final year at the time). Boys, however, greatly outnumbered girls in all other classes. He explained that many of those who attend only occasionally are girls, because their parents are less willing to spend the school fees, to release them from chores at home, and to send them on the long journey to school. The teachers feel these students do not know enough to pass beyond first grade, but for students who keep coming back

---

[13] Preferential policies for minorities meant that schools could not charge their children for tuition, but they made up for it with all kinds of miscellaneous fees.

each year, the teachers eventually feel embarrassed about having such old first-graders, and allow them to move through the system. They get stuck again at fifth grade because teachers feel they cannot be awarded diplomas. This entire highly gendered dynamic, however, is hidden by the statistical summary.

Are higher-level education officials also party to these fictions of enrollments and gender? I have no direct evidence, but it seems most likely that education officials at the township and county level know exactly what is going on. Many such local officials came from the relevant schools, although knowledge of this particular maneuver may fade out as such "sheep's head" data work their way up toward national statistics.

Many ethnographic studies of local politics show related maneuvers. Two very different studies of villages in the early 1980s – Hinton and Gordon's films about Long Bow village in Shanxi and Huang Shu-min's study of Lin Village in Fujian – show village leaders unwilling to give up relatively successful collective economies, and thus continuously dragging their feet on the introduction of the agricultural responsibility system even after all communities had been ordered to carry out the reforms.[14] Both leaders also speak of the importance of a sort of tricky cleverness in dealing with officials as they worked to build up their villages' collective economies. The Long Bow leader, for example, cites his desire to build a cement factory because he saw a strong market opportunity. Knowing the government would say no, though, he requested instead to build a phosphate fertilizer plant. He knew that Long Bow would soon exhaust the raw materials that would allow it to make fertilizer, but he was confident that officials would approve because farmers need fertilizer. He knew also that he could easily convert the factory to produce cement later, and that the officials would not complain at that point. He describes this as a trick, but it seems highly unlikely that anyone is fooled. Local officials at the township/brigade level, and to some extent at the county/commune level, are usually natives of the villages they control. Such maneuvers are thus not really deceptions, but rather part of governance with a wink and a nudge.

This kind of process has not been at all uncommon, and it was followed in the 1980s by the massive registration of private businesses as if they were township and village enterprises (挂靠). This took advantage of tax breaks for communal organizations, and provided political protection at a time when there was still some discomfort with something that looked all too close to capitalism. As Unger and Chan document for one township, this subjunctive arrangement lasted for just over a decade, until a

---

[14] Hinton and Gordon, *All under Heaven*; Huang, *The Spiral Road*.

combination of new factors made it less attractive: the tax law changed, higher levels of government were thought to be more likely to enforce existing rules, and companies concluded there would be less red tape if they were fully private.[15] While it lasted, however, this system fostered a massive tacit bargain to allow such a major warping of the legal framework.

Very high numbers of false registrations continue to characterize other sectors, including the world of NGOs. China's basic legal framework for dealing with NGOs is corporatist – it allows for one organization to represent each social sector. In principle, the organization trades its autonomy for a monopoly on representing those interests. While even the most nominally independent groups had ceased operation during the Cultural Revolution, the reform period created a new space for NGOs, and they grew rapidly beginning in the 1980s, and even faster after Chinese saw the broad international NGO participation in the United Nations World Conference on Women in 1995. Right from the beginning, however, the corporatist goals and structures were compromised.

Friends of Nature, for instance, which is often cited as the first genuine environmental NGO (that is, not a direct government creation), was unable to register with the Environmental Protection Ministry because the Ministry had already granted the single slot for a national environmental organization to a tame group of their own. After several other unsuccessful attempts, Friends of Nature finally managed to register in 1994 with the Academy of Chinese Culture. Liang Congjie, the founder, had no particular interest in Chinese environmental culture. He simply found a place willing to let him hang his hat. The arrangement allowed the group to earn some national prominence, but it also undercut the corporatist spirit of the regulations.[16]

They were not alone. The Ministry of Civil Affairs had registered 354,000 NGOs by the end of 2006, for instance, but the World Bank estimated that there were in fact well over a million already in 2004, and the number has only grown since then. Even among those officially registered groups, many are just like Friends of Nature in that their supervising government unit is really just a flag of convenience. Similarly, many of the "missing" NGOs are in fact legally registered, but they have chosen to register as for-profit corporations because the procedure is so much easier. That is, of well over a million such organizations in this booming and politically important sector, we can guess that very roughly 60–70 percent, perhaps even more, are extra-legal in the

---

[15] Unger and Chan, "Inheritors of the Boom."   [16] Weller, *Discovering Nature*.

sense that they have not registered, registered falsely as for-profit companies, or registered improperly with inappropriate sponsors.[17]

The Ren Ai Charitable Foundation, with which I began, is an example of just this kind. Just as I argued in their case, a very large number of these extra-legal NGOs are neither actively resisting the registration system nor trying to change it. And just like Ren Ai, they are not fooling anyone with these maneuvers. Friends of Nature, for example, is a prominent group, well known among high officials who surely know its registration status perfectly well. At the local level, while central authorities may be unaware of the status of organizations, local officials typically do know. As Wu Keping has documented, for instance, several non-profit old age homes in Changzhou (Jiangsu) had direct links to Buddhist or Christian groups.[18] This is again not legal and like Ren Ai, they registered as purely civil associations, but their actions and motivations were nevertheless grounded in religion.

On paper, at least, religious groups and NGOs are governed quite differently from each other. All Chinese religions were organized into five national organizations in the 1950s – one each for Buddhists, Daoists, Muslims, Protestants, and Catholics. There was no legal room for anything else. There could thus be no Jews, Mormons, Hindus, or even Confucians. Village temple worship was simply superstitious and backward, and not counted as religion at all. This system was rebuilt after the Cultural Revolution and continues to provide the legal framework for religion today.

This system had serious problems from the beginning, including its rejection by large numbers of Catholics and Protestants who organized their own underground churches instead, and its subversion by the continued practice of village religion and the continuation of many kinds of "heterodoxies." With the greatly increased social space during the reform period, there has been a huge growth in the practice of religion, and the majority has taken place in the gray zone outside of the five legal religious organizations. Numbers are even harder to estimate than for NGOs, but no one doubts that the clear majority of Christians are in unregistered churches, that the most actively growing Buddhist influences are lay organizations and followers of the monk Chin Kong (both outside the official Buddhist Association), and that the descendants of older religious redemptive societies also number in the millions.[19] As a guess, perhaps

---

[17] This is consistent with Hildebrandt's survey showing 59 percent of NGOs are unregistered; he does not break out inappropriately registered groups. Hildebrandt, "The Political Economy," 975.

[18] Personal communication, May 2015.

[19] For more detail, see Weller and Sun, "Religion: The Dynamics of Religious Growth."

60–70 percent of religious activity takes place in the extra-legal gray zone beyond the supervision of the five religious associations.[20] That is, such groups are a large majority constituting very roughly the same proportion of the field as extra-legal NGOs.

In some cases, we can see the process through which decisions about registering village temples get made. Fang Ling, for example, analyzes a temple in Hangzhou that tried unsuccessfully to register with the Daoist Association, and later tried the Buddhist Association instead, after first painting its front wall with huge characters reading "In the Name of Amidha Buddha" (南无阿弥陀弗). When that also failed, they decided just to remain unregistered.[21] Adam Chau similarly documents the long struggle of a Shaanxi temple to get registered with the Daoist Association. They finally succeeded, but only because the temple had been so entrepreneurial about bringing benefits to the community and praise to the local officials. They built a village school, for instance, and brought in NGO support from both Beijing and Japan to construct an arboretum.[22]

Gao Bingzhong has documented what he calls "double naming" at a temple in rural Hebei.[23] The local elders raised money for the project by telling the villagers that they would construct a temple to honor the "dragon board" that they had long worshiped. They told local government officials that they intended to build a "museum of dragon culture." The building itself bears one plaque for each identity, flanking either side of its main entrance. In a very similar way, a huge and ornate lineage hall in rural Wenzhou (also extra-legal) bears a plaque identifying it as the local Old People's Association (老人协会). These are very clear examples of hanging a sheep's head. Both local officials and villagers know exactly what these buildings are intended for and how they are used. At their least successful, these maneuvers allow local officials to save face and to be able to deny knowing what was happening if necessary. At best, officials can claim credit for the construction of museums, arboreta, and old people's associations while keeping the local population satisfied and to some extent governing itself.

We saw this again with the early reconstruction of religious pilgrimage in Fujian, as Taiwanese temples began to visit their temples of origin on the mainland. Local officials tended to look the other way because they saw the promise of future business investment in their community from Taiwan, and in some cases were able to extract promises of medical clinics

[20] See Wu, "Religious Believers," for a 2006 survey that found about 31 percent of the population described themselves as religious; roughly triple the official figure at the time.
[21] Paper presented at the Workshop on Religion in the Lower Yangzi Region, Shanghai, 2013.
[22] Chau, *Miraculous Response.*   [23] Gao Bingzhong, "An Ethnography of a Building."

or other public services.[24] In another region, we know of a Hong Kong medium who founds temples across southern China. According to Liu Tik-sang, her followers contact local officials in advance, who make sure they will be out of town when the shaman visits to open each temple.[25]

Hans Steinmüller adds several examples from ritual life rather than temple construction. He gives one case, for instance, of a very large and elaborate funeral held for the father of a county-level official in Hubei. The sheep's head in this case was the enactment of appropriate ritual behavior and expression of filial piety. The dog's meat was the enormous expense and the rumors of even more enormous gifts given to the family by people attending. Such a tension is inherent in the nature of rural funerals like this for both officials and locals. Steinmüller thus sees no important opposition in these dynamics between people and state. Instead, he identifies an opposition between "an official, outside representation and a vernacular, inside practice."[26] A public discourse thus plasters over a practice that lies just beneath the surface.

The situation with Christian house churches has sometimes been more fraught and embattled than these cases of village temple religion. In some cases, house churches have refused the bargain of this form of governance, unwilling to accept the hypocrisies that it entails. There are not many of these cases, but they have achieved a great deal of publicity, as in the recent uproar over the displacement of Beijing's Shouwang Church from its worship place, and the group's insistence on continuing worship outside and in public. Such actions are intended to pressure the state into a fundamental change in its management structures for religious groups (and by extension for all social organizations), but in fact many other house churches have criticized them for rocking the boat and increasing the pressure on everyone. That is, most house churches have found ways of living with the hypocrisy of the system, as the official system usually lives with them. Many cities now boast "underground" unregistered house churches that in fact occupy large buildings with a cross on the outside and hundreds of people who show up to worship every Sunday. Shouwang Church really is involved in a form of resistance – an active attempt to change the system – but most other house churches have adopted a different strategy. Perhaps the Chinese metaphor of governing with one eye open and one eye closed (睁一只眼，闭一只眼) is more accurate than the English one of turning a blind eye.

---

[24] For an example of some of the issues involved in the early 1980s renewal of such rituals in the region, see Dean, *Taoist Ritual and Popular Cults.*
[25] Liu, "Associating Local Traditions with the State Apparatus."
[26] Steinmüller, "Communities of Complicity."

When I interviewed a recently retired official of the United Front Department, which is the Communist Party office responsible for religion, she spoke of having visited a large number of churches in the recent past.[27] Somewhat freed by her retirement, she said she had open discussions with the local Christians about registration status. She had spent much of the last two decades as a party official worrying about unregistered churches, but in fact most people seemed not to care. In many cases, she reported, people did not even know if their church was affiliated with the official Protestant organization or not. This supports the idea that a kind of extra-legal equilibrium has been reached in most places, even though the laws remain unchanged. On an even more public scale, we can see something similar in Wenzhou, which has an unusually high proportion of Christians, and where some prominent and wealthy Christian entrepreneurs have become Communist Party members. This is also illegal, but dissatisfied people who reported the abuse to party authorities were apparently told that no one cared.[28]

Why?

While many observers have documented the results of governing with one eye closed, there has not been much systematic analysis of why we see this so frequently and in so many different aspects of life in contemporary China. A few recent articles on NGOs have begun to address the significance of the massive numbers of apparent scofflaw organizations. Anthony Spires, for instance, quotes an NGO leader on how she negotiates the gray area in her relations to the government: "In China, if the government doesn't say 'no,' you can experiment and understand their failure to say 'no' to mean 'yes,' or you can say 'I thought since you didn't say no, I could do this.' That's the way things work here. So we do take some risks here in our work."[29] Spires sees these maneuvers as evidence of a successful authoritarian adaptation, in spite of the surface appearance of a failure of corporatist state policy. The constant threat of suppression, he argues, encourages such groups to limit their democratic claims and to act generally in support of the state's welfare goals.

Timothy Hildebrandt is one of the few recent writers who directly address the problem of the massive numbers of unregistered NGOs. For him, three factors lead local officials and NGO leaders to pursue such a strategy.[30] First, officials increasingly rely on NGOs to provide

---

[27] This took place in Shanghai, August 2011.   [28] Cao, *Constructing China's Jerusalem*.
[29] Quoted in Spires, "Contingent Symbiosis and Civil Society," 23.
[30] Hildebrandt, "The Political Economy."

important services, but the corporatist regulatory system would vastly limit their numbers, and so officials are encouraged to look the other way. Second, just as in Spires' analysis, unregistered groups are easy to suppress, and therefore tend to be more pliable and cautious. Third, for those groups able to bring in significant foreign funding, the money must flow through a government agent, providing opportunities to profit. This is not the case for registered organizations.

The first two of his factors seem just as relevant for misleading school entrance rates, unregistered religious groups, or any of the other examples I have cited as they are for NGOs. They show how the benefits of creating these subjunctive worlds can outweigh the very real risks (to both officials and citizens) of enforcing the letter of the law by shutting down social groups, razing temples and churches, and arresting officials for corruption and collusion – all of which happen regularly. By accepting the deal, members of society gain a limited ability to organize independently to pursue their own goals, from worshiping gods to striving for clean water supplies. They also benefit directly from the politics of hypocrisy when it successfully delivers needed social goods (like the Christian or Buddhist old age homes), emergency relief (like Ren Ai and many other groups after the Wenchuan earthquake), economic benefits (like falsely registered "collective" township and village enterprises), or just entertainment (like temple festivals). Officials benefit too when their populations are less restive and better served with social goods, and when their monitoring costs are lower. If they can leverage these arrangements into museums, botanical gardens, schools, or medical clinics, they are even better off in their careers. Even when social organizations are more annoying, as when they monitor pollution from an income-generating factory, officials still gain an independent information source that may help them respond early and effectively to potentially career-damaging problems like social unrest.

If the benefits of turning a blind eye often outweigh the costs, however, it raises a new question: why not simply change the laws and regulations to gain the same benefits, decrease the risks, and avoid a form of governance that relies on hypocrisy and scofflaws? Why not end the corporatist fiction behind NGO registration and abolish the monopoly of the five religious associations, for instance? This is, after all, more or less what happened with private companies falsely registered as collectives, as government rule changes lowered the tax benefits of being a collective and removed many of the risks of being a private enterprise.

It is always difficult to determine why something does not happen, but let me suggest some possible motivations. To begin with, legal and regulatory systems have purposes that can go well beyond regulating behavior by making clear rules. Most relevant to the cases under discussion here, law can also serve as a public statement of ideals and moral goals, even when no one expects real behavior to live up to those ideals. One obvious case is the law governing prostitution in countries like the United States, which bans the practice everywhere, but in fact tolerates it within generally unspoken limits. No politician dares to take a moral stand in defense of prostitution, and the tacit agreement in the United States is that on this issue, hypocrisy is a better choice than either legalization or strict enforcement.

If we understand much of Chinese law as a statement of how things ought to be in an ideal world, rather than how the state will force them to be in this world, the techniques of governing with a blind eye make more sense. China after the Cultural Revolution built the legal structures of a corporatist relationship between state and society, and the government has maintained that image against alternative possibilities. Nevertheless, the state recognizes that it may in fact govern more effectively by having a flexible relationship between state and society in practice, giving it a repertoire of techniques of governance that includes closing an eye. Thus, for example, the government insists in principle that religious groups should only conduct religious activities for adult believers (and thus ideally with no broad philanthropies and none of the very common religious summer camps and retreats aimed at children), and that they act only as parts of large and closely supervised institutions. Yet it accepts a completely different situation on the ground.

Above all, patrolling the state/society boundary with one eye closed allows China to retain the fundamental ideological claims and formal institutions of a one-party, authoritarian regime where the state incorporates a full range of social interests made fully harmonious with the state's needs through mechanisms like the legal NGOs imagined in the law or the older mechanisms of the United Front. Although there have been some experiments (creating "popular belief" as a sixth religion for a while in Zhejiang and Fujian, or the current attempts at less corporatist NGO registration requirements in Shenzhen), Chinese authorities have not been willing even to take what would appear to be small steps in changing this system at a national level because any of them would imply a fundamental rethinking of the relationship between state and society. For now, and perhaps for the long term, the central state insists on maintaining this formal vision of itself, and turning a blind eye provides the best compromise between that vision and the advantages of greater societal independence.

Actually enforcing that corporatist vision, however, would carry a very high cost, and risks losing significant benefits. Like all hypocrisies, this one creates a small subjunctive world – tolerating a wide range of religious behavior while everyone acts as if it fits into the five big categories, allowing hundreds of thousands of extra-legal social organizations while acting as if the arrangement were corporatist, and so forth – that allows them to claim their ideals while acting with considerably more freedom.

Modes of Repression

Like any form of governance, this one entails underlying modes of repression and control. Turning a blind eye runs a wide range of risks, especially because its subjunctive worlds are so simply reread as lies and deceptions. State actors may be tempted to expose the system out of sincere devotion to the ideals stated in the legal system, or because the status quo is not serving their personal interests, or simply (like the United Front people I spoke to) because they are tired of the daily hypocrisies of trying to provide effective governance with a system of rules that just does not fit real life. Social actors can sometimes also be eager to overturn the system, no longer willing to put up with the "don't ask, don't tell" needs of hanging a sheep's head. Beijing's Shouwang Church is just one of many examples of groups no longer willing to accept the bargain. Governing by turning a blind eye, and being governed by putting acceptable disguises on behavior, thus offers only a frail equilibrium, which requires regular reinforcement. Shared subjunctives can be fragile, because everyone needs to agree to maintain the illusion.

In addition, the improvised and ad hoc nature of many of these mechanisms fosters the idea that people can always push a little harder for what they want – make their church or temple even more obvious, campaign harder for gay rights, or perhaps march the streets in opposition to a factory. Because all of these adaptations by definition take place beyond the letter of the law, the line between what is tolerated and what is repressed is never entirely clear to anyone. Social attempts to push that fuzzy line outward will eventually be answered, however. The groups that push the system the hardest may become the first targets for repression, but attacks can also be essentially random or ad hominem. The main point of such an attack can be less to drive out a particular group than to send a message to all groups. We can see this in apparently random acts of repression, as in the August 2011 shutting down of some schools for children of migrant workers in Beijing on the grounds that they were not properly registered.[31] We can also see it when the government actively chooses to redefine the lines around the tolerated gray zone, for example

[31] "Beijing's Migrant Workers," 40.

in the large-scale deregistrations of NGOs after the Tiananmen demonstrations of 1989 or the Falun Gong demonstrations of 1999. It happened in the religious world most recently in 2014, when a high official in Zhejiang expressed dismay at all the large temples and churches in the province, and began a campaign destroying religious buildings that were said to violate zoning codes. One of the most powerful effects of this mode of repression is that it encourages self-censorship, thus helping stabilize a system that might otherwise threaten to collapse.[32] Maintaining subjunctive worlds thus reinforces all the inequalities that are part of those worlds. As a form of governance, such worlds also contain their own forms of violence, which may usually lie just over the horizon, but whose threat is inherent to the system.

Comparisons

Contemporary China is by no means the only place where governance with a blind eye plays an important role. To some extent, it occurs everywhere, as implied by the prostitution example I mentioned above. Just as I have argued for China, anti-prostitution laws tend to declare a moral stance rather than an intention to enforce a set of rules. And just as in China, they carry a mode of repression that can appear arbitrary, but whose deeper purpose is to show where the line of tolerance lies at the moment rather than to create a social reality that actually accords with the law.

Taiwan under its long colonial (1895–1945) and authoritarian (1945–1987) periods saw some adaptations that resemble the situation I have described for China, especially for religion. The annual festival to appease ghosts during the seventh lunar month, Pudu (普度), for example, typically attracted large crowds in the late Qing Dynasty, who sometimes became unruly. The worst moment was when people were allowed to climb tall poles, at the top of which were platforms of offerings and some flags, all of which would bring people good luck for the coming year. The ensuing chaos often led to injury. The Japanese colonial government was never friendly toward Taiwanese temple religion, and it was unhappy about the large crowds and this annual near-riot. They thus made the pole-climbing ritual illegal. In Sanhsia, the town where I first did field-work in Taiwan, the people responded by avowing their willingness to obey the law. In fact, they explained to the officials, they would instead promote strong and healthy imperial subjects through physical competition. That is, during the Pudu festival, they would stage a pole-climbing

---

[32] Stern and Hassid, "Amplifying Silence."

contest for food and flags at the tops of the poles. It might look identical to what they were doing before, but it was, they assured the government, really about physical education.

Something very similar happened early during the Republican period. The new KMT government in Taiwan was also unfriendly toward temple religion, and tried to discourage what they considered its most wasteful and unsanitary practices. One of these was offering enormously fattened pigs to local gods on their birthdays and other major occasions. The KMT in the early 1950s campaigned strenuously to discourage the practice. Once again, the people of Sanhsia agreed completely. Instead, they introduced an agricultural competition to encourage the best pig-raising practices, and would display the winning pigs in the temple plaza on the god's birthday. In other words, they changed nothing except what they were telling the state.[33]

It is tempting to interpret these activities as a "hidden transcript," a kind of smirking resistance taking place beyond the limits of authoritarian control, which is in fact an argument I made when I first wrote on this. Yet it is important to realize that the rulers, at least the local ones, understood exactly what was going on. The township offices in Sanhsia are just down the street from the temple plaza where these activities took place, and most of the officials were locals. No one is being fooled. Instead, the people are offering a flimsy disguise for their rituals, which allows local officials to save face – everyone can claim that they complied with the state campaign, while no one has to pay the high price of actual enforcement. The parallels to a People's Republic of China temple that calls itself a museum are very close indeed.

We can see parallels even much farther afield than Taiwan. One of the most striking examples of hypocrisy as a philosophy of governance occurred in Holland from the late seventeenth century to the late nineteenth. This was just after the Thirty Years' War, which pitted Protestants against Catholics in a massively destructive and deadly confrontation of mutual intolerance. The Westphalian treaties that ended the war solidified a new formula for religious peace: *cuius regio eius religio* (whoever rules determines the religion). While this is a formula for religious cleansing, the treaties in fact left room for the "private" practice of other religions. Within a few decades, the result was a broad range of what the historian Benjamin Kaplan calls "semi-clandestine churches" – mostly Catholic but also Jewish and alternative Protestant houses of worship.[34] These were called *schuilkerken* in Dutch, but they also extended much more broadly through Western Europe.

---

[33] Weller, "The Politics of Ritual Disguise."   [34] Kaplan, "Fictions of Privacy."

These churches were not identifiable from the outside, and generally occupied upper floors of what appeared to be private houses. Inside, however, they could be as elaborate as any cathedral. Most importantly, there was nothing secret about them. Local officials knew exactly what went on, but tacitly agreed to tolerate it as long as people maintained the fiction that these were not churches. Just as I suggested for China, the law stating that there was only one religion, that of the state, was more a statement of moral principle than of a mode of governance. And just as in China, people pushed at the limits of state tolerance. Sometimes they succeeded, but sometimes the facade broke down and churches or synagogues were razed. In spite of the inherent tensions and frailty in such subjunctive worlds, this system allowed for peace and a certain kind of strained religious tolerance for well over two centuries.

These scattered examples are not enough to establish a pattern, of course, but they do suggest that there may be certain situations that particularly lend themselves to this form of governance. In soft authoritarian regimes, it provides a kind of pragmatic flexibility that elections provide in democracies. On the other hand, harder authoritarian and totalitarian regimes appear to have little use for such techniques. Holland during the Thirty Years' War had no space at all for the tolerance of insincerity and hypocrisy; the war was justified in terms of loyalty to a single truth. Similarly, China under Mao, and especially during the Cultural Revolution, had little room for governance by winks and nudges. Thus, while governing with a blind eye may occur to some extent in almost every state, it has become especially important in a few cases like China, where it contributes to a form of resilience in authoritarian regimes that might otherwise lack the flexibility to cope with rapidly changing social conditions. While much earlier work on the resilience of authoritarian rule in China has focused on institutional structures, here I have tried to show how the measure of flexibility that is required can also come from the practice of actual governance rather than from formal rules and institutions themselves.[35]

Conclusion

I suggested at the beginning that it might be useful to compare this kind of subjunctive governance with the practice of ritual or etiquette. In each case, social convention makes real something that may be false in the context of everyday life. Within its conventional context, saying "please"

---

[35] On authoritarian resilience, see for example Nathan, "Authoritarian Resilience"; Shi, *Political Participation in Beijing*.

really does posit us as equals, the wafer really is the body of Christ, and the temple really is a museum. As Rappaport explained, rituals can be seen as a response to the inherent human capacity to lie and deceive.[36] One either takes part in a ritual or refuses to do so, but truth or falsehood are simply irrelevant. Taking part in a ritual and acting politely do not express any truths about the participants, they do not even tell us what participants believe. What they do show, however, is a willingness to accept the convention. This above all may be what is accomplished by hanging a sheep's head. As I have discussed, that acceptance often lies above an underlying threat of state violence, but it is nonetheless a performative act of claiming to respect the rules, even though actual behavior may have little to do with those rules.

Such conventions are always open to mockery as mere hypocrisy or empty ornament. Criticisms of this sort have been crucial in the history of religion: early Christianity was a reaction against Jewish ritualism, the Protestant Reformation reacted against the re-ritualization of Catholicism, Buddhists against Hindu ritualism, and Mozi against Confucian ritualism. The tension between perceiving these subjunctive worlds as respect for proper convention or as hypocrisy is especially powerful in the cases I have been discussing because the falsehood is so close to the surface and so improvised. The house church really is visible even if everyone claims they cannot see it, the religious group really is providing general social services, and people really are burning incense in the museum. Unlike much religious ritual, the techniques I have been discussing are obviously recent inventions and not parts of long traditions.

They work, however, because participation indicates acceptance – in this case, acceptance of the fundamental legitimacy of the state and of its ideals about how state and society should relate to each other. The split between churches like Shouwang, which is fighting for an official legitimacy outside the official Three Self movement, and the many other unregistered house churches, which keep their heads down, centers around whether those conventions should be accepted. Shouwang refuses, thus implying that other Christians are acting hypocritically, and at the same time refusing to acknowledge the state's power to control them. Other Christians prefer the de facto freedom that the convention and acceptance have been allowing them.

This is a sort of cultural intimacy, where well-known behaviors that do not fit cultural and moral ideals are widely practiced but never mentioned out loud. In the Chinese context, though, it is also worth noting that this is very much a political process as well – miscalculating what can and cannot

[36] Rappaport, *Ritual and Religion*, 11–17.

be said and done leads to visits from public security forces, and possibly arrest and destruction of property. The zone of governing by turning a blind eye, which I have argued is very large in contemporary China, is inherently ill-defined, changing over time and across contexts.

Life in a political gray zone is subject to occasional and sometimes arbitrary repression. Yet, that liminal space also offers one of the most creative and fertile experimental zones in China today. I was at a meeting on religion in China in the summer of 2012 where the Chinese partici-pants debated what to call this space. Most (including me) had begun by calling it a gray zone, but several soon protested that "gray" was far too pessimistic a term, emphasizing only its extra-legal status and occasional repression. Why not call it a zone of creativity or a free zone? There was no final decision, largely because both the pessimistic and optimistic under-standings are correct. This is a space of great flexibility in part because the Chinese state is complex and plural and in part because the boundaries between state and society are under constant renegotiation. It offers innovation and new kinds of openness, along with dangers for both the state and the people. If China ever chooses to move toward a democratic model of civil society, and thus to draw the boundary in a completely different way, this wide zone of gray creativity may shrink considerably. For now, however, the sheep's head is likely to remain hanging over the shop because it provides significant advantages to all concerned.

References

"Beijing's Migrant Workers: School's Out," *The Economist*, September 3, 2011.

Cao, Nanlai. *Constructing China's Jerusalem: Christians, Power, and Place in Contemporary Wenzhou*. Stanford: Stanford University Press, 2011.

Chau, Adam. *Miraculous Response: Doing Popular Religion in Contemporary China*. Stanford: Stanford University Press, 2005.

Dean, Kenneth. *Taoist Ritual and Popular Cults of Southeast China*. Princeton: Princeton University Press, 1993.

Deng, Guosheng. "The Hidden Rules Governing China's Unregistered NGOs: Management and Consequences," *China Review*, 10, 1: 2010, 183–206.

Gao Bingzhong (高丙中). ("An Ethnography of a Building both as Museum and Temple: On the Double-Naming Method as an Art of Politics"). "一座博物馆/庙宇建筑的民族志–论成为政治艺术的双名制," 社会学研究, 121: 2006, 154–168.

Herzfeld, Michael. *Cultural Intimacy: Social Poetics in the Nation-State*. New York: Routledge, 1997.

Hildebrandt, Timothy. "The Political Economy of Social Organization Registration in China," *China Quarterly*, 208: 2011, 970–989.

Hinton, Carma and Gordon, Richard. *All under Heaven*. Brookline, MA: Long Bow Group, 1985.

Huang, Shu-min. *The Spiral Road: Change in a Chinese Village through the Eyes of a Communist Party Leader*. Long Grove, IL: Westview Press, 1998.

Hu Ping (胡平). ("Absurd China"). "荒诞中国," 北京之春, 197: 2009 年10 月, 3.

Kaplan, Benjamin J. "Fictions of Privacy: House Chapels and the Spatial Accommodation of Religious Dissent in Early Modern Europe," *American Historical Review*, 107, 4: 2002, 1031–1064.

Liu, Tik-sang. "Associating Local Traditions with the State Apparatus: A Way of Revitalizing Popular Religion in South China." Paper presented at Workshop on "'Religion' in China," Harvard University, 2005.

McCarthy, Susan K. "Serving Society, Repurposing the State: Religious Charity and Resistance in China," *China Journal*, 70: 2013, 48–72.

Nathan, Andrew J. "Authoritarian Resilience," *Journal of Democracy*, 14, 1: 2003, 6–17.

Rappaport, Roy A. *Ritual and Religion in the Making of Humanity*. New York: Cambridge University Press, 1999.

Seligman, Adam B., Weller, Robert P., Puett, Michael J., and Simon, Bennett. *Ritual and Its Consequences: An Essay on the Limits of Sincerity*. New York: Oxford University Press, 2008.

Shi, Tianjian. *Political Participation in Beijing*. Cambridge, MA: Harvard University Press, 1997.

Spires, Anthony J. "Contingent Symbiosis and Civil Society in an Authoritarian State: Understanding the Survival of China's Grassroots NGOs," *American Journal of Sociology*, 117, 1: 2011, 1–45.

Steinmüller, Hans. "Communities of Complicity: Notes on State Formation and Local Sociality in Rural China," *American Ethnologist*, 37, 3: 2010, 539–549.

Stern, Rachel E. and Hassid, Jonathan. "Amplifying Silence: Uncertainty and Control Parables in Contemporary China," *Comparative Political Studies*, 45, 10: 2012, 1230–1254.

Stern, Rachel E. and O'Brien, Kevin J. "Politics at the Boundary: Mixed Signals and the Chinese State," *Modern China*, 38, 2: 2012, 174–198.

Unger, Jonathan, and Chan, Anita. "Inheritors of the Boom: Private Enterprise and the Role of Local Government in a Rural South China Township." *China Journal*, 42: 1999, 45–74.

Wedeen, Lisa. *Ambiguities of Domination: Politics, Rhetoric, and Symbols in Contemporary Syria*. Chicago: University of Chicago Press, 1999.

Weller, Robert P. *Discovering Nature: Globalization and Environmental Culture in China and Taiwan*. New York: Cambridge University Press, 2006.

Weller, Robert P. "The Politics of Ritual Disguise: Repression and Response in Taiwanese Popular Religion," *Modern China*, 13, 1: 1987, 17–39.

Weller, Robert P., and Sun, Yanfei. "Religion: The Dynamics of Religious Growth and Change," in Joseph Fewsmith, ed., *China Today, China Tomorrow: Domestic Politics, Economy, and Society*, 29–50. Lanham, MD: Rowman & Littlefield, 2010.

Wu, Jiao. "Religious Believers Thrice the Estimate," *China Daily*, February 7, 2007, at www.chinadaily.com.cn/china/2007–02/07/content_802994.htm.

III

Expedients of the Local State: Bargains and Deals

Buying Order

6   Seeing like a Grassroots State: Producing Power and Instability in China's Bargained Authoritarianism

Ching Kwan Lee and Yong Hong Zhang

If the puzzle demanding analysis in the 1980s and 1990s was how to account for the Chinese state's capacity to fuel economic growth, then since the turn of the century, that puzzle has been displaced by the need to explain instead the state's capacity to manage social conflict and maintain stability amidst widespread popular protest. The China studies literature today depicts on the one hand an adaptive and resilient authoritarian state and on the other the rise of an assertive rights-conscious citizenry, while failing so far to explain how and why this paradoxical duality exists. This essay draws on ethnographic and interview data gathered in Beijing and Shenzhen, to analyze the quotidian yet transformative processes of non-zero sum bargaining between grassroots officials and aggrieved citizens in moments of unrest; processes that quite effectively produce but also depoliticize large numbers of social protests while allowing officials to capitalize on instability to advance their career and department interests.

The Puzzle of "Stability Preservation"

After thirty years of sustained economic growth, China continues to fascinate the world with an unfolding "miracle" story that has recently taken a socio-political turn. Increasingly, the riddle of China has become one of fathoming the capacity of the ruling Communist Party (CCP) to maintain social stability while capitalist economic development has been engendering a range of class-based conflicts and enabling a plethora of collective mobilizations not found before, under state socialism. Even for a government normally averse to reporting the seamy side of its society, there is no avoidance of the "facts" of social instability.[1] In the mid-2000s, the Ministry of Public Security released stylized statistics of

---

[1] On the other hand, the results of Martin Whyte's decade-long surveys indicated widespread social acceptance of inequality and disputed the image that Chinese society is a restive volcano ready to erupt into chaos. Whyte and Im, "Volcano still Dormant."

"mass incidents," showing staggering increases in the volume of popular protests from 10,000 in 1993 to 60,000 in 2003, and then to 180,000 in 2010.[2] The Beijing leadership under Hu Jintao and Wen Jiabao vowed to construct a "harmonious society," a euphemistic allusion to the actuality of social instability as a top national concern. Overall, notwithstanding palpable regime anxiety displayed in politically sensitive moments, such as the 2008 Olympics and the Arab Spring in 2011, the Chinese state has been largely successful in containing the numerous incidents of social unrest and preempting them from developing into organized dissent that transcends class, location, or issue boundaries.[3]

Scholarship in contemporary China studies has tended to underscore this duality of heightened political stability and intensified popular activism, without explaining how they come about and coexist. On the one hand, political scientists write about the Chinese communist regime's "authoritarian resilience," or "adaptiveness."[4] They attribute these features to the party's ability to engineer peaceful leadership and economic transition, coopt social and economic elites into its ranks, achieve a unified vision of rule, as well as to the state's methodical control and use of the media, its tight grip on non-governmental organizations and the increasing use of deliberative practices (e.g. public hearings and polls) to persuade and influence the public.[5] Along similar lines, Chinese scholars have pointed to the rationalization of the Chinese state bureaucracy, the new incentive and responsibility accounting systems to explain its professionalization and effectiveness.[6] While all these are important factors contributing to regime resilience and adaptability, the existing literature has largely left unexamined the important question of *how* the government accomplishes social stability *at the moment* of popular unrest. In authoritarian societies, public display of defiance generates disproportionate risks for the regimes. That is why an account of regime stability in China must also explain the state's time- and place-sensitive capacity to

---

[2] Sun Liping, "Social Disorder Is a Present and Serious Challenge." The official definitions and parameters of these statistics have been inconsistent and vague.

[3] In this essay, popular unrest refers to the large numbers of "ordinary" social protests grassroots governments handle. These are to be distinguished from at least two other types of contentious politics that often galvanize more media attention and are dealt with differently by the state. They are: political dissent sustained by intellectuals, lawyers, and artists on the one hand, and mass riots involving violent outbursts of rage and rampage against the government on the other.

[4] Nathan, "Authoritarian Resilience"; Chen, "China's Reaction to the Color Revolutions"; Shambaugh, *China's Communist Party*; Walder, "Unruly Stability."

[5] He and Warren, "Deliberative Authoritarianism."

[6] Wang and Wang, "Goal Management"; Cao Zhenghan, "Vertically Decentralized Authoritarianism."

handle, contain, and absorb collective mobilizations *when and where they occur.*

Looking more from the perspective of society, scholarly studies of collective mobilization by peasants, workers, middle-class homeowners, and other social movement actors have revealed a wide range of organizational and rhetorical strategies used by different social classes demanding labor, land, housing, and environmental rights. Framed around notions of rights consciousness, resistance, class formation, and citizenship, these studies have painted a Chinese society with a remarkable capacity and willingness to challenge state authority.[7] However, most of these studies explain the emergence of protests, giving short shrift to official responses that decisively determine the effects and effectiveness of these mobilizations.[8]

Using the moment of unrest as a unique aperture, taking into account the interests and interpretations of both officials and citizens, here we offer an analysis of the molecular processes of state–society *interaction*: i.e. how Chinese officials negotiate with aggrieved citizens, how citizens confront officials, and how the nature of state authority and citizens' rights is being transformed by and through these processes of power. In these political trenches, we find bargaining to be the foundation of domination and subordination, which is a sea change from the days of state socialist authoritarianism when clientelism was the main nexus between the Chinese state and society. Moreover, we see bargaining that is not by any means purely an instrumental or impersonal process; importantly it involves delicate "emotion work" or "mass work" that has long been a part of the repertoire of communist rule in China.[9]

From Clientelism to Bargaining

Andrew Walder's *Communist Neo-Traditionalism* trained a sharp Weberian focus on patron-clientelism as the foundation of communist state authority. Meshing economic and political control, the CCP penetrated society through its numerous party branches staffed by party

---

[7] Bernstein and Lü, *Taxation without Representation*; O'Brien and Li, *Rightful Resistance*; Perry and Selden, eds., *Chinese Society*; Hsing, *The Great Urban Transformation*; Lee, *Against the Law*; Chan and Pun, "The Making of a New Working Class"; O'Brien, "Villagers, Elections and Citizenship."

[8] An exception is Cai's *Collective Resistance in China* which attempts to explain how the Chinese government chooses between accommodation and repression in dealing with mass incidents. But the disparate and uneven newspaper accounts that form his database do not offer adequate good-quality data about these encounters, much less about the methods and meanings of "accommodation" and their effects on aggrieved citizens.

[9] Perry, "Moving the Masses."

officials and managers of the socialist work unit. In the absence of a market that would have provided an alternative source of livelihood resources, the party-state organized the material, political, and social dependence of the entire populace, and spawned a stable, vertical network of party activists and loyal clients who exchanged political loyalty for preferential material rewards, career, and life chances. Power relations were based on dependence, deference, and particularism, hence Walder's application of the term "traditional" to this configuration, to be distinguished from more modern configurations that might have pivoted around bargaining, personal independence, social conflict, and contract.[10]

Yet, how can state domination be secured today when market reform has broken the material dependence of the majority of the population who now have access to alternative sources of income, status, and life chances, and when the direct presence of the party-state apparatus in non-state workplaces has been extensively attenuated? At the beginning of urban reform in the mid-1980s, Walder already observed the development of informal negotiations on the Chinese shop floors as enterprises gained more autonomy in control over revenue and its allocation as incentive pay. Concluding his book, he wrote presciently, "In the exercise of their recently enhanced autonomy, managers must deal with their workforce in a way that is functionally analogous to more formal collective bargaining ... This pattern of negotiation, however real, remains socially amorphous, unorganized."[11]

As a matter of fact, bargaining under authoritarianism is anything but new. Instead of society's supposed dependence on the state, a second perspective on state socialism has highlighted autonomy and the spaces for pervasive bargaining. Charles Sabel and David Stark found "hidden forms of bargaining"[12] or what Michael Burawoy and Janos Lukacs called "shop floor games" symptomatic of the power relations between the party-state and the working class.[13] These analysts suggest that adaptation to the planned but shortage economy (shortage in labor, materials, parts, and breakdowns of machinery) compels management to cede autonomy and leverage to workers who then use these to bargain with management. Everyday work life was dominated by worker–management negotiations over production norms, wages, and opportunities to participate in various collectives (the second economy) using state factory resources. Sabel and Stark emphasized the economic structural power

---

[10] Walder, *Communist Neo-Traditionalism*, 10.   [11] Ibid., 240.
[12] Sabel and Stark, "Planning, Politics and Shop-Floor Power."
[13] Burawoy and Lukacs, *The Radiant Past.*

of the working class under state socialism: they cannot be fired or dismissed.[14] On the other hand, Burawoy and Lukacs focused on workers' oppositional consciousness emerging from the contradiction between ideology and reality: the party-state organizes the shop-floor ritual of celebrating its virtues to affirm its legitimate domination, ironically reminding workers of the contradiction between the ideology of justice, efficiency, and equality, and the reality of exploitation, inefficiency, and inequality.[15] These scholars concur that state domination resulting from bargaining is fragile. Given the right conditions, ever-present and systematically produced dissent will find expression in counter-hegemonic organization to challenge despotism, or else workers in key firms would up the ante by demanding the bargaining gains be spread to other plants. "Even limited rights give subaltern groups hidden power to paralyze the economy . . . it is a perpetual threat to those in command."[16]

The similarity between Eastern European state socialism and China today is in the political monopoly of the communist party-state, or as Sabel and Stark put it "a blockage of democracy." But the protest bargaining we document in this essay differs from workers' shop-floor bargaining with management under state socialism. First, because most Chinese citizens have access to the market for alternative sources of livelihood, their autonomy and leverage is greater. Whereas only privileged and skilled workers had bargaining power within the shrouded abode of state socialist production, now aggrieved Chinese citizens hail from different class backgrounds, pursue public and visible actions, and, most importantly, they can opt for "exit" by rejecting or derailing the bargaining routine. Second, citizens' bargaining chips are no longer limited to the skills needed for fulfillment of the plan and production targets, but include acts of civil insubordination. What is exchanged in these encounters is state authority and citizens' rights, through processes we will elaborate below as a "commodification of politics," leading to very different consequences from the critical consciousness and dissent anticipated by previous analysts.

At the Frontier of Stability Preservation: The "Grassroots" State

For James Scott, authoritarian states armed with high modernist ideology (rational design) practice "transformative simplification," making society

---

[14] Sabel and Stark, "Planning, Politics and Shop-Floor Power."
[15] Burawoy and Lukacs, *The Radiant Past.*
[16] Sabel and Stark, "Planning, Politics and Shop-Floor Power," 475.

legible and standardized for central record-keeping and monitoring. He contrasts these state ways of seeing and doing with the "indispensable role of practical knowledge, informal processes and improvisation in the face of unpredictability outside the state."[17] Yet, such flexible and informal ways of power, rather than necessarily residing outside the state, are quite compatible with even notable characteristics of the grassroots level of the Chinese state. A Chinese expression poignantly captures the political significance of the basic-level (基层) state: "A thousand threads from above, one needle point below." We term this "needle point," the lowest level of the Chinese government, the "grassroots state" to spotlight (1) its direct interaction with aggrieved citizens attempting to make claims on the government and (2) the roots it extends deeper into the local community through its practices of stability maintenance. In urban and peri-urban areas where we have done our research, the grassroots state consists primarily of the street government and its executive arm the Community Work Station (社区工作服务站).[18]

The political logic and practices of the grassroots state remain obscure, largely because it has often been subsumed in academic writings under the general category of the "local" state, which conventionally encompasses the provincial authority and all the levels below it. Also, most theoretical constructs of the Chinese state, such as "local-state corporatism,"[19] "local government as industrial firms,"[20] and "Chinese style federalism"[21] speak to the economic role of the local states, be it developmental or predatory, not to their political responsibility for maintaining stability. We know that the institutional logic of the Chinese polity gives grassroots officials a fair amount of flexibility and autonomy,[22] as with street-level bureaucracies found in other systems.[23] But we know little about what they do with this discretion. Our field research has sought to fill this empirical gap by enhancing our understanding of the

---

[17] Scott, *Seeing Like a State*, 6.

[18] A Community Work Station is the executive arm of the street government, and is usually staffed by a dozen or so full-time civil servants supported by a large contingent of part-time staff. It aims at integrating resources of many functional departments of the grassroots state and it is charged with 130 tasks, in which stability maintenance work is given particular emphasis. In many places, the staff members of the Community Work Station are actually the same as for the residents' committees which, since the founding of the PRC, have supposedly been mass initiated community organizations. See Read, *Roots of the State*.

[19] Oi, *Rural China Takes Off.*   [20] Walder, "Local Governments as Industrial Firms."

[21] Montinola et al., "Federalism, Chinese Style."

[22] Zhou, "The Institutional Logic of Collusion"; Heilmann and Perry, eds., *Mao's Invisible Hand.*

[23] Lipsky, *Street-Level Bureaucracy.*

strategies, incentives, and constraints of grassroots officials' stability maintenance work.

Over the years, the focus of "stability preservation" (维稳) has shifted from "strike hard campaigns" targeting criminals, vices, and cults in the 1980s and 1990s, to the more recent notion of "social management," a vague and all-encompassing term that entails the building of a "people-centered" and "services-centered" government, to resolve the masses' legitimate and rational appeals," all under the leadership of the CCP.[24] First officially enunciated in 2003, social management as a strategic priority is piloted by two dragonhead organs at the center: the Politics and Law Committee and the Ministry of Civil Affairs. "The heart of social management," however, "is decisively the grassroots government, especially the one at the community level."[25] Accompanying this shift in the core tasks of stability preservation was a downward transfer of responsibility for stability maintenance which began in the early 1990s, right after the Tiananmen Incident. Several foundational documents issued by the Central Committee of the Chinese Communist Party and the State Council on strengthening social control and public security laid down the administrative principle of "jurisdictional management" (属地管理).[26] During the 2000s, the trend toward localizing the responsibility for maintaining social stability has increasingly become codified, most prominently in the 2005 National Petition Regulation and the 2008 CCP decision on Strengthening the Implementation of Integrated Public Security Management. Intended to overcome the longstanding conflicts and overlaps of authority existing in the Chinese bureaucracy between the hierarchies of functional departments and of geographical jurisdictions, the policy of "jurisdictional management" gives to municipal governments and above the power to evaluate, reward, or punish lower-level officials for their performance in core social policy areas. For instance, if social disturbances, industrial accidents, or over-quota births occur in a jurisdiction, the hierarchy of leaders responsible for that jurisdiction will *all* be subjected to the "one veto rule" (一票否决); i.e. their failure in that one policy area will negate all other accomplishments by the government unit and deprive officials serving there of bonuses, promotions, and the eligibility of the unit to compete for organizational honors. In practice, the cascade of bureaucratic pressure has tended to fall most heavily on those working in the lowest rank in the state hierarchy – rural township and urban street officials. It is these officials who carry out the actual work of building connections with the local populace, arriving at the

[24] Xu and Li, "The Machinery of Stability Preservation."
[25] Gong Weibin, "Ten Major Relationships in the Innovation of Social Management."
[26] Central Committee of the Chinese Communist Party, "Decision."

scenes of social unrest, negotiating with aggrieved citizens and gathering information about the local communities. The power processes that transpire in these interactions form the empirical subject of this essay.

Sources of Instability: Commodification and Counter-movements

Here, we draw on data collected through participant observation and in-depth interviews between 2008 and 2011 in two Chinese cities and their peri-urban areas which have borne the brunt of the challenge of stability maintenance.[27] Shenzhen is a major industrial powerhouse in China, and the most popular destination of the country's 250 million strong migrant workers. The rapid, ever-expanding urbanization of Shenzhen, as in Beijng and other Chinese cities, has spawned a ferocious new enclosure movement. As the host city of the Summer Universiade, the Shenzhen government's concern for social stability reached its zenith in 2011. Beijing, because it is the capital, is the leading destination of many aggrieved citizens from around the country seeking official redress to a plethora of injustices and conflicts. The host city of the 2008 Olympics, it also became the location of intense housing and property conflicts thanks to a sizable class of affluent homeowners and the many Olympics-related demolition and road projects.

In both cities, the major types of social conflicts causing protests have been related to labor, land, and property rights violations. First, labor strife, especially in Shenzhen, intensified with the implementation of the Labor Contract Law in 2008. The law has emboldened workers to demand compensation when employers refuse to sign written contracts, or make severance payments at the end of a contract, or repay defaulted overtime wages earned in the past two years, etc. Labor discontent was also aggravated in the wake of the 2008 global financial crisis as widespread plant closures caused by the sudden contraction of overseas orders made local governments reluctant to enforce the new law, in an attempt to stabilize the local economy. Typically, disgruntled workers would demonstrate at factory gates, organize strikes, traffic blockages, or sit-ins in front of government buildings. The vast majority of labor actions have been about economic compensation.

---

[27] One of us has shadowed officials in five street governments in Shenzhen since 2008, participating in their meetings, appearing on site with them when protests and negotiations took place, and talking with officials in their offices. The other author has interviewed district, street, and township government officials responsible for stability maintenance in Beijing in 2008 and 2009. We have also jointly carried out fieldwork in Shenzhen, interviewing officials and citizens involved in protests.

The second type of protests in both cities has been triggered by land requisition. Building new infrastructure in the run up to the Olympics has dislocated many peasants in Beijing's rural counties. Similarly, in Shenzhen, forced conversion of farmland into non-agricultural land (for more lucrative uses such as university campuses, high-tech parks, or intercity motorways) fanned discontent. In both Beijing and Shenzhen, the pressure to complete an expressway or a stadium in time for the Olympics, or to fulfill the needs of investors, meant that these projects would start even before all the necessary legal requirements (e.g. consultation with village committees, land requisition permits, environmental impact evaluations, etc.) were met. Such forced-pace projects were dubbed "3-ongoing constructions" (三边工程) – meaning that planning, land requisition, and construction all proceeded simultaneously. Just as in labor disputes, it has usually been monetary compensation that is at the heart of these mobilizations, taking the forms of demonstrations, sit-ins, and traffic blockages. In a few exceptional cases, aggrieved citizens also made charges of corruption and administrative malpractice.

The third type of disputes has been caused by property rights violations. Massive demolitions in Beijing in preparation for the Olympics occasioned collective disputes and violent clashes between demolition officials and residents who refused to move out or threatened to commit suicide. In newly built condominium neighborhoods, now reaching a total of more than 5,000 inside the four ring roads of Beijing, property disputes mostly involved conflicts between homeowners and developers or their affiliated property management companies over the quality of construction and management service, and property rights over commonly owned spaces and facilities. In Shenzhen, the quality of newly built residential complexes also triggered mass incidents. The introduction of the Property Rights Law in October 2007 has induced a spike in litigations and collective petitions stemming from these conflicts, as well as new conflicts surrounding the election of homeowners' committees.

In short, following the analysis of Karl Polanyi,[28] these three types of social unrest, caused by violations of labor rights, land use rights, and property rights, can be understood as "counter-movements" carried out by the classes dislocated respectively by the commodification of labor, land, and housing. As power is centralized in the state, social unrest arising from commodification always turns to the state as both the source and solution of people's dislocation and deprivation. Moreover, as some Chinese sociologists have pointed out, the vested interests of the ruling bureaucratic-business elite have stalled political reform that would allow

---

[28] Polanyi, *The Great Transformation.*

for institutionalized channels of interest representation of the subordinate classes.[29] Therefore, counter-movements have no other institutional channels to pursue except direct action, aggravating the problem of "stability preservation." These "movements" have so far not taken the forms of sustained and organized mobilizations but have remained instead cellular, localized, ephemeral episodes of collective defiance.

Buying Stability: Non-Zero Sum Protest Bargaining

The strategy of "buying stability" (花钱买平安), literally meaning "paying cash for peace," is the most prevalent means of pacifying aggrieved citizens involved in labor, land rights, and property disputes. In our research in Beijing, all district governments have reported the existence of a "stability maintenance fund" with annual budgets varying between RMB 2 million and 1 billion.[30] In Shenzhen, we were told that the municipal government has demanded each district government allocate RMB 20–30 million each year for stability maintenance.[31] The aggregate size of these "stability maintenance" funds has ballooned in recent years. Nationwide, in 2010, according to the Finance Minister, for the first time ever, spending on public security (RMB 549 billion) overtook spending on national defense (RMB 533.4 billion), and it would be more than the combined budgets for health care, diplomacy, and financial oversight in 2011.[32] "Buying stability" had its origin in the central government's concern for preserving stability prior to and during the 2008 Olympics Games. Aggrieved citizens seized the sensitive moment of the Games to put pressure on officials to resolve historical

---

[29] Sun et al., "Realizing Long-Term Stability."

[30] Our interviewees reported the following amounts (in RMB) by district in 2008 in Beijing: XW 10 million, FT 5 million, CW 49 million, HD 1 billion, SJS 20 million, CP 30 million, YQ 4 million, DQ 3 million, HR 2 million, FS 2 million. Overall, rural counties/districts have smaller funds than urban districts. In both Shenzhen and Beijing, the stability maintenance fund has been financed by the city and district governments, and charged to the account of the government unit responsible for causing a particular incident. Every time the fund is used, local party committee approval is required *ex post facto*. Street-level officials could also use extra-budgetary incomes (e.g. transaction fees collected from factory rental contracts, or fines from over-quota births) to cover the costs of stability maintenance. In both cities, officials were less concerned with the financial burden the task of stability maintenance incurs than whether or not money could indeed buy stability.

[31] Interview in T Street, Shenzhen, November 23, 2011. However, officials also emphasized that there was no precise balance sheet for stability maintenance expenses billed as payments for environmental protection, demolition costs, low income household subsidies, or other kinds of government expenditure.

[32] Hook, "Beijing Raises Spending."

grievances expediently. The practice seemed to have worked and became a lasting mechanism.[33]

Besides cash payments to people who stage direct and public acts of defiance, "buying stability" could take the form of grassroots governments paying for urgent services and utilities (e.g. water supply, electricity, garbage collection, building a new school) when these became the subject of disputes. For instance, in order to prevent angry residents from demonstrating in the streets, a street government located in the embassy district in Beijing had to use its own fund to repair the water pipes during a protracted dispute between homeowners and a management company.[34] In another neighborhood, the street government brought in tanks of water to service homeowners after their water supply was suspended by the property management company as retaliation against the homeowners' mass default on payment of the management fee.[35] More generally, whenever severe confrontation between the developers and property owners occurred, paralyzing the provision of basic services like garbage disposal and heat and power supply, the street government would have to pay for and send in a government-owned interim property management company to secure neighborhood stability. In a property management dispute in T Street, the Shenzhen Bureau of Housing and Construction paid a hefty RMB 20 million, or three years' worth of property management fee, on behalf of the homeowners.

Expenses for stability maintenance often remain hidden behind more routine government expenditures and do not allow a straightforward accounting of the actual amounts spent on this purpose. In a housing quality dispute, when the local government reached its limit of monetary compensation, officials sweetened the deal by building a new primary school for homeowners' children (counted as an education expenditure) and improving the environment by planting shrubs (an environmental improvement item), and other "services" such as augmenting community security by adding a guarded gate, assisting unemployed residents to find jobs, even providing some petty employment in the Community Work Station (run by the street government) for family members of the protest leaders.

Deceptively ad hoc and arbitrary, dishing out cash payments or other material benefits in exchange for compliance has become a patterned and routinized response to popular unrest, summed up in a widely circulated popular jingle, "Big disturbance big resolution, small disturbance small resolution, no disturbance no resolution." The grassroots state has turned

[33] Hu Ben, "The Codification of Weiwen Mechanisms."
[34] Interview in Beijing, December 16, 2009.   [35] Interview in Beijing, October 26, 2009.

into a marketplace where gamesmanship (博弈), meaning strategic game playing, between officials and citizens, determines the price tag of stability. But as the following examples throw into sharp relief, the essence of buying stability is not the final delivery of cash and other forms of material benefits, but the *processes* leading to it. One Shenzhen official put it most succinctly, "Cash is only the outcome. The key is in the process. It is through processes of mass work, thought work, and education work," he explained, that state power is practically realized. "With the passage of time, we turn confrontations (交锋) into dialogues (交流), [and] personal understanding (了解) into cognitive alignment (理解)."[36] Rather than residing in objective institutions of law, government bureaucracy, or the armed forces, state power realizes itself as and through a transformative, non-zero sum bargaining process of fragmenting protesters, protecting and harassing activists, defining and limiting citizens' "realistic" rather than "legal" rights, controlling and capitalizing on instability, and turning leaders of dissent into informants for the government, all leading to a pragmatic but precarious alliance between state and citizens.

Based on cases of protest bargaining collected from our field sites, we can break down "buying stability" into these component and typically concurrent processes: (1) categorization of unrest and emotion control, (2) fragmentation and cooptation, (3) joint construction of citizen's rights, (4) use or threat of force, and (5) coordinated capitalization of instability.

Categorization of unrest and emotion control

Since the run up to the Olympics in 2008, street-level governments in both Beijing and Shenzhen have set up "Integrated Security, Petition and Stability Maintenance Centers" (综治信访维稳中心) with the explicit mandate to handle conflicts and disputes. Sometimes these centers are located in stand-alone buildings, with huge signs announcing their presence. Alternatively, as is the case at T Street in Shenzhen, the center is prominently located on the ground and first floors in the 10-story headquarters of the street government, with a twenty-four-hour emergency call center. Staffed by officers on shifts, this is the nerve center that receives all kinds of information about instability incidents and responds according to a triage system. Street and district governments have developed an elaborate classification of four or five types of events, according to the "number of people" participating, the "amount of money" involved, and the "contagious potential" of the incident. For each type, there are

[36] Interview in Shenzhen, November 23, 2011.

designated officials of primary and secondary responsibility who are required to arrive on the scenes immediately as well as other higher-ranking officials who would be informed. In an hour-long PowerPoint presentation given by the director of stability maintenance in T Street to officials from another street government in Guangzhou, he showed detailed flowcharts and spreadsheets of the names and numbers to call for each category of event. Often, when we were having dinner with street officials, text messages came in constantly to their cell phones, which they jokingly nicknamed "stability maintenance cell phones" and to which they paid constant and undivided attention even when eating, drinking, and socializing. The efficiency of this system is impressive as this official recalled, with palpable pride, a labor protest he handled:

At 11:15pm, about five hundred workers blocked the main road leading to the hotel hosting leaders from Beijing. By 11:35pm, we had assembled on the scene officials from the street, the district, the trade union, the police, together with 200 of our hired security officers. By 11:45pm, we cleared the road. Only 30 minutes. Then we started working and negotiating.[37]

Upon arrival at the scene of a mass incident, the typical first move is to accomplish "emotion control." Grassroots officials display remarkably astute sensitivity to people's psychology, character, and social dynamics. They used metaphors of "making friends" and "talking love" to describe the social skills entailed in stability preservation work. Even emotional confrontations, such as threats of suicide by homeowners resisting a demolition order, or workers threatening to jump off high rises to demand wage payment, are handled calmly by grassroots officials who see such displays as routinized performances by citizens trying to strengthen their bargaining position. A grassroots official with seven years of experience in handling demolition and property compensation in Beijing stressed the importance of emotion in official and citizen interactions:

The period from 2000 to 2007 was the climax of demolition for the Olympics. We were given annual demolition targets of 8,000 to 13,000 households. As demolition officials, we have to be thoroughly in touch with people's psychology. It's twenty-four-hour work. Demolition and relocation are more about psychological gamesmanship than anything else. All you need to do is to let people see the hope of making some profit and solving their real livelihood problems. Once, a woman threatened to drink poison in front of me. I had come to know her pretty well through the long negotiation process. I knew she did not want to die. So I said, "okay, drink, Big Sister. You know you will not die. I will call the police and the ambulance will come immediately to take you to the hospital. Why do you

[37] Interview in Shenzhen, November 24, 2011.

want to punish yourself?" I personally think that Chinese people are really easy to govern because all they want from you is some economic benefit. But dealing with different kinds of people, we will have to use different languages and methods. For instance, teachers. They are shy to talk about money. So they talk about the law and regulations, beat around the bush, but their real goal is still money. Peasants are straightforward, they make direct demands for money.[38]

A Shenzhen labor dispute official corroborated with his emphasis on the priority of emotion control.

Money is workers' only motive. But on site, the first thing is to manage their emotion, keep them calm. I also always give my cell phone number to the workers, to increase their sense of security, to give them an outlet to voice their grievance. This will eliminate the need for them to launch a petition to a superior level of government, and give me access to their thoughts.[39]

Fragmentation and Cooptation

Channeling passion and emotion into rational discussion of interest is the next step. As making scenes of instability and disorder is the major leverage the protesters have, grassroots officials waste no time in creating order out of chaos. Many talked about the urgency of finding an "access point" to the crowd – identifying their leaders. If no one comes forth, officials would ask them to elect their representatives, usually not more than five. The imperative is to aggregate interests so that demands are expressed in an orderly manner and to create target intermediaries between the state and the aggrieved. To generate the desired effects, the election of representatives has to be handled with tactful considerations, as this labor dispute official at T Street explained after resolving a labor dispute involving 400 workers protesting at the factory gate.

The next critical thing is to mobilize them to elect their representatives. Disorder is their bargaining chip. Electing representatives is the beginning of a process of orderly negotiations, because only then would everyone know what the demands are about. But we have to avoid having all representatives coming from the same native-place. So we ask them to elect "workshop" representatives.[40]

Experienced officials realize that ordinary citizens are fearful and indecisive in moments of conflict, but protest leaders are the elite who are more recalcitrant, bold, articulate, educated, and knowledgeable about how the world works. The emergence of these representatives is the beginning of

---

[38] Interview in Beijing, December 18, 2009.
[39] Interview in Shenzhen, October 19, 2010.   [40] Ibid.

a process of cooptation and fragmentation. A Beijing official offered this illustration:

In 2005, when a developer of luxurious villas obtained a piece of (peri-urban) land without the proper permit, 200 peasants surrounded the government demanding compensation for illegal demolition. I first asked them to select ten representatives, and then talked to these representatives individually about their own domestic and personal situations. I know I can fragment them and exploit their conflict of interest. As soon as they see some opportunity for making a profit, they will eventually agree.[41]

The significance of protest leaders as handles for cooptation and fragmentation can be demonstrated by a "negative" case where the government almost failed to maintain stability because officials failed to identify leaders, or leaders were rejected by their constituencies. In December 2011, a strike broke out in a Japanese factory in Shenzhen where 4,000 workers demanded overtime wage payment and restructuring of compensation in anticipation of the company's merger with an American company. It developed into the longest strike ever in Shenzhen's history, dragging on for twenty-two days, and escalated into warehouse blockages and clashes with the police widely reported in the press. The crux of the problem, from the perspective of officials handling this incident, lay in the lack of "handles." The absence of any party organization or union in this factory forced the government into a defensive position. At the beginning, officials asked workers to elect representatives but they were later on rejected by workers who claimed that they had been corrupted by the company.

We were not able to identify the organizers behind the scenes. We suspected some higher-level managers and "black lawyers" were involved in planning and mobilizing the workers. Right from the start, officials tried to seek out the real organizers ... Because the representatives we negotiated with were not the real organizers, they were not able to channel workers' demands and emotions .... When the district and street governments sent a work team into the dormitory to do thought work, workers chased the team out, and destroyed copies of the agreements posted on the walls ... Finally, when we found the crucial organizers, the incident was resolved (the leader was arrested).[42]

Joint Construction of "Rights"

Once simmering emotion and disruptive action are defused, bargaining will begin with officials making conscious attempts to "steer citizens from irrational to rational demands," a process of transforming citizens'

---

[41] Interview in Beijing, December 18, 2009.
[42] Fieldwork in Shenzhen, December 22, 2011.

imagined "legal" rights stated in the law book into realistic and feasible rights under the circumstances. On the part of the citizens, negotiation is a process of adjusting their strategies and demands, upon discovering the extent and limits of state power at various levels. Some would come to realize that if the conflict was caused by higher-level governments, there would be less or little wiggle room for bargaining while others learn how to exert the right amount of pressure on the right departments to maximize results. In any case, the point is that "rights consciousness" is jointly constructed by both officials and citizens through a transformative and malleable process of engagement. It is not, as is often assumed in the current China studies literature, a static state of mind that is fully formed prior to protests and to which protesters are committed from beginning to end.

The lived experience of bargaining as one of discovery and cognitive adjustments regarding their "rights" was most clearly conveyed to us by a representative in a case of homeowners' struggle against the construction of a major highway in Shenzhen. The "Western Corridor" was a central government project intended to boost Hong Kong's economy after the SARS epidemic hit the city in 2003. Tens of thousands of residents living in different residential neighborhoods along the highway mobilized to complain about noise and environmental degradation brought about by the construction. One of the elected leaders of several thousand residents in one segment of the road project was a retired navy intelligence officer, a proud twenty-year veteran member of the CCP. His investigation into the project led him to discover ever more irregularities and vested interests by various government departments (e.g. environmental evaluation of the project was undertaken by a company owned by the Environmental Protection Bureau). Meetings with the police chief and street-level Party Secretary sometimes escalated into verbal confrontations, and also convinced him that there was little chance for citizens to reverse the decision. Instead of seeking an end to the project, which he and others increasingly came to regard as an illusionary goal because the decision to build the road came from Beijing, he adjusted his perspective and settled for an "optimization of policy": "The government has increased its budget for optimizing this road, from RMB 700 million to RMB 2.1 billion. We stopped making noise because the government has made a concession."[43]

Most of the time, officials preach pragmatism to the parties involved in disputes, explaining to them why their legal rights cannot be realized. The conflict-prone construction industry creates notoriously acute problems for stability maintenance because of the informal and multiple

---

[43] Fieldwork in Shenzhen, December 1, 2011.

subcontracting employment system involving a large number of workers who are not legally employed. Factory workers protesting against wage defaults may not have labor contracts, pay slips, or time cards to legally support their claims, or the factories concerned are illegal and unregistered to begin with. Under such circumstances, when unrest occurs, officials strain to persuade both workers and employer to see and agree on some discounted compensation as their best option, regardless of the law.

> To the boss, we talk about potential losses if the standoff continued. We ask the boss, "how much would you lose if they stop working for one day?" and once he calculates, he will agree to pay ... To the workers who refuse to accept a reduced payment by the boss, we make them see the possibility of the factory going under. In the end, both sides would usually come to a compromised rate of compensation.[44]

Toward the end of the aforementioned twenty-two-day long strike in Shenzhen, with augmented pressure exerted from the municipal government to end this protracted labor strife, the union official responsible for handling the incident made a passionate plea with workers' representatives, marshaling legal, moral, and strategic arguments to define and limit their "right" and "interest":

> Our national law does not say whether the strike is legal or illegal. But the union is against this method because we prefer a better, win–win method and not a lose–lose method to resolve workers' problems and demands ... It is not in our workers' interests to make the company go under. Our biggest interest is maximizing income. We want a win–win result ... We have bargained a compensation package that is higher than what the law stipulates ... I have been here many days to negotiate with the company. Any one among you thinks you are a better negotiator? With this result, you should stop pressing and calm down. I have to be frank: besides the ACFTU, different government departments are already involved, and we are still investigating. But I know everything every one of you has done has been recorded, and you have to be responsible for that. Occupying the warehouse and stopping others from work are illegal. Distributing handbills and instigating strikes are illegal. You cannot escape (from the law). We do not want to see you get hurt. As the Vice-Chair of the Union, I implore you, my worker brothers and sisters, it's time to quit. For the few organizers behind the scenes, I tell you to stop now. What you are doing is very dangerous. We know who you are.[45]

Use or Threat of Force

Protest bargaining does not happen on a level playing field for citizens and officials because the latter could resort to the use or the threat of police

---

[44] Interview in Shenzhen, October 19, 2010.
[45] Fieldwork in Shenzhen, December 23, 2011.

force. The invocation of coercive power is never too far from the realm of possibility, an ever-present factor that armors the construction of consent through bargaining. However, since the Weng'an incident in Guizhou in June 2008, the Beijing authorities have imposed the injunction "to use force judiciously" (慎用警力). Only when "disruption of public order" occurs, such as blocking highways or vandalizing public property, can the police arrest protesters. Stability officials reported that most of the time, the police arrive to watch, and are reluctant to take action lest they become responsible for any casualty or escalation of conflict. To enhance their range of options and flexibility, street governments deploy security officers who are employees of security companies and normally work full time as guards at factory gates or residential neighborhoods. For instance, T Street government has about 2,000 hired security officers at its disposal. When an incident requires a show of force to maintain order, street officials could call on them and pay for their service on a piece rate basis, e.g. RMB 100 per person per incident.

We can use the largest ever land requisition project in Shenzhen to illustrate the several occasions when police force was used. The construction of a new "University City" in Shenzhen to house satellite campuses of several higher education institutions involved land requisition of 1.47 million square meters, with 700 enterprises and a total population of 50,000. In March 2008, the arduous process of compensation negotiation started, with the government proposing a compensation scheme used for non-profit projects, claiming that the land was for educational facilities. The district government proposed that either a household should obtain a new housing unit of 480-square meters or a monetary compensation at the rate of RMB 6,000 per square meter of their existing village homes for native villagers and a lower rate for village residents who moved in more recently as property owners of illegally built village houses. Conflicts flared when native villagers wanted higher rates, pointing to other cases in the same district where the compensation rate was twice that of this project, and when newer villagers demanded the same rates as the natives. The protest leader was the chairman of the shareholding company owning and controlling the land owned by the village collective. He organized villagers to protest in front of the Shenzhen City government, banging on the main entrance of the Shenzhen Municipal Government Building. According to villagers, police deliberately dragged villagers away from the surveillance cameras before beating them up and arrested six activist villagers. The district government which initiated the project also ordered an investigation into the financial records and commercial activities of the village shareholding company, with an eye to discovering irregularities that it could use as leverage against the village leader. With what officials claimed to be evidence of embezzlement of collective income, the village leader was forced to sign a move-out agreement on behalf of all the villagers, and some of the other village leaders were arrested by the police on charges of fraud. Finally, the day before the ground-breaking ceremony officiated by the Provincial Governor was to take place, more than a thousand police were sent to rip off protest banners hoisted by the remaining 160 non-native households and encircled the village to prevent villagers from disrupting the ceremony. Two months later, when the final deadline for signing compensation documents approached, and when the government had sweetened the deal with an additional award, the leaders of the last remaining 'nail households' were arrested.

Arrests like these were the exceptions rather than the rule. Normally, a display of force by police on the scene would suffice to convey to the masses the peril of pushing too hard. As this official explained, striking a balance between force and protection toward protesters is a recurrent tactic for turning dissent into cooperation:

We usually tolerate minor infractions at the beginning, but we will also collect evidence of such behavior so we can use the evidence against them later on if they go beyond a certain reasonable limit ... We officials have to sing both red songs and black songs. We have to order their arrest when they violate the law, but also secure their release afterwards ... We do not normally arrest the leaders because we want them to persuade their people. We arrest mostly the minor characters, unimportant airheads. To the leaders, I would tip them off, to show that I protect them in critical moments so they would listen and be thankful to me. This requires tact and skills. Only after experiencing this process will they trust you.[46]

Capitalizing on Instability

One surprising discovery for us in this research is that grassroots officials and aggrieved citizens can actually share a common interest in sustaining a certain level of instability. That is, both state and society capitalize on instability to generate power. We came to realize officials' interest in maintaining a persistent but controllable level of instability through incidents in which stability maintenance officials instructed aggrieved workers in the correct and effective ways to protest (e.g. blocking the warehouse to prevent goods from reaching the buyers), or counseled peasants to petition one and not the other government department. They would advise protesters with whom they bargain on how to push but not exceed the boundary of the legally permissible, in order to

---

[46] Interview in Shenzhen, November 23, 2011.

generate the maximum political effect. Also, during a "quiet" period without much unrest in their jurisdiction, officials would prolong the resolution of existing cases, by channeling them into the court. Why?

As citizens use instability as the bargaining chip, grassroots officials also capitalize on instability to augment their departmental and personal career interests. The existence of instability justifies demands for augmented budgets for the departments and personnel involved in preserving stability. Both figuratively and literally, as one official admitted, "without popular unrest, we (officials) won't have good meals to enjoy," referring to the lavish dinners in one of the most upscale club-house restaurants officials routinely arranged for "cooperative" representatives of protests. Other than justifying requests for larger budgets and expenses at their disposal, officials capitalize on instability to confirm the importance of their department, thereby facilitating their career mobility. In the past few years, we have observed that officials receiving promotion from the street to the district and municipal governments have come from the line of stability maintenance work. More routine and ordinary rewards for good performance take the form of annual bonuses that could amount to one third of their salaries, in addition to symbolic honors and prizes. Negative incentives exist to punish officials who fail to maintain stability, but these are usually dodged with the same ingenuity and flexible improvisation that officials apply to bargaining with citizens. For instance, the seemingly harsh policy of "one veto rule" can be dealt with by keeping the district informed of unfolding difficult cases, seeking a superior's advice, and thereby sharing or shedding responsibility in the event of a negative outcome.

In short, protest bargaining is a non-zero sum game through which officials seek to transform what is originally a conflictual relationship between the grassroots state and aggrieved citizens into a pragmatic albeit precarious alliance. Several salient political consequences follow. First, "buying stability" allows the grassroots state to absorb unrest but leaves intact the root causes of unrest (e.g. defective policy-making, the lack of institutional representation and resolution of class interests, weak enforcement of the law, etc.). The constant shuffling of leading cadres across localities as they move up the bureaucratic ladder means that they are disposed to demand from their subordinates only short-term pacification. Therefore, this kind of "passive stability maintenance," as one official described it, is conducive to persistent instability, both because of its avoidance of underlying problems and of the opportunity it creates for joint capitalization by lower-level officials and protesters.

Second, "buying stability" amounts to a commodification of state authority and citizens' rights that undermines both. Money is the medium of exchange in this depoliticizing process. However, authority and rights are "fictitious commodities," according to Polanyi, because turning them into commodities with a price tag for sale in the marketplace necessarily destroys their essence and purpose. What is state authority if official orders are followed only after payment is made? Equally, what does it mean to have labor rights when workers are routinely compelled to negotiate for discounted wage compensation? And even after obtaining compensation, protest bargaining tends to undermine citizens' sense of efficacy as well as state authority, as this reflection by a protest leader illustrates.

We ordinary citizens can never successfully fight the government. They set the price and you either take it or leave it ... The power holders can use all kinds of methods. At times they listened, and sent you away with their buses. Other times, they used scare tactics, taking some influential villagers or villagers with problematic businesses into custody for interrogation. They returned, shaken, and it makes everyone nervous. We don't trust the government anymore ... we won't threaten suicide or pursue any radical behavior, because we Shenzhen villagers actually have decent livelihoods. But as a village, we have been crushed.[47]

On the side of the officials, buying stability as a pragmatic means of preserving stability epitomizes the erosion of state authority. As one Shenzhen official puts it bluntly,

The people don't trust the government and they don't respect the authority or the law. The government's authority has been eroded for a long time, that's why the masses use every opportunity to eke out more benefits for themselves.[48]

Our analysis therefore casts doubt on the prevailing argument in the China studies literature that postulates an augmentation in both state authority and citizens' rights' consciousness in the post-socialist period. Despite the maintenance of short-term stability and the reaping of material gains, the bargaining process has also left both officials and citizens diminished, resentful, and reticent. The authority of the authoritarian state suffers, with uncertain implications for regime durability. Looking ahead, the materialist expectation and exchange relations that protest bargaining cultivate may backfire if the Chinese regime ever finds itself in a fiscal crisis and can no longer buy stability expediently.

Conclusion

In stark contrast to the era of state socialism, the market economy in China has substantially reduced popular dependence on the authoritarian state, compelling the state to make concessions to elicit citizen compliance,

---

[47] Interview in Shenzhen, December 17, 2010.
[48] Interview in Beijing, December 17, 2009.

fostering citizens' capacity and interest to pursue collective mobilization. As the use of force is not politically desirable and ideological indoctrination is ineffective, the Chinese government has resorted to routinized bargaining to maintain stability. Even as authoritarianism is still transparent, power concentrated in the hands of the CCP, and the use of repression always an imminent possibility, it is now mediated by the logic of market exchange. Non-zero sum bargaining preserves stability by depoliticizing official–citizen confrontations, i.e. transforming contestations about political power and values into bargains of material interests.[49] This explains why the majority of social unrest in China seldom challenges the legitimacy and system of one-party rule, but has mostly focused on issues of livelihood and material interests. We maintain that this is not a result of any deep-seated tendency in Chinese political culture[50] but at least partly a consequence of the state's strategy of domination.

While our data show that the state's ideological affirmation of "harmonious society" produces among aggrieved citizens a critical consciousness that Chinese society is anything but harmonious, we also found that such critical consciousness does not preclude adaptation to, even a keen desire to work for, the one-party-state. A poignant moment in our fieldwork well illustrates this contradictory subjectivity: a demobilized soldier, who staged protests with several dozen others demanding higher pensions, was asked by a street official to state his demands in exchange for stopping the protests. The demobilized soldier said, "Why can you be a civil servant and I cannot? I want my daughter to be a civil servant too."[51] Notwithstanding the large numbers of mass incidents, polls show that government employment has consistently been the most preferred career option among university graduates in China. A government post brings employment security, a handsome salary, and superior benefits (especially in terms of housing), in addition to family prestige and personal status.

But domination by bargaining is precarious: as power resides in the process of bargaining, stability maintenance is wrought with uncertainty and unpredictability. There is always the possibility for unsuccessful bargaining, or the emergence of some particularly recalcitrant, cohesive, and daring groups of protesters, and hence explosive events such as those in Wukan and Weng'an.

Careful study of micro-politics and ways of governing at the grassroots level are necessary, albeit not sufficient, ingredients in understanding Chinese stability maintenance, which also depends on macroscopic forces and institutional reforms. On the one hand, selective but

---

[49] See also Thornton, "Retrofitting the Steel Frame."
[50] Perry, "Chinese Conceptions."   [51] Fieldwork in Shenzhen, July 31, 2010.

systematic repression is still meted out to dissident intellectuals, human rights lawyers, and organized religious and political dissent that show any inkling of cross-class and cross-locality mobilization. On the other hand, the government has launched policy reforms to address the most salient socio-economic grievances. Eliminating the millennia-old agricultural taxes, introducing a rural social insurance scheme, and imposing programmatic increments in minimum wages indicate the Chinese state's responsiveness, albeit one without accountability, to decades of farmer and worker unrest. More recently, the state's reactions, at least at the rhetorical level, to popular livelihood concerns such as pollution, food safety, land grabbing, and income inequality have seemed to become even more expedient and proactive. Last but not the least, the Chinese state's overall capacity to orchestrate and maintain economic growth, even as the global economy slows, has allowed it to continue making claims of performance legitimacy. These non-crisis moment institutional and macro policy factors must be considered alongside the molecular absorption of popular unrest by bargaining.

References

Bernstein, Thomas and Lü, Xiaobo. *Taxation without Representation in Contemporary Rural China*. New York: Cambridge University Press, 2003.

Burawoy, Michael and Lukacs, Janos. *The Radiant Past: Ideology and Reality in Hungary's Road to Capitalism*. Chicago: University of Chicago Press, 1992.

Cai, Yongshun. *Collective Resistance in China: Why Popular Protests Succeed or Fail*. Stanford: Stanford University Press, 2010.

Cao Zhenghan (曹正漢). ("Vertically Decentralized Authoritarianism and the Mechanisms of Political Stability in China"). "中国上下分治的治理体制及其稳定机制," 社会学研究, 25, 1: 2011, 1–40.

Chan, Chris and Pun, Ngai. "The Making of a New Working Class? A Study of Collective Action of Migrant Workers in South China," *China Quarterly*, 198: 2009, 287–303.

Chen, Titus. "China's Reaction to the Color Revolutions: Adaptive Authoritarianism in Full Swing," *Asian Perspective*, 34, 2: 2010, 5–51.

Central Committee of the Chinese Communist Party and State Council (中共中央). ("Decision on Strengthening the Integrated Governance of Public Security"). "国务院关于加强社会治安综合治理的决定," February 19, 1991, at www.chinalawedu.com/falvfagui/fg22598/7081.shtml.

Gong Weibin (龚维斌). ("Ten Major Relationships in the Innovation of Social Management"). "社会管理及其创新中的十大关系," 2011, at http://theory.people.com.cn/GB/49154/49156/14661549.html.

He, Baogang and Warren, Mark. "Deliberative Authoritarianism: The Deliberative Turn in Chinese Political Development," *Perspectives on Politics*, 9, 2: 2011, 269–289.

Heilmann, Sebastian and Perry, Elizabeth J., eds. *Mao's Invisible Hand: The Political Foundations of Adaptive Governance in China*. Cambridge, MA: Harvard University Asia Center, 2011.

Hook, Leslie. "Beijing Raises Spending on Internal Security," *Financial Times*, March 6, 2011.

Hsing, Youtien. *The Great Urban Transformation: Politics of Land and Property in China*. New York: Oxford University Press, 2010.

Hu Ben (胡贲). ("The Codification of Weiwen Mechanisms"). "维稳:体制隐然成型," *南方周末*, 2010-3-4, at www.360doc.com/content/10/0305/11/142_176 36520.shtml.

Lee, Ching Kwan. *Against the Law: Labor Protests in China's Rustbelt and Sunbelt*. Berkeley: University of California Press, 2007.

Lipsky, Michael. *Street-Level Bureaucracy: Dilemmas of the Individual in Public Services*. New York: Russell Sage Foundation, 1983.

Montinola, Gabriella, Qian, Yingyi, and Weingast, Barry R. "Federalism, Chinese Style: The Political Basis for Economic Success," *World Politics*, 48, 1: 1995, 50–81.

O'Brien, Kevin. "Villagers, Elections and Citizenship in Contemporary China," *Modern China* 27, 4: 2001, 407–435.

O'Brien, Kevin and Li, Lianjiang, eds. *Rightful Resistance in Rural China*. New York: Cambridge University Press, 2006.

Oi, Jean. *Rural China Takes Off*. Berkeley: University of California Press, 1998.

Nathan, Andrew. "Authoritarian Resilience," *Journal of Democracy*, 14, 1: 2003, 6–17.

Perry, Elizabeth. "Chinese Conceptions of 'Rights': From Mencius to Mao – and Now," *Perspectives on Politics*, 6: 2008, 37–50.

Perry, Elizabeth. "Moving the Masses: Emotion Work in the Chinese Revolution," *Mobilization: An International Quarterly*, 7, 2: 2002, 111–128.

Perry, Elizabeth and Selden, Mark. *Chinese Society: Change, Conflict and Resistance*. 3rd edn. London: Routledge, 2010.

Polanyi, Karl. *The Great Transformation: The Political and Economic Origins of Our Time*. Boston: Beacon Press, 1944 [2001].

Read, Benjamin. *Roots of the State: Neighborhood Organizations and Social Networks in Beijing and Taipei*. Stanford: Stanford University Press, 2012.

Sabel, Charles and Stark, David. "Planning, Politics and Shop-Floor Power: Hidden Forms of Bargaining in Soviet-Imposed State Socialist Societies," *Politics and Society*, 11, 4: 1982, 439–475.

Scott, James. *Seeing Like a State: How Certain Schemes to Improve the Human Conditions Have Failed*. New Haven: Yale University Press, 1999.

Shambaugh, David. *China's Communist Party: Atrophy and Adaptation*. Berkeley: University of California, 2008.

Sun Liping (孙立平). ("Social Disorder Is a Present and Serious Challenge"). "社会失序是当下的严峻挑战," 2011, at www.21ccom.net/articles/zgyj/ggzhc/article_2011022830678.html.

Sun Liping, Jin Jun, and Ying Xing. (孙立平、晋军、应星). ("Realizing Long-Term Stability through the Institutionalization of Interest Aggregation"). "以利益

表达制度化实现长治久安，" 领导者, 3: 2010, at blog.sina.com.cn/s/blog_4e4e23 f6010176x3.html.

Thornton, Patricia. "Retrofitting the Steel Frame: From Mobilizing the Masses to Surveying the Public," in Heilmann and Perry, eds., *Mao's Invisible Hand*, 237–268.

Walder, Andrew. *Communist Neo-Traditionalism: Work and Authority in Chinese Industry*. Berkeley: University of California Press, 1986.

Walder, Andrew. "Local Governments as Industrial Firms: An Organizational Analysis of China's Transition Economy," *American Journal of Sociology*, 101, 2: 1995, 263–301.

Walder, Andrew. "Unruly Stability: Why China's Regime Has Staying Power," *Current History*, September, 2009, 257–263.

Wang Hansheng (王漢生) and Wang Yige (王一鸽). ("Goal Management and Responsibility System: The Logic of Practice in Rural Governance"). "目标管理责任制 – 农村基层政权的实现逻辑," 社会学研究, 2: 2009.

Whyte, Martin and Im, Dong-Kyun. "Is the Social Volcano still Dormant? Trends in Chinese Attitudes toward Inequality." *Social Science Research*, 48: 2014, 62–76.

Xu, Kai and Li, Weiao. "The Machinery of Stability Preservation," *Caijing*, June 6, 2011. Translation www.duihuarjournal.org/2011/06/translation-machinery-of-stability.html.

Zhou, Xueguang. "The Institutional Logic of Collusion among Local Governments in China," *Modern China* 36, 1: 2010, 47–78.

Selling off Entitlements

7 Finding China's Urban: Bargained Land Conversions, Local Assemblages, and Fragmented Urbanization

Luigi Tomba *

Where Does the City Begin?

Returning from Nanhai (Foshan) to Guangzhou, after a day of interviews with local officials, the car left us at the Nanhai station of the GuangFo metro line, one of the transportation engineering stops towards the long-anticipated integration of the two metropolises of the Western Pearl River Delta (PRD), Guangzhou, and Foshan. As has been the case for many of the new rail and metro hubs in the region (integration of the Greater Delta in the national transport network is proceeding apace), this station is in the middle of an unbuilt nowhere, surrounded by cranes, piles of construction materials, newly built roads, and dust. Most people need a private car or a taxi to reach it. These messy surroundings, nonetheless, promise that the city will be there, soon.

But the city is not there yet. Nanhai is an urban *district* (区) that was formerly, briefly, an autonomous *city* (市), and before that a rural *county* (县). It is "urban" because of massive industrialization in its villages (driven here mostly by small and medium domestically invested enterprises) and because the administrative wand has been waved at its classification and names. The municipal government has decided to turn some of its rural townships (镇) into urban "street offices" (街道办) and to rename some villages as "urban communities" (社区 or居委会). These name changes are generally the first sign of "urbanization." Except for the awe inspired by the frenetic pace of construction as well as by its intense concentration of economic activities, however, the occasional visitor might hardly associate the scenery in this part of non-metropolitan PRD with any familiar idea of an urban landscape. And this remains the case even though the PRD is today widely regarded as one of the largest

* This essay is based on four months of fieldwork between 2009 and 2011 in urbanizing villages in the Western Pearl River Delta. Funding was provided by a German Research Foundation Grant (TO 638 1–2 and TO 638 2–1) and by an Australian Research Council Discovery Project Grant (2009–2012).

conurbations on the planet, with 40 million human inhabitants crawling over its vast, riverine and dangerously polluted territory.

Traveling around the industrializing countryside of the Delta, I have wondered where that megacity actually is, what its emergence means beyond a renaming and a remapping of economic activities on the territory. Urbanization, after all, is far from a simple linear process during which people and territory just change functions.

State-dominated processes of economic and territorial transformation, planning, and administrative renaming are accompanied, importantly, by the return of exasperated localisms. Almost counter-intuitively, such localisms appear quite crucial to this particular style of urbanization. They are fueled by the emergence of land-based elites who owe their positions to the long-lasting effects of collective ownership of the land and to the processes of village-level industrialization that took place during the 1980s and 1990s.

At the same time, the power of the state is visible and significant. A virtually uninterrupted stream of governance experiments keeps local officials in townships and districts busy (with cadres in competition among themselves for the "best practice" that will assist in their promotion to higher ranks). This leads to ever-changing varieties of governance solutions. Officials deploy differing, flexible tactics – ranging from collaboration and bargaining, to allowing villages control over the conversion of their land and strategies for industrialization, to all-out violent conflicts.

Despite the apparently homogenizing effects of official "governance speak" that beats the drum for improved efficiency and social order in urbanizing villages, the PRD is, at best, a highly fragmented megacity. Tailored solutions to local problems are often the results of bargains struck between different levels of government and numerous other players. Enterprises and investors, both local and international, can and do inject resources, fostering competition in township and village economies. Entrepreneurial village collectives devise their own strategies in accord with local political-economic opportunities and conditions. In the course of such complex processes, townships and municipal governments try to enforce now-worn-out categories like "city" and "countryside," "urban" and "rural," "state and collective ownership." These binary distinctions are enshrined in the Chinese constitution and inscribed on the ground thanks to China's rigid administrative classification of what is urban and what is not. But these lines, drawn over six decades of planning, are now becoming increasingly blurred.[1]

---

[1] The most recent studies on the highly fragmented nature of China's urbanization and land practices are Hsing, *The Great Urban Transformation*, and Lin, *Developing China*.

Given the involvement of such a large number of players and interests as well as material and policy conditions, the processes of urban place-making today are characterized by the *repackaging of fragmented realities* onto the territory, rather than by *a linear process of transition*. The city and the non-city would be very hard to discriminate, therefore, were it not for the ceaseless efforts of the Chinese authorities, through population policies, land laws, and planning, to reproduce such a distinction. The distinction is often symbolized in the imposition of names and ranks on a territory that resists them. Asking ingenuously "where the city begins" or "where it ends" implies taking administrative labels at face value, accepting that while the boundaries of the city are blurred, the labeling itself does produce real consequences. The PRD megacity is thus the product of very particular assemblages emerging out of contingent factors (both indigenous and global), which recombine locally. In the specific contexts created for them by the national priority being given to urbanization, the megacity is in fact in continuous turmoil. To understand "the urban" we therefore have to see it as more than simply the city. Not only does the ideological and symbolic power of the urban extend well beyond those places that exhibit the spectacle of the metropolis and of modernity; but urbanization itself becomes a site of negotiation among diverse actors, which are neither in nor of the city.

The very act of classifying a territory as rural or urban remains the monopoly of the state, but is increasingly becoming contested, because a change in classification implies substantial alterations in the ways territory is governed. Such acts of classifying the urban have become part of an arena for the accommodation of complex interests rather than simply an instrument of state domination, although coercion is one of the tools local governments do use. The goal of bestowing such a distinction is no longer "capital accumulation" as it was during the fifties and sixties. It seems now to aim, instead, at "rationalizing" the local use of land and other resources, addressing social instability, containing conflicts, and finding reasonable solutions to the host of new problems presented by rapid urbanization. The main goal is to govern urbanization by dealing with each of its local manifestations.

Administrative hierarchies in China are, in turn, also a function of the distinction between collective/rural (集体), and state-owned/urban (国有) land. Seen from this perspective, the government's rationale for promoting urbanization is relatively simple: the higher the rate of urbanization (that is, the greater the amount of land owned by the state), the stronger the state's capacity to govern.

The practices of collective land use frequently form the main arena of contention. Collectives are the formal owners of agricultural land but are also prohibited from autonomously developing it for profitable commercial purposes. Yet they have done so for decades, thereby creating the foundations for the PRD's economic boom. Formally, in order to reclassify collectively owned land to "construction land," it first has to be "urbanized," or turned into state-owned land. Frequently, however, the state negotiates its way to an agreement with the rural collectives involved, circumventing existing regulations to find a tailored solution (shared-income arrangements, financial concessions, or rental) and preventing overt conflicts. While few farmers object to a more profitable use of their cultivated land (by converting it, for example, into an industrial park or a real-estate development) villagers do object to the limitations imposed by state ownership on their traditional entitlements.[2] They are also increasingly well aware that state officials often reap the lion's share of the benefits of land conversion. Regulations on these matters still favor the state as a land monopolist.

Urban officials I interviewed in Guangdong justify their strategies with the need to facilitate planning and large-scale development, and are lured to the urban growth argument by the prospect of financial and political gains. They often argue that industrialization brings more wealth but also requires greater efficiency, standardization, and rationalization of governing and financial processes, for which rural communities are assumed to be ill-prepared. Collective entitlements are often seen as hindering the overall development of the city and the region, and as making the process more expensive. It is not uncommon to hear township and district officials complain about what they regard as the excessive parceling of their territories. They complain about their own powerlessness to bring order to such a fragmented political economy, where even the smallest of players – hamlets and families – maintain sufficient formal or customary rights over land distribution and use to make higher-level officials sweat for results.

The classifying language of the state is the result of the reification of urbanization as a process of rationalization, an inevitable transition towards a higher phase of development. This idea is not, of course, only a Chinese invention. During a visit to China in September of 2013 the President of the World Bank Group, Jim Yong Kim, who was then consulting with the Chinese government on the best strategies to urbanize the country, handed his support to this argument by saying that urbanization often "happens haphazardly. People move in, they invade an area and

---

[2] This goes beyond land. Until recently, for example, farmers converting collective land also lost the more relaxed birth-control policies they were entitled to.

things sprout up ... China wants to do this based on evidence, based on the best experience from around the world."[3]

This centralized logic of rationalization also contributes to the discourse of civilization (文明). Cities are regarded as sitting on a higher step of the evolutionary ladder and are challenged to compete with one another for the label of "civilized cities" on the basis of a complex set of parameters that extends to the behavior of their citizens.[4] These rationalizing arguments take for granted the civilizing value of the urban. In the hands of self-interested urban authorities, the same arguments justify many of the land grabs and transfers of assets from collectives to the state.

The apparently homogenizing effect of such rhetoric stands in stark contrast to the fragmented experiences of urbanization one encounters on the ground, however. Becoming urban means one thing to farmers-turned-billionaires in many Guangzhou *chengzhongcun* (城中村, villages in the city) that were transformed from peripheral, agricultural territory to prime real-estate land in the city's Central Business District;[5] but something else to rural villagers now organized into shareholding cooperatives who are trying to maximize the financial advantages of a self-managed conversion of land to commercial use;[6] and still something else to residents of newly "urbanized" (*cungaiju* 村改居) villages that receive only a fraction of the welfare benefits traditionally reserved for urban folks, and bitterly envy their fellow farmers in nearby villages who maintained control of collective land; and again something else to most of the "rural to urban" migrants who, in their daily lives, never experience the high modernity of China's twenty-first-century cities, remaining trapped in the rural-yet-industrial hinterland of the metropolis.

In the remainder of this essay, I discuss how urbanization becomes characterized by a proliferation of localized solutions requiring new adaptations in governing practices. Historical, territorial, and economic factors all dictate that while urbanization is a national project, its practices and outcomes are determined locally. In the final section, I suggest a possible approach to recomposing this fragmented experience, by referring to some insights from the literature on assemblages.

---

[3] www.worldbank.org/en/news/speech/2013/09/18/transcript-world-bank-group-president-jim-yong-kim-closing-press-conference-beijing.

[4] On the on-going campaign to turn cities into national "civilized" models, see Cartier, "Building Civilized Cities."

[5] Zhang et al. "Self-help in housing"; Zheng Mengxuan, *The Urbanization*; Li,"The *Chengzhongcun* Land Market."

[6] Hsing, *The Great Urban Transformation*; Yang and Wang, "Land Property Rights."

Making and Contesting the Territorial Hierarchy

Maintaining a territorial hierarchy between urban and rural places has long been common practice in socialist China. After the revolution, the making of a comprehensive national plan for development required that people and places be classified according to their economic function. Since this classification also determined how resources were distributed, the territorial and administrative boundaries that derived from this logic were always contested.[7]

The idea behind this approach was to disentangle the process of industrialization from the processes of urbanization of people and resources, through a "rational" allocation of human and economic assets to industrial accumulation. Following the flood of rural migrants into the cities during the Great Leap Forward,[8] from the early 1960s the trend was reversed, with farmers sent back to their villages, and with tight controls over mobility that kept the urban population in check for the next two decades.

By containing mobility and urbanization for over two decades, China also entrenched and hardened the definition of where and what the city is. Partly because of this rigid definition, in the 1980s, when rural industrialization began spreading in the PRD, the spaces "in-between" became both the most dynamic and the hardest to govern.

When Guangdong, the first province allowed to do so,[9] opened up to the international economy, it did so with a selective territorial strategy blessed by central policies – the Special Economic Zones (SEZ). SEZs were aimed at institutionalizing territorial distinction through the implementation of flexible governance rules in strategically located pockets of Chinese territory. Initially, this was about large areas that underwent substantial infrastructural upgrade funded by state investments.

The national strategy rapidly turned local as local governments and even village collectives tried to grab opportunities made available to them by the opening up of the economy by extending the use of zoning.[10] Aihwa Ong suggests that zoning aimed at creating transnational connections that would fit the production models of global capitalism, and produce a "variegated sovereignty." In her view, by applying the logic of exception, it was possible to tailor financial, fiscal, and labor regulations without affecting the legitimacy of the socialist system.[11] However, by

---

[7] Schurmann, *Ideology and Organization*; Lewis, ed., *The City in Communist China.*
[8] Schurmann, *Ideology and Organization*, 405; Brown, *City Versus Countryside.*
[9] Vogel, *One Step Ahead.*
[10] Cartier, "'Zone Fever'"; Li and Yeh, "Analyzing Spatial Restructuring."
[11] Ong, "The Chinese Axis."

formalizing the right of landholders to set rules on the use of their territory, zoning also became the basis of the current fragmented nature of PRD urbanization. In other words, the present fragmented megacity, where a myriad of different governance modes coexist, has its origins in how the hard distinction between urban and rural established during the Maoist period became blurred, allowing the reemergence of localism.[12]

While the distinction between "state-owned" and "collective" has, in many ways, been rendered obsolete by countless examples of local innovation in land management that weaken the rigid distinction and create spaces in-between, these categories cannot be ignored, as they form the basis for the significant local interests generated over three decades of gradual market reform and rural industrialization.[13] With industrial activities located increasingly outside of metropolitan areas, the functional distinction implied by the socialist rural–urban divide was progressively eroded by a proliferation of actors, competition over resources and territory, antagonism among localities, inflow of capital, and the transformation of the region's demography due to the rapid injection of millions of migrants. Local practices became more malleable but an administrative distinction between rural and urban land and people remains in place. As the geography of urbanization shifts, and rural land and people are progressively reclassified as urban, the boundary itself has become an object of contestation.

One result was also to empower the village collectives that had long been seen as resource-less and vulnerable prey for a predatory government. Prevailing local conditions and historical factors mattered for the success of villages during this process of industrialization. When they controlled sufficient resources, collectives often considered urbanization (either formal or substantive) unnecessary to advance their economy. Using their land for development was a way to wrestle resources away from the advancing urban governments. By renting land to industries directly, they could retain the profits of land conversion, rather than relying on the limited compensation offered by township and district governments when land is expropriated. Villagers also tended to secure their interests against the encroachment of the state by accelerating construction of housing and commercial activities that would make any takeover more expensive for the township and district governments.

I encountered one such village in a less-developed township of the Western Delta. The collective derived a conspicuous part of its wealth from the success of one village-enterprise-turned-large-corporation – one of only two "national brand enterprises" in the township. As a

---

[12] Tomba, "Awakening of the God."   [13] Tomba, "A New Land Reform?"

consequence of this investment, the village has a thriving economy and a significant collective rental income from the industrial and commercial land (about 1,000 *mu* out of a total of 6,000 *mu*). Besides higher income, residents of successful villages such as this also enjoy improved employment opportunities in the new industries. Unlike what has occurred even in some closely neighboring communities, in this village the company has favored employing a local workforce for many of its managerial jobs. It also attracted over 2,000 migrant workers to the village, particularly from Sichuan, whose consumption requirements boosted a healthy service economy that further favors local villagers who control rental housing and petty trade. At the time of this research housing occupied about 2,000 *mu* of village land. Local building regulations in these rural areas still require that privately built residential buildings be no taller than 14 meters on each allocated 80 square meter block. Villagers, however, tend to build up to the highest limit if not higher (in violation of the regulations – fines are not very significant), to be able to rent additional residential space to migrants or to include commercial spaces on the ground floor. Villagers themselves also control local markets, trade agricultural products, and maintain control over those commercial activities with the highest value added (such as restaurants or mobile phone resellers, as well as most of the shops selling religious and ritual goods). Most importantly, the village has achieved this without surrendering its land to the municipal government, but rather establishing a collective shareholding corporation to manage the land and conducting active bargaining with the township government.

In this case, by retaining control over greater shares of the income generated on their land, farmers were able to resist and contest the axiomatic subordination of collectives to the state. They also challenged the validity and applicability of governance regulations, which became increasingly dependent on local practices and interests. As one urban planning official put it, "Rules are of no use if no one is willing to play by them."[14] This village elite's position vis à vis the government is strengthened by its history of early industrialization, which placed it in a position to assert control over its own land. Villages that were "convinced" to surrender this privilege in the 1990s, by contrast, generally find themselves with declining resources today and limited control over the income generated on their land. They have become "urban" but also more dependent on the state.

Village leaders in the case mentioned above are driving a hard bargain for their share of the spoils of industrialization and urbanization,

---

[14] Wang, "Transfer of Collectively-Owned Rural Land."

increasing the transaction costs of state land expropriation. Local authorities, however, do not regard them only as troublemakers for this entrepreneurial approach. Accommodating to their "special conditions" also allows appropriation of the success stories of constituent villages into the narrative of a township's success. They perform an exemplary role and higher levels of government often use them to exemplify the success of local development practices. Successful villages thus have an important place in the township economy that results in a greater capacity to lobby the township or even district government for resources, or for more flexible rules. Effective accommodation of local interests (which results in an endless stream of different arrangements often referred to as "each village, its own policy" (一村一策) returns some legitimacy to the local governments involved as well. The need to respond to local interests is also the reason for significant bending of national regulations. In August 2013, for example, responding to a further increase in informal practices of land transfer, Guangdong's provincial authorities became the first to allow, albeit with conditions, rural residents to sell use rights on the land where their housing was built (宅基地), a practice specifically prohibited by the State Council since 1999.[15]

Mixed Blessings of Land Conversion

The rural–urban administrative boundary no longer has the goal of regulating the extraction of resources from rural economies to subsidize industrialization. It plays, however, an important role in governing the process of urbanization that leads to a concentration of resources in the hands of the municipal government.

Scholars have placed emphasis on different aspects of how the conflict between the entitlements of the collective economy and the dominant role of the state play out in the process of urbanizing China. Chan and Buckingham, for example, observe that the process of redefining the status of farmers from rural to urban to make them eligible for social welfare in exchange for their land amounts to a "de facto looting" of their entitlements, with significant consequences for their long-term livelihood.[16] The pace of *cungaiju*, the turning of villages into urban communities, which also implies turning collective land into state land, has in fact been very significant in Guangdong: 1,312 villages had become urban communities by 2005, while by the same year in the municipality of Foshan over 300,000 farmers had become urban residents. Much of this

---

[15] Li Xuena, "Guangdong Plans to Allow."
[16] Chan and Buckingham, "Is China Abolishing the Hukou System?"

transformation has been forced, bargained, and contested, to the point that, still in 2011, the State Council published a circular that explicitly prohibited both the unauthorized use of *cungaiju* and the illegal transfer of collective land to non-agricultural use, both very common practices in the Delta and elsewhere.[17] The new policy was characterized in one comment as "stop using *cungaiju* to force farmers to walk up the high rises."[18]

Other scholars have suggested instead that in the Pearl River Delta, the collective system of land ownership serves to protect farmers' interests during urbanization and industrialization better than in other parts of the country. You-Tien Hsing has defined the conflicts between villages and urban governments as expressions of "civic territoriality," that is the defense of the interests embodied in the territorial prerogatives of villagers against the abuses of higher levels of government.[19] Others have noted that more popular modes of governance in Cantonese villages (for example, village shareholding cooperatives) have produced far better economic returns and autonomy for villages and villagers than in other parts of the country.[20]

The capacity to protect village interests has not resulted, however, in a slowing down of the pace of land conversion. Despite regulations in place since 1997 to prevent the loss of agricultural land, constructed areas in the Pearl River Delta have grown from 5,973 square kilometers in 1996 to over 7,000 in 2002, with a predicted constructed area of 21,700 square kilometers by the year 2020. This was accompanied by an increase in productivity that may have benefited both the villages and the local state: between 1996 and 2002, the average GDP contributed by each square kilometer of constructed land went from 78 million yuan to 136 million yuan.[21]

This is not a process driven only from above. The active agency of village collectives in this process is producing variable outcomes and governance models, with some villages thriving and others significantly declining as a result of their choices of how to deal with the advance of the city.

What I am arguing here is that the two processes (predatory expropriation and consolidation of village interests) coexist, rather than being two different explanations for the nature of the Guangdong model.[22]

---

[17] "State Council Notice." Local authorities in the province also reacted to the perceived widespread violations of administrative procedures in the process of land requisition and conversion. The Luogang district government in Guangzhou, for example, published a compilation of such violations accompanied by a list of "ten forbiddens" (十不准), to guide the action of township governments. Ren Chaoliang, "Luogang District."

[18] re.icxo.com/htmlnews/2012/02/24/1406430_0.htm.

[19] Hsing, *The Great Urban Transformation.*   [20] Chan et al., *Chen Village.*

[21] Liu Xiaoling, *Research on the Growth*, 271.

[22] Chung and Unger, "The Guangdong Model."

Collective land tenure is having contradictory effects on the governance of urbanization. On one hand, it provides a legal and political basis on which local leaders may work to resist the attempts of urban state actors to grab resources and impose development plans. On the other, village elites formed locally through alliances of traditional clan structures and new economic interests have progressively become directly invested in the process of urbanization. They are today significant interlocutors of the state bureaucracies when problems arise. In a very flexible policy environment, stronger and legitimate resource-controlling village elites contribute to an efficient governance structure and work to control and contain conflicts. Resource-rich villages not only reap substantial economic advantages for their residents when land is converted to more profitable activities. They also have to assume responsibilities and costs for services, infrastructure, and maintenance of social order connected to industrialization and migration. They thus help in containing the costs of social change to the state, and in achieving tailor-made solutions for the complex realities of the PRD.[23]

Institutional Innovation, Shareholding Cooperatives and the Risks of Localism

One characteristic common to the governance structure in many of the industrializing villages of the Delta is the corporatization of collective land tenure. Conversion of land (土地流转) has happened through three methods: rental (出租), subcontracting (转包), and shareholding arrangements (入股). In the whole of the Delta, subcontracting and shareholding arrangements have been used to convert about 3.05 million *mu* or 60 percent of the converted land in the province. In the four districts of the city of Foshan, shareholding arrangements were used for about 92 percent of all converted land.[24]

Despite the prevailing legal limitations on leasing out collective farmland for profit, village collectives were encouraged to pool land use rights so as to create large shareholding cooperatives (股份合作社). The shareholding system, initially intended to facilitate the conversion of collectively owned agricultural land from small farms into more profitable uses in rapidly industrializing areas across the region, also had the effect of consolidating properties, and thus facilitating the pursuit of villagers' own

---

[23] Tomba, "Awakening of the God." Studies of village-level governance have appeared in recent years that can complement this analysis and add complexity to the understanding of this transition. See for example Tsai, *Accountability without Democracy*.

[24] Zhang Zheng, "Report on the Situation."

economic interests, often in opposition to the interests of their township and district governments.

Under the shareholding system, agricultural, commercial, and reserved housing land all become assets of the cooperative. Individual villagers (rather than families as under the household responsibility system) receive equal shares in the cooperative and are entitled to the distribution of dividends. The cooperatives have a chairman, a management committee, and a representative assembly that approves a yearly plan on how the income generated should be redistributed or reinvested. The shareholding cooperative, with its control of the village's most important resources, operates in tandem with the village committee, and while the two bodies do not entirely overlap, some of the services and welfare provided by the village committee are funded out of coop income.[25]

While the PRD featured, as early as the mid-1990s, several different forms of this experimental policy "model,"[26] the district of Nanhai is generally considered the place where the system was first experimented, with some now referring to Nanhai as the "second Xiaogangcun" or the site of a "second rural leap forward" (农村第二跃进),[27] following the de-collectivization of the early 1980s. The city of Nanhai (today a district of the city of Foshan), introduced shareholding cooperatives in 1993, following experiments carried out during the 1980s. According to official data, in the first five years of implementation some 1,870 such share-holders' cooperatives were created in Nanhai, distributing dividends of over 13 billion yuan to 766,000 farmers. As a result, the average income of Nanhai rural residents was reported to have increased 150 percent to over 6,200 yuan per capita.[28] The economic success of the Nanhai experiment encouraged village collectives in many other parts of the PRD to adopt similar strategies. Since the creation of these shareholding cooperatives did not require fundamental changes in the land laws, decisions concerning them continued to be taken at the municipal level. Cities like Foshan and Dongguan (administering large territories still formally classified as "rural") adopted the new system at different times and in different ways. The system has never explicitly become a national policy, but similar experiments are now widespread in other parts of the country. It has

---

[25] See for example Bo Chen, "Property Rights Arrangements"; He and Shang, "The Shareholding Cooperative"; Huang Li, "The Impact."

[26] At least a Nanhai model, a Guangzhou model, and a Zhanjiang model were all popularized during the 1990s, in the name of adapting the system to the specific local conditions and the different municipalities' land conversion processes, see Zhou and Wang, "Theory and Practice."

[27] *Xiaogangcun* (小岗村) was the first experimental site in Anhui for the household responsibility system. Huang Yanhua, "Nanhai, Guangdong."

[28] Feng Shanshu, "The Bitter Changes."

also received endorsements from numerous central leaders. In November 2011, the Vice-Minister of Land and Resources, Wang Shiyuan, after carrying out inspections in Foshan and other PRD localities, encouraged "all localities with the right conditions" to adopt this "Guangdong model."[29] The regulations promulgated allowed for great variation in implementation of the new shareholding system both between and within different municipalities, districts, and townships. In Dongguan, for example *shareholding co-ops* were formalized in 2004. By 2006, reportedly, over 99 percent of the village collectives in the city's territory had completed the transition to the new system, with 1.192 million farmers formally becoming shareholders.[30]

Such a swift pace of transition inevitably gave rise to criticism. While this new form of governance was officially heralded and praised as "voluntary" (自愿), some observers have compared it to the forced collectivization movement of the 1950s, when the whole of the Chinese countryside was hurriedly reorganized into increasingly "socialist" forms of production cooperatives, often despite the opposition of farmers.[31] While the overall picture of the PRD rural economy is significantly rosier more than a decade after the experiments began, it remains to be proven that the shareholding cooperatives were the main institutional driver of such improvement. The areas where the new system was seen as more successful, in fact, also happened to be those that experienced the highest levels of investments, economic construction, and industrialization, and therefore had the strongest interest to protect the wealth created locally. The dramatic improvement in incomes and living standards might, thus, well be attributed more to the changed conditions of the economy than to administrative innovation. Also, villages were affected differently by the corporatization of collective land, with some flourishing and others remaining sluggish in their economic outlook. Economic outcomes were significantly affected by location: villages whose territory was progressively enclosed into the core urban areas have experienced the greatest improvements in their economic position. Many of the original residents of these so-called "villages in the city" in Guangzhou or Shenzhen, for example, saw the value of their land use rights increase many fold when the municipality decided to use it for signature real-estate projects. In the case of such projects, the municipality was willing to make significant financial concessions to landholders to avoid protests that might have derailed other significant urban projects. In these cases, the consolidation of collective use rights through shareholding cooperatives helped the collectives to strengthen their position vis à vis the

---

[29] Li Yue, "Land Ministry Survey."   [30] Feng Shanshu, "The Bitter Changes."   [31] Ibid.

municipality, and the capital returns from their real estate catapulted some old farmers onto the Olympus of the PRD's super rich.[32]

In other cases, however, especially farther away from the urban core, results were not as spectacular, with villages struggling to achieve returns on their shares or giving up their rights entirely in exchange for short-term gains guaranteed by a real-estate or industrial deal and the sale of land to the urban authorities.

GZ, a village in Shunde, was, for example, particularly rich in available land but with a weak local economy and a divided leadership. Bargaining with the local state was eventually successful when villagers accepted a good and advantageous offer for compensation, but the final result was an almost complete takeover by the district government. The village controlled the largest available amount of agricultural land in the township, and is split in two by a new road and near the border with a neighboring, more developed township. GZ is one of only three very large villages in the district and, as has happened in other parts of the Delta, it is the product of the merger of six neighboring villages. The 1990 merger was a complex political operation orchestrated by the township government, which sent down a high-ranking official to sort out the differences between the different leaderships of the merged villages. As one of the deputy party secretaries of the village said: "We suddenly found ourselves with seven party committees and six party secretaries, all at the same level. I am a secretary, you are a secretary, so who is in charge? Once the township sent down a 'general' secretary, all secretaries became deputies, and in charge of one of the sub-committees in the village. It is complicated but it has historical roots."

The land here is still controlled by the production teams. "[I]t is like having thirty-seven different *shareholding co-ops*," said one cadre. This situation made it particularly hard to find a solution for the expropriation of the land, despite the pressures from the district government, and delayed the process for much longer than the township and district authorities had hoped. The discussion about the expropriation of village land to create a new district-level industrial zone lasted eight years, amid stiff resistance and heated discussions. Because every team was endowed with a different amount of land, and had different expectations, reaching a collective agreement was hard. The district government was originally only interested in a portion of the land but villagers requested (and eventually obtained agreement) that the district purchase the whole of the agricultural land in the village, to make sure that benefits could flow to all villagers. Some teams had a larger population and thus a smaller

---

[32] Chung and Unger, "The Guangdong Model."

amount of land per capita, and the variation was significant, between one and two *mu* per capita. In 2009, the village leadership was still reluctant to mention the state of the discussion, but by the time of our visit in 2010 the final deal with the district government had become a reason for self-congratulation. The deal reached in 2010 with the district government for the sale of all the village's land included a payment of between RMB 54,000 and 90,000 per *mu* for the land and the preservation of collective use rights over the residential land, while 15 percent of the land was "reserved" for direct development by the village collective. The preservation of the residential setting after expropriation is also a common feature in this part of the country as it is a more economical solution than physical relocation, which is common in other places.[33] A thirty-year annual payment by the district to each family was also included in the deal, to compensate for the loss of agricultural income. Another consequence of the agreement was that the villagers would become urban residents and that the district, not the township, would be directly responsible for the development of the area. Urban social regulations however, including a stricter implementation of the one-child policy, would be required to take effect for residents after a five-year transitional period.

The experiences of villages in neighboring townships, which had surrendered their land in exchange for compensation, also accounted for a greater public awareness of the potential value of industrial and commercial land in the urbanizing PRD. George Lin, for example, reports that in one case in a nearby county in 2006 the compensation paid to the collective had been 35,000 yuan per *mu*, and that a subsequent sale of the land for 120,000 yuan per *mu* to a real-estate developer had sparked serious incidents between the expropriated villagers and the local authorities.[34]

Considering that GZ villagers controlled slightly more than one *mu* per capita of agricultural land (10,800 *mu* for 10,355 residents), many families found themselves with cash in their pocket corresponding to several decades of their agricultural income. In late 2010, almost all private houses were being renovated or rebuilt, often with lavish finishes and high fences. The availability of cash and the loss of agricultural land did not encourage an exodus from the village (although some interviewees suggested that they would buy an apartment in the city) but rather its renewal and upgrading. Villagers also expected the village to experience a significant growth in population once factories replaced agriculture and fisheries, and consequently a significant increase in opportunities for commercial activities and rental income as migrant workers flowed into

[33] Sargeson and Song, "Land Expropriation."   [34] Lin, *Developing China*, 5.

the village. (At the most recent count, migrants amounted to only about 10 percent of the population here, which was much less than the average in the eastern corridor of the Delta). Local shop owners, however, could easily see the advantages of the new situation: "There are not many migrants today, but wait until all of the big factories start producing, and there will be tens of thousands of industrial and commercial workers." Villagers were also voicing their expectations that further planning of still more real-estate developments will follow, and were trying to maximize the value (and the future potential compensation) of the assets they continued to hold on the collective land by upgrading their houses.

In the case of GZ, then, it was not only the distance from the metropolitan area that mattered but a combination of historical and structural conditions, accidents of geography, elite cohesion, and political economy that all had a role in determining a specific outcome. I have observed important differences among villages within the same county in the western PRD, where both governing practices and economic rewards varied substantially between adjacent villages. My observations suggest that those communities with cohesive elites that had developed their rural industry early, during the 1980s, obtained the best results. Those that had relied on small-scale agricultural activities, or were guided by divided and conflict-prone elites (often due to protracted clan conflicts), were often affected negatively by the introduction of shareholding cooperatives.[35] The corporatization of the village's economy does not appear to weaken or supersede but rather reinforces preexisting structures of community politics: the collective remains the corporate title holder, and older informal networks, clan interests, and customs continue to overlap the formal institutions of power in the villages.

While *shareholding cooperatives* can put villages in a position to protect collective land from predatory expropriation, they can also generate new forms of inequality and social friction, which in turn adds fuel to the arguments of those who are critical of the shareholding system. In the township of Humen (Dongguan), for example, after the introduction of cooperatives and the transformation of villages into residents' committees, the average income for farmers had increased dramatically from 9,508 yuan in 2004 to 16,439 yuan in 2010 (73 percent). However, significant differences among villages also emerged, revealing that the shareholding cooperatives were also tending to entrench inequalities *between* villages. Humen's six top performing villages averaged an income of over 30,000 yuan, while in the bottom nine the average was only 8,420 yuan (almost a four-to-one ratio). The percentage of an individual's

---

[35] Tomba, "Awakening of the God."

income derived from the shareholding system also varied significantly. Residents in the wealthiest villages received almost half their income from dividends, while the bottom communities only received about 29 percent of their yearly revenues from dividends. The survey also showed that this difference in income between villages was directly proportional to the number of enterprises in the village (average 272 in top villages and 45 in bottom villages), and consequently to the numbers of migrants living in each village (7.46 times more than villagers in bottom villages and 10.74 times in top villages). While the system, as some have argued,[36] has been strengthening wealthy villages' capacity to resist expropriation from the state, it has also, in the absence of a progressive tax system, been the source of new and different types of inequality.

Shareholding cooperatives are also criticized for redirecting the wealth produced by industrialization out of shareholders' pockets and into the provision of services for the collective economy. In Nanhai, for example, the total income of the *cooperatives* in 2007 was 26.7 times higher than in 1993, when the system was first established. In the same period, farmers' average incomes only grew 4.17 times, and the dividend distributed to shareholders grew just 9.91 times.[37] This has led in recent years to increasing numbers of farmers wanting to opt out of the system and go back to a family by family land lease system (分田退股).[38]

This situation points to yet another outcome of corporatization: communities feel called upon to invest heavily to attract and support the industries that guarantee their dividends. Between 1993 and 2007, Nanhai's cooperatives, for example, took their economic decisions more like enterprises than like social communities, reinvesting 4 billion yuan to "develop production" and only 3.2 billion in services for villagers. Findings like this make it clear that villages and their economic organizations are shouldering a significant portion of the costs (and associated risks) of the PRD's industrialization.

Relatedly, investment in welfare has become very segregated or fragmented. Collectives establish exclusive welfare systems for their members. While it is not surprising that such arrangements result in discrimination against the migrant majorities (non-local residents who do not have access to community welfare), they also entail significant consequences for local farmers' differential access to quality service. Shareholding arrangements prevent the wealth produced in one village or in a cluster of successful villages from contributing to the welfare of other citizens in the same township, or municipality, and instead result in

[36] Unger, "Status Groups."   [37] Wang et al., "Transformation."   [38] Ibid.

the territorially based accumulation of wealth in the hands of certain collectives and local elites.

One consequence of this has been the devolution of some welfare responsibilities to highly localized agents and actors who are primarily concerned with the well-being of one community. This priority given to the members of the village community is embedded in both traditional village and clan solidarity and in the collective arrangements of the socialist period. When applied to an economic system that relies heavily on industry and outside labor force, it produces a segregation and privatization of the wealth created in the process of urbanization, and risks excluding from economic and social citizenship large slices of the people who have contributed to the very creation of that wealth.[39]

But even villages blessed with good services can be fragile. The overall devolution of the burden of welfare and service provision to the village-level economy is seen as one of the key reasons behind the recent debt crisis of villages in Dongguan. Having borrowed heavily to establish a rental economy (that in 2011 made up more than 70 percent of the income of Dongguan's rural collectives[40]), both village shareholding cooperatives and individual villagers have found themselves exposed very directly to the risks of an economic crisis – like the one that accompanied the 2008 global financial downturn, hitting hard at export-oriented industry. Villages were also increasingly required by higher authorities to expand their security (治安) apparatus, especially in view of the perceived increase in social risks with the presence of large numbers of migrants. Xue and Wu report cases of villages carrying up to 300 security officers on their payrolls, and an average spending of almost 60 percent of their income in public services.[41] Such schemes are difficult to scale back in response to a crisis precisely because they represent important employment opportunities for members of the village community.

While shareholding cooperatives are widespread across the whole Delta, specific practices vary significantly, even between neighboring villages. In some villages, the unit of ownership of the collective land is still the hamlet or (as it is still often called) the "production team" (生产队) of communal memory. In other, generally more industrialized, villages, the unit of ownership is the administrative village (the former "production brigade," 大队), and the redistribution of collective income is based on shares that cannot be transferred but can be inherited. At least one district government in Foshan has been experimenting with the

---

[39] Examples of such exclusive welfare systems are described in Chan et al., *Chen Village*.
[40] According to Xue and Wu, "Failing Entrepreneurial," this compared to a mere 9 percent generated through profits from collective enterprises.
[41] Ibid.

complete separation between "economic" and "political" governance at the village level, with two different committees elected separately to take care of the different functions. The transition to an "urban" classification, that is the relabeling of certain villages as neighborhood committees, entails the expropriation of the land, but not necessarily the complete loss of control over the territory by the villagers. The local government thus often engages in bargaining with villages over significant lots of well-located land. The conclusion is generally foregone, but the ability of villagers to achieve long-lasting and significant concessions has been increasing in this part of China, as a consequence of the greater resources available to local governments and investors.

As a consequence of three decades of "industrialization without urbanization" (非城市化的工业化), the specific strategies adopted by village collectives are now shaping substantially the process of urbanization in the Delta. Resourceful village collectives have achieved significant, albeit uneven and divided, agency. As the basic unit of collective land ownership and management, collectives compete with higher-level authorities for control over the profits of land conversion, sometimes with very significant advantages for their communities, some other times exposing their communities to significant costs and risks. Like corporations taking collective risks to achieve profits for their shareholders, villages have transformed their governance structures and competed with other villages to attract and retain economic opportunities. In the process, these collectives have challenged and resisted (when conditions allowed) the formal urbanization planned by the municipal authorities; but their fortunes have become also more precarious, and their strivings have created new forms of inequality.

Guangdong's urbanization does not show the hallmarks of a carefully implemented national or even provincial plan. Rather, it appears negotiated and fragmented. The incremental nature of land reform, the entrenched and reemerging interests of local actors, and the important and legitimate role played historically by local policy experiments during the socialist period all combine to decide local outcomes.[42] With numerous competing claims to the land, every locality seems to negotiate its own way toward industrialization or urbanization, in what is often called a "fire brigade" (救火队)[43] approach to land issues, focused on short-term, tailored solutions. While many of the underlying conditions can be quite similar in each locality – centrality of land use rights, a comparable regulatory environment, abundant economic opportunities and

[42] Heilmann, "From Policy Experiments."   [43] Cao Xiuying, "The Pressure of Land."

availability of capital, strong local elites, growth coalitions that involve the state, etc. – different localities assemble these in different ways.

Re-assembling the Urban

The recent focus on urbanization across the nation by China's new leaders has tended to reinforce the idea that the process of urbanization is one directed by the center. While a massive effort at city building is most certainly on the agenda after Prime Minister Li Keqiang called for the urbanization of 250 million Chinese and the construction of one new city per year in the next twenty years, understanding urbanization merely as the straightforward result of central planning, as some commentators like to do,[44] seems to disregard the reality that one sees on the ground. Nor would it be enough, at the other end of the scale, to portray urbanization only in terms of struggle: with the center pushing the urban to new limits, even as localities and rural collectives do their best to resist it. The processes on the ground suggest instead that accommodation and bargaining remain the rules of the game. While the focus of this essay has been on the central role that land plays in the process, what is ultimately at stake in all the bargaining are the terms and conditions on which to "become urban." The Pearl River Delta reveals a proliferation of local solutions, a revival of localism, and a de facto risky fragmentation of what on the surface appears as a centrally guided process of urbanization. Settling only for the descriptive term "fragmentation" to *explain* urbanization and its role in the governance of China, however, would be akin to tearing a toy apart, scratching one's head over how complicated it looks, then leaving it on the ground for someone else to put back together.

One possible way to more acutely analyze and understand such non-linear processes of urbanization may be found in borrowing the concept of *assemblages*. Starting from the work of Gilles Deleuze, and in a critique of social research that focuses on "totalities" (social formations where components only exist in relations with the whole), Manuel De Landa defines assemblages as formations in which factors exist in a "relation of exteriority," meaning that "component parts of an assemblage may be detached from it and plugged into a different assemblage in which interactions are different."[45] In relation to the urban in particular, De Landa has paid attention to how the idea of assemblages helps in explaining processes of territorialization ("that define or sharpen the spatial

---

[44] Gordon Chang for example, www.forbes.com/sites/gordonchang/2013/06/23/chinas-mao ist-vision-a-city-of-260-million-people/.
[45] De Landa, *A New Philosophy*, 10.

boundaries of actual territories") and deterritorialization ("that destabilize spatial boundaries or increase internal heterogeneity").[46]

De Landa's method encourages us to look at factors first and to assemble them to make sense of visible (and variable) wholes. This method emboldens the idea that the analysis of a social system should embrace its complexity, not aim at simplification; it also suggests to me that such complexity can yield useful narratives to make sense of the complex social processes involved in urbanization, and the different roles actors play under different circumstances (farmers, village elites, local governments, geographic locations, policy environments, and political histories). Finally, it urges scholars of China to bring all the elements of the story to bear, rather than focusing only on identifying the dominant one. The latter approach is often tempting in China, where the state appears always and again as the point of arrival of any analysis of social change.

Instead, I propose that, in the process of urbanization, the role and condition of each unit of the territory are determined by the combination of at least four sets of factors: land classification and other conventions associated with the institutions that define the administrative hierarchies of "the urban"; geographic and infrastructural conditions; the local political economy; and global factors.

A narrative of the ways in which the PRD recombines into an assemblage may thus look like this. A rigid distinction between urban and rural was the most significant "territorializing" factor in socialist China, as it projected boundaries onto the territory and established the rules of exchange between the city and the countryside. This produced a binary classification of land (state/collective), people (urban/rural) and economic activities (industry/agriculture) that slowed down the transformations generally associated with urbanization (population movements and concentrations of resources) and defined socialist cities as protected areas of capital accumulation. The rezoning of the territory that began with the creation of the SEZs in the 1980s responded to two needs: preserve the legitimacy of the regime while bending the rules (by creating zones of "exception"[47]); and allow the flow of global capital in the country's industrial economy. This ultimately produced a de facto deregulation of land practices and a significant "destabilization" of the rigid territorial and administrative boundaries between city and countryside, territorial functions, and classification of the population. Increased flows of population, communication technologies, and trading networks also contributed to undermining the original classification of city and countryside. The conflicts over territorial classification both weakened the dominant role of

---

[46] Ibid., 13.   [47] Ong, *Neoliberalism as Exception.*

the state and empowered local elites. Collective ownership of village land turned some communities with significant landholdings and cohesive elites into significant players in this process. In this process, villages tried to take advantage of the very logic introduced by the SEZ, and autonomously (and at times illegitimately) reallocated part of their land to industrial or real-estate projects. The success of village strategies depended on historical and infrastructural factors that, at times, appear almost serendipitous. The construction of a road, the presence of a wealthy local entrepreneur, access to a specific market, the availability of flat land, all affected the capacity of the villages to take advantage of the new situation. Equally, the capacity to bargain with the state became crucial. A divided leadership (often the consequence of historical conflicts among village clans) produced poor results, while cohesive collectives often obtained better terms and more autonomy for themselves. A culturally informed localism reasserted itself, revitalizing kinship networks, producing new coalitions and becoming harder for the state to ignore.

In each village, such factors recombined in a different way. State actors, in response, also recombined differently. In Dongguan, for example, a more decentralized configuration of interests meant that villages became parts of coherent industrial districts and the township level of government became the most powerful one for coordinating and providing infrastructural inputs to the local industrial system. It also meant, however, that villages had to take on much greater levels of risk, rendering their positions more tenuous. In other parts of the Delta, the higher municipal or district levels maintained control over regional planning and economic growth. More likely to intervene in determining investment outcomes, they also worked to shift the balance of power to their advantage. This difference was, not incidentally, also a result of the internal hierarchy of municipal governments, and of geographic conditions (the East has more natural boundaries that favor industrial district structures and is closer to Hong Kong which facilitates international, larger-scale investments). While Guangzhou was and remains a well-established urban polity, Dongguan is an example of a more decentralized governance structure where today's townships are the traditional market towns and remain the seats of actual power. A stronger role for the state allowed Guangzhou to survive unscathed when the financial storm hit, while autonomous Dongguan townships and villages were ill-prepared and floundering in debt.

While the region became "deterritorialized," villages relying on their own strategies also strengthened the boundaries of their territory, by consolidating their control over resources, and fortifying rules of membership, as well as forms of economic solidarity. The "corporatization" of villages has hardened the barriers between villagers–shareholders and outsiders and, where the resulting wealth allowed, produced decidedly exclusive and potentially unequal welfare systems.

In all this, of course, the state does matter. In fact, the relationship to the state remains the most important factor in determining the success or failure of any territorial unit, village, or region. The state's presence and action are, however, not guided by a single rationality or primarily by the national or regional goals of urbanization. Its actions are therefore not always predictable. While the shared goals of state actors remain growth and stability, the way in which they produce such outcomes depends on how they interact with the localities. In other words, while the state is in itself an autonomous, powerful player (with goals and rationalities and relatively stable ideology), its effects are not homogeneous and in many places are not visible unless they are considered in combination with physical and human factors manifested at the local level.

References

Barmé, Geremie R. and Goldkorn, Jeremy, eds. *Civilising China*. Canberra: Australian Centre on China in the World, 2013.

Bo Chen (傅晨). ("Property Rights Arrangements in China's Rural Cooperative Organizations"). "我国农村社区合作经济组织的 产权制度安排," 农村经营管理, 11: 2008.

Brown, Jeremy. *City Versus Countryside in Mao's China: Negotiating the Divide*. Cambridge and New York: Cambridge University Press, 2012.

Cao Xiuying (操秀英). ("The Pressure of Land: How do we Advance Development and Protect the 'Red Line' at the Same Time?"). "土地的压力：保发展与保红线如何兼顾," 科技日报, February 1, 2013, at digitalpaper.stdaily.com/hwww.kjrb .com/kjrb/html/2013–02/01/content_190200.htm?div=-1.

Carrillo, Beatriz and Goodman, David S. G., eds. *Peasants and Workers in the Transformation of Urban China*. Cheltenham: Edward Elgar, 2012.

Cartier, Carolyn. "'Zone Fever', the Arable Land Debate, and Real Estate Speculation: China's Evolving Land Use Regime and its Geographical Contradictions," *Journal of Contemporary China*, 10, 28: 2001, 445–69.

Cartier, Carolyn. "Building Civilized Cities," in Barmé and Goldkorn, eds., *Civilising China*, 256–285.

Chan, Anita, Madsen, Richard, and Unger, Jonathan. *Chen Village: From Revolution to Globalization*. Berkeley: University of California Press, 2009.

Chan, Kam-Wing and Buckingham, Will. "Is China Abolishing the Hukou System?" *China Quarterly*, 195: 2008, 582–606.

Chung, Him and Unger, Jonathan. "The Guangdong Model of Urbanisation: Collective Village Land and the Making of a New Middle Class," *Chinese Perspectives*, 3: 2013, 33–41.

De Landa, Manuel. *A New Philosophy of Society: Assemblage Theory and Social Complexity*. New York: Continuum, 2006.

Feng Shanshu (冯善书). ("The Bitter Changes of the 'Nanhai Model'"). "南海模式: 遭遇变局," *中国乡村发现*, 9: 2009, at www.zgxcfx.com/Article/17734.html.

He Shuyi (何淑仪) and Shang Chunrong (商春荣). ("The Shareholding Cooperative System and the Rights of Women: A Guangdong Province Survey"). "土地股份合作制与农村妇女土地权益 – 基于广东省的调查研究," *广东农业科学*, 2: 2010.

Heilmann, Sebastian. "From Policy Experiments to National Policy: The Origins of China's Distinctive Policy Process," *China Journal*, 59: 2008, 1–30.

Hsing, You-Tien. *The Great Urban Transformation: Politics of Land and Property in China*. Oxford: Oxford University Press, 2010.

Huang Li (黄丽). ("The Impact of Rural Land Shareholding Cooperatives on Social Security"). "农地股份制度的社会保障效应研究," *中国集体经济*, 4: 2008.

Huang Yanhua (黄艳华). ("Nanhai, Guangdong: The Rural Shareholding System Reaches Three Boundaries"). "广东南海: 农村股份合作制触到三个边界," *中国改革*, 7: 2004.

Lewis, John Wilson, ed. *The City in Communist China*. Stanford: Stanford University Press, 1971.

Li, Tian. "The *Chengzhongcun* Land Market in China: Boon or Bane? – A Perspective on Property Rights," *International Journal of Urban and Regional Research*, 32, 2: 2008, 282–304.

Li, Xia and Yeh, Anthony Gar On. "Analyzing Spatial Restructuring of Land Use Patterns in a Fast Growing Region Using Remote Sensing and GIS," *Landscape and Urban Planning*, 69: 2004, 335–354.

Li Xuena (李雪娜). ("Guangdong Plans to Allow the Conversion of Housing Land in Townships"). "广东拟允许宅基地在镇域范围内流转," *财新*, August 6, 2013, at china.caixin.com/2013–08–06/100565899.html.

Li Yue (李乐). ("Land Ministry Surveys the 'Guangdong Model' of Land Shares"). "国土部调研土地股改 '广东模式'," *中国经营报*, 26, November 2011.

Lin, George C. S. *Developing China: Land Politics and Social Conditions*. London and New York: Routledge, 2009.

Liu Xiaoling (刘小玲). (*Research on the Growth of Urban and Rural Land Markets at a Time of Structural Change*). *制度变迁中的城乡土地市场发育研究*. 广州: 中山大学出版社, 2005.

Ong, Aihwa. "The Chinese Axis: Zoning Technologies and Variegated Sovereignty," *Journal of East Asian Studies*, 4, 1: 2004, 69–96.

Ong, Aihwa. *Neoliberalism as Exception: Mutations in Citizenship and Sovereignty*. Durham and London: Duke University Press, 2006.

Ren Chaoliang (任朝亮). ("Luogang District, Guangzhou: Build a 'Protective Wall' for Clean Requisitions and Demolitions"). "广州萝岗区: 为廉洁征拆建' 防护墙'," *广州日报*, July 16, 2013.

Sargeson, Sally and Song Yu. "Land Expropriation and the Gender Politics of Citizenship in the Urban Frontier," *China Journal*, 64: 2010, 19–45.

Schurmann, Franz. *Ideology and Organization in Communist China*. Berkeley: University of California Press, 1968.

"State Council Notice on the Active and Reliable Implementation of the Reform of Household Registration Management." "国务院办公厅关于积极稳妥推进户籍管理制度改革的通知," at www.gov.cn/zwgk/2012–02/23/content_2075082.htm.

Tomba, Luigi. "The Awakening of the God of Earth: Land Place and Class in Urbanizing Guangdong," in Carrillo and Goodman, eds., *Peasants and Workers*, 40–61.

Tomba, Luigi. "A New Land Reform?," in Barmé and Goldkorn, eds., *Civilising China*, 234–241.

Tsai, Lily. *Accountability without Democracy: Solidary Groups and Public Goods Provision in Rural China*. Cambridge: Cambridge University Press, 2007.

Unger, Jonathan. "Status Groups and Classes in a Chinese Village: from the Mao Era through Post-Mao Industrialization," in Carrillo and Goodman, eds., *Peasants and Workers*, 15–39.

Vogel, Ezra. *One Step Ahead in China: Guangdong under Reform*. Cambridge, MA: Harvard University Press 1990.

Wang, Kai. "Transfer of Collectively-Owned Rural Land Revisited," *Caijing*, October 8, 2013, at english.caijing.com.cn/2013–10–08/113381366.html.

Wang Peiwei (王培伟), Du Juan (杜鹃) and Xiao Sisi (肖思思). ("Transformation in the Pearl River Delta: from 'Land Shareholding' to 'Return the Shares and Redistribute the Land'"). "珠三角变局： 从土地入股到分田退股," *新华每日电讯*, July 20, 2008.

Wu, Fulong, ed. *China's Emerging Cities: The Making of New Urbanism*. London and New York: Routledge, 2007.

Xue, Desheng and Wu, Fulong. "Failing Entrepreneurial Governance: From Economic Crisis to Fiscal Crisis in the City of Dongguan, China," *Cities*, 43: 2015, 10–17.

Yang, You-ren and Wang, Hung-Kai. "Land Property Rights Regimes in China: A Comparative Study of Suzhou and Dongguan," in Wu, ed., *China's Emerging Cities*, 26–43.

Zhang Li, Zhao, Simon, and Tian, J. P. "Self-help in Housing and *Chengzhongcun* in China's Urbanization," *International Journal of Urban and Regional Research*, 27, 4: 2003, 912–937.

Zhang Zheng (张征). ("Report on the Situation of Land Conversion in Guangdong Province"). "广东省农村土地流转状况调研报告," *宏观经济*, 1: 2009.

Zheng Mengxuan (郑梦煊). (*The Urbanization of Shipai Village*). 城市化中的石牌村. 北经: 社会科学文献出版社, 2006.

Zhou Zhenguo (周振国) and Wang Jiangtao (王江涛). ("Theory and Practice of Guangdong's Rural Land Shareholding Cooperative System"). "广东农村土地股份合作制的理论与实践," *中凯农业技术学院学报*, 8, 1: 1995.

IV

Governance of the Individual and Techniques of the Self

Idealizing

8   Governing from the Middle? Understanding the Making of China's Middle Classes

Jean-Louis Rocca

In the mid-1990s, a new consensus suddenly emerged in China concerning the necessity of including "middle classes" as a segment of Chinese society. This new social paradigm, which prevails in Chinese academic circles, in the popular media, and even within the political apparatus, is very similar to the universal agreement which arose in Europe decades ago that the presence of middle classes was a necessary element of modern society. In both these cases, how to define the "concept" of the middle classes was the subject of much controversy. Researchers talk about a middle class, middle classes, middle strata, old middle classes, new middle classes, upper middle classes, lower middle classes, and upper classes.[1] In Western countries, the middle classes were perceived by mainstream theorists as agents of modernity, stimulating domestic consumption, introducing new lifestyles anchored in individual preferences, and playing an important role in propelling political change. For many, the agenda of this new focus on the middle class was to "Americanize" (a synonym for "modernize") certain segments of European societies. For Marxist theorists, the agenda was, rather, the overthrow of capitalist regimes.[2]

As a social scientist, how is one to analyze this new consensus? One way would be to participate in the debate about the "concept" of the middle classes, to supply one's own definition, and to seek evidence or not of the existence of an "authentic" Chinese middle class. This is the approach taken by most scholars, both Chinese and non-Chinese, who have dealt with the Chinese middle classes so far. An alternative route, which I will follow, adopts a deliberately constructivist approach, and considers the

---

[1] Howe, *Political Ideology and Class Formation*; *China Statistical Yearbook – 2009*.

[2] Ehrenreich, *Fear of Falling*; Bruce-Biggs, ed., *The New Class?*; Block, *Post-Industrial Possibilities*; Bell, *The Coming of Post-Industrial Society*; Poulantzas, *Classes in Contemporary Capitalism*; Wright, *Class Structure*; Aronovitch, *False Promises*; Mallet, *The New Working Class*; Offe, *Disorganized Capitalism*; Abercrombie and Urry, *Capital, Labor*.

middle-class discourse as an imaginary phenomenon. By "imaginary," I do not mean "fantasy": the emergence of a new or distinct social group is a strong and undeniable reality. In this essay, the term "imaginary" has to be understood in the manner used by Castoriadis when he points out that a society is always an *imaginary institution*, a mental construction.[3] A social phenomenon cannot be analyzed independent of the manner in which it is interpreted. Put simply, the definition of the middle class is never neutral and objective. In the following, we will see that the attempts made by Chinese scholars to provide objective definitions have contributed more to confusion than to clarification. Nearly every one offers a particular definition mainly because behind each definition lies a hidden agenda, either conscious or unconscious. On the other hand, some working definition is required – beyond the common-sense understanding that to be middle class is to be neither rich nor poor.

According to Luc Boltanski, "rather than look for criteria in terms of which the group ought to be defined ... one can investigate the workings of group-making (*travail de regroupement*), the processes of inclusion and exclusion, that produce it."[4] Boltanski took this approach in *The Making of a Class: Cadres in French Society*. As he demonstrates so well there, "cadres" (that group of middle-rank people who have constituted and symbolized the core of the French middle classes since the 1950s) began to emerge in the 1930s. They came from very diverse social backgrounds, but gradually learned to see themselves as members of a specific class. Simultaneously, they came to be recognized, by both state and society, as a symbol of modernity and social stability.

To analyze the making of this class, Boltanski traces the intertwining genealogies of the phenomenon.[5] Here, then, my goal will be to trace the historical processes that led similarly, in China, to the production of a political, ideological, and cultural representation of a new social group.[6] I do not contend that "governing from the middle" is a "political project" driven by the top in a strategically well-defined manner, or some new trick of the ceaselessly resilient authoritarian party-state. My point is simply that from different parts of Chinese society, through a series of actions (conscious or unconscious) and phenomena (some of which may have had unexpected results), there emerged the idea that China *should be* a middle class country governed according to the supposed characteristics and mores of this new category. These processes did not occur to benefit only the interests of any specific category for, in the long run, almost all can expect to be "middleized." "Governing from the middle" can be

---

[3] Castoriadis, *The Imaginary Institution*.   [4] Boltanski, *The Making of a Class*, 30.
[5] Ibid., 472.   [6] Ibid., 475.

conceived as a point of convergence for four phenomena, which will be
analyzed successively in the sections to come. First, there is an increase in
living standards which contributes to the emergence of people situated in
the middle of society as a whole. Second, various micro-initiatives, local
policies, and other diffused actions trigger processes of class production
and reproduction, transforming the old middle classes into "new middle
classes." Third, a phenomenon resembling what Elias called a "civilizing
process"[7] begins to unfold in which new norms of behavior and moral
values are redefined around an imaginary of what the middle classes are
"supposed to be." And fourth, there surfaces a new representation of
politics, the actual effect of which is to *depoliticize* incipient social conflicts. These phenomena are neither linear nor unidirectional but simultaneously generated from above (in public policies, official discourses,
and the actions of the ruling classes) and from below (in the everyday
practices, activities, and self-representations of diverse groups all across
Chinese society). In Foulcaudian fashion, therefore, the production of a
new way of governing China and the creation of new subjectivities are
viewed as mutually reinforcing processes that cannot be decoupled or
disaggregated. Thus, I resist counter-posing "society" and "state" here:
the two cannot be separated. In China, as I have argued elsewhere, the
gap between state and society is filling in gradually.[8] Furthermore, even if
"governing from the middle" can be understood in part as a strategy to
modernize Chinese society while avoiding conflicts and instability, we
cannot assume there is any guarantee of its success. Unlike research that
approaches Chinese society in terms of "transition" or "authoritarian
resilience," my aim is to keep all future political options open.

As for the materials on which I base this analysis, I examine the
scholarly literature but also incorporate the findings of interviews with
130 professionals and executives working in the communications and
high-tech sectors that I conducted in Beijing and Shanghai between
2006 and 2014. I also draw here upon a survey I conducted in 2011 of
501 Tsinghua University students.[9] The objective of the questionnaire
developed for that survey was to gather insights into the social origins of
the students, their tastes, hopes, and political opinions. Finally, the
analysis of middle-class collective actions presented here relies on fieldwork carried out during my six years in Beijing as well as on the data
presented in dissertations written by some of my students at Tsinghua
University.

---

[7] Elias, *The Civilizing Process*.   [8] Rocca, "The Rise of the Social."
[9] I conducted this survey with the help of three students of the department of sociology of
Tsinghua University, He Xuebing, Sarah Hoessler and Liu Cui.

The Making of Prosperity

As elsewhere, the emergence of new middle classes in China is the out-come of rapid social and economic change. Living standards have increased markedly throughout most of the country since the middle of the 1990s. More importantly, a group of middle incomers has emerged which enjoys "small prosperity" (小康), a modest degree of comfort.[10] This group which has to be clearly distinguished from those who are "rich" and those big private entrepreneurs who, contrary to common belief,[11] belong to the upper classes both encounters and contributes to the creation of a new social world. For them, once all their basic needs have been more than fully met, new crucial and worrying questions arise: what to do with the surplus money? What to do with the new luxury of free leisure time? China's sports and leisure sectors have developed at a phenomenal rate.[12] In big cities, cafés and night bars have blossomed, and more and more Chinese people travel for pleasure both within China and all over the world. Going out for a good time (出去玩) has become an important activity in urbanites' everyday life.[13] A new world of cultural consumption is gradually opening up to such individuals. In performing their modern subjectivities, members of the urban middle class may pursue novel tastes, trends, and interests such as collecting vintage fur-nishings and ornaments, or taking classes in yoga or belly dancing. There is also the emergence of new techniques of domination that entrust individuals with new responsibilities for social control. As in other mod-ern societies,[14] values like freedom, "entrepreneurial spirit," and auton-omy have become determinant norms of acceptable social behavior. Individuals now have to find a job and to choose a partner by themselves; they have to act as subjects,[15] that is, to produce their own subjectivities. This injunction to be self-reliant in a world of competition and constraints is, for many, a source of anxiety. Above all, individuals are now expected to be responsible for the condition of their bodies. In China, as in Europe or the US,[16] urbanites adopt the practice of working on themselves, reshaping their bodies, and improving their fitness in order to conform to socially accepted images of the body. Identification with new, more leisurely lifestyles is revealed also by the middle classes' strong

---

[10] Lu, "The Chinese Middle Class."   [11] Goodman, ed., *The New Rich.*

[12] Davis, *The Consumer Revolution*; Zhao Weihua, *Status and Consumption*; Zhou, "Eat, Drink and Sing"; Fleischer, *Suburban Beijing*; Gerth, *As China Goes.*

[13] Interviews with executives working in media and communication sectors, Beijing, Shanghai, 2008–2010; Tsinghua University Survey.

[14] Rose, *Inventing Our Selves*; Dean, *Governmentality*; Boltanski and Chiapello, *The New Spirit of Capitalism.*

[15] Elias, *The Civilizing Process.*   [16] Rose, *Powers of Freedom.*

commitment to public holidays. In 2007, rumors circulating concerning the possible cancellation of certain public holidays led to torrents of insults and protests on the web.[17] In brief, a new social group has emerged, composed of educated, middle-income knowledge workers who, like the new middle classes described by the "post-industrialism" theorists,[18] have the ability to change their life expectations. They can invest not only in new living areas, new spaces of consumption, but also in new forms of self-cultivation and self-identification.[19]

In seeking to name and evaluate this nascent social grouping, Chinese social scientists employ diverse criteria. The first criterion is income level, a measure that poses particular problems in the Chinese case, in part because there is no reliable means of measuring the "gray" and "black" components of total incomes, which are often as important as the "white" ones. Furthermore, it is widely recognized that vast differences in standards of living continue to persist across different types of communities and the country at large. To earn 1,500 yuan a month makes you comfortably well-off in a small city of a remote province but in a major metropolis like Shanghai you would be ranked as a member of the lower classes.

The second criterion, since access to higher education has been widely eased since the end of the 1990s, is educational attainment. The gross higher education enrolment ratio (the ratio of those enrolled in university to those of the corresponding university enrolment age (高级教育毛入学率) was 1.56 percent in 1978, and 30 percent in 2013.[20] Finally, occupational status can be taken as a criterion and, as such, can shed interesting light on the emergence of a new category of people, as we will see below. According to Chinese researchers themselves, the results of this effort to delineate the middle classes in statistical terms have been quite disappointing, and the picture remains blurred. According to Li Peilin and Zhang Yi, the number of people possessing all three kinds of "capital" (education, job, and income) that can be regarded as key criteria is extremely low compared to the number of people having two or just one of these sorts of capital: respectively 3.2 percent, 8.9 percent, and 13.7 percent of the whole population and 7 percent, 18.4 percent, and 24.3 percent of the urban population. On this basis, therefore, they propose dividing the middle classes into three groups: the core (核心) middle class (three kinds of capital); the semi-

---

[17] Rocca, "A Tortuous Trajectory."
[18] Touraine, *The Post Industrial Society*; Bell, *The Coming of Post-Industrial Society*; Inglehart, *The Silent Revolution*; Inglehart, *Culture Shift*.
[19] Rofel, *Other Modernities*; Hanser, *Service Encounters*.
[20] News.ifeng.com/mainland/detail_2013_08/19/28774327_0.shtml.

Table 1: *Social stratification in China based on ten occupational categories as defined by Lu Xueyi*

	2001	2006
Upper classes	4.7%	6.2%
Middle classes	18.9%	22.8%
Lower classes	76.4%	71%
Total	100%	100%

Source: Lu Xueyi, *Mobility of Social Strata*; Lu Xueyi, *Social Structures in Contemporary China.*

core (半核心) middle class (two kinds); and the marginal (边缘 *bianyuan*) middle class (one kind).[21]

The interviews I conducted in 2010 and 2013 with prominent Chinese specialists doing research on the middle classes confirm the continuing extreme difficulty encountered by scholars seeking to define and clarify these issues. Probably the criterion that has been most widely used is Lu Xueyi's negative definition of middle classes based on occupations: members of the middle classes are *not* peasants, *not* migrant workers or industrial workers, *not* unemployed, and *not* part of the elite. This amounts to stipulating that the Chinese middle classes are composed of individual entrepreneurs, office workers, and professionals/technicians.

Based on that definition, the middle class constituted 22–23 percent of the population in 2006 and probably reached 25 percent in more recent years.[22] Lu's figures rest on the broadest possible definition of middle classes. However, the price to pay for using this negative and broad definition is that the resulting group is composed of a range of very diverse people. Among researchers studying the subject in China today, everyone seems able to perceive the shade of the middle classes, but as soon as they try to capture it, it disappears.

Class Production and Class Reproduction

Still, the difficulties entailed in defining the group have not deterred researchers from continuing to try. Until the middle of the 1990s, research on the middle strata published by Chinese sociologists did not look at China but focused almost exclusively on Western countries. Analysis of China's own middle strata only began to emerge in the year 1994–1995, at the onset of the second and most radical wave of reforms.

[21] Li and Zhang, "The Scope, Identity, and Social Attitudes."
[22] Lu Xueyi, *Mobility of Social Strata*; Lu Xueyi, *Social Structures in Contemporary China.*

Li Qiang, one of the researchers who had previously published on social stratification in developed countries, recalls that, at that time, there was a strong demand that came from official circles to collect more information and generate more analysis of this social phenomenon in China itself.[23] The number of articles devoted to this topic suddenly soared around 1997–1998, when the abolition of the work units (单位) system and the increase in standards of living entirely reshaped urban society.[24] In that context, the official picture of social stratification as it had earlier been defined by the Communist Party lost its relevance. Once the socialist working class disappeared, the fiction of two classes (peasants and workers) and one stratum (intellectuals) could no longer be sustained. At the same time, the growing income gap between the poor and the rich presaged the possibility of political turmoil. Consequently, intellectuals (including people working for research centers affiliated with ministries, scholars with the CASS and prominent universities) have produced numerous works devoted to the topic.[25]

From the beginning, the matter of defining the middle class in China involved normative, political, and performative elements. "Normative elements" because the discourse on the Chinese middle classes defines a norm or an ideal of which groups might be regarded as belonging to the middle classes and, as a second step, identifies segments in Chinese society that correspond to the ideal type. "Political elements" because the question of what impact the reforms will have on middle-class formation is partially driving the research agenda. "Performative elements" because the discourse on the middle class opens up the possibility of identifying oneself with it, thus contributing to the making of the middle classes as an actually existing social reality in China.[26] From the mid-1990s, scholars in China have been publishing papers and giving interviews on the subject in newspapers, journalists have been writing articles, media groups have created journals and magazines for consumption by the "middle classes," political leaders have discussed the subject, and finally, as a result, a broad social consensus has emerged that the middle classes do (or should) exist in China.

In my survey of students from Tsinghua University, for example, 22 percent consider that their parents belonged to the upper middle (中上) class, 42 percent to the middle middle class (中中), and 22 percent to the lower middle class (中下).[27] Despite the commonly held belief that the

[23] Rocca, *La Société Chinoise*, 121–130.   [24] Rocca, "Power of Knowledge."
[25] Rocca, "Political Interaction."
[26] Performativity is a process in which language expressions result in actions, see Austin, *How to Do Things with Words*.
[27] Tsinghua University Survey, 2010.

middle classes are "new," today's middle incomers are in fact mostly members of the old middle classes or their offspring. The "middleization" of Chinese society therefore is also partly due to the *class reproduction* of old socialist middle classes. During the Maoist period, urban workers and employees of state enterprises and low-level cadres, that is to say, the vast majority of urban dwellers, were situated in the middle of socialist society in terms of income, prestige, and status. They were neither part of the ruling classes nor part of the lower classes (peasants). They had close and complex relationships with higher-ranked cadres (the ruling elite) and enjoyed far better living and working conditions than peasants.[28] Today, all studies show that the middle-income group is composed of registered urban dwellers. So the new middle strata can be estimated as composed very largely of ex-"employees and workers" (职工) and small cadres (小干部), or their children.

Several factors explain this phenomenon. First, good jobs and big money were, and now remain, concentrated in the cities. Secondly, social capital is a determinant factor in finding a job. Even university graduates have difficulties in getting a position when they lack local social networks.[29] But, above all, as education capital has become the main asset on the road to success,[30] the control exerted by urban dwellers and members of the middle classes over the education system provides them with an enormous advantage.[31] At Tsinghua University, students who come from the three big cities (Beijing, Shanghai, and Tianjin) represent 14.8 percent of the entire student body whereas the populations of these cities count for only 3.6 percent of the national total. 72.4 percent of undergraduates come from urban areas and only 22.3 percent from rural areas. The percentage of students whose fathers belong to lower classes (less than 30 percent) is very low compared to those whose fathers belong to middle and upper classes.[32]

This form of control relies on different mechanisms. Every university determines enrolment quotas for each discipline according to students' place of residence. Big cities and rich provinces are systematically given generous enrolment quotas. The best secondary schools – (those which have the best success rate) and the best primary schools – (those which give the best chance of entering "elite secondary schools") are all in the cities. Universities attempt to secure a supply of good students by dealing

---

[28] Walder, *Communist Neo-Traditionalism*; Whyte and Parish, *Urban Life in Contemporary China*.
[29] Lian Si, *The Ants*.
[30] Chen Shuhong, "The Problem of Cultural Reproduction"; Lu Xueyi, *Social Structures*.
[31] Li Chunling, "The Expansion of Higher Education."
[32] Tsinghua University Survey, 2010.

directly with "elite schools" without relying on examination scores.[33] The fact that urbanites continue to have far easier access to higher education is partly due to pressure coming from local governments. According to information I have collected in different cities, local governments exert pressure on universities and on the education administration to preserve and even increase the number of positions reserved for locals.[34] Beijingers contend that these quotas reflect an objective fact: the higher quality of the Beijing population[35] and the attitudes of local governments mirror this position.

The absence of any real reform offsetting this discrepancy between rural and urban populations is also linked to public order concerns, however. In the mid-1990s, the dismantling of the public sector led to the redundancy of scores of millions of middle-aged urban workers. Thousands of incidents, some violent, broke out in industrial cities around the country.[36] Very quickly, central and local governments adopted social policies aimed at limiting the impact of workers' anger.[37] In that context, it is easy to understand why officials were not keen to withdraw the huge advantage in access to higher education still possessed by urban dwellers. Not only would calling this into question have led to new expressions of discontent, but sustaining the lopsided monopoly of urban dwellers in education helped guarantee longer-term social stability in China's cities. In most rustbelt cities and even in municipalities like Beijing, many older workers have succeeded in preserving a middle-class position because their offspring have graduated from superior schools, enabling them to get good jobs, and putting them in a position to help their parents avert a sharp decline in class position.[38]

Finally, the process of reproduction of urban dwellers in the new category of middle classes is linked to the quasi monopoly of middle strata on public discourse itself. As the prominent sociologist Li Qiang states, "middle strata have power over discourse" (话语权力).[39] Undoubtedly it is the upper strata who ultimately control the mass media, but those who produce and read the media belong to the middle class. In media discourse, "middle strata" chiefly refers to a very specific group of people: lawyers, researchers, journalists, technicians, intellectuals, etc., whose parents were urban, well-educated, "networked" people. They are people

[33] Fieldwork, Beijing, 2010–2011.
[34] Interviews with officials, bureaus of education, 2009–2010.
[35] Fieldwork investigations, 2010–2011.
[36] Rocca, "'Three at Once'"; Lee, *Against the Law*; Rocca, "Formation of the Middle Class"; Cai, *Collective Resistance*.
[37] Kernen and Rocca, "The Social Responses to Unemployment"; Rocca, "Old Working Class Resistance."
[38] Rocca, *La Condition Chinoise.*   [39] Rocca, *La Société Chinoise*, 121–130.

who know how to manipulate language and who have good knowledge of the machinery of Chinese society. They differ in almost every way from other types of middle-class people including middle-rank officials, small-scale businessmen, and rural middle strata; but in monopolizing the voice of the whole class, they have, in fact, succeeded in imposing a certain image of the middle strata in China: an image which is very close to what they are. It is certainly not by chance that the media and the academic world have pointed out homeowners as best representing the middle classes. Homeowners are like them: well-educated, modern, rational, supportive of rule of law, etc. And thus the much-reported struggle of homeowners against the arbitrariness of local government authorities has also become one prominent symbol of the rise of the middle class.

A Process of Civilization

The third phenomenon contributing to the making of the middle classes is the growing importance given to the process of civilizing the Chinese people, in which the middle classes play a major role. As has been widely noted, Chinese society is experiencing a deep and complex movement for the improvement of the "quality" (素质) of the population and the normalization of certain associated behaviors. In official discourse, behind the propaganda for promoting "civilization" (文明) rests the idea that the quality of the population must be improved in order to allow China to enter modernity.

The state expends much money and energy in the drive to civilize people. The residents' committees press urbanites to observe proper behavioral norms in public places, such as refraining from spitting or littering. During the Olympic Games and the World Exhibition, a flood of propaganda appeared that aimed to teach Chinese people how to behave correctly, for example, by queuing in an orderly fashion and speaking politely in measured tones.[40] More recently, the reintroduction of the Qingming holiday (清明) in the official calendar has offered a new opportunity for reminding people of this civilizing ambition: the cemeteries are festooned with banners calling for a "safe and sound," civilized *holiday* (平安清明, 文化清明). People are asked to make "low-carbon offerings" to their ancestors and to hold "green funerals" (低碳祭祀, 绿色殡葬).[41] On television, "etiquette experts" present special programs in which they explain to viewers how to behave according to circumstances. One such expert, Zhang Xiaomei, explains in a book that the

[40] Chen and Liu, "After HIGH, Good Taste Has Risen"; Xu Bo, *World's Fair Etiquette*.
[41] Rocca, "A Tortuous Trajectory."

body of "urban dwellers is involved, from the top to the bottom, in a deep process of modernization. They are noble-minded individuals, people of quality but they still need to improve in terms of tastes and 'class', in other words they need to learn modern social graces."[42]

The making of the middle classes relies, furthermore, upon an effort at "distinction" in the two meanings of the word. In contrast to the Maoist period, where an ascetic working-class lifestyle was the norm, people now must not only display their acquisition of good manners and good taste, but also do all they can to distinguish themselves from the lower classes and *also* from the elite.[43] This distinction of the middle from the elite is pursued through a "moral war" against the practices associated with the upper class. As elsewhere, the Chinese middle class' imaginary is characterized by the "acceptance of the ideology of merit over inheritance, of legitimacy based on competence and success rather than money, of the authority of managers over the power of owners."[44] In my interviews as well as in the results of the Tsinghua survey, it is clear that the success of middle-strata members is based on a particular ethics, a moral economy that emphasizes hard work, acquired talents and skills, and rational choice-making in consumption and lifestyle. By contrast, the elite, the very rich, and very powerful are viewed as "dishonest people." They rely on personal relations (political, kinship, etc.) or even on illegal means. Everything in life is easy for them and they do not need to make any effort to enjoy privileged positions in society.

Prominent Chinese sociologists read such attitudes as a form of criticism of the monopoly exerted by a "unified elite," comprising prominent groups from political, economic, and intellectual fields.[45] The rich deliberately hinder the middle strata from joining the ranks of the elite by using social connections.[46] To a certain extent, this moral judgment is supported by the state, which affirms that public policies must guarantee that the only means for achieving success will be through the acquisition of personal skills and hard work. At the same time, according to figures like Zhang Xiaomei, people "in the streets of big cities" must compare themselves against negative sets of behaviors if they are to regard themselves as "well-mannered." "Bad manners" are those of the lower classes: urban dwellers still living in traditional housing, peasants, or migrant workers.

A widespread public discourse on the bad quality of the population (素质不好) takes aim at "popular (vulgar) culture": various unrefined, spontaneous, casual behaviors like spitting on the ground, speaking

---

[42] Zhang Xiaomei, *Zhang Xiaomei Talking about Etiquette*, 4.   [43] Bourdieu, *Distinction*.
[44] Boltanski, *The Making of a Class*, 21.
[45] Sun Liping, "Common Spirit," 22; Sun Liping, *Reconstructing Society*.
[46] Rocca, "Political Interaction."

loudly, eating noisily, dressing carelessly, treating other people rudely, etc.[47] I have been witness to countless small incidents in the Beijing underground arising from conflicts over "manners": urban dwellers criticizing rural workers bearing huge and unsightly bundles (instead of having proper suitcases), young *ayi*s (housemaids) suspected of spreading strange smells, old Beijingers jostling other people to get a seat, etc. In traditional housing areas where such people live, everything is said to be dirty and deprived, the children wander about the neighborhood instead of studying, their clothes are smelly, the environment is messy (乱).

Of course, alongside this contemptuous discourse, we can find a more positive approach to lower-class culture. In particular, academic articles, media productions, and interviews reveal strong feelings of compassion for migrant workers. Adult migrants are depicted as exploited, their children, who are barred from attending city schools, as humiliated and sad, deprived of all access to a proper education. The great majority of Tsinghua students say they are in favor of social policies improving living and working conditions for migrant workers. All these broad generalizations are reasonably founded and true to a certain extent, but they rely largely upon a superficial glance from above. The opinions of migrant workers themselves on such matters are rarely taken into account.[48] Even those progressives in China today who support popular protest movements – researchers, lawyers, intellectuals, artists, members of local assemblies – will still advocate the need for proper political behavior. They regard migrant workers as needing to strengthen working-class consciousness in order to defend their rights. Since the future for migrant workers is to enter the ranks of the middle strata, today's discourse of compassion toward them aims first to neutralize this potentially dangerous class. They are to be instructed and guided to normalize their attitudes and conduct, to behave as civilized people. This anxious focus on popular education is comparable to the way in which the notion of the *évolués* (the enlightened, civilized natives) in ex-French-speaking African colonies was once deployed.[49] In this way, expressing *both* contempt *and* compassion have emerged as crucial normative techniques for promoting the production/reproduction processes of the middle strata. Together, they allow the middle strata to keep an ethical distance from the lower classes.

It would still be a mistake, however, to consider that the civilizing process is only an effect of policies from above. In the "gardens" (花园)

---

[47] Anagnost, "The Corporeal Politics"; Pun, *Made in China*; Jacka, "Cultivating Citizens."
[48] Salgues, "La Chine, entre Cadre et Contexte."
[49] Onana, *Le Sacre des Indigènes Èvolués*.

of today, homeowners and residents set out a code of conduct and standardized behavior concerning all aspects of community life. In order to protect harmony, outsiders are generally prevented from entering the compound. Moreover, the "outsiders" will most often appear to accept the stigmatized image of themselves provided by official and new middle-class discourses. In interviews with migrant workers, many freely declared: "we are peasants, we are of bad quality," "we have to educate ourselves," etc.

Evading Politics

The necessity of "depoliticizing" the issue of middle-class formation is the final element we need to consider here. The problem with politics appeared from the very start, complicating even the proper translation into Chinese of the expression "middle class." The quite literal 中产阶级 poses two problems. The first being that 产 refers to property or estate and, by extension, to capital. People have been understandably quite reluctant to identify themselves with something like property which, in China, is still not firmly guaranteed by law. The second problem, politically even more sensitive, concerns the term "class" (阶级) and its association with political class struggle. Zhou Xiaohong uses middle class (中产阶级) when he is dealing with middle classes elsewhere in the world and middle strata (中产阶层) when he deals with the Chinese case. Others use middle strata (中间阶层), which helps to circumvent the historical association with the Marxist vocabulary of class struggle (阶级斗争), but even more "depoliticized" is the expression "those with middle-range income" (中等收入者), commonly used in official speeches. It has no political overtones, referring blandly to a group of people who have a unique and objective characteristic in common.

The use of "middle strata" (中产阶层) is, however, no longer taboo in official publications such as party theoretical journals and party school journals.[50] And nowadays, the thrust of the "depoliticizing" process where the middle classes are concerned is not based on vocabulary alone, but takes several other forms as well. First, there are the discourses and processes of idealizing the middle classes. It became commonplace in the Chinese media to say that the middle classes fit perfectly with what China now needs in terms of political change: a social force that fights for rights, more freedom, and greater justice without jeopardizing the stability of the country. This works to depoliticize the implications of middle-class emergence by retaining the party in the position of deciding what is

---

[50] See, e.g., Zhao Jie, "A Summary of Research on Middle Strata."

and is not threatening to the regime, while simultaneously asserting that much can be challenged, just as long as the regime itself is not brought into question.

Second, in their analyses, some Chinese intellectuals do try to convince the state that a stable society is not a society without discontent but, rather, one that is able to institutionalize channels for orderly protest.[51] For them, given that the political realm, especially anything involving a challenge to the Communist Party, is effectively off-limits, the only way to change the face of politics is to intervene in the social realm with the hope that, eventually, political change will follow.[52] "In Chinese society, since 1989, politics is a forbidden field."[53] As a consequence, "the only method to change politics is to mobilize people in the social realm so as to force the government to recognize rights to protest."[54] This is the sort of script being followed by homeowners when they have fought against real-estate developers felt to be reneging on earlier promises and understandings. They aim to act as model citizens, scrupulously respectful toward laws and regulations, behaving as civilized persons, advocating for moderate reforms, contributing to social stability.[55] What has been at stake in such neighborhood dramas is an effort to disconnect politics from social problems, postponing politics to a later time, when it is expected that Chinese society will have become a modern society; one in which urban immigrants will have become first workers and then move on into the ranks of the proper middle classes.

Finally, the depoliticization of the middle classes has hinged also on a more general but evident lack of confidence in the ability of a free election system to ensure a safe future for the country. "The quality of Chinese people is too low to introduce elections in China," is so often repeated. Whoever you are talking to in China, this is now the common view. The vast majority of the Chinese population, composed of farmers, migrant workers, and urban lower classes is considered unqualified for choosing China's leaders. Farmers can manage village affairs but have no capacity to decide weightier matters such as the future of nation. Because of the Chinese people's low level of education, an election-based political system would give opportunities to powerful and wealthy people to buy votes. The conduct and behavior of the Chinese people may be

[51] Tsinghua University, Sociology Department Social Development Study Group, *Reach a Long Period of Stability.*
[52] Zhang Yi, "The Political Attitudes." www.cssn.cn/news/424315.htm; and interviews with Chinese sociologists, 2010–2011.
[53] Interview, M. Liu, university professor, Beijing, 2009.
[54] Interview, M. Zhang, university professor, Beijing, 2009.
[55] Rocca, "Chinese Homeowners' Movement."

improving, but not enough to attain international standards.[56] According to some Chinese researchers, representative democracy would weaken the decision-making process, and what China needs instead is urgent social reforms so as to reduce the income gap and alleviate inequalities.[57] In the same vein, Han Han, the celebrity liberal blogger, in his published reflections on revolution (谈革命) has stated his view that Chinese people are not ready for democracy:

"Cultured people" (文化人) link democracy with freedom. But ... for most Chinese people, freedom has nothing to do with publications, news, literary and artistic creation, election, public opinion, or politics. For example, people without social relations consider that to be free means to be able to shout, to cross a street or spit at will; those with a little bit of social relations consider that being free is to break rules at will, to take advantage of loopholes in the laws and regulations, perpetrate whatever evil one pleases. Perfect democracy cannot emerge in China, the only thing we can do is to seek democracy step by step."[58]

What then are the consequences of this tendency to want to avoid politics or political participation where the middle classes are concerned? Some surveys do show that the middle classes are more critical and less satisfied with government policies,[59] more determined to defend their rights and more keen to protest than other segments of Chinese society.[60] However, contrary to expectations, in new middle-class gardens (花园), residents' protest movements are not putting pressure on the regime itself. From this point of view, the behavior of the middle class is not very different from that of farmers, migrants, or workers. But with the middle class, the political consequences of such behavior are more significant. As in the "new social movements" of Europe, middle-class consciousness tends to be strongly linked to a highly specific identity,[61] and most such actions have no broader motive than solving very local, very specific conflicts.[62] For example, the protest movements of homeowners against illegal practices of developers and new residence management companies are limited to the defense of residents' property interests and the promotion of harmonious community (小区), characteristics that

---

[56] The recent controversy about a teenage Chinese tourist having carved his own name on an Egyptian relic is a revealing incident.

[57] Interviews, Chinese researchers, Beijing, Shanghai, 2010, 2011, 2012.

[58] Han Han, "On Revolution," blog.sina.com.cn/twocold.

[59] Yuan and Zhang, "2008 Survey on Living Quality," 62; Li and Zhang, "The Scope, Identity, and Social Attitudes."

[60] Liu Xin, "Middle Classes and Community Governance"; Zhang Yi, "The Political Attitudes"; Fang Jinyou, "Social Functions and Evolution."

[61] Melucci, *L'Invenzione del Presente*; Baggurley, "Social Change, the Middle Class"; Dalton and Kuechler, *Challenging the Political Order*.

[62] Rocca, "Chinese Homeowners' Movement."

align them more with NIMBY movements than with genuine political action.[63]

But, it is not by chance that what participants want to protect is "our garden" (我们花园). In the past, the status of urbanites depended largely on what work unit they belonged to; today it is a matter of the particular neighborhood in which they dwell. The shift from one kind of urban space to another has not changed the central characteristic of the middle classes' subjectivity – i.e. the importance given to a local identity; it has only changed the particular nature of the link to this identity. At present, it is true they are *individuals* (rather than work-unit-defined collectives) who are defending their particular localized identities. But this particular form of identity appears to be advancing at the expense of other kinds – based on work, geographic origin, cultural practices, consumer interests, etc. The fact that developers and management companies, which take advantage of their position for swindling homeowners, are usually supported by local governments does give these movements a certain political aspect. But such movements do not aim at "changing the world," only at "modernizing" archaic aspects of the social reality.

Above all, such protesters are acting as "proprietors" searching to secure their assets and to enjoy a stable and comfortable life. From this point of view, the rights defense movement (维权) is not at odds with government policies. On the contrary, the central government's effort to promote rule of law is in tune with the homeowners' desire to see their rights properly and firmly established. These conflicts are provoked by the inchoate process of implementation of the regime's new legal norms which are calling into question the privileges of local officials and powerful interest groups in the real-estate industry. These vested interests and privileges are perceived, and branded, both by the central government and the middle classes, as "archaïc" and potentially dangerous for social stability.[64] Furthermore, any attempts to aggregate such protests into a unified movement are confronted with hosts of difficulties.

In urban China today, as in Europe, "new middle class individualism is personal rather than political."[65] Nor, at its core, is it a "universalistic" form of individualism defined in terms of a series of *rights*,[66] but a "particularistic and solitary individualism."[67] People's participation in social movements hangs on whether they feel that they, and their community, will or will not benefit from it. These movements can mobilize people as long as they maintain a strong link with the interests of

---

[63] Zhang, *In Search of Paradise.*   [64] Rocca, "Chinese Homeowners' Movement."
[65] Sulkunen, *The European New Middle Class*, 5.
[66] Bell, "Resolving the Contradictions of Modernity."
[67] Sulkunen, *The European New Middle Class*, 43.

individuals. Most participants would not object to the extension of these same benefits to people living in other communities. Yet problems have cropped up in the "professionalization" of such movements. Movement leaders tend to become experts, and as such are gradually integrated into the prevailing political system. In Beijing at least, leaders of homeowners' movements have succeeded in convincing local officials to adopt new regulations concerning the management of housing estates. And who can be better advisors on that matter than movement representatives? The same situation seems to exist in Chinese environmental protection movements. Numerous associations have been created but their effectiveness is proportional to their ability to keep up strong ties with government institutions.[68] The Friends of Nature is a leading example. They aim at changing things from within the system.

In brief, homeowners' movements have contributed to the improvement of the situation of homeowners in Beijing. New regulations have been adopted and it is far more difficult than before for developers and management companies to rip off citizens. But, this limited success had no impact on politics since, from the beginning, protesters present themselves as reasonable people, aiming to negotiate and helping the government find new means to solve conflicts. Many intellectuals supporting these movements have recently been expressing their disappointment at the reduced levels of anger to be found now among homeowners.[69] But, how could we expect these movements, as analyzed above, to fight for more significant political change?

From Aristotle to the 18th Congress

What, then, is the significance of "governing through the middle"? Let us start with what it is not. First, it is not a new form of authoritarian state, proving once again that the China trajectory must be culturally determined to remain in some kind of limbo, between democracy and the darkness of authoritarianism. It is not a stage on the virtuous path of democratic transition, a notion dear to those who conceive of democratization as akin to a form of religious conversion. "Governing from the middle" cannot be understood in such a teleological framework, wherein the present must always be assessed according to an already determined future.

Second, this new technique of governing is the result neither of a "top-down" nor a "bottom-up" movement. The actions of many people and

[68] Lu Yiyi, *Non-Governmental Organizations in China*.
[69] Interviews, Beijing, 2012–2013.

groups coming from many different strata of society contribute to its emergence. Certainly, the report of Hu Jintao to the 18th Party Congress is unambiguous: the main objective of the regime is to "build a moderately prosperous society" (建成小康社会). But becoming middle class – having good manners, pursuing the right lifestyle, consuming rationally, acting as citizens – is already the objective of most people in China. And this desire is only marginally the consequence of state propaganda.

Third, this new way of governing China cannot be perceived as springing from or serving only the interests of those whose social status is situated in the middle of the society. The "social identity" model that now dominates the planned trajectory of Chinese development is universal in the sense that almost everyone, eventually, is anticipated to become "middle class": registered urban dwellers first, of course, but later also migrant workers, and even farmers. On this projection of future trends and transformations in social development, the middle class of today is not only the social category that has benefited from reforms so far. It is, more momentously, the category that is designed and expected to gather together gradually all the categories that will benefit from reform.

Affirmatively assessed, governing from the middle is "a model" in the sense that it demands certain behaviors and policies be followed, in order to imitate the so-called modernization paradigm. The modernization imaginary, spread so vigorously in China by both foreign and Chinese media, has contributed to the popular conception that to be "middle class is beautiful." Like many Western politicians in the past, Chinese leaders have a dream, a dream of the middle class as "the class of citizens which is most secure in a state, for they do not, like the poor, covet their neighbors' goods; nor do others covet theirs, as the poor covet the goods of the rich; and as they neither plot against others, nor are themselves plotted against, they pass through life safely."[70] In summary, "governing from the middle" is the consequence of the *convergence* of several phenomena linking diverse social forces and diverse elements of the society: a significant (but ambivalent) *alteration in the pattern of social stratification inherited* from the socialist period, accompanied by the *perceived necessity of reproducing the urban population* as the social basis of the regime, along with the *normalization of certain social attitudes*, behaviors, and norms of conduct and the *depoliticization* of social conflicts and of political change.

Even if the nature and the scope of this group of people are impossible to define, middle incomers have undoubtedly succeeded in imposing themselves as a pressure group pushing for social recognition through a

---

[70] Aristotle, *Politics*, IV-11.

kind of class struggle. Not only do journalists, researchers, writers, and most officials regard themselves as members of middle classes, from both social and ethical points of view, but their readers doubtless belong to the same social milieu. Who chats, who reads magazines, who appears on television programs? In other words, on the internet, in newspapers, on television, members of the middle classes are talking to other members of the middle classes. Moreover, since the "new" middle classes have originated from the old (socialist) ones, the former has maintained the privileged relationships the latter had been enjoying with the political apparatus before the period of reform. Even if the middle classes do not yet represent the majority of the population, they constitute the most precious part of the society. This idea of the middle classes has become an *illusio*,[71] a fiction and yet also a "rule of the game" that everyone accepts. The middle class exerts a moral hegemony over society at large. In such a situation, the question of drawing class "boundaries" becomes a pointless one. As Sulkunen noted about European mass society, "the new middle class is hard to locate because it is everywhere. Its thoughts are difficult to recognize because they are our own."[72]

Nonetheless, if we insist that the future is not determined but yet to be written, then "governing from the middle" as a strategy cannot work without encountering many difficulties and contradictions. First of all, the fact that the government now governs from the middle does not mean that class conflicts have disappeared. Prominent sociologists are calling for the rapid reshaping of the pattern of social stratification and in particular for a sharp increase of the numbers in the population who belong to the middle classes;[73] they want public policies conceived to help incorporate the maximum possible number of lower-class members into the middle classes. The 12th Five Year Plan (2011–2015), for example, stipulated the official intention to reduce the burden on low and middle incomers, to increase tax pressure on high incomers and to extend the group of middle incomers. A system of low-rent housing is to be established for low-income families. But second, such policies as these, if designed and pursued, cannot but lead to conflicts regarding control over resource accumulation. The ruling classes rely upon social capital and illegal or immoral tricks and deals to accumulate wealth, whereas the main source of money for most middle incomers is earned wages, access to higher education and middle-level social networks. As the main competitors of the lower classes, these two strata maintain control over the

---

[71] Bourdieu, *Distinction*.   [72] Sulkunen, *The European New Middle Class*, 3.
[73] Lu Xueyi, *Social Structures in Contemporary China*; Liu Xin, "Developing the Function of Middle Strata."

education selection system and the powerful networks of personal relations (关系网) in the big cities.

Furthermore, this class struggle is also a moral one. As moral subjects, members of the middle classes defend a certain conception of the meaning of a "good life," a "moral economy," and modern lifestyles. Against the ruling classes, they favor fairer and more open access to wealth and prestige, as stipulated in numerous central government rules and regulations. Chinese authorities are committed officially to turning the nation into a meritocracy where people acquire power and prestige thanks to their abilities and intelligence, rather than because of their wealth or political status. The making of the middle classes is then a new *governmentality* that links techniques of economic and social domination (consumption, savings, labor, leisure, etc.) with the cultivation of new moral subjects.

Finally, the "depoliticization" of middle-class political action is not tantamount to guaranteeing the political conservatism of the class as a whole. On that point, as well as the question of class boundaries, it is important that we avoid any *a priori* assumptions and, instead, practice political science as events unfold. The middle classes have no political or historical "nature per se." The middle classes may be judged to be politically "conservative" if we focus on the fact that they do not envisage overthrowing the party/regime. But these same middle classes can be quite radical where particularistic interests are at stake. The rights defense movements observed so far, for example, tend to support democratization but not direct elections (直接选举).[74] The middle classes, it is clear, have very ambivalent attitudes towards concepts like democracy, rule of law, rights, democratization, and protest. They typically support democratization as long as it works to enable them to defend their interests and their social imaginary.

In brief, relying on a process of integrating the middle classes gradually into politics must postulate that the middle classes will continue to be satisfied by the Chinese party-state bureaucracy, which is becoming increasingly adept at controlling social conflicts. Local governments may buy off protesters with cash payments; the central government may pressure local officials to bargain and negotiate "to find solutions"; or to adopt new and better regulations; or to find ways to coopt protest movement leaders into roles as unofficial advisors. All of these tactics, and more, have already been well observed. And yet, it seems that many members of the Chinese middle classes, and in particular the youngest

---

[74] Li and Wang, "Social Existence of Middle Strata." www.sociologyol.org/yanjiubankuai/tuijianyuedu/tuijianyueduliebiao/2009–01–02/7001.html.

members, are having serious difficulties in maintaining their newly won social status. Nothing surprising here, since middle classes everywhere are perpetually concerned by possible losses in status. The media are full of stories about middle-class confusion, troubles, or what Li Chunling calls the "disease" of middle-class anxiety (中产阶级焦虑).[75] According to a story from the *Financial Times* republished in the Chinese online edition, anxiety and a general feeling of insecurity are becoming a question of public health.[76] Young people, in particular, are finding it increasingly difficult to live according to their own expectations. So, however much its goal may be one of maintaining stability, pursuing a strategy of "governing through the middle" classes would seem to have no chance at all of resembling a dinner party.

References

Abercrombie, Nicholas and Urry, John. *Capital, Labor and Middle Classes*. London: Allen and Unwin, 1983.

Anagnost, Ann. "The Corporeal Politics of Quality (Suzhi)," *Public Culture*, 16, 2: 2004, 189–208.

Aristotle, *Politics*, classics.mit.edu/Aristotle/politics.4.four.html, translated by Benjamin Jowett.

Aronovitch, Stanley. *False Promises*. New York: McGraw-Hill, 1973.

Austin, John. *How to Do Things with Words*. Oxford: Oxford University Press, 1975.

Baggurley, Paul. "Social Change, the Middle Class, and the Emergence of New Social Movements: a Critical Analysis," *Sociological Review*, 40, 1: 1992, 45–61.

Bell, Daniel. *The Coming of Post-Industrial Society: A Venture in Social Forecasting*. New York: Basic Books, 1973.

Bell, Daniel. "Resolving the Contradictions of Modernity and Modernism Part Two," *Society*, 27, 4: 1990, 66–75.

Block, Fred. *Post-Industrial Possibilities: A Critique of Economic Discourse*. Berkeley: University of California Press. 1990.

Boltanski, Luc. *The Making of a Class: Cadres in French Society*. Cambridge: Cambridge University Press, 1987.

Boltanski, Luc and Chiapello, Eve. *The New Spirit of Capitalism*. London and New York: Verso, 2005.

Bourdieu, Pierre. *Distinction: A Social Critique of the Judgement of Taste* (translated by Richard Nice). Abingdon: Routledge and Kegan Paul, 1986.

Bruce-Biggs, B., ed. *The New Class?* New Brunswick, NJ: Transaction Brooks, 1979.

Cai, Yongshun. *Collective Resistance in China: Why Popular Protests Succeed or Fail*. Stanford: Stanford University Press, 2010.

---

[75] Li Chunling, "Conditions of Development of the Middle Class."
[76] Xi Jialin, "Anxiety among Young Chinese."

252   *Jean-Louis Rocca*

Castoriadis, Cornelius. *The Imaginary Institution of Society*. Cambridge, MA: MIT Press, 1998.

Chen Ming (陈鸣) and Liu Gaoyang (刘高阳). ("After HIGH, Good Taste Has Risen, the World Expo Opened up the 'Rite of Passage' of the Quality of the Nation"); "HIGH 过之后 优雅起来 世博开启国民素质'成人礼,'" 南方周末, 9 月2日2010, 6.

Chen Shuhong (陈曙红). ("The Problem of Cultural Reproduction in the Education Inheritance of the Middle Class"). "中产阶级教育传承中的文化再生产问题," 社会纵横, 8–9: 2008, 143–7.

China Statistical Yearbook – 2009. 中国统计年间 2009.

Dalton, Russell and Kuechler, Manfred. *Challenging the Political Order: New Social Movements in Western Europe*. London: Polity Press, 1990.

Davis, Deborah. *The Consumer Revolution in Urban China*. Berkeley: University of California Press, 2000.

Dean, Mitchell. *Governmentality: Power and Rule in Modern Society*. London: Sage, 1999.

Ehrenreich, Barbara. *Fear of Falling*. New York: Pantheon Books, 1989.

Elias, Norbert. *The Civilizing Process*, vol. I: *The History of Manners*. Oxford: Blackwell, 1969.

Fang Jinyou (方友). ("Social Functions and Evolution of Middle Classes"). "中产阶级的演变及社会功能," 国外社会科学, 3: 2007, 54–57.

Fleischer, Friederike. *Suburban Beijing: Housing and Consumption in Comtemporary China*. Minneapolis: University of Minnesota Press, 2010.

Gerth, Karl. *As China Goes, So Goes the World: How Chinese Consumers Are Transforming Everything*. New York: Hill and Wang, 2010.

Goodman, David, ed. *The New Rich in China: Future Rulers, Present Lives*. London and New York: Routledge, 2008.

Goodman, David and Chen, Minglu, eds. *Middle Class China: Identity and Behaviour*. Cheltenham: Edward Elgar, 2013.

Han Han (韩汉). ("On Revolution"). "谈革命," 2003, at blog.sina.com.cn/twocold.

Hanser, Amy. *Service Encounters: Class, Gender, and the Market for Social Distinction in Urban China*. Stanford: Stanford University Press, 2008.

Howe, Carolyn. *Political Ideology and Class Formation: A Study of the Middle Class*. Westport, CT: Praeger Publishers, 1992.

Inglehart, Ronald. *The Silent Revolution*. Princeton: Princeton University Press, 1977.

Inglehart, Ronald. *Culture Shift in Advanced Industrial Society*. Princeton: Princeton University Press.

Jacka, Tamara. "Cultivating Citizens: Suzhi (Quality) Discourse in the PRC," *Positions: East Asia Cultures Critique*, 17, 3: 2009, 523–535.

Jaffrelot, Christophe and Van der Veer, Peter, eds. *Patterns of Middle Class Consumption in India and China*. Los Angeles, London, New Delhi, and Singapore: Sage, 2008.

Kernen, Antoine and Rocca, Jean-Louis. "The Social Responses to Unemployment: Case Study in Shenyang and Liaoning," *China Perspectives*, 27: 2000, 35–51.

Kuah-Pearce, Khun Eng and Guiheux, Gilles, eds. *Social Movements in China and Hong Kong: The Expansion of Social Space*. Amsterdam: ICAS/Amsterdam University Press, 2006.

Lee, Ching Kwan. *Against the Law: Labor Protests in China's Rustbelt and Sunbelt*. Berkeley: University of California Press, 2007.

Li, Cheng, ed. *China's Emerging Middle Class: Beyond Economic Transformation*. Washington DC: Brookings Institute, 2010.

Li Chunling (李春玲). ("Conditions of Development of the Middle Class in China"). "中国中产阶级的发展状况," 黑龙江社会科学, 1: 2011, 45–56.

Li Chunling (李春玲). ("The Expansion of Higher Education and the Inequality of Education Opportunity"). "高等教育扩张与教育机会不平等," 社会学研究, 2010, at www.sociology.cass.cn.

Li Chunling (李春玲), ed. (*Formation of the Middle Class in Comparative Perspective: Process, Influence and Socioeconomic Consequences*). 必要视野下的中产阶级形成. 北京: 社会科学文献出版社, 2009.

Li Lulu (李路路) and Wang Yu (王宇). ("Social Existence of Middle Strata in Contemporary China: Social Living Conditions"). "当代中国中间阶层的社会存在: 社会生活状况," 社会视野网, 一月二日2009, at www.sociologyol.org/yanjiubankuai/tuijianyuedu/tuijianyueduliebiao/2009–01–02/7001.html.

Li Peilin (李培林) and Zhang Yi (张翼). ("The Scope, Identity, and Social Attitudes of the Middle Class in China"). "中国中产阶级的规模. 认同和社会太读," 社会, 2: 2008, 1–19.

Lian Si (廉思). (*The Ants*) 蚁族. 桂林: 广西师范大学出版社, 2009.

Liu Xin (刘欣). ("Developing the Function of Middle Strata in the Construction of Urban Society"). "发会中产阶层在城市社会建设中的作用," 探索与证明, 1: 2010, 45–58.

Liu Xin (刘欣). ("Middle Classes and Community Governance in Urban China"). "中国城市中产阶层与社区治理,"paper prepared for the conference Middle-Class Studies in the Chinese Societies, 长春, 7月22日2008.

Lu, Hanlong. "The Chinese Middle Class and Xiaokang Society," in Li, ed., *China's Emerging Middle Class*, 104–132.

Lu Xueyi (陆学艺). (*Mobility of Social Strata in Contemporary China*). 当代中国社会阶层流动. 北京: 社会科学出版社, 2004.

Lu Xueyi (陆学艺). (*Social Structures in Contemporary China*). 当代中国社会结构. 北京: 社会科学文献出版社, 2010.

Lu Yiyi. *Non-Governmental Organizations in China: The Rise of Dependent Autonomy*. London: Routledge, 2009.

Mallet, Serge. *The New Working Class*. Nottingham: Spokesman Books, 1975.

Melucci, Alberto. *L'Invenzione del Presente: Movimenti Sociali nelle Società Complesse*. Bologna: Il Mulino, 1970.

Mengin, Françoise and Rocca, Jean-Louis, eds. *Politics in China: Moving Frontiers*. New York: Palgrave, 2002.

Offe, Claus. *Disorganized Capitalism. Contemporary Transformations of Work and Politics*. London: Polity Press, 1985.

Onana, Janvier. *Le sacre des indigènes évolués: Essai sur la profesionnalisation politique. L'exemple du Cameroun*. Chennevières sur Marne: Dianoïa, 2004.

Poulantzas, Nicos. *Classes in Contemporary Capitalism.* London: New Left Books/ Verso, 1978.

Pun, Nai. *Made in China: Women Factory Workers in a Global World.* Durham. NC, and Hong Kong: Duke University Press and Hong Kong University Press, 2005.

Rocca, Jean-Louis. "Chinese Homeowners' Movement: Narratives on the Political Behaviors of the Middle Class," in Goodman and Chen, eds., *Middle Class China,* 110–134.

Rocca, Jean-Louis. *La condition chinoise. La mise au travail capitaliste des chinois.* Paris: Karthala, 2006.

Rocca, Jean-Louis. "Old Working Class Resistance in Capitalist China: A Ritualised Social Management (1995–2006)," in Kuah-Pearce and Guiheux, eds., *Social Movements,* 117–134.

Rocca, Jean-Louis. ("Political Interaction, Empirical Characterization, and Academic Intervention: Formation of the Middle Class in China"). " 政治交叉, 社会便章与 学术干预：中产阶级在中国阶级在中国的形 成," in Li Chunling, ed., *Formation of the Middle Class in Comparative Perspective,* 59–83.

Rocca, Jean-Louis. "Power of Knowledge: The Imaginary Formation of the Chinese Middle Class Stratum in an Era of Growth and Stability," in Jaffrelot and van der Veer, eds., *Patterns of Middle Class Consumption,* 127–139.

Rocca, Jean-Louis. "The Rise of the Social and the Chinese State," *China Information,* 17, 1: 2003, 1–27.

Rocca, Jean-Louis. *La société chinoise vue par ses sociologues.* Paris: Presses de Sciences Po, 2008.

Rocca, Jean-Louis. "'Three at Once': The Multidimensional Scope of Labor Crisis in China," in Mengin and Rocca, eds., *Politics in China,* 3–30.

Rocca, Jean-Louis. "A Tortuous Trajectory: Patriotism and Traditional Festivals in Reform-Era China," *Critique internationale,* 58: 2013, 73–92.

Rofel, Lisa. *Other Modernities: Gendered Yearnings in China after Socialism.* Berkeley: University of California Press, 1999.

Rose, Nikolas. *Inventing Our Selves.* Cambridge: Cambridge University Press, 1996.

Rose, Nikolas. *Powers of Freedom: Reframing Political Thought.* Cambridge: Cambridge University Press, 1999.

Ru Xin (汝信)et al., eds. (*Society of China: Analysis and Forecast for 2009*). *2009 年中国社会形势分析与预测.* 北京： 社会科学出版社, 2009.

Salgues, Camille. "La Chine, entre cadre et contexte: une recherche sur les enfants de *Mingong,* plusieurs constructions du savoir," *Terrains et Travaux,* 16: 2009, 175–193.

Sulkunen, Pekka. *The European New Middle Class: Individuality and Tribalism in Mass Society.* Aldershot: Avebury, 1992.

Sun Liping (孙立平). ("Common Spirit and Sharp Rise of Middle Strata"). "公共 精神与中产阶层崛起," 绿野, 12: 2009, 22.

Sun Liping (孙立平). (*Reconstructing Society: To Rebuild Order in Transitional Society*). 重建社会：转型社会的秩序再造. 北京：社会科学文献出版社, 2009.

Touraine, Alain. *The Post-Industrial Society – Tomorrow's Social History: Classes, Conflicts and Culture in the Programmed Society.* New York: Random House, 1971.

Tsinghua University, Sociology Department Social Development Study Group (清华大学社会学系社会发展研究科技组). (*Reach a Long Period of Stability through Institutionalization of the Expression of Social Interests*). 以利益表达制度化实现社会的长治久安, 清华大学社会发展论坛, 2010.

Walder, Andrew. *Communist Neo-Traditionalism: Work and Authority in Chinese Industry,* Berkeley: University of California Press, 1986.

Whyte, Martin and Parish, William. *Urban Life in Contemporary China.* Chicago: University of Chicago Press, 1984.

Wright, Erik Olin. *Class Structure and Income Determination.* New York: Academic Press, 1979.

Xi Jialin (席佳淋). ("Anxiety among Young Chinese"). "中国年轻人的焦虑," FT 中国文网, 2月1日2012.

Xu Bo (徐波). (*World's Fair Etiquette*). 世博礼仪. 北京：东方出版社中心, 2009.

Yuan Yue (袁岳) and Zhang Hu (张慧). ("2008 Survey on Living Quality of Life among Chinese Citizens"). "2008年中国居民生活质量调查报告," in Ru Xin et al., eds., *Society of China: Analysis and Forecast for 2009.*

Zhang Li. *In Search of Paradise: Middle-Class Living in a Chinese Metropolis.* Ithaca, NY: Cornell University Press, 2010.

Zhang Xiaomei (张小梅). (*Zhang Xiaomei Talking about Etiquette*). 张小梅说礼仪. 北京：中国青年出版社, 2007.

Zhang Yi (张翼). ("The Political Attitudes of the Middle Strata in Contemporary China"). "当代中国中产阶层的政治态度," 中国社会科学, 3: 2008, 117–131.

Zhao Jie (赵洁). ("A Summary of Research on Middle Strata Done by Chinese Scholars in the Recent Years"). "近年来我国学者关于中产阶层的研究综述," 福建党校学报, 6: 2009, 57–9.

Zhao Weihua (赵卫华). (*Status and Consumption*). 地位与消费. 北京：社会科学文献出版社, 2007.

Zhou, Xiaohong and Qin Chen. "Globalization, Social Transformation, and the Construction of China's Middle Class," in Li, ed., *China's Emerging Middle Class*, 84–103.

Zhou Xun. "Eat, Drink and Sing, and Be Modern and Global: Food, Karaoke and 'Middle Class,'" in Jaffrelot and van der Veer, eds., *Patterns of Middle Class Consumption*, 170–185.

Patronizing

9 A New Urban Underclass? Making and Managing "Vulnerable Groups" in Contemporary China

Patricia M. Thornton

The Chinese Communist Party's relationship to labor has undergone a dramatic transformation in the wake of market reform. The "Open Door" and the "Four Modernizations" policies paved the way for a fundamental restructuring of the social contract between worker and state in the PRC. Whereas the 1950s witnessed the creation of a state-directed, centrally planned economy organized around spatially anchored sites of industrial production characterized by the so-called "old three iron-clads" (旧三铁) – the "iron rice bowl" (铁饭碗), "iron wages" (铁工资), and "iron-clad posts" (铁交椅)[1] – the piecemeal rollout of market reform has subjected increasing numbers of workers in China to occupational instability and impermanence.

The party leadership has greatly facilitated the shift from "organized dependency" to "disorganized despotism" across a variety of workplaces that span the Chinese economy.[2] Without disavowing its role as the "vanguard of the proletariat," it has nonetheless overseen the repositioning of a significant proportion of the urban labor force "from master to mendicant,"[3] refashioning it into what Standing recently labeled "the engine of the global precariat, denizens in their own country ... forced to live and work precariously, denied the rights of urban natives." Unlike the Mao-era proletariat, which arguably exchanged long-term, stable, fixed-hour jobs defined by the "old three iron-clads" for political subordination and acquiescence to party rule, Standing's new precariat subsists primarily under conditions defined by labor impermanence, informality, and insecurity, "without a bargain of trust or security in exchange for subordination."[4] Others observe that the combination of

---

[1] Ding and Warner, "China's Labour-Management System Reforms."
[2] Tomba, *Paradoxes of Labour Reform*, 7, 190; Walder, *Communist Neo-Traditionalism*; Lee, "From Organized Dependence to Disorganized Despotism."
[3] Solinger, "The New Crowd of the Dispossessed."
[4] Standing, *The Precariat*, 106; see also Standing, "The Precariat?"

free market expansion and social welfare retraction has downshifted large swathes of the former working class into a state of "advanced marginality" characterized by the de-proletarianization of the workforce.[5] In *Punishing the Poor*, Wacquant describes the new urban underclass as the "destitute and disruptive fractions of the postindustrial proletariat," and its most marginalized segments, forced to seek a livelihood at the lowest end of the labor market.[6]

As analytical concepts, neither Standing's "precariat" (危险无产者) nor Wacquant's "underclass" (底层阶级) has gained traction with Chinese scholars and policy-makers, who use the less plainly politicized "marginal groups" (边缘群体) and "households in special difficulty" (特困户) to refer to those requiring special "assistance" and "care" from the party-state.[7] In popular parlance, the new faces of urban poverty are denigrated as members of "tribes" subsisting parasitically on the margins of urban society: members of the "ant tribe" (蚁族), the "snail house tribe" (蜗居族), the "cupboard tribe" (柜族), and the "gnawing away at the elders tribe" (啃老).[8] More recently collectively christened "vulnerable groups" (弱势群体) in official discourse, this loosely aggregated social stratum includes landless peasants, rural migrants, laid-off workers, disabled adults, retirees, and, since the late 1990s, increasing numbers of university graduates without stable employment.[9] According to one 2009 estimate, members of "vulnerable groups" numbered between 140 million and 180 million nationwide, comprising as much as 14 percent of the population.[10] Unlike the urban poor of the pre-reform period, who suffered from the "three nos" (no working capacity, no relatives, and no stable income),[11] this newly immiserated urban underclass is chiefly formed as a direct result of the shifting developmental agendas and policy choices of the center,[12] and whose existence presents a particular challenge to the legitimacy of the party-state in the reform era.

Chinese leaders have responded to these developments by reviving urban residents' committees (城市居民委员会) as part of a broader community building (社区建设) initiative designed to shore up the party's power and legitimacy at the urban grassroots.[13] The *shequ* (社区), a community-level unit of state administration, was conceived as a grass-roots institution of urban governance capable of taking on not only many

---

[5] Wacquant, "The Rise of Advanced Marginality."
[6] Wacquant, *Punishing the Poor*, 69.
[7] Wu, "The Poverty of Transition," 2674; Solinger, "The Phase-out of the Unfit," 308.
[8] "China's New Tribes"; Liu Shantao, "The 'Ant Tribe'."
[9] For example, see Huang Chunmei, "An Exploration of the 'Ant Tribe' Phenomenon."
[10] *Party and State Cadre Reader*, 89.   [11] Wu, "The State and Marginality," 842.
[12] Liu et al., "The Making of the New Urban Poor."   [13] Monteil, "Communities," 176.

of the tasks formerly fulfilled by the work unit,[14] but also of managing and surveilling members of the new urban underclass. As early as 1986, the Ministry of Civil Affairs proposed developing "community services" (社区服务) as a viable alternative to state-owned and regulated goods, facilities, and services. "Residential and community service enterprises" (社区居民服务业) were aspirationally designated as a primary channel for the reemployment of workers laid-off from their public sector jobs. Three years later, urban residents' committees – an institution established in the early years of the People's Republic that was quickly eclipsed by the urban work unit system – were restored with an expanded remit that included citizens' self-management, self-education, and self-service, in order to relieve pressure on higher levels of government for service provision.[15] By 2000, under the guidance of the revived residents' committees, the *shequ* was officially designated as the new grassroots unit of urban social, political, and administrative organization, and tasked with "harmonious community building" (和谐社区建设), and the provision of basic social welfare, including the care of "vulnerable groups" within their jurisdictions.[16] The net result of these developments has been to make these grassroots urban organizations responsible for managing social tensions and of containing them *at the level of the neighborhood,* instead of allowing them to refract to higher levels of state power.[17]

However, whereas the state apparatus has scaled back its role at the urban grassroots, the party has been busily expanding under the aegis of community building, using it to enhance its legitimacy, extend recruitment, and strengthen party political control. Heberer and Göbel recently described "harmonious community building" as a vast "regrouping" of the party's efforts to enhance its "infrastructural power" in the era of reform.[18] Working through the dense network of capillary "administrative grassroots engagement" institutions,[19] the party has utilized its expanded presence to ensure policy compliance and spur recruitment, including from underrepresented "vulnerable groups" like migrant workers and retirees.[20] At the same time, urban party activists have refashioned the traditional practice of "mass work" (群众工作) in order to promote, secure, and enforce social stability. Party branches in urban areas champion both self-help and charitable assistance to those in need, generating a

---

[14] Derleth and Koldyk, "The *Shequ* Experiment."   [15] Monteil, "Communities," 183.
[16] Ministry of Civil Affairs, "Opinion."
[17] Xu, "New Modes of Urban Governance," 29; Monteil, "Communities," 176.
[18] Heberer and Göbel, *Politics of Community Building in Urban China,* 3–4.
[19] Read, *Roots of the State,* 3–7.
[20] Lu Yuemian, "Investigatory Analysis of Foundational Patterns."

discourse of care, concern, and, where possible, enabling, at the urban grassroots.[21]

The latest iteration of urban social policy, rolled out at the 18th Party Congress under the slogan of "party-building helps the people" (党建惠民), recombines traditional party-building with party-led social outreach including "mass work" among the disadvantaged.[22] On the party-building side, new recruitment efforts target "floating party members" (流动党员) who have left their original work units as a result of lay-offs, bankruptcies, or reorganizations. However, even more important has been the goal of raising the party's visibility at the urban grassroots, particularly in those locations where the urban poor and socially vulnerable are likely to be seeking services and help from the state. The centerpiece of the campaign is the public performance of acts of social care for vulnerable urban residents by party members and party-organized teams of volunteers, who seek to build the party's "brand," and make the party a more visible, prominent, and positive presence in urban neighborhoods.[23]

At the same time, such activities clearly also increase the party's control and surveillance over those on the lower rungs of the socio-economic ladder. Grassroots cadres coordinate traditional "mass work" activities like "heart-to-heart talks" (谈心) and "house calls" (家访)[24] – also described in Perry's contribution to this volume – with the work of local public security forces, residents' committees, and public security management teams. These new joint activities expand the party's points of contact with those living precariously in China's cities, and control, curtail, and contain the potential for collective action by vulnerable groups. The combined effect of these new overlapping initiatives is, as one grassroots party activist observed, "to weave an interlocking safety net"[25] within which to "catch" members of the urban poor and at-risk populations, in the interest of preserving social harmony and stability.[26]

Thus, despite being cloaked in a benign official discourse of caring concern, "reinforcement," and "help,"[27] the party's latest interventions at the lower rungs of the socio-economic ladder involve strategies of targeted surveillance, frequent and routine structured encounters with local authorities and agents of the party-state, and preemptive cum

---

[21] See Gleiss, "From Being a Problem to Having Problems"; Leung et al., "The 'Person-Centred' Rhetoric."

[22] Qiao Yun, "Raising the Happiness Index."

[23] Li Dongxiao "Using the Brand Effect."

[24] Task Force, "Problems with and Solutions to the Party's Present Mass Work."

[25] Wu Airan, "Weave an Interlocking Safety Net for the Urban Poor."

[26] CCP Organization Department, "Opinion on Strengthening Party Construction Work."

[27] As described, for example, in Edelman, "The Political Language of the Helping Professions."

coercive strategies of control that serve to subdivide and subdue the poor, all practices with roots in the pre-reform era. Although official and policy discourses regarding "vulnerable groups" are relatively new, the techniques used to manage them in urban society owe much to past practice. Taken as a whole, the party's contemporary governance of the new urban underclass has served to reinforce, reproduce, and extend the intrusive information-gathering capacities of what Read dubs the "inquisitive and coercive" urban grassroots state,[28] beneath a guise of paternalistic care and concern.

China's Urban Underclass in Historical Perspective

Contrary to common assumptions, informal, temporary, and migrant workers without full access to the so-called "old three iron-clads" comprised the majority of the Mao-era proletariat: when the PRC's new labor insurance system guaranteeing social welfare benefits was initially implemented in 1952, it covered a mere 7 percent of the nation's workers. In 1958, following the socialization of industry, the percentage of workers fully covered peaked at 30 percent, but at the beginning of market reform in 1978, the percentage had dipped to 22 percent.[29] Furthermore, the distribution of welfare provision during the Mao era was far from uniform: as Frazier has shown, throughout the 1950s, workers in state-owned enterprises in heavy industry enjoyed generous benefits compared to those in the private and urban handicraft sectors, where wages were low and welfare benefits were negligible. Following the full collectivization of industry (1955–1957), many workers actually suffered declines in income and benefits following the closure, consolidation, and mergers of smaller plants and workshops. Mounting pressure on enterprise managers to meet production quotas prompted periodic waves of "hiring from society" to meet shifting targets.[30] Later, during the post-Great Leap economic recovery period, Liu Shaoqi and other party leaders promoted the use of temporary and contract labor to boost production and keep costs low. Temporary, contract, and "non-contract" workers (外包工) were excluded from pensions, subsidies, and other benefits, including party, trade union, and Communist Youth League membership. Wages, too, were considerably lower: whereas a worker on the bottom rung of the permanent worker wage scale earned at least 40 yuan per month, many contract and temporary workers had to make do with less than 30 yuan.[31]

---

[28] Read, *Roots of the State*, 105–116.   [29] Perry, "Labor's Love Lost," 67.
[30] Frazier, *The Making of the Chinese Industrial Workplace*, 140–142, 153–156.
[31] Perry and Li, *Proletarian Power*, 100.

These wage and benefit asymmetries sparked roiling conflicts that periodically destabilized Chinese cities over the course of the Mao era. In 1956 in Guangzhou and across the Pearl River Delta, some newly recruited "working masses" used a campaign to oppose bureaucratism and waste to demand that welfare subsidies paid to permanent full-time employees be eliminated.[32] Less than a year later, similar labor protests paralyzed the city of Shanghai.[33] During the early stages of the Cultural Revolution at the end of 1966, Shanghai's labor force erupted again when so-called "conservative" Scarlet Guards – populated largely by older state workers from the Jiangnan region – faced off against the self-declared "Revolutionary Rebels" comprised of mostly younger, unskilled contract and temporary workers.[34] Siding with the latter in late December, Jiang Qing lambasted the system of contract labor as a "corrupt" product of the bourgeois line. Two months later, she reversed herself when organizations representing temporary workers were disbanded, having concluded that temporary and contract labor were "rational" after all.[35]

As the Cultural Revolution came to an end, many of the students and others who had been "sent down" to the countryside began trickling back to urban areas to become a new temporary and contract labor pool, often finding jobs in what were known as "street collective enterprises" (街道集体企业) or "street or alley production groups" (街道, 里弄生产组).[36] One January 1979 article in Shanghai's *Wenhui bao* described the conditions for such employees as poor and uncertain, sparking a poster campaign and a new wave of mass protests led largely by the city's unemployed and underemployed "educated youth."[37] The precariously employed returnees quickly overwhelmed municipal offices to the tune of 9,000 protesters a day, posing serious challenges to social order in the cities.[38] By 1981, many Chinese sources estimated that between 1966 and 1976, some 13 to 14 million peasants had entered Chinese cities, taking up posts at the same workplaces that were prevented from hiring returned students. The result was a roughly balanced wave of inward and outward urban migration, with the number of rural migrants moving into the cities roughly offsetting the number of educated youths being "sent down" to the rural areas; both groups were forced to accept precarious employment.[39]

[32] Frazier, *The Making of the Chinese Industrial Workplace*, 196–212.
[33] Perry, "Shanghai's Strike Wave," 9.   [34] Ibid., 22.
[35] Walder, "Chang Ch'un-ch'iao," 70.
[36] Jiang Liang, ed., *Changning District Gazetteer*, 395.
[37] McLaren, "The Educated Youth Return"; Gold, "Back to the City."
[38] Hua Wei, "From the Work Unit System."   [39] Bonnin, *The Lost Generation*, 38–41.

With the introduction of market reform, the numbers of informal, temporary, and migrant workers swelled again, expanding from an estimated 22 percent in 1978 to 46 percent or more of the national labor force in 2005.[40] As a result of lay-offs in the state-owned sector, predatory taxation in the countryside, and the en masse privatization of formerly collectively owned Township and Village Enterprises (TVEs), millions of dispossessed rural workers migrated into the cities in search of work from the late 1980s through the 1990s.[41] A concomitant steep rise in higher education enrollment, which increased 5.6 times between 1998 and 2008, added another new subgroup to China's teeming urban underclass: unemployed and underemployed college and university graduates subsisting precariously in Chinese cities without official permission or proper papers. In 1997, the gross university enrollment rate represented a mere 5 percent of the population; by 2002, it had tripled, expanding to 15 percent of the population, marking the "popularization" (大众化) of higher education in China.[42] But this expansion was not accompanied by an equal growth in white-collar jobs: Ministry of Education statistics show that while the employment rate for university graduates in 1996 was 93.7 percent, by 2009 only 68 percent were able to find stable employment.[43] In early 2009, it was reported that 20 million migrant workers had not only lost their jobs but were also unable to return home due to the 2008 financial meltdown; university graduates fared even worse that year, with nearly one in six unemployed.[44]

One 2009 Ministry of Education-sponsored survey of over 3,100 "new urban migrants" found that many were unwilling to return to their homes in the countryside following graduation, and opted to remain in urban areas without stable employment. Fewer than 30 percent of such graduates found stable employment in the cities: over a third (34.7 percent) reported having changed jobs at least once a year, with more than two-thirds (70.2 percent) having changed jobs at least once every three years. Most self-identified as "outsiders" (外来人) in the cities in which they were living when polled, and nearly a third as "temporary urban dwellers" (暂时待在城里的人) unassimilated into established networks at the urban grassroots.[45]

Clustering in low-rent peri-urban neighborhoods where they frequently share overcrowded flats, "new educated migrants" came to

---

[40] Park and Cai, "The Informalization of the Chinese Labour Market," 20.
[41] Solinger, *Contesting Citizenship in Urban China.*
[42] Xia Fei, "A Rational Look at the Expansion of Admissions."
[43] As cited in Han Heng, "University Graduates," 45.
[44] Li Ming, "The Power of 'Anticipatory' Social Stability Factors."
[45] Han Heng, "University Graduates," 47.

popular attention following the 2009 publication of Lian Si's *Ant Tribe: A True Record of [Urban] Villages Inhabited by University Graduates*. According to Lian's investigation, an estimated 100,000 university graduates – either unemployed or underemployed – were living illegally in certain Beijing neighborhoods. At the national level, more than 3 million "ant tribe" members were suspected of living in major and "second tier" Chinese cities, with their numbers increasing by 0.2–0.3 million annually.[46] According to some, the disenfranchisement of these educated migrants, when combined with their facility with new communications technologies, predisposes them toward collective unrest: 87.9 percent of "ant tribe" members admitted having participated in online "mass action" (网络群体活动), a percentage notably higher than the general population.[47] Another analyst cited the 2005 wave of anti-Japanese demonstrations in Beijing and the 2008 boycott of Carrefour as typical "ant tribe"-fomented unrest, and warned that their "resentment, when built up to a certain level, will likely ... lead to large-scale collective action" that could destabilize urban society.[48] Unlike other migrant workers, who petition or turn to their own kinship networks to resolve difficulties, "ant tribe" members generally vent their discontent online. As Lian and Zhang noted, "ant tribe" members manifest "anti-establishment and anti-authority, and even extreme anti-social sentiments" that could easily spread, and some express "anti-monopolistic, anti-corruption (views) ... even to the point of advocating liberal democracy and the like." Against the backdrop of a recent rising tide of economic growth that failed to "raise all boats," Lian and Zhang ominously predict that the resentment of underemployed and unemployed youth will breach the economic sphere, ultimately manifesting in overt political action.[49]

"Vulnerable Groups" in Contemporary Urban Society

The inclusion of unemployed or underemployed recent university graduates marked a watershed in the composition of China's social stratification. Liang Xiaosheng's widely read 1997 study identified several emerging social strata (阶层) and popularized a new conceptual language for describing social inequality delinked from either social antagonism or revolutionary political mobilization. In his introduction, Liang proposed that the old concept of socio-economic class (阶级) could no longer describe   the   burgeoning   complexity   of   market-driven   social

---

[46] Zhang, "China's Ant Tribe."   [47] Wang Huan, "Operational Research," 155.
[48] Shen Peng, "An Initial Exploration of Public Security Management."
[49] Lian Si and Zhang Linna, "'Ant Tribes" Feelings of Social Injustice." I am grateful to Yi Chengzhi for sharing this article with me.

differentiation in reform-era China. Like a gap-toothed comb (齿稀齿缺的梳子), the Mao-era concept of class crudely divided society into opposing camps trapped in an endless dialectic of class struggle. However, in Liang's view, the more recent market-driven development of productive forces has allowed not only for more finely differentiated gradations of strata, but also enhanced the possibility – and therefore, the expectation – of movement up the rungs of the ladder for the less advantaged.[50] Jiang Zemin also underscored the new mutability of socio-economic status during his controversial 2001 National Day address, when he acknowledged that there were "those among the masses who encounter temporary (暂时) difficulties in work and in life" who required special assistance from the party. By recasting economic hardship as a merely transitory condition rather than a grim, structurally determined position for a significant proportion of the laboring multitudes, Jiang did not commit the party to continuing to carry out revolutionary struggle on behalf of the working poor, but instead to expressing care and concern for those "masses who had unexpectedly encountered hardship in their work and in their lives."[51]

The term "vulnerable groups," used to describe temporarily economically disadvantaged strata in Chinese society, initially emerged in Premier Zhu Rongji's government work report delivered a few months later, in March 2002.[52] He Ping, the research director of the Labor and Social Security Ministry's Institute of Social Security promptly identified four key groups conceived as forming the core of this newly minted stratum: laid-off workers, the itinerant self-employed subsisting "outside the system" of formal employment, migrant workers, and pensioners whose meager retirement benefits put them below the poverty line.[53] Within months, the National People's Congress was to put the protection of so-called "vulnerable groups" at the top of the national agenda, spurring new waves of scholarly research on social stratification and increased polarization in Chinese society,[54] with advocates for various disadvantaged groups arguing on behalf of their inclusion in the category.

Yet, notwithstanding the flowering of a new public discourse of social care and concern, the party's practical management of vulnerable groups became noticeably more securitized. Zhu Rongji's original March 2002

[50] Liang Xiaosheng, *A Comprehensive Analysis of Social Stratification in China*, 2; see also Anagnost, "From 'Class' to 'Social Strata'."
[51] Jiang Zemin, "Jiang Zemin's Address."
[52] Zhu Rongji, "2002 State Council Government Work Report."
[53] He Lei, "To Whom Does the Premier's Use of the New Term 'Vulnerable Groups' Refer?"
[54] Note from the Editor, "Pay Close Attention to the Problem(s) of Vulnerable Groups."

work report comingled two themes: the possibility of extending social
assistance to "vulnerable groups" undergoing temporary economic hardship, and the preservation of national security and stability from sabotage
by "hostile forces." Zhu's proposed response involved "a combination of
punishment and prevention" (打防结合) that accorded priority to
prevention, and the creation of a comprehensive system of social order
maintained through prevention and control (社会治安防控体系)[55]
that involved expanding the oversight of the party in urban neighborhoods (社区) over grassroots policing and public security. The newly
installed Hu-Wen administration subsequently elevated the power and
position of the central party political Legal Committee by appointing two
successive Politburo Standing Committee members to chair it and over-
see its work, and to strengthen its efforts in the direction of "social
management."[56] By November 2003, the Party's Central Committee,
moreover, called for party committees at all levels to appoint public
security chiefs at provincial, prefectural, and county levels to positions
within the party's commensurate Standing Committee, thereby elevating
their stature over that of their local counterparts within the state and
judicial apparatuses.[57] As Wang Yuhua has shown, the cumulative effect
of these measures increased the control of the party apparatus over the
comprehensive maintenance of social order. By 2004, party activists in
many areas began working more closely with neighborhood police
personnel,[58] and urban community office party branches and personnel
increasingly fused party-building, urban social control measures, and the
more traditional practices associated with "mass work."

Much of this effort focused on enhancing the party's control over
migrant workers. Municipal Party Committees initiated programs
designed to meet the needs of "mobile party members," including a
new campaign to encourage members to "leave their homes without
leaving the party" (离乡离土不离党).[59] One 2007 program to issue
"party activities cards" to mobile members resulted in the distribution
of 2.19 million swipe cards nationwide, covering about 3.3 percent of the
party's total membership.[60] By 2010, a survey conducted in Shanghai's
Songjiang district found that 88 percent of the new "floating party members" were employed by either privately owned or non-profit enterprises,

[55] See "The Appearance of 'Vulnerable Groups'."   [56] Pieke, "The Communist Party."
[57] CCP Central Committee, "Decision on Strengthening and Improving Public Security Work."
[58] Wang, "Empowering the Police," 630–631.
[59] Li Shengjie, "Manage Party-Building as a Brand."
[60] Other estimates of party members among the migrant worker population are considerably higher, ranging from 5 to 10 percent of the party's total membership. Li Zhangjun
and Tian Doudou, "Managing Party Trends."

and that nearly 40 percent of these had been issued "floating party member activities cards" that permitted them to participate in party-organized activities in multiple locations,[61] but also, of course, permitted the party to track the participation and movement of its ordinary members.

Some Party Municipal Committees have upgraded not only their communications systems, but also developed new tools specifically for transmitting information to mobile members. In greater Beijing, the Shilihe Chamber of Commerce introduced a web-based social networking service, regular text messaging between grassroots branches and their "floating" members, and online party study activities that allow members who are migrant workers to keep their party education up-to-date.[62] In 2009, Shanghai's Hongqiao District (Street-Level) Party Committee organized a daily "Red SMS" text message aimed at mobile party members, sending single-line messages "introducing the party's concept and theory of "scientific development," promoting [宣扬] the exemplary methods and deeds associated with practice and study, and circulating news of the practice and study activities" of new party branches in order to "penetrate deeply into the hearts of every single" party member among the migrant laborers in Hongqiao.[63] In 2009, Liaoning's Yingkou Municipal Party Committee rolled out a "fast food text messaging" (短信快餐) service for its "mobile party members" with messages designed to communicate party committee business updates, party news and information, advertise services provided by the party committee, and extend holiday greetings, in order to encourage two-way interactive communication between migrant workers and municipal party officials.[64] In Qingdao City, the Municipal Party Committee rolled out an ambitious program of "party-branded" services for highly skilled mobile workers, including job-seeking and professional training for temporarily unemployed members, and even conflict mediation for those attempting to collect back wages.[65]

Updating "Mass Work"

In addition to these new recruitment efforts, party activists working with and through the new residents' committees have been developing more heavily securitized iterations of "mass work" to defuse social tensions outside the party's ranks, particularly among members of vulnerable

[61] Songjiang Social Work Task Force, "Investigation."
[62] Li Shengjie, "Manage Party-Building as a Brand."
[63] Hongqiao Community (Street Office), "Bulletin."
[64] Yingkou Municipal Party Committee Organization Department, "Mass Mailing," 11.
[65] Li Dongxiao, "Using the Brand Effect."

groups. Accordingly, whereas "mass work" in the early years of the party's history traditionally involved the dissemination of propaganda and outreach efforts aiming to build broad, popular support for the party, contemporary versions frequently combine preventative strategies of social control with propaganda dissemination specifically targeting socially marginal and other troublesome groups at the lower rungs of urban society. The new comprehensive "punishment and prevention" agenda is overtly designed to delimit both traditional expressions of protest as well as "weapons of the weak" forms of resistance – on the rise in recent years[66] – by the urban dispossessed, and to prevent the rise of what are increasingly recognized as "malicious [vulnerable] groups" (恶势群体)[67] who disrupt social order.

At the party's direction, the new community offices fuse their provision of services with public security work. In Shenyang Municipality, community offices not only provide "socialist education" or "civilized citizen quality education" (文明市民素质教育) to local residents, but also coordinate neighborhood security work with local police and security guards. These responsibilities include arranging security patrols of the entire community territory, disseminating information on household security, monitoring the behavior of "higher-risk" residents, and mobilizing "neighborhood watch"-type organizations with an eye to reducing, deterring, and controlling crime. In Shanghai, community office cadres and party volunteers coordinate traditional "mass work" activities like "heart-to-heart talks" (谈心) and "house calls" (家访)[68] with the work of local "comprehensive public security management leading small groups" (社会治安综合治理领导小组) – teams organized under the command of party political Legal Committees to detect and punish illegal activities and prevent social unrest in the name of "stability maintenance" (维稳). In workplaces, enterprise party committee cadres cooperate with official labor union staff to organize monthly "heart-to-heart" sessions with migrant and temporary workers to encourage workers to bring forth concerns and requests in order to circumvent labor unrest and to suppress independent labor activism.[69] As the report of one high-ranking party task force recently observed,

under new conditions of social stratification and differentiation, the party's mass work has already shifted beyond traditional thought work, the dissemination of

[66] Zhang Yigang, "The Strength of the Vulnerable."
[67] See, for example, "Why Disadvantaged Groups Become 'Malicious Groups'"; Zhou Yinzu, "Harmonious Ecology and Harmonious Society"; Lu Fang, "On the Legal Protection."
[68] Task Force, "Problems with and Solutions to the Party's Present Mass Work."
[69] Lu Zhang, "Labor Force Dualism," 127.

simple information and dispute resolution to aspects involving the understanding of interest-based demands, the harmonizing of conflicts of interest, and the allotment of relatively complex social and public capital . . . leading to the prevention and management of the worsening difficulties of the problems of the masses from every social strata.[70]

Many of these new duties are broadly consistent with traditional, long-standing "mass work" practices (作风) involving party officials and activists "going down" to the social grassroots in order to receive the complaints and hear the concerns of the masses. As in the Mao era, present-day grassroots cadres make periodic "house calls" on residents to hold "heart-to-heart talks" with them about their worries and problems; an emphasis is placed on the "one-on-one, face-to-face" nature of such exchanges, during which cadres are enjoined to abandon "officialese" (官腔) and join with the masses "hand-in-hand, heart linked to heart" (手拉手, 心连心) as a way of demonstrating sympathy and support for those facing extraordinary burdens.[71] However, contemporary grassroots cadres engaged in mass work particularly at the *shequ* level are urged to "listen attentively to the voices of the people, respect the popular will, grasp popular feelings, and improve people's livelihood" (倾听民声、尊重民意、掌握民情、改善民生) so as to circumvent the paradoxical "strength of the weak"[72] at the lower rungs of urban society, interweaving solicitous, charitable and patronizing measures with surveillance and community policing practices. In some areas, local party officials have developed a practice of making regular rounds of "popular sentiment house calls" (民情家访), with city-level officials paying visits at least once a month, county or district-level cadres at least twice a month, and township or street-level party workers visiting, on average, at least three times a month. The frequency can be stepped up under certain circumstances: in 2012, when Jiangxi's Nanchang City encountered stiff opposition to levies imposed on 532 households in the city's West Lake District, it called upon more than 600 party activists to descend upon them for "all night in-depth conversations" (彻夜深谈) with the households in question during which the cadres "played on the emotions of the residents, to convince them through reason in order to increase their confidence" in the party, and attempted "to demonstrate [the party's] resolve" to all of the households visited. Shortly after the nocturnal visits, all of the households paid the levy in full without further incident. The Nanchang Municipal Party Committee proudly noted that

[70] Task Force, "The Influence of Changes in the Formation of Social Strata."
[71] Li Junru, "On the Party's Mass Work."
[72] Zhang Yigang, "The Strength of the Vulnerable."

its mass work effort on this occasion had resulted in a "three zeros" success: zero petitions filed with authorities in Beijing, zero incidents of mass protest or resistance, and zero casualties were incurred.[73]

In a similar vein, the Ministry of Public Security's Border Control Department initiated a "three visits and four sees" (三访四见) campaign beginning in July 2005 to mobilize grassroots public security and police officials to conduct "mass work" in the form of house-to-house surveys. The stated goals of the program included paying visits to the poor to gather information about their level of hardship; calling upon the handicapped in their homes to hear about their challenges; and to pay house calls to new migrants to the area in order to ascertain whether they might be classified as members of a "vulnerable group." Furthermore, local public security officials were ordered to carry out home visits and house-to-house surveys annually among the elderly, the impoverished, the disabled, and members of "vulnerable groups" (laid-off workers, the "left-behind" children, and other family members of migrant workers).[74]

These multi-stranded governing practices, although certainly intrusive, are being rolled out alongside new discourses of "people-centeredness" (以人为本) and "humanized management" (人性化管理), terms often used to describe the work of the new community offices.[75] In deftly combining the policing and patronizing aims of social governance, contemporary "mass work" among socially vulnerable groups is being conducted with a more highly securitized agenda than in the past. Community office cadres serving on comprehensive public security teams likewise engage in monitoring, either as "barometers" (晴雨表) of grassroots popular sentiment, or "early warning" (预警) nodes capable of portending danger levels of social discontent or threats to system stability. Those engaged in mass work report to higher levels any activities that obviously deviate (偏离) from the party line, potential violations of national or local regulations, evidence of irregularities in financial matters, as well as the implication of involvement in any "significant political plots" (重大政治图谋).[76] For example, in 2003, Xigong Provisional Party branch activists conducting "house calls" in Shanghai uncovered an underground cell of Falun Gong practitioners. The following year, another group engaging in home visits under the rubric of engaging in "mass work" broke up a practice site for the banned

[73] Jiangxi Province Organization Department, "Popular Sentiment."
[74] Zhou Lijun, "Examination of and Reflection."
[75] In late 2005, the *People's Daily* reported that the number of volunteer organizations existing in Chinese *shequ* was already 75,000, with approximately 16 million members. Heberer and Göbel, *The Politics of Community Building*, 83.
[76] Ma Xiheng, "The Development of Civic Organizations."

"Fragrant Gong" (香功) sect in their area.[77] In 2008, one new party branch operating with a community public security management team in Shanghai's Putuo District mobilized forty-six "community leaders" to participate in an "early warning" information exchange network. The team quickly discovered twelve illegal and unregistered grassroots societies operating in the district as well as plans for no fewer than twenty illegal collective protest activities. All were reported to party and municipal authorities.[78]

In addition to conducting more frequent and more intrusive forms of surveillance over members of "vulnerable groups," new community and party organizations at the urban grassroots interweave political and patriotic education into their broader social agenda, mixing outreach efforts, charitable works, and propaganda, particularly in poorer neighborhoods where pensioners, migrant workers, and "ant tribe" members congregate in inexpensive rented housing. For example, in Shanghai, the Daning Road Street Office Society for the Elderly (大宁路街道老年协会), established in September 2002 as a social service center and party branch for pensioners, engages in the political and patriotic education of senior citizens and retirees in the neighborhood, for which they have been recognized with four model civic association awards. According to their party branch website, they focus on

integrating resources, taking service as the foundation, excelling at doing the party's work among civic associations, bringing into play the party's political core, strengthening the organization of the party's branch among social organizations, leading, mediating and serving, and unceasingly simultaneously strengthening both the party's cohesion and combat effectiveness (战斗力).[79]

In order to deliver the party's political message to its core audience, the center provides regular rounds of patriotic education lectures, helpfully organized by a retired People's Liberation Army political commissar who is also a district resident. Recent topics included current events and broader interpretive themes, like "China's peaceful rise" and the "Three Represents"; outings to revolutionary heritage sites and "nostalgia tours;" and a public education campaign, "a million families learning etiquette," designed to boost the profile of Zhabei District residents in advance of the Shanghai Expo.[80] In many cases, generational bridging activities are encouraged in order to foster social contact between the

---

[77] Zhou Jiafeng, "Solidify Party-building in Civic Associations."
[78] Meng Qian, "The Changshou Model."
[79] Zhabei District Daning Community (Street-Level) Elder Assistance Party Branch, "Brief Introduction."
[80] "Daning Elder Assistance Reviews Information Report."

younger workers and older residents. For example, just after National Day 2010, a team of five youthful white-collar volunteers working with elderly residents in Shanghai's Changshou Road district "braved the rain" to engage in house calls to "search out red memories" (寻找红色记忆) from among local retirees. The group set out with digital recorders to visit old soldiers in their homes, and to exchange needed items, small gifts, and services for the stories, as part of an ongoing outreach effort targeting former veterans in the district.[81] Likewise, the enterprise party committee for the Guangzhou Metropolitan Subway system set up a "logistical service center" in 2009 staffed by party activists who provide services that are particularly in demand among members of "vulnerable groups" in Guangzhou – migrant workers, "ant tribe" members, and pensioners – including a phone-ahead chaperone service for those using the metro late at night or early in the morning, as a first step toward facilitating "face-to-face ideological and political work" with metro users in need.[82]

Policing and Patronizing the New Urban Underclass

As many have noted, China's new "authoritarian resilience" rests, at least in part, on the adaptive capacity of the party-state to accommodate socio-economic change, including the rise of new social groups and classes within a robustly autocratic party-state framework. Indeed, despite profound socio-economic changes which have led to "the embourgeoisement of cadres and the patronization of capitalists, the semi-proletarianization and segmentation of the working class, the depoliticization of the new middle class, and the professionalization of cadres,"[83] the post-Mao party-state has nonetheless managed to maintain the upper hand by fostering "tailor-made governance," portraying itself to those on lower rungs of the socio-economic ladder "as the last defense against the deregulation of the market," while at the same time projecting an image of the party to the upwardly mobile middle classes "as the champions of [their] newly acquired 'rights'."[84]

The party is deftly managing impoverished urbanites in part, as Cho recently pointed out, by consistently "dividing the poor." This is accomplished chiefly through differential policies that distinguish between urban laid-off workers who, as officially registered urban residents, are at least potentially deserving of public welfare benefits and "laboring

---

[81] Changshou Road Alliance of Street-Level Civic Associations General Party Branch, "Seeking Out Red Memories."

[82] An Heyi, "Speaking from the Experience of Doing Thought Work."

[83] So, "Beyond the Logic of Capital," 493.   [84] Tomba, "Making Neighborhoods," 61.

migrants," whose incomes may or may not differ significantly from beneficiaries of the minimum livelihood guarantee (低保) program, but nonetheless eke out precarious lives on the margins of urban society.[85] Beneath the discourses of help and social assistance that underlie the 18th Party Congress' "Party-building helps the people" program, the patronizing and policing aspects of "mass work" practices reproduce social divisions in a manner that accords with the central party-state's agenda of securing urban stability alongside accelerated market reform. Despite the discursive framing of the new outreach programs targeting members of "vulnerable groups," the political agenda of "divide and rule"[86] persists through the continued tactics of classifying, penetrating, monitoring, and closely governing the urban underclass. These methods, honed in response to the specific needs and social demands of contemporary society, nonetheless carry "a signature Maoist stamp that conceives of policy-making as a process of ceaseless change, tension management, continual experimentation, and ad-hoc adjustment."[87] Traditional "mass work" practices – like heart-to-heart talks and home visits by party activists to members of vulnerable groups – coexist at the urban grassroots with high-tech innovations, like "red SMS text messaging" and "linked heart messaging" between party cadres and their mobile members that seek to tether China's mobile workforce to the party.

Given its expansive reach, the point to stress is that the Chinese Communist Party has proved the key medium through which comprehensive governance reforms are being disseminated and implemented, effectively overhauling what Yang dubbed "the sinews of governance."[88] The party's specific role in drawing together the disparate offices and branches of government across both horizontal and vertical axes through the articulation of a shared set of social governance policy objectives has arguably contributed much to the overall functional coherence of reform, and improved implementation by integrating efforts across state departments, and coordinated government action at various levels. Insofar as the party has "remained in the driver's seat" of both the state's political machinery and the strategic planning process, it appears to be taking at least some steps to redress some of the more glaring weaknesses of policy implementation described by the "fragmented authoritarian" model.[89]

This is not to suggest that the policies and initiatives crafted by the party at higher levels for governing socially "vulnerable groups" are unquestioningly and uniformly applied at the urban grassroots.

[85] Cho, "Dividing the Poor," 192.   [86] Perry, "Studying Chinese Politics," 10–17.
[87] Heilmann and Perry, "Embracing Uncertainty," 4.   [88] Yang, *Remaking Leviathan.*
[89] Mertha, "'Fragmented Authoritarianism 2.0'."

Although the foregoing analysis, drawing chiefly from scholarly and official sources, provides a fairly consistent and coherent portrait of an
authoritarian party-state adapting well-worn governing techniques to
the rise of new social phenomena, when viewed from below, the picture
is far more mixed. Under the auspices of "harmonious community
building," the urban residents' committees also frequently pursue
accommodative strategies, treating members of "vulnerable groups"
with what Read characterizes as "a mixture of paternalistic solicitude
and administrative sternness, and receive gifts and cooperation from
them in return."[90] Some of these symbiotic exchanges may include the
provision of temporary accommodation, the sponsorship of small businesses and, occasionally, employment opportunities for migrant workers,
welfare recipients, and other socially vulnerable groups. Yet, as Read
acknowledges, such opportunities are extended to only a tiny fraction of
the new urban underclass,[91] more suggestive of idiosyncratic, un-orche-
strated instances of grassroots accommodation than of deliberately coordinated patterns of adaptation and change.

Despite the potentially greater policy coherence that the party's efforts
to reinstitutionalize the urban grassroots can bring, the worrying trend
toward the securitization of social governance policies – particularly with
respect to disadvantaged "target populations" – is indicative of an increasingly bifurcated model of urban governance. The reinvigoration of the
shequ has afforded a select tier of urban residents the opportunity to play a
greater role in self-governance at the very lowest levels of the urban state
by including them in the management, operation, and supervision of their
communities. However, as Koldyk has demonstrated in his survey analysis
of the impact of "community-building" efforts among over 800 urban
residents in Shandong and Hubei in 2008, whereas nearly half of all wealthy
households enjoyed the benefits of self-administration (自我管理),
self-education (自我教育), self-service (自我服务), and self-supervision
(自我监督) at the community level, only 19.7 percent and 22.4 percent of
poor and average-income households could boast access to the same level of
autonomy. His conclusion is that whereas better-off urban residents
are increasingly able to empower and protect themselves through participation in self-organized resident groups that facilitate the mobilization,
articulation, and defense of their newly legislated rights, poorer residents
generally experience far more intrusive management from local agents of
the party-state.[92]

---

[90] Read, *Roots of the State*, 118.   [91] Ibid., 116–122.
[92] Koldyk, "Central Plan, Local Jam."

As I have shown, the situation for underpaid and unemployed denizens living precariously in China's cities without urban household registration is generally even more dire.[93] Lei Guang's work on precariously employed informal-sector migrants helps in understanding just how this subgroup experiences the party-state "simultaneously as an irrelevant institution at the site of production and as an omnipresent coercive apparatus bent on preventing their social reproduction in the cities." In his view, because precariously employed migrants experience the state neither through its regulatory functions at the workplace, nor as a provider of welfare benefits, they therefore have little or no sense of solidarity with urban laid-off workers and other marginal groups that comprise the urban poor.[94]

The current leadership's affinity for "governing through the middle" may indeed be allowing those who now enjoy moderate levels of prosperity and a relatively privileged relationship with the political apparatus to exert their moral hegemony as the "most precious part" of contemporary Chinese society, as Rocca's research here demonstrates. At the same time, however, the party-state's stunning recasting of the working poor as members of a "vulnerable group," people who have fallen behind and now require both paternalist care and constant supervision, emphatically strips them of the political primacy they once enjoyed, in the era of revolutionary struggle, as the irreproachable "heroes" of history. It also spotlights the ever-widening gulf between the poor and the privileged that, however ironical it may be, so clearly complicates the pursuit of a more "harmonious" society in China today.

References

An Heyi (安合义). ("Speaking from the Experience of Doing Thought Work among Subway Logistics Employees under the Networked Environment"). "谈网络环境下做好地铁后勤员工思想工作的体会," 东方企业文化, 16: 2013, 1–2.

Anagnost, Ann. "From 'Class' to 'Social Strata': Grasping the Social Totality in Reform-Era China," *Third World Quarterly*, 29, 3: 2008, 497–519.

"The Appearance of 'Vulnerable Groups' and Other Neologisms Attracting Attention in Government Work Reports." "政府工作报告中出现'弱势群体'等词引人关注," 3,月06 日2002, 工人日报, at news.sina.com.cn/c/2002–03–06/1443497138.html.

Bonnin, Michel. *The Lost Generation: The Rustification of China's Educated Youth (1968–1980)* (translated by Krystyna Horko). Hong Kong: Chinese University Press, 2013.

---

[93] For an alternative view, see Solinger's trenchant analysis of recipients of the new Minimum Livelihood Guarantee (MLG) in "The New Urban Underclass."

[94] Guang Lei, "Guerrilla Workfare," 495, 498; see also Cho, "Dividing the Poor."

CCP Central Committee. "Decision on Strengthening and Improving Public Security Work," "中共中央关于进一步加强和改进公安工作决定," 9月18 日 2003, at cpc.people.com.cn/GB/64184/64186/66691/4494638.html.

CCP Organization Department (中共中央组织部). ("Opinion on Strengthening the Party Construction Work in Individually- and Privately- and Other Non-Publicly Owned Economic Organizations"). "关于在个体和私营等非公有制经济组织中 加强党的建设工作的意见(试行)]" (2000年9月13日印发), at cpc.people.com.cn/GB/64162/71380/71382/71383/4844924.html.

Changshou Road Alliance of Street-Level Civic Associations General Party Branch (长寿路街道民间组织联合党总支). ("Seeking Out Red Memories"). "寻找红色记忆" (12月 06 日2010), at h.shlxhd.gov.cn/Front/BranchSite/article_detail.htm?articleId=80309.

"China's New Tribes." "中国的新族群," 世界博览, 4: 2012, 10.

Cho, Mun Young. "'Dividing the Poor': State Governance of Differential Impoverishment in Northeast China," *American Ethnologist*, 39, 1: 2012, 187–200.

"Daning Elderly Assistance Reviews Information Report of 'Five Goods' Party Organizations," "大宁老协创评'五好'党组织的申报材料," 8月29日2007, at h.shlxhd.gov.cn/Front/BranchSite/article_detail.htm?articleId=3213.

Derleth, James, and Koldyk, Daniel R. "The *Shequ* Experiment: Grassroots Political Reform in urban China," *Journal of Contemporary China*, 13, 41: 2004, 747–777.

Ding, Daniel Z. and Warner, Malcolm. "China's Labour-Management System Reforms: Breaking the 'Three Old Irons' (1978–1999)," *Asia Pacific Journal of Management*, 18: 2001, 315–334.

Edelman, Murray. "The Political Language of the Helping Professions," *Politics and Society*, 4, 3: 1974, 295–310.

Frazier, Mark. *The Making of the Chinese Industrial Workplace: State, Revolution, and Labor Management*, Cambridge: Cambridge University Press, 2002.

Gleiss, Marielle Stigum. "From Being a Problem to Having Problems: Discourse, Governmentality and Chinese Migrant Workers," *Journal of Chinese Political Science*, 2015, 1–17.

Gries, Peter and Rosen, Stanley, eds. *State and Society in 21st-Century China: Crisis, Contention, and Legitimation*. New York and London: Routledge-Curzon, 2004.

Gold, Thomas B. "Back to the City: The Return of Shanghai's Educated Youth," *China Quarterly*, 84: 1980, 755–770.

Guang, Lei. "Guerrilla Workfare: Migrant Renovators, State Power, and Informal Work in Urban China." *Politics and Society*, 33, 3: 2005, 481–506.

Han Heng (韩恒). ("University Graduates from the Countryside Drift to the Cities – the Formation and Special Characteristics of Educated Migrant Workers"). "漂在城市的农村籍大学毕业生–智力型民工的形成与群体特征," 中国青年研究, 9: 2010, 43–47.

He Lei (何磊). ("To Whom Does the Premier's Use of the New Term 'Vulnerable Groups' Refer?"). "总理使用新名词'弱势群体'说的是哪些人?" 中国青年报, 3月7日2002, at news.sina.com.cn/c/2002–03–07/0427497805.html.

Heberer, Thomas and Göbel, Christian. *The Politics of Community Building in Urban China*. London: Routledge, 2011.

Heilmann, Sebastian and Perry, Elizabeth J. "Embracing Uncertainty: Guerilla Policy Style and Adaptive Governance in China," in Perry and Heilmann, eds., *Mao's Invisible Hand*, 1–29.

Heilmann, Sebastian and Perry, Elizabeth J., eds. *Mao's Invisible Hand: The Political Foundations of Adaptive Governance in China*. Cambridge, MA: Harvard University Asia Center, 2011.

Hongqiao Community (Street Office) (虹桥社区（街道）). ("Bulletin on the Second Round of Activities to Deepen the Study and Practice of the Concept of Scientific Development"). "第二批深入学习实践科学发展观活动 简报，" 学习实践活动办公室编, 3, 9月25日 2009.

Hua Wei （华伟）. ("From the Work Unit System to the Return of the Community System – 50 Years of Change in the Grassroots Administrative System of China's Cities"). "单位制向社区制的回归单位制向社区制的回归 – 中国城市基层管理体制50年变迁，" 战略与管理, 1: 2000, 86–99.

Huang Chunmei (黄春梅). ("An Exploration of the 'Ant Tribe' Phenomenon from the Perspective of Social Mobility"). "社会流动视角下的'蚁族'现象 探析，" 东西南北·教育观察, 4: 2012, 10–11.

Jiang Liang (姜梁), ed. (*Changning District Gazetteer*). 长宁区志. 上海市：上海社 会科学院出版社, 1999.

Jiang Zemin (江泽民). ("Jiang Zemin's Address to Celebrate the 80th Anniversary of the Founding of the Chinese Communist Party, 01 July 2001"). "在庆祝中 国共产党成立八十周年大会上的讲话 2001 年 7 月 1 日，" in Jiang Zemin, ed., *The Theory of the "Three Represents*," 162–163.

Jiang Zemin, ed. (江泽民). (*The Theory of the "Three Represents"*). 论 "三个代表." 北京市: 中央文献出版社, 2001.

Jiangxi Province Organization Department (中共江西省委组织部). ("Popular Sentiment House Calls"). "江西 '民情家访'," 中国党政干部论坛, 2013 年2 月, 79–82.

Keister, Lisa, ed. *Work and Organizations in China after Thirty Years of Transition*. Bingley: Emerald Publishing Group, 2009.

Koldyk, Daniel. "Central Plan, Local Jam: Reorganizing the Grassroots from Above." Presented at Oxford University (October, 23, 2010).

Kuruvilla, Sarosh, Lee, Ching Kwan and Gallagher, Mary E., eds. *From Iron Rice Bowl to Informalization: Markets, Workers, and the State in a Changing China*. Ithaca, NY: Cornell University Press, 2011.

Laliberté, André and Lanteigne, Marc, eds. *The Chinese Party-State in the 21st Century: Adaptation and the Reinvention of Legitimacy*. Abingdon: Routledge, 2008.

Lee, Ching Kwan. "From Organized Dependence to Disorganized Despotism: Changing Labour Regimes in Chinese Factories," *China Quarterly*, 157: 1999, 44–71.

Leung, Terry, Fong, Tse, and Tam, Cherry Hau Lin. "The 'Person-Centered' Rhetoric in Socialist China," *British Journal of Social Work*, 45, 5: 2015, 1–19.

Li Dongxiao (季冬晓). ("Using the Brand Effect to Elevate the Level of Grassroots Party Construction – the Means and Inspiration for Qingdao

City's Creation of the Party-Building Brand"). "用品牌效应提升基层党的建设水平–青岛市创建党建品牌的做法与启示," 理论学刊, 3: 2010, 26–27.

Li Junru (李君如). ("On the Party's Mass Work – Discussing Both the Party's Tradition of Mass Work and the Special Characteristics of Mass Work in the New Period"). "论党的群众工作 – 兼论党的群众工作和新世纪群众工作的特点," 毛泽东邓小平理论研究, 6: 2011, 5–10.

Li Ming (季明). ("The Power of 'Anticipatory' Social Stability Factors"). "预期'性'社会稳定因素的力量," 瞭望, 3: 2010, 23–24.

Li Shengjie (李晟杰). ("Manage Party-Building as a Brand – Elevating the Brand to a Culture"). "把党建经营成品牌 – 让品牌升华为文化," 企业党建, 10: 2010, 36.

Li Zhangjun (李章军) and Tian Doudou (田豆豆). ("Managing Party Trends – Emigrées Have a 'Home'"). "党员动态管理–外出异地有'家'," 人民日报, 9月26日2007, 6.

Lian Si (廉思) and Zhang Linna (张琳娜). ("Research on the 'Ant Tribes'' Feelings of Social Injustice in the Transitional Period"). "转型期'蚁族'社会不公平感研究," 中国青年研究, 6: 2011, 20.

Liang Xiaosheng (梁晓声). (*A Comprehensive Analysis of Social Stratification in China*). 中国社会各阶层分析. 北京市: 经济日报出版社, 1997.

Liu Shantao (刘善涛). ("The 'Ant Tribe' and 'Cupboard Tribe' as 'Snail House Dwellers'"). "'蜗居' 中的 '蚁族' 和 '柜族,'" 术语标准化与信息技术, 2: 2011, 21–23.

Liu, Yuting, Wu, Fulong, and He, Shenjing. "The Making of the New Urban Poor in Transitional China: Market versus Institutionally Based Exclusion," *Urban Geography*, 29, 8: 2008, 811–834.

Lu Fang (卢方). ("On the Legal Protection of the Rights of the Objects of Community Rectification in China"). "论我国社区矫正对象权利的法律保障," 皖西学院学报, 29, 3: 2013, 42.

Lu Yuemian (鲁月棉). ("Investigatory Analysis of Foundational Patterns in Party Organization-Building in the 'Two News' Domain"). "两新' 领域党组织设置模式创新探析 – 基于上海市'两新' 组织党建实践的理性思考," 上海党史与党建 (8月), 2004, 49–51.

Lu, Zhang, "The Paradox of Labor Force Dualism and State–Labor–Capital Relations in the Chinese Automobile Industry," in Kuruvilla, Lee, and Gallagher, eds., *From Iron Rice Bowl to Informalization*, 107–137.

Ma Xiheng (马西恒). ("The Development of Civic Organizations and Constructing the Ruling Party – a Reflection on the Practice of Party-Building in Grassroots Organizations in Shanghai"). "民间组织发展与执政党建设 – 对上海市民间组织党建实践的思考," 求实, 1: 2009, 29.

McLaren, Anne. "The Educated Youth Return: The Poster Campaign in Shanghai from November 1978 to March 1979," *Australian Journal of Chinese Affairs*, 2: 1979, 1–20.

Meng Qian (孟 谦). ("The Changshou Model: The Creation of the Resident Association's 'Civic Organization Service Center'"). "长寿模式: 民间组织服务中心 '的社区创新 社区'," 社区, 2: 2009, 10.

Mertha, Andrew. "'Fragmented Authoritarianism 2.0': Political Pluralization in the Chinese Policy Process," *China Quarterly*, 200: 2009, 995–1012.

Ministry of Civil Affairs (民政部). ("Opinion Regarding the Promotion of Urban Community Building throughout the Country (2000)"). "民政部关于在全国推进城市社区建设的意见 (2000)," at www.cctv.com/news/china/20001212/366.html.

Monteil, Amandine. "Communities: A Lever for Mitigating Social Tensions in Urban China," in Schuerkens, ed., *Globalization and Transformations of Social Inequality*, 175–192.

Note from the Editor (编者按). ("Pay Close Attention to the Problem(s) of Vulnerable Groups in the Transitional Period"). "关注转型时期的弱势群体问题," *中国党政干部论坛*, 3: 2002, 19.

Park, Albert and Cai, Fang, "The Informalization of the Chinese Labor Market," in Kuruvilla, Lee, and Gallagher, eds., *From Iron Rice Bowl to Informalization*, 17–35.

Party and State Cadre Reader on the Prevention and Management of Mass Incidents. 预防于处置群体性事件党政干部读本. 北京市：人民日报出版社, 2009.

Perry, Elizabeth J. "Labor's Love Lost: Worker Militancy in Communist China," *International Labor and Working-Class History*, 50: 1996, 64–76.

Perry, Elizabeth J. "Shanghai's Strike Wave of 1957," *China Quarterly*, 137: 1994, 1–27.

Perry, Elizabeth J. "Studying Chinese Politics: Farewell to Revolution?" *China Journal*, 57: 2007, 1–22.

Perry, Elizabeth J. and Li, Xun, *Proletarian Power: Shanghai in the Cultural Revolution*. Boulder: Westview Press, 1997.

Pieke, Frank N. "The Communist Party and Social Management in China," *China Information*, 26: 2012, 149–165.

Qiao Yun (乔云). ("Raising the Happiness Index in Deepening 'Party-Building Benefits the People'"). "在深化'党建惠民'中提升民生幸福指数," *前进*, 11: 2013, 34–36.

Read, Benjamin. *Roots of the State: Neighborhood Organization and Social Networks in Beijing and Taipei*. Stanford: Stanford University Press, 2012.

Schuerkens, Ulrike, ed. *Globalization and Transformations of Social Inequality*. London and New York: Routledge, 2010.

Shen Peng (申鹏). ("An Initial Exploration of Public Security Management of the 'Ant Tribe' in the Beijing Area"). "北京地区"蚁族"治安管理初探," *辽宁警专学报*, 5: 2010, 54.

So, Alvin Y. "Beyond the Logic of Capital and the Polarization Model," *Critical Asian Studies*, 37, 3: 2005, 481–494.

Solinger, Dorothy J. *Contesting Citizenship in Urban China*. Berkeley: University of California Press, 1999.

Solinger, Dorothy J. "The New Crowd of the Dispossessed: The Shift of the Urban Proletariat from Master to Mendicant," in Gries and Rosen, eds., *State and Society in 21st-Century China*, 50–66.

Solinger, Dorothy J. "The New Urban Underclass and its Consciousness: Is it a Class?," *Journal of Contemporary China*, 21, 78: 2012, 1011–28.

Solinger, Dorothy J. "The Phase-out of the Unfit: Keeping the Unworthy out of Work," in Keister, ed., *Work and Organizations in China*, 307–336.

Songjiang Social Work Task Force (松江区社会工作党委课题组). ("Investigation and Analysis of Mobile Party Members in Shanghai's Songjiang District"). "上海市松江区流动党员队伍的调查与分析,"*上海党史与党建*, 2010 年 11 月, 29–30.

Standing, Gary. "The Precariat: From Denizens to Citizens?" *Polity*, 44: 2012, 588–608.

Standing, Gary. *The Precariat: The New Dangerous Class*. London: Bloomsbury Academic, 2011.

Task Force (课题组). ("The Influence of Changes in the Formation of Social Strata on the Party–Mass Relationship, and Countermeasures"). "社会阶层构成变化对党群关系的影响及对策," *中国延安干部学院学报*, 5, 2: 2012, 73.

Task Force (课题组). ("Problems with and Solutions to the Party's Present Mass Work"). "当前党的群众工作的问题与对策," *中国延安干部学院学报*, 4, 2: 2011, 64.

Tomba, Luigi. "Making Neighborhoods: The Government of Social Change in China's Cities," *China Perspectives*, 4: 2008, 48–61.

Tomba, Luigi. *Paradoxes of Labour Reform: Chinese Labour Theory and Practice from Socialism to Market*. Honolulu: University of Hawaii Press, 2002.

Wacquant, Loïc. *Punishing the Poor: The Neoliberal Government of Social Insecurity*. Durham, NC: Duke University Press, 2009.

Wacquant, Loïc. "The Rise of Advanced Marginality: Notes on its Nature and Implications." *Acta Sociologica*, 39, 2: 1996, 121–139.

Walder, Andrew. "Chang Ch'un-ch'iao [Zhang Chunqiao] and Shanghai's January Revolution," *Michigan Papers in Chinese Studies*, 32: 1977.

Walder, Andrew. *Communist Neo-Traditionalism: Work and Authority in Chinese Industry*. Berkeley: University of California Press, 1986.

Wang Huan (王欢). ("Operational Research into the Tendency of the 'Ant Tribe' to Lead Mass Actions"). "引导'蚁族'群体行动倾向的策略研究," *鸡西大学学报*, 10: 2013, 155–156.

Wang, Yuhua. "Empowering the Police: How the Chinese Communist Party Manages its Coercive Leaders," *China Quarterly*, 219: 2014, 625–648.

"Why Disadvantaged Groups Become 'Malicious Groups'." "劣势群体为何变成了'恶势群体,' 深圳法律网, 3月11日 2009, at lvshi.sz.bendibao.com/news/2009311/93621.shtm.

Wu Airan (吴爱然). ("Weave an Interlocking Safety Net for the Urban Poor – A Chronicle of Jiangsu's Yancheng's Care for the City's Vulnerable Groups"). "编织一张完整的城市贫民安全网 – 江苏省盐城市关注城市弱势群体纪事," *社区*, 13: 2002, 50–51.

Wu, Fulong. "The State and Marginality: Reflections on Urban Outcasts from China's Urban Transition," *International Journal of Urban and Regional Research*, 33, 3: 2009, 841–847.

Wu, Fulong. "The Poverty of Transition: From Industrial District to Poor Neighbourhood in the City of Nanjing, China," *Urban Studies*, 44, 13: 2007, 2673–2694.

Xia Fei (夏斐). ("A Rational Look at the Expansion of Admissions at Universities"). "理性客观看待大学扩招," *光明日报*, 12月10 日2008, at www.gmw.cn/01gmrb/2008–12/10/content_867560.htm.

Xu, Feng. "New Modes of Urban Governance: Building Community/Shequ in Post-Danwei China," in Laliberté and Lanteigne, eds., *The Chinese Party-State in the 21st Century*, 22–38.

Yang, Dali L. *Remaking Leviathan: Market Transition and the Politics of Governance in China*. Stanford: Stanford University Press, 2004.

Yingkou Municipal Party Committee Organization Department (营口市委组织部). ("Mass Mailing 'Five Types' of SMS Text Messages, Serving Mobile Party Members"). " 群发 '五型' 短信, 服务流动党员, " 共产党员, 1: 2009, 10–12.

Zhabei District Daning Community (Street-Level) Elder Assistance Party Branch (闸北区大宁社区（街道）老年协会党总). ("Brief Introduction"). " 支部简介, " 8月13日2007, at h.shlxhd.gov.cn/Front/BranchSite/branchDetail.htm?branchId=6090.

Zhang, Xiaosong. "China's Ant Tribe Present Social Survival Situation and Personal Financial Advice," *Asian Social Science*, 9, 2: 2013, at www.ccsenet.org/journal/index.php/ass/article/viewFile/24350/15405.

Zhang Yigang (张益刚). ("The Strength of the Vulnerable – on the Relationship between the Stability of the Government and the Preservation of the Rights of Vulnerable Groups"). "弱者的'强势'–政府维稳与弱势群体的权利保障关系论," 齐鲁学刊, 236: 5月 2013, 85–88.

Zhou Jiafeng (周嘉艳). ("Solidify Party-Building in Civic Associations, Promote the Building of Harmonious Residents Associations"). "夯实民间组织党建, 促进和谐社区建设," 7月31日2009, at stj.sh.gov.cn/Info.aspx?ReportId=c915ef27-e978–4c2d-8bea-d0a3ff31ec6e.

Zhou Lijun (周立军). ("Examination of and Reflection on the Development of Innovations in Public Security Mass Work under New Circumstances – Inspiration from the 'Three Visits and Four Sees' and 'Great Surveys'"). "新形势下公安群众工作创新发展的思考与探索 –基于 '三访四见' 和 '大走访' 的启示," 湖南警察学院学报, 8: 2011, 20–24.

Zhou Yinzu （周荫祖). ("Harmonious Ecology and Harmonious Society"). "生态和谐与和谐社会, " 南京社会科学, 11: 2005, 97.

Zhu Rongji (朱镕基). ("2002 State Council Government Work Report"). "2002 年国务院政府工作报, " at www.gov.cn/test/2006–02/16/content_201164.htm.

Haunting

10 The Policy Innovation Imperative: Changing Techniques for Governing China's Local Governors

*Christian Göbel and Thomas Heberer**

Introduction

In this essay, we argue that the recent appearance in China of an unanticipatedly large number of local governance policy innovations can be explained by an alteration of the cadre assessment rules in combination with the stimulation of what Foucault has termed "techniques of the self." These two strategies not only provide incentives for local cadres to generate policy innovations, but to do so in line with the central government's preferences. In contrast to policy experimentation, where desired policy outcomes are clearly defined, local officials engaging in policy "innovation" need to decode central government documents and directives to assess whether their planned innovation is likely to meet with the approval of the highest leadership stratum. Instead of being told what to do, they are led to judge by themselves whether their project will earn them praise or criticism.

Our analysis rests on three propositions: first, that there has been a change in the central government's governance strategy; second, that this change has resulted in an alteration of cadre performance evaluation rules; and third, that the central government has sought to instill in local cadres a "will to improve" in order to motivate them to proactively pursue non-economic policy innovations.

We do not examine whether increased training and indoctrination has indeed changed the preferences of local officials, nor do we claim that the policy innovations produced by local officials are indeed solving China's manifold problems. Our aim, rather, is to establish the *theoretical preconditions* for examining these questions by demonstrating that the central

* The research for this contribution was funded by the Swedish Science Council (Vetenskapsrådet Project No. 2011–1495) and the German Ministry of Education and Research (BMBF).

government did react to increasing governance complexity with a change in policies, and that local actors then altered their behavior to accommodate these new policies. We thereby show how strengthening local agency does not result in a loss of central government power: the relationship is not zero sum. If cadres can turn a unique mix of local problems, resources, and motivations into very specific local policy innovations that are in line with the preferences of the central government, the result of their agency represents not a loss, but a gain for central state capacity. The center has not yielded power to the localities, but instead made the exertion of power more flexible.

Central–Local Relations and Policy Innovation

Previous work highlights institutional configurations like the cadre responsibility system that have impeded the improvement of local governance. In a seminal contribution, Kevin O'Brien and Lianjiang Li convincingly show that policies with outcomes that are easily quantified by superordinate authorities are more likely to be implemented than policies with more intangible outcomes, because officials are evaluated and ranked according to their fulfillment of "hard" targets. While O'Brien and Li find that quantifiable policies like birth control and taxation tend to be "unpopular,"[1] John James Kennedy points out that "popular" policies like tax reforms and village elections can be made quantifiable as well.[2] Maria Edin reconciles the two positions, showing that it is not the characteristics of a certain policy, but the central government's resolve that determines if the policy will be implemented or not.[3]

What these findings have in common is that local officials emerge as more or less faithful implementers of central government policy. By highlighting the potential of local leaders to design and implement solutions on their own initiative, however, more recent work adds another perspective on the dynamics of central–local relations. Most notably, Sebastian Heilmann illustrates the important role local experimentation has played in testing and refining policies mandated by the central government that are later implemented nationwide.[4] However, Heilmann points out that such proactive experimentation is confined to policies that promise short-term economic rents. Policies in which this is not the case, such as those mandating provision of social and public goods, tend to be sidelined. "[P]roviding these goods requires a combination of societal interest

---

[1] O'Brien and Li, "Selective Policy Implementation in Rural China."
[2] Kennedy, "The Implementation of Village Elections."   [3] Edin, "State Capacity."
[4] Heilmann, "Policy Experimentation"; Heilmann, "Maximum Tinkering"; Heilmann and Perry, eds., *Mao's Invisible Hand.*

articulation and imposition of national policy priorities that goes against the short-term interests of most local elites," he argues, "and is therefore not easily reconciled with the entrenched mode of economic experimentation."[5] Thus, the design and implementation of social and public policies takes a back seat to the stimulation of economic growth, because economic growth increases rent-seeking opportunities and, one must add, is also one of the most important indicators for assessing cadre performance.[6]

A number of recent studies seem to confirm this phenomenon. In his study of an Anhui county, Graeme Smith finds that "the county government only takes up initiatives wholeheartedly when three conditions are met: 1) the initiative is important to the annual assessment system . . . ; 2) the initiative raises revenue . . . ; 3) the initiative benefits individual cadres . . . financially."[7] On the county level, he finds a "shadow state" in operation where "party leaders, their personal assistants, and their friends and relatives in the local business community" collude in rigging government contracts and trading government posts.[8] In an in-depth analysis of "County X," Ben Hillman finds similar mechanisms at work, and discovers that such "factions" are not confined to single counties, but operate at the "inter-state" level.[9] At the township level, Graeme Smith finds leaders squeezed between higher-level demands to fulfill achievement targets, and lower-level demands to "enforce family planning policies and maintain social stability,"[10] leaving no spare capacity for service provision.[11]

By contrast, Gunter Schubert and Anna Ahlers' study of three counties in Shaanxi, Zhejiang, and Jiangxi shows that "1) local development blueprints are taken seriously, and 2) win–win situations are often created for all parties concerned: county and township cadres, upper government levels and villagers."[12] There is also evidence that local governments are now proactively engaging in policy innovation. In 2000, the China Center for Comparative Politics and Economics (CCCPE), a think-tank organized under the CCP Central Compilation and Translation Bureau (中共中央编译局), presented its first "Government Innovation Award" to ten local governments that were selected from among 320 applicants. By 2013, the CCCPE program had received and evaluated more than 2,000 applications, among which innovations geared toward improving

---

[5] Heilmann, "Policy Experimentation," 19.
[6] Whiting, *Power and Wealth in Rural China*; Heberer and Schubert, "County and Township Cadres."
[7] Smith, "Political Machinations," 30.   [8] Ibid., 49.
[9] Hillman, "Factions and Spoils," 17.   [10] Smith, "The Hollow State," 601.
[11] Ibid., 618.   [12] Schubert and Ahlers, "County and Township Cadres," 68.

the accountability and service of administrative departments were especially prominent.[13]

Of course, these overall figures tell us little about the quality of these innovations. Examining several of the cases that received awards, Joseph Fewsmith shows that many, and perhaps most, of them are in fact unsustainable.[14] This is an interesting finding, which perhaps signifies that local leaders are incentivized to innovate, but not necessarily to do it well. A recent volume edited by Jessica Teets and William Hurst found that while policy diffusion does take place, it is not necessarily the "best" policies that are chosen for emulation.[15]

The foregoing indicators paint a picture of Chinese governance in flux: some localities are responsive to social grievances, others less so, but an increasingly vocal, rights-conscious, and internet-savvy public creates tremendous pressure on the regime to enhance its performance. Here, we will show that the central government has reacted to this challenge: by changing its techniques for governing local officials, it has sought to incentivize local policy innovation.

Defining Policy Innovation

In China, the term "innovation" is used in inflated ways, and in different contexts, leaving distinctions between policy, economic and technical, administrative and political, social and government or governance innovations not always clear. We define policy innovation as entailing the development of new ideas or concepts and the conversion of these ideas and concepts into new policies or policy instruments. It refers to the "introduction of new decision rules, new technology, new approaches to organizing," that is, it entails some "qualitative difference from existing routines and practices."[16] Application and implementation of innovations is aimed at facilitating change in economic and social development, social management, public services, and the interaction between a local government and its citizens.

As we are interested more in the mechanisms of local policy change than in the novelty of the resultant policies, we follow Merilee S. Grindle's definition of policy innovation as "actions of government that have not been undertaken before in a given place and whose promotion is a result of local action."[17] Hence, it is irrelevant whether such measures have already been invented or applied by other localities[18] – policy innovation

---

[13] Chen and Göbel, "Regulations against Revolution."
[14] Fewsmith, *The Logic and Limits.*
[15] Teets and Hurst, eds., *Local Governance Innovation.*   [16] Nice, *Policy Innovation,* 5.
[17] Grindle, *Going Local,* 146.   [18] Ibid., 5–7.

may well involve a learning effect, wherein local governments are learning by watching and copying effective policies from other governments, albeit without being instructed to do so by the central government.

Policy innovation is related to, but different from, the "point to surface" experiments analyzed by Heilmann. In policy experimentation, the central government defines desired outcomes, and localities find the instruments to achieve them. The ultimate aim is to generate "policy instruments" that can be applied elsewhere.[19] By contrast, policy innovation is less concerned with policy instruments and does not aim at replication, but at satisfying the specific demands of local constituencies. Both desired outcomes and policy instruments are defined by local governments. Whereas experimentation is a crucial component of state building, policy innovation is about the production of public goods for increasingly demanding consumer-citizens who are no longer satisfied with economic growth alone. In that sense, policy innovation represents a process of trial and error not at the national but the local level. The replication of such policies is not of chief concern, but it is not ruled out, either. Occasional exceptions notwithstanding, it is local authorities, and not the central government, who decide how far a policy innovation travels. The central government's role in this process is to encourage policy innovation and to use various means to outline a vague and changing opportunity space in which policy innovations are deemed possible and even desirable.

Facets of Power

This essay aims to show that party-state leaders have understood the shortcomings of past methods and have taken steps to make local cadres more responsive to social demands. In particular, we find that the central government has imposed what we call a "policy innovation imperative" on local leaders: it has taken measures to increase both the extrinsic and the intrinsic motivation of local officials to come up with innovative solutions to local difficulties. Foucault defines "government" as the "totality of institutions and practices by which one steers people." This includes both the setting and enforcing of rules and the stimulation of "technologies of the self." In China today, a combination of these techniques structures the possible fields of action available to local cadres and thereby impacts the probabilities of their conduct.

Max Weber defined power as "making someone do something he would not have done otherwise."[20] While power is often equated with coercion,

---

[19] Heilmann, "Policy Experimentation"; Heilmann, "From Local Experiments."
[20] Weber, *Grundriß der Sozialökonomie III*, 28.

288   *Christian Göbel and Thomas Heberer*

Michel Foucault has presented a more nuanced understanding of how power is wielded. We draw on his concept now to advance our analysis. According to Foucault, power implies a "will to dominate."[21] In a hierarchical political system, power is expressed as the ability to "make subjects behave in a specific way." This can take the form of an act of *coercion* followed by an act of obedience, or by *disciplining* actors to behave in a certain way even when a direct stimulus is absent: actors behave in a certain way because they might be punished if their rule violation is discovered. Institutionalist approaches typically examine just these two dimensions of power.[22] Foucault's concept of "governmentality" adds a third dimension. According to Foucault, the most effective, lowest-cost form of wielding power occurs when those who are dominated can be persuaded to accept the preferences of those who dominate *as their own*. Acquiescing in the alteration of their own preferences, they may eventually become active accomplices in their own domination, not only upholding but even helping to improve prevailing structures of domination. In other words, the "will to dominate" will be met by a "will to improve."[23]

Concurrently, this aim that cadres should not merely supervise innovation projects but "internalize" them leads to an individuation or personification of power relations at the local level, since each and every cadre is to be made to feel "haunted" by the constant sense that there remains something more, and more effective – something better – that must be found, or done, or be developed. "Haunted" by this perpetually felt need to do better, cadres internalize and cultivate a personal "will to improve."[24] The notion of "haunting" is borrowed from Derrida's "Spectres de Marx" and with regard to China, we use it to refer not only to the impact of Confucian discourses (such as the "civilizing" mission of the center, or "self-cultivation") but also to Maoist discourses (such as "struggle" and "reeducation") and other discourses aimed at instilling certain concepts of modernity and development among local cadres ("modernization," "betterment," "improvement"). Techniques of "haunting" help ensure that lower-level cadres do feel under pressure to comply with central expectations.[25] Thus, to guarantee the internalization of the center's own concepts and policies, upper levels today can be seen to deploy a combination both of standard political-administrative protocols and of such "techniques of the self."[26]

Haunting involves two principal aspects: (1) the development of a "will to improve," and (2) the creation of a system of pressures. As a Party Secretary of a county in Guizhou explained, local cadres are facing "a pressure

---

[21] Foucault et al., *Analytik der Macht*.   [22] Lukes, *Power: A Radical View*.
[23] Li, *The Will to Improve*.   [24] See Derrida and Bernd, *Specters of Marx*.
[25] Gordon, *Ghostly Matters*, xvi.   [26] Foucault, *The History of Sexuality*.

system" (压力型体制), with pressure coming primarily from three sides: (a) rising performance demands by higher authorities and a stricter monitoring of policy implementation (not only through target, responsibility, and evaluation systems, but also through a ranking system now applied to the governments of counties and townships); (b) rising demands for "rights" from local people; and (c) a heightening sense of interior or personal pressure – pressure to pursue one's own career successfully within the hierarchy of the nomenclatura system.[27] An important part of this system of pressures is the so-called "one item veto rule" (一票否决), a periodic assignment of "hard" targets for goals which must be successfully fulfilled and for crises or mistakes which must be prevented from happening locally. Major emphases in the "one item veto rule" system have been, for instance, preserving social stability (i.e. preventing mass protests or other instances of popular unrest locally), fulfilling birth planning quotas, increasing per capita income in the locality, preventing major industrial accidents, and other focal policies particular to a given locality (such as environmental protection/ remediation, rural social security, etc.).[28] If one of these key targets should not be successfully accomplished, all other achievements of the local leadership would be regarded as void; making a county or township leading group ineligible for classification as "advanced," and promotion of the county and township Party Secretary or Mayor to a higher post almost impossible. Through these devices, the specific rank that county and township cadres hold in China's hierarchically structured political system and their exposure to pressure from both higher-level governments and the rural populace in the process of local decision-making and implementation work to force the local leadership core and all other group members into strategic alignment and cooperation.[29] Under such interlocking pressures in their work, local cadres can now often be heard to complain about suffering from depression and other psychic syndromes such as eating disorders, insomnia, aggressiveness towards their families, etc.[30]

The prevalence of such a system of pressures, of this sentiment of being "haunted," and the development of such a "will to improve" are strongly linked together within the cadres' responsibility and evaluation routines. The routine discipline of signing annual "cadres' responsibility contracts" sets the agenda for what must be accomplished by each locality in the following year. Local leading cadres and government offices are held

[27] Interview, Xifeng County Party Secretary, September 6, 2010.
[28] Heberer and Trappel, "Evaluation Processes," 1053; Heberer and Senz, "Streamlining Local Behaviour," 87–94.
[29] Heberer and Schubert, "County and Township Cadres."
[30] See, for example, N. N., Decision-Making, 192; N. N., "Grassroots Cadres"; and Jia Jianyou, "Township Cadres."

responsible for the fulfillment of dozens of complex and challenging development goals in these responsibility contracts. At the end of each year, leading local cadres must verify for higher authorities that things have "improved" within their jurisdictions, giving evidence that, among those cadres, a "will to improve" does exist.

The Emergence of the Policy Innovation Imperative

The first proposition underlying our analysis is that perceived threats to the survival of the party-state have led the central government to change its techniques for governing China's local administrators.

Perceived Threats to Regime Survival and the Need to Innovate

The most explicit expression of a prevailing fear of regime collapse is found in the "Decision on Enhancing the Party's Ability to Govern," which the CCP's Central Committee passed at the Fourth Plenum of the 16th Party Congress in September 2004. The Decision reflects the results of an inner-party evaluation of the collapse of the Soviet Union and other communist states,[31] identifies challenges to the legitimacy of the CCP, and outlines possible solutions. Most importantly, it declares a need to strengthen the party's ability to govern. In quite dramatic terms, the document warns that this undertaking will determine "the success or failure of establishing Socialism in China, the future of the Chinese people, the life or death of the party, and the long-term stability of the country."[32]

Zeng Qinghong, then head of the CCP's powerful Organization Department and the person responsible for drafting the Decision, reiterated its importance in a lengthy *People's Daily* article. One of the central messages of the Decision, which Zeng confirmed in his editorial, is that the quality of the cadre force was then too low to tackle the many new challenges with which a rapidly developing China was being faced. In particular, the Decision deplores cadres' "low level of ideological and theoretical knowledge, weak ability to govern according to law, weak capacity to solve complex contradictions," and asserts that their "degree of personal refinement (素质) and ability do not match requirements needed to [implement central party programs]." Accordingly, the need to "rotate, retire and change leading personnel" and to "improve cadre competence and recruitment into the party" are two among ten key "lessons" identified in the Decision.

---

[31] Shambaugh, *China's Communist Party*, 124.
[32] CCPCC, "Decision on Strengthening the Party's Governing Capacity."

The Need to Improve the Quality of China's Cadre Force

As a consequence of these findings, a major part of the Decision focuses on measures to "intensify the reform of the cadre system [in order to] construct a cadre force with high personal refinement (素质) that is good at managing state affairs."[33] While the Decision itself promoted only the "professionalization" of the cadre force along with certain institutional reforms such as the improvement of checks and balances, it was followed in January 2005 by a campaign to "maintain the advanced nature of CCP members."[34] This campaign complemented institutional changes by increasing the intrinsic motivation of local officials to become better cadres. Joseph Fewsmith correctly identifies this as "an old-style rectification campaign,"[35] because cadres underwent "study sessions, lectures, and criticism and self-criticism"[36] intended to "increase the personal refinement (素质) of party members," "improve grassroots party organization," "serve the masses," and thus "promote all kinds of work."[37]

In the first half of 2005, virtually all cadres at the county level and above underwent this training; followed by township-level officials during the latter part of the year. Shortly before the campaign was extended to village-level administrations in early 2006, the CCP intensified its strategy of coupling general institutional reforms with attempts to instill in its cadre force a "will to improve." On December 23, 2005, the CCP's Central Committee and the State Council jointly released "Several Opinions regarding the Deepening of Reforms of the Cultural System" which reminds readers that "socialist culture" is a productive force, and that reforms and innovations in the "cultural system" (文化体制) are important preconditions for China's further modernization and for strengthening the party's hold on power. The general public and officials alike were enjoined to improve themselves by "incessantly strengthening their practice, mass, market, and innovation orientations."[38]

Beyond Management Skills: Personality Engineering

It was a hallmark of the Hu-Wen government that it sought to improve party-state performance by extending the focus of politics beyond institutional reform as such to include what we might call "personality engineering." And this was to continue under Xi.

---

[33] Zeng Qinghong, "Strengthening the Party's Governing Capacity."
[34] CCPCC, "Opinion on Having the Entire Party."
[35] Fewsmith, "CCP Launches Campaign."   [36] Ibid., 5.
[37] CCPCC, "Opinion on Having the Entire Party."
[38] CCPCC and SC, "Some Opinions on Deepening Cultural Restructuring."

In a fascinating study of the reorganization of China's national leadership training system, Gregory T. Chin has examined the significance of the three cadre training academies established in 2005 under the party's Central Organization Department. In the Shanghai-Pudong academy, leaders learn about modernization; in Jinggangshan, about party history; and in Yan'an about party strategy.[39] Chin finds that the reform of China's leadership training system, from that time, departed from the previous understanding of leadership: "the present aim is to develop leadership skills that are both comprehensive – by providing training on a broad range of issues that a leading cadre or official might encounter, not just executive or management training per se – and also practical and case-specific skills."[40] Leaders now are envisioned not only as managers, but also as innovators, with roles as much akin to those of businesspeople operating in competitive markets as to government bureaucrats.

With the campaign to "Maintain the Advanced Nature of Communist Party Members" still underway, the central government issued its Trial Regulations for Cadre Education and Training Work (干部教育培训工作条例（试行）) in 2006.[41] This document identifies a lack of "ideological and political conviction, talent and knowledge" within the cadre force as a bottleneck in the "construction of a moderately well-off society and the speedy modernization of socialism." To remedy the situation, it called for "large-scale training programs for cadres and the significant improvement of cadre personal refinement" to be made a part of local economic and social development plans. In effect, this lodged the effort to rectify and improve cadre behavior at the local level and gave it a firm basis in development planning itself.

These documents, mainly concerned with cadre "quality" or personal refinement, also articulated a need for officials to become innovators. The Sixth Plenum of the 16th Central Committee in October 2006 proclaimed "a national spirit with patriotism at the core, and a spirit of the time with reform and innovation at its core" to be the essence of a System of Socialist Core Values (社会主义核心价值体系). From then on, raising a cadre's aptitude for innovation became an end in itself – summoning talents crucially different from the more instrumental tasks cadres must fulfill in the course of policy experimentation. The document further extends the meaning of "reform and innovation" to include "the construction of the economy, politics, culture, and society."[42] In these efforts too, officials, and especially leading cadres, are expected to shoulder

---

[39] Chin, "Innovation and Preservation," 24–25.   [40] Ibid., 22.
[41] Zeng Qinghong, "Strengthening the Party's Governing Capacity."
[42] CCPCC, "Decision on Important Questions."

responsibilities, improve their own skills, and serve as role models and teachers for the general population. It follows from this narrative that China's future development is perceived to hinge importantly on its capacity to generate economic, political, cultural, and social innovation, which in turn hinges on bettering the overall quality and personal refinement of China's cadres.

In a more recent iteration of this broad endeavor, a "Mass Line Education and Practice Activities" campaign (群众路线教育实践活动),[43] was initiated in June 2013 and carried out over a full year. Its focus was on activating the individual will of the "self" in rectifying party members, encouraging them to engage in *self*-purifying (自我净化), *self*-perfection (自我完善), *self*-reformation (自我革新), *self*-elevation (自我提高), *self*-criticism (自我批评), *self*-education (自我教育), and *self*-analysis (自我剖析).[44] And senior officials, the campaign emphasized, should serve as role models in this quest for moral self-reformation.

This campaign emphasized the responsibility of each *individual* with respect both to actual behavior and the continual rectification of one's own thinking. One message of this campaign clearly was that where mistakes are made, it is the individuals involved who should be held responsible: not society at large, and not the general party-state political system.

The required "mass line activities" of the campaign were time limited – each unit carrying it out for at most three months, with each locality exercising discretion on how precisely to orchestrate the proceedings. It was, in contrast to some of Mao's earlier "mass line" concepts, more flexible. It expressly did not aim to mobilize the masses themselves for any political or utopian goals, but rather to engender a new contingent of "clean" cadres who would *both* prioritize the needs of the people *and* develop a "learning," "innovation," and "problem-solving" mentality in order to enhance overall state capacity.[45] Its final goal, having secured the compliance and cooperation of the majority of party members and officials, was to focus their activities on finding innovative solutions for concrete local problems.[46]

Frank Pieke aptly sums up the logic behind the massive personality engineering efforts entailed: "Cadres continue to be bound by the ideology and practice prescribed by Leninist party discipline, but should also

[43] See N. N., "The Party Center Strives."
[44] Xi Jinping, "Speech at the Work Conference on Mass Line Education"; see also Liu Yunshan, "Education and Practice."
[45] The promotion of innovation in local politics was particularly emphasized in Liu Xiaojun, "Vehicles of Innovation Activity."
[46] Heberer, "China in 2013."

become modern, competent managers of increasingly complex organizations."[47] This is not all, however: as Chin has shown, and as all of our interviewees stressed, cadres are now also expected to be "innovative" problem-solvers.[48]

Setting Incentives through Disciplining and Evaluation

This novel "innovation imperative" was put into practice via the cadre "target responsibility system" and the cadre "evaluation system" applied to those working in state offices and enterprises in the annual responsibility contracts that are signed (since the 1980s) between local officials and their administrative supervisors at the next higher level. The performance and behavior of leading local cadres, in each policy area, are compared against their contracted targets, to generate their collective and personal evaluations. Meeting performance targets and receiving good evaluations heavily determine the career prospects and the remuneration scales of local cadres. Throughout the 1990s and early 2000s, achieving local economic growth was the single most heavily weighted performance item for officials, with other policy priorities taking a back seat.[49] While economic growth performance *remains* very important to this day, local officials must now also perform well in other domains. Consequently, three instruments are now employed to encourage them to innovate in these other public policy arenas: (a) setting minimum standards for performance in non-economic domains without, however, prescribing policies; (b) turning policy innovation from a means into an end in itself; and (c) giving additional, (career) rewards to them – outside the evaluation system – explicitly for innovation.

Setting Minimum Standards in Domains without Rent-Seeking Potential

First, the center has set minimum standards to encourage conscientious implementation of non-growth-related policies. These minima take the form of veto items that, if not fulfilled, prevent an official from being evaluated as "excellent," which is a precondition for promotion. One particularly important veto item has been *maintaining social stability*: even if officials have displayed good performance under their responsibility contracts in other respects, any outbreak of public protests in their district, or even a high number of citizen complaints and petitions sent

[47] Pieke, *The Good Communist*, 51.   [48] Chin, "Innovation and Preservation."
[49] Whiting, *Power and Wealth.*

from the district or personally delivered to higher-level governments, may prevent that official's promotion.[50]

This is spelled out in recent policy documents demanding local officials come up with "innovations in social management" (社会管理创新).[51] The "better social management program" calls for improvements in the quality of public services, and encourages the local formation of self-governing functional and territorial organizations, i.e. special-interest groups or neighborhoods and communities that will assist and promote provision of public goods. Of course, local officials must demonstrate that they have played a leading role in designing and regulating these innovations, which, as Hu Jintao put it, "must play a facilitating role in upholding social stability and in creating a favorable environment for the people to live and work in peace and happiness."[52]

Another example has been embedded in the center's program of "Constructing a New Socialist Countryside." Initially, in 2006, the central government issued one terse document, just twenty characters in length, to prompt all local governments in rural areas to engage in a new round of "advancing agrarian production," "improving overall living conditions," "civilizing rural life," "tidying up villages," and improving democratic administration.[53] All local levels were called upon to specify guidelines, adapted to their local conditions, for implementing this framework of rural policy objectives. The innovative aspect here was that local leaderships could set their own specific targets of emphasis, as long as their policy implementation choices were compatible with the "20 characters" and associated higher-level guidelines. Allowing this degree of discretion was viewed as beneficial in fostering a wider range of localized policy experiments and added opportunities for innovation within China's counties, townships, and villages.

Our interviewees confirmed, as expected, that an inability to be "innovative" in the sense of devising new solutions for pressing problems results in lower cadre evaluation scores and can hinder individual career advancement. Many cadres have complained, also not unexpectedly, that the evaluations, which are conducted frequently, place them therefore under enormous personal pressure to be innovative. One county-level Organization Department leader we interviewed insisted that only officials who demonstrate their ability to come up with creative solutions to local problems can be evaluated as "excellent" (优秀)

[50] Heberer and Trappel, "Evaluation Processes."   [51] N. N., "Hu Jintao."
[52] Hu Jintao, "Speech at the Research Seminar."
[53] For more details on the program and its implementation in rural China, see Ahlers and Schubert, "'Building a New Socialist Countryside'"; Schubert and Ahlers, "'Constructing a New Socialist Countryside'."

296 Christian Göbel and Thomas Heberer

officials.[54] For generating outstanding ideas or solutions, leading officials can even be awarded an "Innovation Prize."[55] And on the level of townships and street committees, cadre innovation competitions have been initiated by the local leadership.[56] In these and other ways, cadre evaluations work as components of the haunting system now applied to career-minded lower-level bureaucrats. This setting of targets they know they must meet, and would do better even to exceed, contributes to fostering within them, as teams and as individuals, a "will to innovate improvements."[57]

Transforming Policy Innovation from a Means into an End

Second, it is now evident that policy innovation has progressed from being seen by officials as a means to solve problems to being regarded as an end in itself. Changes in the regulations for cadre evaluation – implemented in 2006 on a trial basis and formalized in 2009 – indicated that local officials were expected to demonstrate their capacity to produce context-specific policy innovations even where no pressing problems were present. Now, "innovation," as an indicator of good cadre quality, features in four domains. First, leaders are evaluated along five personality characteristics: 德 (moral quality), 能 (capability/skills), 勤 (work attitude/diligence), 绩 (achievements) and 廉 (integrity/incorruptibility). A quality referred to as "innovation awareness" (创新意识) has become one item in the individual personality evaluation of a leader under the category of capability (能).[58]

A second evaluation criterion is the instigation of "practical innovations" as a sign of "leadership ability" (领导水平). Here, actual policies, which should be characterized by "realism and pragmatism, courageous exploration, the tackling of difficulties" (求真务实, 勇敢探索, 攻坚克难) serve as a base for the judgment. Third, administrative innovations (管理创新) are one element contributing to positive scores in the domain of "work achievements" (工作实绩).

And finally, these regulations provide for limited public participation in the evaluation of local leaders, during which exercise scores are assigned for their reforms and innovations (改革创新). Of course, policy innovations need to adhere to existing regulations and should reflect the preferences of the central government. During the annual evaluation of policy implementation and cadre performance, higher-level bodies examine and

---

[54] Interview, Jilin Province, July 23, 2013.
[55] See, e.g., Taizhou Municipality Party Committee Office, "Notice." [56] Ibid.
[57] Heberer and Trappel, "Evaluation Processes."
[58] See Jiangyin Municipal Committee, "Survey on Democracy among Leading Cadres."

disseminate the progress of previous policy innovations and, in doing so, put even more pressure on local leaders to strive, themselves, to create such successful "models" of innovation in their own jurisdictions. Counties are evaluated not only with respect to their ability to solve their own problems, but also in comparison to the performance achieved in other locations. This discourages the mere adoption of "best practices" devised and honed elsewhere and forces leaders to come up with their own distinct policies.

Jiangyin and Wuxi, for instance, have already developed annual plans for policy innovations and evaluation of innovative behavior defining which problems local cadres have to develop solutions for in a given year and tightening the assessment of these innovative solutions.[59] It is specifically demanded that leading cadres identify local problems themselves, determine goals, specify concrete steps for implementation, and solve the problems through innovative measures.[60] These, then, are among the disciplining techniques being used to develop a cadre's "will to improve."

In 2012, Jiangyin City's party committee and government issued a joint document on developing innovations in the context of structural reforms in various administrative fields. Among the thirty-two flagged fields in which innovative reforms should be developed (or already existing experiments be disseminated) were: administration of the cadre selection and appointment system; restructuring of street offices; restructuring of local public services; acceleration of government permits and approvals procedures; establishment of companies charged with managing the property and other assets of villages; mergers of villages with urban neighborhoods; reform of local pharmaceuticals management systems; and restructuring of environmental management systems in townships.[61] The document emphasized the need to intensify the evaluation of cadre innovation. In less-developed areas, "learning" among local cadres is conceived of as a first step to trigger innovative thinking. There, workshops with and lectures on innovative policies by externally invited experts are organized, and local cadres regularly travel to policy and social innovation ("model") counties and locations that have received awards for specific innovations. In addition, local governments arrange regular meetings with local

---

[59] See "Jiangyin Municipality ... Joint Circular ... 2011"; and "Jiangyin Municipality ... Joint Circular ... 2012"; Interview, secretary–general, Wuxi Party Committee, August 21, 2011; and also Wuxi Municipality, Bureau of Science and Technology, "On the Trial Methods for Evaluating 'Three Creates' Agents."

[60] Wuxi Municipal Party Committee, Organization Department, "Party Building Leadership Group ... Document."

[61] "Jiangyin Municipality ... Joint Circular ... 2012."

entrepreneurs and representatives of various social groups asking them to make suggestions of where innovative reforms are necessary in order to improve the administrative setting and investment climate for entrepreneurs or other services for townspeople.[62]

Though cadre visits to "model units" is a longstanding practice of the CCP, the current aim is not merely to copy existing "political models" but to stimulate innovative problem-solving among local cadres now under pressure to develop their own innovations according to the specific conditions and environment of their own localities.

Rewards beyond the Evaluation System

Finally, there now exist, outside the cadre evaluation system itself, additional incentives for making public policy innovations. Our interviews make it clear that the initiation and successful implementation of innovative public policies draw the attention and support of an official's superiors. No matter whether a policy innovation is initiated top-down or bottom-up, it requires frequent communication and coordination between leading cadres. A local official who implements an idea as an experiment, or sponsors what becomes a new "model," thereby demonstrates individual worth and is seen as a candidate for promotion. In addition, a proven capability to produce and implement innovative policies can help local officials to secure earmarked funding to enhance the implementation of the new policy or to engage in still further experiments. By helping a higher-level official to enhance performance in the district, a lower-level official will increase the likelihood of being rewarded in other ways as well. Especially in regions or departments where faster economic growth policies are not feasible or already exhausted, public policy innovations can serve as an important means of gaining favor and obtaining political rewards.

In sum, the evaluation system stimulates public policy innovations in two ways. First, it provides career incentives for conducting policy experiments, creating models, and implementing innovative policies that are not restricted to the economic realm. Second, performance ratings constitute a system of controls and pressures to discipline cadres. According to Heberer and Trappel, cadres consecutively evaluated as "excellent" and proven to be innovative are chosen over others when it comes to promotions.[63] Furthermore, the evaluation system communicates to

---

[62] Interview, Jiangyin, August 19, 2011. See also Shiquan County, "Basic Methods."

[63] Heberer and Trappel, "Evaluation Processes"; see also Shih et al., "Getting Ahead"; Tao Ran et al., "Can Economic Growth Lead to Job Promotion."

lower authorities the development expectations of superior authorities and provides an optimal frame of reference for local cadres when designing and implementing local development policies. More specifically, the frequent evaluations force local officials to comprehend and conform to the developmental concepts of the central government, which they are to put into practice by means of innovative policies.

Shaping Preferences through Indoctrination and Training

Our third proposition is that the government attempts to shape cadres' behavior by increasing their intrinsic motivation to voluntarily engage in policy innovations commensurate with the aims of the central government. As we have shown, the central government has created a theoretical narrative that links China's pressing social and political problems to the low level of personal refinement of local officials. Now we can turn to examining this narrative in more detail and describe the techniques employed to instill in local officials the desired "will to improve."

The Personal Refinement (素质) Discourse as a Disciplining Instrument

As shown above, the party-state leadership has framed the lack of personal refinement of China's population as a major development bottleneck, and the cultivation of innovation as the path to modernity and self-discipline.[64] Along with engaging in "cultural system reforms" (文化体制改革) for the benefit of the Chinese population, the central government therefore resolved to raise the personal refinement of local officials. Higher personal refinement, in turn, should enable local officials to solve local problems better and improve local governance proactively instead of merely doing what they are told. In this narrative, very broadly speaking, the explanatory focus for the persistence of underdevelopment and bad governance is shifted from structural to individual-level factors, and active self-improvement is represented, instead, as a way out of the conundrum of underdevelopment.

In these discourses, personal refinement and policy innovation are intimately connected. Yu Keping, director of the "Excellence in Local Government Innovation" program and advisor to the CCP's Central Committee, stresses that China's uneven development and the associated increase in inequality are the products of a vicious circle, in which low personal refinement and low development reinforce each other.[65] And

---

[64] See, e.g., Yan, "Neoliberal Governmentality and Neohumanism."
[65] Interview, Beijing, February 21, 2012.

the Party Secretary of Shaanxi's Shiquan County reflects this view of things when he emphasizes that "the aim of innovation is not to show a great performance (作秀) but to solve problems which, due to persistent routine thinking previously, could not be solved."[66]

Hence, personal refinement serves as the link between the individual actor and the central government's vision of what a "modern" China should look like. Without good personal quality, or refinement, there can be no genuine modernization; and the successful modernization of a locality, in turn, serves as an indicator that local authorities there do possess a high level of personal refinement. The reverse is also true: where modernization remains elusive, low personal refinement is thought to be to blame. Policy innovation is one of the acts that can transform individual, personal refinement into modernity.

Calling on local cadres to improve their personal refinement adds to the existing achievement targets, a performance measure that is subjective and non-quantifiable, but intimately tied to the modernization of a locality. In this way, the notion of personal refinement has become a subtle instrument of power. Its purpose is to establish new forms of social control, new patterns of rationality, and new norms and standards of behavior. Local cadres, to be sure, face negative sanctions if they fail in efforts to raise their quality.[67]

Cadre Training: Raising Personal Refinement and Enhancing Learning Capacity

The party-state avails itself of a broad set of tools to instill in local cadres a "will to improve." Local cadres are treated as disciples who need to internalize central government propaganda so as to enable them to intuit the center's intentions when they engage in policy innovation. This includes clever ways of meeting the central government's targets as well as coming up with new policies that are not part of the annual assessments, but are rewarded for their "innovative" nature. These skills are developed through rigorous training and continuous indoctrination, in which cadres internalize a carefully selected tome of propaganda documents, absorb the central government's stance on how certain questions should be handled, and work to develop a variety of management and problem-solving capabilities. We would not, of course, argue that the "techniques" described below are always very deeply, or even straightforwardly, effective in improving the

---

[66] Interview, Shiquan County, August 24, 2011.
[67] On this issue, see Heberer, "The Contention between Han 'Civilisers' and Yi 'Civilisees'."

personal refinement or the learning capacity of the cadres concerned. We aim, in what follows, only to indicate which types of "techniques" are being employed.

Among the most important organizations for imparting such knowledge on a regular basis are the central and local party schools,[68] where leading local cadres are required to take a variety of courses, ranging from training on general political doctrines to concrete issues such as social psychology, economic management, and social management. At the county level, according to our interviews, party schools invite renowned scholars and entrepreneurs to give lectures, and leading local cadres are provided with a set of (translated) foreign best-sellers concerned with innovative practices in various social and policy fields. Local party schools and organizational departments of the CCP regularly organize visits to model counties and cities across the country to get fresh ideas about how to solve social policy and administrative issues. On an annual basis more wealthy counties send leading cadres abroad to attend study courses at renowned US or Singaporean universities on administration and social management issues.[69]

Interviews with professors of party schools at different levels confirm that the schools are indeed conceiving their training as crucial for enhancing the capacity of leading local officials to be innovative.[70] The deputy director of the party school of Jiangyin City (a county-level city in Jiangsu Province) emphasized that all their study materials and techniques serve to raise the personal refinement of leading local cadres, and are regarded as "crucial."[71] In illustrating how a high level of personal refinement among leading cadres at the local level can be demonstrated, she noted:

You have to solve problems locally. The local Organization Department of the party will examine your problem solution capacity every year. If you need, for instance, funding for implementing an innovative project you have to manage it by yourself and get a bank credit. You cannot ask the higher authorities to solve this problem for you. Rather, superior authorities should get the impression that you are a resourceful person successfully figuring out how to solve problems (想办法).[72]

The Party Secretary of a township in Shiquan County also confirmed that the stimulation of innovative ideas lies at the heart of modern cadre education with its emphasis on raising personal refinement: "it shall enable us to solve problems which we could not yet solve due to obstacles

---

[68] Pieke, *The Good Communist.*   [69] Interview, Jiangyin party school, August 18, 2011.
[70] Interview, Beijing, August 16, 2012; Interview, Jiangyin party school, August 18, 2011.
[71] Jiangyin Municipal Committee, "Jiangyin Municipality 2011 Program for Implementation of Work Targets."
[72] Interview, Jiangyin party school, August 18, 2011.

in our thinking . . . and to enhance our operationalization capacity in order to solve practical problems."[73]

Apart from party schools, the center also dispatches higher-level cadres to townships and villages (挂职) to guide and monitor development processes in "backward" villages and townships. Needless to say, these can often be contentious processes, especially in minority regions, or in other circumstances where the center's vision of development can clash with the preferences of the population at the grassroots. County offices may be directed to take over responsibility for several villages in order to guide their "development." In addition, university graduates are sent into villages and townships to instruct the rural population and local cadres.[74] The local party schools too may offer specific training courses for those graduates who are being trained for certain rural jobs.

Moreover, local governments frequently organize training courses on policy innovation and policy learning for officials at the county and township level. Experts from the central and the provincial level teach courses on improving local policies as well as on the construction of environmental or ecological models at the county, township, and village levels. These courses also may include visits to model townships and model villages across the country in order to gain inspiration from their experiences.[75] In addition, county Organization Departments regularly organize inspection tours so that rural cadres may gather new information and knowledge on rural models. One County Party Secretary in Sichuan, for instance, reported having attended inspection tours to Chengdu, Hangzhou, Nanjing, and Suzhou, where the participating cadres encountered some cutting-edge patterns of rural development, processing industries, land policies, and environmental protection.[76]

To enhance their innovative capacity, leading cadres of the counties and townships of Wuxi are sent to special training seminars inside and outside China. Zhejiang Province, for instance, dispatched eighteen county party secretaries to the University of Duisburg-Essen in 2013 where they attended a several-week-long seminar on urban development, urban planning, and sustainability and related best practices in Germany. The rationale behind the seminar was that "innovation means continuously learning. Innovations originate not only from one's own reflections but also from seeing new and

---

[73] Interview, Shiquan County, August 24, 2011.

[74] Du Wenhao, "The Significance and Strategies"; Chen Zhong, "College Graduate Village Cadre"; Duan Zhezhe and Huang Weiren, "The Predicament and the Prospect." Increasing *personal refinement* is of course not the only reason to send students down to the countryside. A welcome side effect of this measure is to ease the political pressure generated by a high number of university graduates who cannot find a suitable occupation.

[75] Interview, Xichang, February 15, 2012.   [76] Interview, Xichang, February 15, 2012.

innovative things."[77] Accordingly, the mayor of one Jiangsu township declared that he had learned innovative thinking from study courses on rural modernization in Shanghai, Singapore, and Stanford. Moreover, opportunities for regular meetings to be arranged with private entrepreneurs and even with scientists are also considered helpful.[78]

Conclusion

Existing scholarship has ably demonstrated that, previously, policies were successful either where the interests of the central and local governments converged, or where the central government applied campaign-style politics to force local implementation of a certain policy. As we have shown, national leaders in Beijing saw the collapse of the Soviet Union and rising unrest in China as signs that this political-developmental path was no longer tenable. Both Hu Jintao and Xi Jinping have put a premium on improving the quality of the cadre force. It was hoped that cadres with better education, higher skills, and motivation would prove more able to proactively solve local problems and thereby enhance the overall legitimacy of the CCP. In particular, cadres have been spurred to produce policy innovations in fields that had previously been neglected, most notably in the areas of social policy and public administration.

Our work shows that such innovations are now being produced in fact, and in great numbers. Moreover, the evidence mounts, as we have argued, that changes in the evaluation regulations for local cadres have reinforced a "haunting" system of pressures upon cadres aimed to stimulate among them a "will to improve" that will likely be responsible for inducing many more such local innovations. It remains very doubtful, of course, that cadres themselves really *want* to be innovative now. At present, rather, their "will to improve" takes the form of a perceived "need to improve" in order to be positively evaluated and to advance along the bureaucratic career ladder. Nevertheless, what is being attempted at this stage in China is different from straightforward technical target fulfillment. Although the creation of policy innovations can be regarded as a simple target to be met, the processes involved are more complex than for example meeting birth control targets: leaders must first identify a problem, come up with a new policy, and, most importantly, market this policy by convincing other departments and the general public to participate. While target fulfillment requires cadres to administer and manage, policy innovation requires more – it requires entrepreneurship.

---

[77] Interview, Jiangyin party school, August 18, 2011.
[78] Interview, Qingyang township, August 19, 2011.

It must be noted, however, that the central government's shift to imposing a policy innovation imperative, and to altering the extrinsic and intrinsic motivation structures of local cadres, does not yet seem to have resulted in many policies that were adopted outside of the locations where they originated. In fact, policy innovations generally do appear to be rather short-lived even in the locations that produced them.

One likely explanation for this is that some, or even most, of these policies were produced exactly for the purpose of receiving high evaluation scores and promotions; they lacked advance planning and consultation with relevant stakeholders, and therefore failed at the implementation stage. Another probable explanation pertains to the nature of the policy innovation imperative itself: as cadres are evaluated not only for the absence of social stability and other problems, but also for their production of policy innovations, new officials are almost forced to discard previous policies even if they had been working fine. Figuratively speaking, the policy innovation imperative tends to produce sand castles that are washed away with each wave of new first-in-commands entering a locality. However, we could also consider this from another perspective: innovations are innovative only within a limited time span, and it is their abandonment and replacement by new ones after a few years that might represent some real "progress."

Future research will be needed to resolve the obvious question of whether the imposition of the innovation imperative has been a gigantic waste of resources, or a genuine means of preventing Chinese local governance from becoming sclerotic. More work is needed also to shed light on the questions of whether this modeling and remodeling of policies yields a positive learning effect, and whether it produces increasingly better policies, or better cadres, over time.

Whatever the answers to these questions are, we hope, as a minimum, to have established that the thousands of policy innovations produced in China these days are not insignificant simply because they are not often replicated. Understanding the processes and outcomes of the new policy innovation imperative gives us a more nuanced and realistic picture of central–local relations in contemporary China, and especially of the range of techniques now in use by central authorities for disciplining and guiding their agents – those who govern China in the localities.

References

Ahlers, Anna and Schubert, Gunter. "'Building a New Socialist Countryside' – Only a Political Slogan?," *Journal of Contemporary Chinese Affairs*, 38: 2009, 35–62.

"CCPCC [Chinese Communist Party Central Committee] Decision on Important Questions Regarding the Construction of a Harmonious Socialist Society."

"中共中央关于构建社会主义和谐社会若干重大问题的决定，" *新华*, 10 月18日 2006 年, at news.xinhuanet.com/politics/2006–10/18/content_5218639.htm.

"CCPCC Decision on Strengthening the Party's Governing Capacity." "中共中央关于加强党的执政能力建设的决定，" at www.china.com.cn/chinese/2004/Sep/668376.htm.

"CCPCC Opinion on Having the Entire Party Take the Practice of the Important Thought of the 'Three Represents' as the Core of Educational Activities to Maintain Party Members' Advanced Nature ." "中共中央关于保持党员先进性教育活动的意见 – 中共中央关于在全党开展以实践'三个代表'重要思想 – 为主要内容的保持共产党员先进性教育活动的意见，" *新华*, 3 月07日 2005年, at www.zynews.com/special/2005–03/07/content_152797.htm.

CCPCC and State Council (SC) of the People's Republic of China. ("Some Opinions on Deepening Cultural Restructuring"). "中共中央、国务院关于深化文化体制改革的若干意见，" *新华*, 6月12日 2006 年, at news.xinhuanet.com/politics/2006–01/12/content_4044535.htm.

Chen, Xuelian and Göbel, Christian. "Regulations against Revolution: Mapping Policy Innovations in China," *Journal of Chinese Governance*, 1: 2016, 78–98.

Chen Zhong (陈忠). ("College Graduate Village Cadre and China's Political Environment: Significance, Problems and Tendencies"). "大学生村官与中国政治生态: 意义, 问题 与取向，" *苏州大学学报 – 哲学社会科学版*, 2009, 1–6.

Chin, Gregory T. "Innovation and Preservation: Remaking China's National Leadership Training System," *China Quarterly*, 205: 2011, 18–39.

Derrida, Jacques and Bernd, Magnus. *Specters of Marx: The State of the Debt, the Work of Mourning, and the New International.* New York: Routledge, 1994.

Du Wenhao (杜文好). ("The Significance and Strategies of Stimulating College Graduate Village Cadres' Achievement Motivation"). "激发大学生村官成就动机的意义和策略，" *徐州师范大学学报*, 2: 2011, 29–31.

Duan Zhezhe (段哲哲) and Huang Weiren (黄伟任). ("The Predicament and the Prospect of the College Graduate Village Official System"). "大学生村官制度的困境与前瞻，" *山东行政学院, 山东省经济管理干部学院学报*, 4: 2010, 30–32.

Edin, Maria. "State Capacity and Local Agent Control in China: CCP Cadre Management from a Township Perspective," *China Quarterly*, 173: 2003, 35–52.

Fewsmith, Joseph. "CCP Launches Campaign to Maintain the Advanced Nature of Party Members," *China Leadership Monitor*, 2005, 13.

Fewsmith, Joseph. *The Logic and Limits of Political Reform in China.* New York: Cambridge University Press, 2013.

Foucault, Michel. *The History of Sexuality,* vols. II–III. New York: Vintage Books, 1988.

Foucault, Michel, Defert, Daniel, Ewald, François, Lagrange, Jacques, and Lemke, Thomas. *Analytik der Macht. "Suhrkamp Taschenbuch Wissenschaft."* Frankfurt am Main: Suhrkamp, 2005.

Gordon, Avery. *Ghostly Matters: Haunting and the Sociological Imagination.* Minneapolis: University of Minnesota Press, 2008.

Grindle, Merilee Serrill. *Going Local: Decentralization, Democratization, and the Promise of Good Governance.* Princeton: Princeton University Press, 2007.

Heberer, Thomas. "China in 2013: The Chinese Dream's Domestic and Foreign Policy Shifts," *Asian Survey*, 54: 2014, 113–128.

Heberer, Thomas. "The Contention between Han 'Civilisers' and Yi 'Civilisees' over Environmental Governance: A Case Study of Liangshan Prefecture in Sichuan," *China Quarterly*, 219: 2014, 736–759.

Heberer, Thomas and Schubert, Gunter. "County and Township Cadres as a Strategic Group: A New Approach to Political Agency in China's Local State," *Journal of Chinese Political Science*, 17: 2014, 221–249.

Heberer, Thomas and Senz, Anja. "Streamlining Local Behaviour through Communication, Incentives and Control: A Case Study of Local Environmental Policies in China," *Journal of Current Chinese Affairs*, 40: 2011, 77–112.

Heberer, Thomas and Trappel, René. "Evaluation Processes, Local Cadres' Behaviour and Local Development Processes," *Journal of Contemporary China*, 22, 84: 2013, 1048–1066.

Heilmann, Sebastian, "From Local Experiments to National Policy: The Origins of China's Distinctive Policy Process," *China Journal*, 59: 2008, 1–30.

Heilmann, Sebastian. "Maximum Tinkering under Uncertainty: Unorthodox Lessons from China," *Modern China*, 35: 2009, 450–462.

Heilmann, Sebastian. "Policy Experimentation in China's Economic Rise," *Studies in Comparative International Development*, 43:2008, 1–26.

Heilmann, Sebastian and Perry, Elizabeth, eds. *Mao's Invisible Hand: The Political Foundations of Adaptive Governance in China.* Cambridge, MA: Harvard University Asia Center, 2011.

Hillman, Ben. "Factions and Spoils: Examining Political Behavior within the Local State in China," *China Journal*, 64: 2010, 1–18.

Hu Jintao (胡锦涛). ("Speech at the Research Seminar of Key Provincial and Ministry-Level Leading Cadres on Raising the Capacity for the Construction of a Socialist Harmonious Society"). "在省部级主要领导干部提高构建社会主义和谐社会能力专题研讨班上的讲话," 2005, at news.xinhuanet.com/newscenter/2005–06/26/content_3138887_3.htm.

Jia Jianyou (贾建友). ("Township Cadres amidst Mass Incidents"). "群体性事件中的乡镇干部," at www.snzg.cn/article/show.php?itemid-8707/page-1.html.

Jiangyin Municipal Committee (江阴市委). ("Jiangyin Municipality 2011 Program for Implementation of Work Targets and Assessments of Results in Municipal Level Offices"). "2011年江阴市市级机关工作目标绩效考核实施方案."

Jiangyin Municipal Committee, Organization Department (江阴市委组织部). ("Survey on Democracy among Leading Cadres, Very Few Appraise it as Imporant"). "领导干部民主测评, 个别谈话评价要点," 2011.

"Jiangyin Municipality Party Committee/Government Joint Circular on Guidelines for Structural Reform Innovation Work in 2011." "中共江阴市委, 江阴市政府关于引发江阴市2011年体制改革创新工作指导意见的通知"。 江阴市, 2011.

"Jiangyin Municipality Party Committee/Government Joint Circular on Guidelines for Structural Reform Innovation Work in 2012." "中共江阴市委, 江阴市政府关于引发江阴市2012年体制改革创新工作指导意见的通知"。 江阴市, 2012.

Kennedy, John James. "The Implementation of Village Elections and Tax-for-Fee Reform in Rural Northwest China," in Perry and Goldman, eds., *Grassroots Political Reform*, 48–74.

Li, Tania. *The Will to Improve: Governmentality, Development, and the Practice of Politics*. Durham, NC: Duke University Press, 2007.

Liu Xiaojun (刘小军). ("Vehicles of Innovation Activity: New Highlights in the Development of Mass Line Education Practices"). "创新活动载体, 开创群众路线教育实践活动新局面," 共产党网, at qzlx.12371.cn/2013/10/10/ART I1381373672470984.shtml.

Liu Yunshan (刘云山). ("Speech of Liu Yushan at the Work Conference on the Party's Mass Line Education and Practice Activities"). "刘云山在党的群众路线教育实践活动工作会议上的讲话," 2013, at qzlx.people.com.cn/n/2013/072 6/c365007–22344080.html, accessed October 1, 2013.

Lukes, Steven. *Power: A Radical View*. 2nd edn. Houndmills: Palgrave Macmillan. 2004.

Nice, David C. *Policy Innovation in State Government*. 1st edn. Ames: Iowa State University Press, 1994.

N. N. (*Decision-making, Internal Reference: Big Country, "Imperial Examinations"*). 决策内参 – 大国 《赶考》. 北京: 华文出版社, 2009.

N. N. ("Grassroots Cadres Have Little Power but Large Obligations, the Mental Pressure Is Enormous, Psychic Problems Tremendous"). "中国基层干部权小责大 精神压力大心理问题突出," 2010, at finance.people.com.cn/bank/n/2012/1129/c202331–19733602.html.

N. N. ("Hu Jintao: Strongly Raising the Level of Social Management Science"). "胡锦涛: 扎扎实实提高社会管理科学化水平," 2011, at news.xinhuanet.com/politics/2011–02/19/c_121100198.htm.

N. N. ("The Party Center Strives to Build Long-Acting Mass Line Mechanism"). "中共着力建设走群众路线的长效机制," at news.xinhuanet.com/politics/201 3–07/12/c_116513966.htm.

O'Brien, Kevin J. and Li, Lianjiang. "Selective Policy Implementation in Rural China," *Comparative Politics*, 31: 1999, 167–186.

Perry, Elizabeth J. and Goldman, Merle, eds. *Grassroots Political Reform in Contemporary China*. Cambridge and London: Harvard University Press, 2011.

Pieke, Frank N. *The Good Communist: Elite Training and State Building in Today's China*. Cambridge: Cambridge University Press, 2009.

Schubert, Gunter and Ahlers, Anna L. "'Constructing a New Socialist Countryside' and Beyond: An Analytical Framework for Studying Policy Implementation and Political Stability in Contemporary China," *Journal of Chinese Political Science*, 16: 2011, 19–46.

Schubert, Gunter and Ahlers, Anna L. "County and Township Cadres as a Strategic Group: 'Building a New Socialist Countryside' in Three Provinces," *China Journal*, 67: 2012, 67–86.

Shambaugh, David. *China's Communist Party: Atrophy and Adaptation*. Berkeley: University of California Press, 2008.

Shih, Victor, Adolph, Christopher, and Liu, Mingxin. "Getting Ahead in the Communist Party: Explaining the Advancement of Central Committee Members in China," *American Political Science Review*, 106: 2012, 166–187.

Shiquan County (石泉县). "Basic Methods for Constructing Party Organizations that Study and Learn." "石泉县推进学习型党组织建设工作的基本做法," 2011.

Smith, Graeme. "Political Machinations in a Rural County," *China Journal*, 62: 2009, 29–59.

Smith, Graeme. "The Hollow State: Rural Governance in China," *China Quarterly*, 203: 2010, 601–618.

Taizhou Municipality Party Committee Office (中共台州市黄岩区委办公室). ("Notice Regarding the 'Responsibility System Evaluation Method' for Party-Building in Counties and City Districts." "关于印发《2013年乡镇街道党委（党工委）党建工作责任制考核办法》的通知," at hynews.zjol.com.cn/hynews/system/2013/05/24/016472414.shtml.

Tao Ran (陶然), Su Fubing (苏福兵), Lu Xi (陆曦), and Zhu Yuming (朱昱铭). ("Can Economic Growth Lead to Job Promotion?"). "经济增长能够带来普生吗?" *管理世界*, 2010, 13–26.

Teets, Jessica and Hurst, William, eds. *Local Governance Innovation in China. Experimentation, Diffusion, and Defiance*. London: Routledge, 2015.

Weber, Max. *Grundriß der Sozialökonomie III, Wirtschaft und Gesellschaft*. Tübingen: Verlag von J. C. B. Mohr, 1925.

Whiting, Susan H. *Power and Wealth in Rural China: The Political Economy of Institutional Change*. New York: Cambridge University Press, 2011.

Wuxi Municipality, Bureau of Science and Technology (无锡市科技局). ("On the Trial Methods for Evaluating 'Three Creates' Agents in Wuxi"). "关于印发《无锡市"三创"载体考核评价办法（试行）》的通知."

Wuxi Municipal Party Committee, Organization Department (中共无锡市委组织部). ("Party-Building Leadership Group (under the Wuxi Municipal Party Committee) Document on Implementing the Municipal Party Committee Opinion on Strengthening and Restructuring the Ideology of the Leadership Core in Terms of Political Construction under the New Conditions"). "中共无锡市委的建设领导小组文件(一). 关于贯彻落实市委《加强和改进新形势下领导班子思想政治建设的意见》的通知."

Xi Jinping (习近平). ("Speech at the Work Conference on Mass Line Education and Practice Activities"). "习近平在党的群众路线教育实践活动工作会议上的讲," 2013, at qzlx.people.com.cn/n/2013/0726/c365007-22344078.html.

Yan, Hairong. "Neoliberal Governmentality and Neohumanism: Organizing Suzhi/Value Flow through Labor Recruitment Networks," *Cultural Anthropology*, 18: 2003, 493–523.

Zeng Qinghong (曾庆红). ("Programmatic Article on Strengthening the Party's Governing Capacity"). "加强党的执政能力建设的纲领性文献," 2013, at news.xinhuanet.com/newscenter/2004–10/08/content_2061716.htm.

Index